The preparation and publication of this book were made possible by generous grants to the American Antiquarian Society from The Gridiron Foundation in honor of the bicentennial of the American Revolution. The Gridiron Foundation is an educational and charitable trust created by The Gridiron Club, an organization of newspaper correspondents, columnists, editors, and cartoonists in Washington, D.C.

The Press &
the American Revolution

The Press &
the American Revolution

EDITED BY

Bernard Bailyn and John B. Hench

WITH A FOREWORD BY

Marcus A. McCorison

AND AN AFTERWORD BY

James Russell Wiggins

WORCESTER
American Antiquarian Society
1980

Contents

Foreword

THIS BOOK OF ESSAYS on the activities, place, and influence of American printers and journalists during the period of our Revolution is the American Antiquarian Society's primary scholarly contribution to the two hundredth anniversary of that pivotal process.

Since its founding in 1812 by Isaiah Thomas, one of the leading journalists of the Revolutionary era, the American Antiquarian Society has expended a very large portion of its energies upon the collection, recording, and dissemination of the fundamental printed records of the American Revolution—its precursing events and its aftermath. The Society has done so in the strong belief that the influence of those who controlled the printed word were the persons crucial to the formation of a revolution within the minds of Americans, as well as to the act of overt revolt. Thus, the history of the Society is inextricably linked with the American press and with the American Revolution and has resulted in our enduring interest in the history of printing and publishing of the country. Thomas, himself, established this focus during his own lifetime, for his narrative of the contribution of American printers to the development of our cultural life during the seventeenth and eighteenth centuries is, after 167 years, still informative, and it remains in print. Thomas also compiled the first list of American imprints of the colonial period, which was edited and published by the Society in 1874. Succeeding Society members and staff have followed our founder by actively enlarging knowledge of the American printed record and, through its interpretation, expanding our understanding of American history and culture. Thus, this book of essays falls squarely within the traditional concerns of the Society and we trust it serves to deepen our understanding of the role of the printers during the Revolution. Isaiah Thomas provides a link between the press, the Revolution, and this Society, a link that may serve to introduce this volume.

I

The record of any human enterprise is convoluted by contradictory motives, wise decisions, poor guesses, and a lack of full understanding by later generations. Thomas's own career in Boston during the years immediately prior to the Revolutionary War demonstrates the conflict of choices that bedevil a person.

It has been accurately observed that the American Revolution had already occurred before the nineteenth of April 1775. The armed conflict that began on that date, difficult as it was to be, only ratified in action and brought to political actuality a revolution that had taken place during the generation preceding 1775 in the minds of many men and women. In short, the British had lost a people before a shot was fired. Printers played a major role in causing that stunning transformation.

Before operators of presses could exert an effective political role, certain of their attitudes had to change. As Stephen Botein observes in his essay in this book, the traditional aim of the newspaperman was to profess political, economic, and social subservience to no faction and to keep his press freely open. That is, the facilities of the public prints should be available to all varieties of opinion that exhibited goodwill and tended toward the improvement of the morals and condition of human society.

The career of a predecessor to Isaiah Thomas exhibits the difficulties in reaching such a goal. In Boston, from 1735 until 1775 Thomas Fleet, succeeded by his sons, issued the *Boston Evening-Post*, a publication that they valiantly attempted to maintain as an independent newspaper. In the first issue of *The Weekly Rehearsal*, the immediate predecessor to the *Evening-Post*, Fleet set forth his editorial policy: 'The publisher of this paper declares himself of no Party, and invites all Gentlemen of Leisure and Capacity, inclined on either Side, to write any thing of a political Nature, that tends to enlighten and serve the Publick, to communicate their Productions, provided they are not overlong, and confined within Modesty and Good Manners.'[1]

Isaiah Thomas held a high opinion of Thomas Fleet, who was a man of courage, as one must be to pursue an independent course. He said of him, 'Fleet was a wit, and no bigot,' and of his newspaper Thomas stated that 'It was the best newspaper then published in Boston.'[2] When

[1] Quoted in Isaiah Thomas, *The History of Printing in America*, ed. Marcus A. McCorison (Barre, Mass., 1970), p. 247.
[2] Thomas, *History of Printing*, p. 251.

the elder Fleet died in 1758, the *Boston Evening-Post* descended to his sons, Thomas and John, both patriots, who continued it under the sign of the Heart and Crown with the same impartial standards of their father until they gave it up in the dread month of April 1775.

In times of passion, voices of impartiality and rationality are not welcomed and are seldom heard. Taking impartial positions, the Fleets' *Evening-Post* was not suited for a period of intense social change and political revolution. Rather, it is the press of dogmatic opinion that commands popular attention in such times and it is a new man of the Revolution, Isaiah Thomas, who better represented the era. Thomas was born in Boston in 1749.[3] In 1770 he had just reached majority. His father was a ne'er-do-well who abandoned his wife and five children. At age six Isaiah Thomas was bound by the Overseers of the Poor of Boston to an eccentric, unambitious printer, Zechariah Fowle. He taught himself to read by learning to set type, and what education he gained came from the texts he set. A brilliant boy with impelling energy, he grew up hating his situation and was desperate to get away from it in order to prove that he was the most remarkable and gifted printer in his world.

Thomas led an adventurous life as a youngster; he was impetuous, bold, and irreverent. One day in September 1765, the sixteen-year-old Isaiah had a 'serious fracas' with his master. He 'left him secretly'[4] the next morning, bound for Halifax and London where he hoped to 'acquire a more perfect knowledge of his business.'[5] When he arrived in the capital of Nova Scotia, Thomas applied for work at the printing office of Anthony Henry where Henry was to pay him at the rate of $3.00 per month and to find him board, laundry, and lodging. According to Isaiah, who was fully confident of his abilities, he immediately assumed sole management of the *Halifax Gazette* of which there were not more than thirty-five subscribers and a total pressrun of but seventy copies. It was, incidentally, the only newspaper then published in Nova Scotia and was the official organ of the provincial government. Thomas did his best to improve its typography and to enliven its columns from 'his' first

---

[3] Sources for details of Thomas's life are Isaiah Thomas, *Three Autobiographical Fragments* (Worcester, 1962); Annie Russell Marble, *From 'Prentice to Patron: The Life Story of Isaiah Thomas* (New York, 1935); and Clifford K. Shipton, *Isaiah Thomas: Printer, Patriot, and Philanthropist* (Rochester, N.Y., 1948).

[4] Thomas, *Three Autobiographical Fragments*, p. 8.

[5] Thomas, *History of Printing*, p. 155.

issue, dated October 3, 1765, until he was fired from the job six months later, a 'victim' of the Stamp Act controversy.

The Stamp Act was passed in March 1765 but it was not until November 7 that the *Gazette* was printed upon stamped paper. According to his autobiographical notes, Thomas had already developed 'high notions of Liberty,' and he found the added cost of the duties on stamped printing paper highly objectionable and an infringement upon the rights of members of the English nation. Thomas printed news items, verse, and the like—all voicing opposition to the act—which he copied from Boston or Philadelphia newspapers. Even more provocative to the Nova Scotia government was the appearance of an effigy of the Halifax stamp collector on the gallows near the Citadel. Also, the *Gazette*'s supply of stamped paper was treated most cavalierly. In the issue of February 20 Thomas reported that because the supply of stamped paper had been totally 'expended,' the price of the paper was being returned to its former price of twelve shillings a year. He had cut off the stamps in the binder's guillotine. With that Anthony Henry lost his government work and Isaiah lost his job. Thomas left Halifax on March 19, 1766.[6] It is obvious that the young man thoroughly enjoyed this escapade. Whether it was due to youthful high jinks or to 'high notions of Liberty' may be debatable. Certainly, it demonstrates that Thomas was no respecter of authority.

Thomas traveled from one place to another for the next four years, before returning to Boston to establish a partnership with his old master Zechariah Fowle. On July 17, 1770, they issued a prospectus for the *Massachusetts Spy*. C. K. Shipton believed that the *Spy* was successful from the start. In fact, it would appear that it was not immediately so, for from August 7, 1770, until the first of March 1771 the schedule and regularity of issues varied considerably. In the meantime, Thomas had been learning the facts of journalistic life. Although he claimed to want to present all shades of political opinion in the *Spy*, he found more support from Whig readers and writers and soon alienated any Tory subscribers he had first attracted. In *The History of Printing in America* he wrote:

> A number of gentlemen supplied [the *Spy*] with political essays, which for
> the time were more particularly calculated for that class of citizen who had

[6] Shipton, *Isaiah Thomas*, pp. 9–13.

composed the great majority of its readers. For a few weeks some communications were furnished by those who were in favor of the royal prerogative, but they were exceeded by the writers on the other side; and the authors and subscribers among the tories denounced and quitted the Spy. The publisher then devoted it to the cause of his country, supported by the whigs, under whose banners he had enlisted. . . .

Common sense in common language is necessary to influence one class of citizens, as much as learning and elegance of composition are to produce an effect upon another.[7]

Thomas's editorial policy for the *Massachusetts Spy* was fitted for the common reader—a mass audience (if such existed in eighteenth-century Boston). This was his natural constituency. At age twenty-one and with minimal formal schooling Thomas was no scholar, yet he had a very good mind and a lively wit. He developed a clever facility for combining editorial comment with news. With these attributes and skills he made a success of his enterprise. He wrote that when he began the *Spy* he had fewer than two hundred subscribers but at the end of two years of work the list had grown to be the largest in New England. However, while he was struggling to attain that happy condition, several things troubled Thomas. His political friends and opponents were making life miserable for him. He was having difficulty in meeting the payments on his debt and he may have been having troubles with a wife of wandering ways. The Thomases lived in Union Street, near Fanueil Hall (their house is now part of the Union Oyster House). Benjamin Thompson, later Count Rumford, lived nearby, a clerk to the wealthy merchant, Hopestill Capen. In view of their trip together to Newburyport in 1775, it may not be too farfetched to infer that Mary Thomas and Benjamin Thompson were seeing more of one another than the printer liked.

Thomas's other troubles were financial and editorial. After the first months of publication, by his own account the Tories had deserted him and we may assume that a Loyalist creditor who held the nineteen-year-old mortgage on Zechariah Fowle's printing equipment called in the loan. Therefore, he entered into an agreement with Joseph Greenleaf to form a partnership early in March 1771, at which time the *Massachusetts Spy* resumed publication. Greenleaf presumably would bear half the load. For his own funds, Thomas went to John Hancock who put up

---

[7] Thomas, *History of Printing*, pp. 266–67.

that half of the capital. Thus, Thomas exchanged a loyalist financier for a Whig, finding himself as tightly bound in this new situation as he had been in the previous one. Furthermore, he now had a partner who played an active role in the management of the newspaper, a situation that inhibited Thomas's natural tendencies toward freedom of action.

Beyond the financial aspects of these arrangements was the commitment to party. Without documentary evidence, we can only infer that Hancock supported Thomas for a purpose, namely, to supply a second radical voice in Boston—one the tone and argument of which was more strident and of greater appeal to readers whose intellectual habits and interests were not as well defined as those who looked to Benjamin Edes's *Boston Gazette* for guidance. It may be, as well, that Hancock expected the *Spy* to further his own political interests.

His colleagues in this enterprise were Dr. Thomas Young and Greenleaf, Hancock remaining discreetly in the rear. Young was the physician from Ulster County, New York, who, although he died when only forty-five years old, crops up in the history of American medicine and philosophy, while playing distinctive roles in the politics of Massachusetts, Vermont, and Pennsylvania. Joseph Greenleaf was a lawyer from Abington, Massachusetts, and a justice of the peace in Plymouth County who had made his reputation by writing the 'Noble Resolves' passed by the Town of Abington immediately following the Boston Massacre. Thomas faintly praised Greenleaf, whose pseudonym was 'Mucius Scaevola,' by saying that he possessed some talents as a popular writer and that his pieces, furnished for the *Massachusetts Spy*, displayed an ardent zeal in the cause of American liberty which 'produced a salutary effect.'[8] One of Thomas's 'admirers' in Draper's loyalist *Massachusetts Gazette and Boston News-Letter* said of the crew of the *Spy*, 'What a wretched Triumvirate! A poor shiftless erratic Knight from Abington, a dunghill-bred Journeyman Typographer, and a stupid phrensical Mountebank.'[9] Also, there were other writers who helped give the *Spy* its sensational nature, although it probably was not John Adams, as Hutchinson thought, who under the name of 'Centinel' from May 1771 to March 1772 wrote forty excellent essays on every possible grievance suffered by the provincials.

[8] Thomas, *History of Printing*, p. 174.
[9] Quoted in Arthur M. Schlesinger, *Prelude to Independence: The Newspaper War on Britain, 1764–1776* (New York, 1958), p. 132.

But, in the thirty-seventh issue, dated November 14, 1771, Greenleaf overwrote himself. Governor Hutchinson, having smarted long enough from the sensational tone of the *Spy*, had had enough. 'Mucius Scaevola' called Hutchinson 'a perjured traitor' and 'a usurper' without legal authority in Massachusetts. Scaevola said that 'a ruler independent of the people is a monster in government' and called on the Council to assume the powers of the governor. Even the readers of Boston, grown callous from a torrent of invective, were astonished. Fleet's *Evening-Post* thought it 'the most daring production ever published in America.' Poor James Otis, of scrambled wit, read it to assess its libellous tendencies and said to Thomas, who must have taken small comfort from his remark, that the matter of his legal vulnerability was 'Touch and go, by God!'[10]

The fat was in the fire. The Council summoned Thomas before them on the sixteenth. Thomas cooly responded to their messenger 'that he was busily employed in his office, and could not wait upon his excellency and their honors.' Following his third refusal to come before them, they then voted to sue Thomas for seditious libel at common law, for, not being licensers of the press, the Council had no statutory authority over him. The attorney general brought the matter before the grand jury of Suffolk County but that body voted 'Ignoramus'; that is, the jury purported that they could not determine the facts of the case. Not being able to avenge themselves on Thomas, the Council punished poor Greenleaf by voiding his commission as a justice of the peace.

The entire matter created the most intense interest throughout the continent. It established Thomas's reputation as a fearless editor, and patriot, and the master of himself. From that time forward his affairs improved.

Thomas was to come to public attention frequently in the next few years. He was hanged in effigy in North Carolina. The British troops in Boston paraded before the *Spy* office and threatened Thomas with a tarring. By 1773 he was fully involved in the radical cause. In his autobiographical notes he stated that he secretly printed handbills at night for the Sons of Liberty. Thomas established a schedule of post riders to the south for the delivery of the *Spy* and other papers with William Goddard of Baltimore, John Holt of New York City, and Thaddeus Burr of Fair-

[10] Thomas, *History of Printing*, p. 272.

field, Connecticut. These proved useful for the delivery of communications between Committees of Safety, as well. Thus, his services to the patriot cause were real and his commitment deep.

Also, Thomas was in demand to establish presses in other places. He established the first press in Newburyport in December 1773. His partner there was Henry Walter-Tinges, who according to Thomas, so mismanaged their affairs that Thomas was obliged to sell out at a loss before a year was out. Late in 1774 he was approached by Timothy Bigelow and William Stearns with a proposition to establish a newspaper in Worcester. Accordingly, Thomas issued in February 1775 a prospectus calling for subscriptions to *The Worcester Gazette, or American Oracle of Liberty.*

At the moment of crisis Thomas was fully involved. On the night of April 16, 1775, he transported to Worcester some of his printing materials although, because he was being closely watched, he had to keep to his house on the sixteenth, seventeenth, and eighteenth. On April 19 he went to Charlestown with Dr. Joseph Warren to urge the town to arms and then journeyed to Medford. On the twentieth he stopped to see his family in Watertown and then kept on toward Worcester where he 'arrived fatigued.' He discovered that his press had come safely to the town on the eighteenth.

But things were still unsettled. The Provincial Congress wanted him to bring the press back to Watertown; then they said he was to go to Cambridge. At length, it was decided the press was safer in Worcester. Thomas fully expected to do the printing for the Revolutionary government. He had, in fact, gone to Worcester on the advice of John Hancock, president of the Congress. Quickly he got his press set up in a cellar room in Colonel Timothy Bigelow's house on Main Street. On May 3, 1775, he issued *The Massachusetts Spy, or American Oracle of Liberty* the 'first thing ever printed in Worcester.' At the top of the first page was the challenge, 'Americans!—Liberty or Death!—Join or Die!'

In July Thomas published the official account of the battles of Lexington and Concord, entitled *A Narrative of the Excursion and Ravages of the Kings Troops Under the Command of General Gage, on the nineteenth of April, 1775.* The pamphlet was distributed as widely as possible by the Congress as propaganda for the cause, but it was the only official printing Thomas was to do for the Provincial Congress. Other printers were closer on the scene. Benjamin Edes had gotten himself to Watertown.

Samuel Hall and his brother, Ebenezer, had come down from Salem and established themselves in Cambridge. Thomas was shut out, and it was a bitter blow. He had abandoned property in Boston of considerable worth. His accounts receivable stood at $3,000, which he never fully collected. With Boston closed, the number of subscribers to the *Spy* dropped by more than half to about 1,500.

In late April, Hancock and Adams stopped in Worcester on the way to Philadelphia. Thomas asked Hancock to intercede for him with the Committee of Safety in obtaining a supply of printing paper. The committee voted him four reams of paper to be sent from the mill at Milton, 'he to be accountable.'[11] He was held accountable indeed. Ten years later he received a demand from Treasurer Thomas Ivers that he pay the bill.

Early in 1779 Thomas returned from various wanderings and began anew in Worcester. He divorced his first wife and married Mary Thomas Fowle in May 1779. His business advanced steadily from that time forward until he retired from active supervision of his printing affairs in 1802. He had become a man of considerable wealth. It is not difficult to understand the reasons for his success. He was possessed of splendid intelligence, great diligence, a handsome appearance, and charming manners. He seemed to know how to obtain financial backing and how to use it to the fullest. His network of partners was a means of establishing centers of commerce in various locations; his system of trading stock between himself and his competitors was a means of enlarging his inventory efficiently and cheaply. All these practices served as coordinated ways of increasing his assets. He was, it may be fair to say, one of the first modern entrepreneurs—by regularizing the means of production, distribution, and sales into a disciplined system.

Thomas holds a rightful place as a father of the American Revolution. The national historical society that he founded was directly related to his involvement in establishing a new nation, to his financially successful dealings with the printed word, and to his intellectual and book-collecting interests. The American Antiquarian Society is chartered to collect the 'Antiquities of our country' in order 'to enlarge the sphere of human knowledge.' In unique ways Thomas's own publication, *The History of Printing in America*, his outstanding personal library consisting of about

---

[11] Marble, *From 'Prentice to Patron*, p. 98.

8,000 volumes that includes files of eighteenth-century newspapers, and his purchase and gift to AAS in 1813 of the Mather family library and manuscripts have set the course and style of the institution. We trust that this book of essays will act as a suitable acknowledgement of our concerns with the still lively influences of the art of printing upon political and social events.

The Council and the members of the Society are pleased to here acknowledge the very generous financial support from the governors of The Gridiron Foundation of Washington, D.C., which was used to defray the costs of publishing this book. Bernard Bailyn, a former vice-president of the Society, bore the responsibility of editing each essay and working with its author to correlate the essays with each other. James Russell Wiggins, past president of AAS, read all the essays and commented upon them. It was the duty of John B. Hench, the Society's editor, to copy edit the essays and each has profited by his close reading of it. To all these persons and to the authors of the essays we are most grateful.

MARCUS A. McCORISON

Antiquarian Hall
August 16, 1979

Printers and the American Revolution

STEPHEN BOTEIN

ᔓᕽ ᔓᕽ ᔓᕽ ᔓᕽ ᔓᕽ ᔓᕽ ᔓᕽ ᔓᕽ ᕽᔓ ᕽᔓ ᕽᔓ ᕽᔓ ᕽᔓ ᕽᔓ ᕽᔓ ᕽᔓ

1. Introduction

AMONG THE MISCELLANEOUS MATERIAL that Isaiah Thomas appended to his exhaustive *History of Printing in America* was a list of more than 350 American newspapers published in 1810. All but approximately 50 were classified according to political affiliation, Federalist or Republican.[1]

Reflected in this information was a powerful new trend in American journalism. As the Reverend Samuel Miller had observed at the start of the century, the newspapers of republican America were 'immense moral and political engines' that advanced opinions as well as reported occurrences.[2] The press had become capable at once of greater good and more serious mischief, depending on the perspective of readers, than in the colonial period. To a nostalgic conservative like James Fenimore Cooper, writing from the vantage point of midcentury, this seemed to be a development as inevitable as it was ruinous. Not the least of the evils to undermine the island paradise that Cooper imagined in *The Crater* was the press. 'Fortunately,' in the happy early days of Cooper's fictional community, 'there was yet no newspaper, a species of luxury which, like the gallows, comes in only as a society advances to

The author wishes to thank Michael T. Gilmore, Christopher M. Jedrey, and Harriet N. Ritvo for valuable criticism and suggestions.

[1] Isaiah Thomas, *The History of Printing in America*, 2 vols. (Worcester, Mass., 1810), 2: 517–52; citations throughout are to the original version of this work, but see also Marcus A. McCorison's 1-volume annotated Imprint Society Edition (Barre, Mass., 1970).

[2] Quoted in Thomas, *History of Printing*, 2: 403. Earlier, according to Miller, newspapers had been mostly restricted to 'mere statement of *facts*.'

the corrupt condition; or which, if it happens to precede it a little, is very soon to conduct it there.' Eventually, after a newspaper had been introduced, this utopian experiment collapsed.[3]

It was almost as if Cooper meant to confirm or vindicate the fearful predictions of British authorities in the very infancy of American society. In a declaration of 1671 that has won him much historical notoriety, Gov. William Berkeley of Virginia had been moved to 'thank God' that his colony lacked a press—which he associated with 'disobedience,' 'heresy,' 'sects,' and 'libels against the best government.'[4] For almost a century, Berkeley's alarm had appeared unjustified. In Virginia and the other mainland British colonies of the eighteenth century, it proved difficult to prevent the establishment of printing houses, many of which published newspapers; but these were normally innocent of controversial matter. By the time Isaiah Thomas wrote his *History*, however, virulent political partisanship had become characteristic of American journalism.

Drawing on the personal experience of its author, that pioneering chronicle focused knowingly on the crucial period and process of transformation. Although the political press of the early nineteenth century was a product of contemporary party conflicts, the origins of controversial journalism in America could be traced back to the decade of Revolutionary turmoil that preceded Independence. In the changing business and political strategies of printers, who ran the eighteenth-century press, were registered the circumstances that accounted for the new partisan practices. Revealingly, as an aside in his bitter narrative of the 'American Rebellion,' the loyalist Peter Oliver had called the art of printing 'black,' adding that Benjamin Franklin—for one—had made it 'much blacker.'[5] Many others were of the opinion, at the time, that the behavior of the trade as a whole had aggravated divisiveness and violence, thus hastening the movement of events toward war. Printers, reported one Pennsylvanian at the outset of the crisis, 'almost without exception, stuffed their papers weekly . . . with the *most inflammatory pieces* they could procure, and *excluded every thing that tended to cool the*

---

[3] James Fenimore Cooper, *The Crater*, ed. Thomas Philbrick (Cambridge, Mass., 1962), pp. 374–75, 432–38.

[4] Thomas, *History of Printing*, 2: 139.

[5] *Peter Oliver's Origin & Progress of the American Rebellion*, ed. Douglass Adair and John A. Schutz (San Marino, Calif., 1963), p. 79.

minds of the people.'[6] However exaggerated, this pointed quite accurately to those who were responsible for the unprecedented level of partisan controversy in American journalism during the Revolutionary years.

Throughout, too, Benjamin Franklin played a central part, as Oliver understood. It was a part more characteristically ambiguous, however, than angry loyalist feelings would allow. Franklin's career and reputation as a printer were illustrative of traditional practices in the colonial trade as well as the new patterns that emerged in the Revolution. By examining not only printers as a group but the curiously complicated role of Franklin as their most prominent 'brother type,' it is possible to appreciate some of the larger forces reshaping the public forum of a provincial society convulsed by political crisis. It is possible, furthermore, to understand how that crisis ultimately reshaped the self-imagery, or 'occupational ideology,'[7] of the printing trade. For it was the figure of Franklin, already legendary, that loomed most impressively in the rhetorical efforts of American printers after Independence to affirm and honor the contribution of the press to the Revolutionary movement. Appropriately or not, he became the symbol of a new identity that they formulated for themselves in the new republic. This identity they would continue to promote even in the face of contrary realities, as they struggled with deteriorating business conditions in the early decades of the next century.

2. Colonial Habits

It was Franklin's custom, in later years, to speak fondly of the craft that he had practiced as a young man but abandoned in middle age. For one of his grandsons, he predicted, printing might be 'something to depend on,' an independent source of income that happened to have been 'the original Occupation of his Grandfather.' Meanwhile, at Passy, 'Benjamin Franklin, Printer,' would amuse himself with a private press, in emulation of aristocracy.[8]

[6] John Hughes to Stamp Office Commissioners, Oct. 12, 1765, as reprinted in *Pennsylvania Journal*, Sept. 4, 1766; appointed to the office of stamp distributor in Philadelphia, Hughes was unable to put the new Stamp Act into practice.

[7] By 'occupational ideology' is meant the general system of values and beliefs espoused by printers, arising out of but not limited to trade activities. See Vernon K. Dibble, 'Occupations and Ideologies,' *American Journal of Sociology* 68 (1962–63): 229–41.

[8] Franklin to Richard Bache, Nov. 11, 1784, *The Writings of Benjamin Franklin*, ed.

If the inverted snobbery of this ritual pleased Franklin, it was pardonable. That the most illustrious American of the eighteenth century was also a printer, at least by training, seemed incongruous by European norms. Franklin's remarkable career can only be appreciated in the distinctive context of American social and economic realities, particularly as found in the conditions of the colonial printing trade. Despite limitations on the status that printers could claim in the social hierarchy, the circumstances of the American trade encouraged upward mobility. Probably Franklin could never have achieved his most spectacular successes in the face of the harsh business realities that increasingly threatened the self-esteem of the printing fraternity in London.[9]

By the middle of the eighteenth century, it was no longer common for printers in the capital city of the empire to function as the major entrepreneurs of the publishing business; for the most part, others had usurped that lucrative and influential role. Initially, printers had controlled the principal stages of production in the English book world. Because they alone could actually put a manuscript into print, they were able to demand the exclusive right to profit by its sale. But as the book business grew and required more capital, in response to an expanding middle-class market for print, its separate stages of manufacture and distribution became more specialized. The bookseller, who dealt in the craftsman's product, emerged as the person who laid out capital in a publishing enterprise and then gathered in the benefits.[10] As early as 1663, a dissident group of printers launched an unsuccessful rebellion against the booksellers who dominated the Stationers' Company in London. Protesting that they were now 'yok'd to the Booksellers,' who once were 'but as an Appendix to the Printers,' the insurgents charged that their rivals had grown 'bulkie and numerous' from

---

Albert Henry Smyth, 10 vols. (New York, 1907), 9: 278–79; Franklin to Madame Brillon, Apr. 19, 1788, ibid., pp. 643–45; John Clyde Oswald, *Benjamin Franklin, Printer* (Garden City, N.Y., 1917), chap. 15.

[9] For more elaborate documentation of what follows, in part 2, see Stephen Botein, ' "Meer Mechanics" and an Open Press: The Business and Political Strategies of Colonial American Printers,' *Perspectives in American History* 9 (1975): 130–211.

[10] Marjorie Plant, *The English Book Trade: An Economic History of the Making and Sale of Books*, 2d ed. (London, 1965), pp. 59–62, and see generally A. S. Collins, *Authorship in the Days of Johnson* (London, 1927).

the 'several other Trades' that they had absorbed and were 'much enriched by Printers impoverishment.'[11]

A few printers in eighteenth-century London—among them William Strahan, Franklin's friend and correspondent—ran large businesses that generated sufficient profit to permit investment in copyright, with which they might hope to 'emancipate themselves from the Slavery in which the Booksellers held them.'[12] But they were exceptional figures. To most of their brethren in the trade, the times seemed hard. In 1750 an eccentric master printer named Jacob Ilive—whom Franklin had known, and remembered for his bizarre religious speculations —addressed a general meeting of the trade in London. 'Where is the Man,' he declaimed, 'be he *Divine, Astronomer, Mathematician, Lawyer, Physician,* or what else, who is not beholden to Us?' What a 'great Pity,' he lamented, that printers 'do not meet with an *adequate Encouragement*, suitable to the Labour and Pains they take in the Exercise of it; but this verifies the old Proverb, '*That true Merit seldom or never meets with its Reward.*' It is certain 'from the present Situation of Affairs,' he concluded, 'that in *Our Case,* it never CAN, nor ever WILL.'[13]

The difficulty was not simply a matter of economics. Many of the first European printers had been accomplished scholars, and this distant heritage seems to have shaped the ambitions of eighteenth-century London printers like Ilive. As their economic importance diminished, so did the credibility of their original reputation as men of independent intellect and learning. The dissident printers of 1663, lamenting their subservience to booksellers, had given early voice to what would later be a common anxiety among London's printers—that they would be considered mere manual laborers. In England, the dissidents said, printers 'have so light an esteem' that they fail to 'finde like respect or care with the meanest of Occupations.' Specifically, they complained of an argument used against them by booksellers in the internal struggles of

---

[11] *A Brief Discourse Concerning Printing and Printers* (London, 1663), pp. 4-5; Cyprian Blagden, *The Stationers' Company: A History, 1403–1959* (Cambridge, Mass., 1960), pp. 147-48.

[12] Strahan to David Hall, July 15, 1771, Miscellaneous Collections, Historical Society of Pennsylvania, Philadelphia, and see generally J. A. Cochrane, *Dr. Johnson's Printer: The Life of William Strahan* (Cambridge, Mass., 1964).

[13] *The Papers of Benjamin Franklin*, ed. Leonard W. Labaree et al. (New Haven, 1959–), 17: 315-16n. (hereafter cited as *Franklin Papers*); *The Speech of Mr Jacob Ilive to His Brethren the Master-Printers* (London, 1750), pp. 4, 6-7.

the Stationers' Company. The printers were 'the Mechanick part of the Company,' it ran, 'and so unfit to rule.' By way of contrast, reported the insurgents, printers in France *are above Mechanicks, and live in the suburbs of Learning.*'[14] At stake were traditions that had sustained the pride and prestige of the English trade. Despite isolated literary achievements by members of the fraternity eager to establish credentials that would distinguish them from the ordinary run of skilled workers, printers as a group failed to make these traditions plausible in eighteenth-century London.[15]

Pre-Revolutionary American printers had some reason to hope that they might rank higher in general public esteem, despite prevailing social conventions to the contrary. Theirs was a delicately ambiguous role, however, the strengths and weaknesses of which were determined to a great extent by the structure of business life in an underdeveloped colonial economy.

Compared with the larger printing offices of London, even the most successful firms in the American colonies were modest enterprises. The decisive difference between American printers and those at the top of the London trade was that the former seldom had occasion or incentive to print books of substantial size, because demand for such items in the colonies was unsteady and oriented toward English products.[16] As a result, colonial printers could not expect to prosper from their craft alone, and poverty was often more than a remote contingency.

In order to compensate for limited printing business, however, it was the normal policy of a colonial printer to expand the scope of his work to include enterprises that were no longer or never had been associated with the craft in London. Like printers in provincial England, perhaps their closest counterparts, printers in the colonies participated in a relatively unspecialized trade that reflected the conditions of an inadequate market.[17] Although they lacked the volume of printing business

[14] Plant, *English Book Trade*, p. 32; *Brief Discourse*, pp. 18, 15, 23.

[15] Samuel Richardson, author of *Pamela*, was the most celebrated literary printer in the mother country; see William M. Sale, Jr., *Samuel Richardson: Master Printer* (Ithaca, N.Y., 1950). A less ambitious figure was Samuel Palmer, an employer of Franklin and author of *The General History of Printing* (London, 1732).

[16] 'All publications of consequence, in point of size and expence,' wrote an English observer as late as 1789, 'are executed in Europe.' *Bibliotheca Americana* (London, 1789), p. 14.

[17] On provincial English printers, see Geoffrey Alan Cranfield, *The Development of*

engrossed by major figures in the London trade, they were in practice far from simple mechanics. The very slenderness of the living that they might expect to earn from their skill led them to diversify and thus play more varied roles in their communities than was customary for their brethren in London.

Colonial printers usually sold whatever they could get their hands on. It was not extraordinary to find a general store appended to a printing house; available there, along with the usual selection of dry goods and other imports, might be a wide assortment of the best books that the mother country had to offer. Not only was the colonial printer often a bookseller as well, unlike a printer in London, but quite possibly he also owned and edited a newspaper, which was a convenient place for him to advertise his various wares and insert himself into the intimate daily dealings of his town. Otherwise, too, printers in America were habitually at the center of things. Many staffed the colonial post office; some were clerks in the governments for which they printed laws and currency. By the sum of such activity, a colonial printer might well become a prominent man, unavoidably involved in a broad range of local affairs.[18]

Yet if prominent, he was also vulnerable, enjoying no more status — based conventionally on his occupation—than a printer in the mother country. However lofty his aspirations or diversified his business, it was inescapable that a colonial printer had been brought up to work with his hands. Isaiah Thomas neatly summed up the problem in a capsule memoir of Franklin's nephew, Benjamin Mecom. 'He was handsomely dressed,' recalled Thomas, 'wore a powdered bob wig, ruffles and gloves; gentlemanlike appendages which the printers of that day did not assume—and, thus apparelled, would often assist, for an hour, at the press.'[19] In the colonies, as in both London and the provinces, printers had to face the hard, discouraging fact that in the eyes of many neighbors, especially those who claimed to be 'gentlemen,' they were by training mechanics, without full legitimacy as men of independent intellect and creed.

---

the Provincial Newspaper, 1700–1760 (Oxford, 1962); Roy M. Wiles, *Freshest Advices: Early Provincial Newspapers in England* (Columbus, Ohio, 1965).

[18] The best general account of the American trade is still Lawrence C. Wroth, *The Colonial Printer*, 2d ed. (Portland, Me., 1938); on diversity of enterprise, see esp. chap. 9.

[19] Thomas, *History of Printing*, 1: 351.

The discrepancy here between social convention and occupational reality was ironical but easily ignored. One reason Franklin had chosen to be a printer, rather than a soapmaker like his father, was to satisfy his 'Bookish Inclination.' And certainly his own experience confirmed the advice he gave William Strahan in 1754, as Strahan's oldest son was learning the business in London. 'If, with the Trade,' Franklin wrote, 'you give him a good deal of Reading and Knowledge of Books, and teach him to express himself well on all Occasions in Writing, it may be of very great Advantage to him as a Printer.'[20] Although Franklin cited 'some Instances' in England to prove his point, it was more frequently the colonial printer, so often a newspaper editor too, who needed and acquired literary facility. More plausibly than their brethren in London, whose work had felt the impact of specialization, printers in America might still take pride in the intellectual dimensions of their craft. Nevertheless, conventional social prejudices tended to persist. A colonial printer was not commonly expected to possess a mind of his own, and this expectation was likely to undercut whatever efforts he made to influence his neighbors.[21]

Even Franklin, perhaps the finest prose writer in the colonies, could not hope to transcend effortlessly the prevailing public image of his occupation. In 1740, when a lawyer in Philadelphia proposed to edit *The American Magazine* for Franklin's chief competitor in the printing trade, Franklin responded to the challenge by claiming that the scheme was originally his; the scornful reply was that Franklin's involvement in the periodical had never been projected 'in any other capacity than that of a *meer* Printer.'[22] Before the decade was over, Franklin had decided to disengage from work that ultimately impeded realization of the very ambitions it stimulated. A managing partner 'took off my Hands all Care of the Printing-Office,' he wrote in his *Autobiography.* Thus released, 'I had secur'd Leisure during the rest of my Life, for Philo-

---

[20] *The Autobiography of Benjamin Franklin*, ed. Leonard W. Labaree et al. (New Haven, 1964), p. 58; Franklin to Strahan, Nov. 4, 1754, *Franklin Papers*, 5: 439–40.

[21] Thus, in 1753, when Hugh Gaine attempted to defend himself against opponents of his *New-York Mercury*, he felt compelled to apologize for his audacity. It was a departure, he conceded, 'to appear in print in any other Manner, than what merely pertains to the Station of Life in which I am placed.' *New-York Mercury*, Sept. 3, 1753.

[22] *American Weekly Mercury*, Nov. 20, 1740. The literary dimension of Franklin's printing career is discussed in James A. Sappenfield, *A Sweet Instruction: Franklin's Journalism as a Literary Apprenticeship* (Carbondale, Ill., 1973).

sophical Studies and Amusements.'[23] Only after ceasing to practice his craft could Franklin become a scientist and statesman.

Thus released, too, Franklin was no longer as vulnerable as he had been to the pressures of powerful men and competing interests in his community. A further weakness in the position of the colonial printer, working as he did an underdeveloped local market where he needed all the business he could get, was that he had to take pains to please all customers at all times. As often in the English provinces, but not in London, a printer in America might face no competition but still have few clients, because local demand for his product was apt to be slight. Usually unable to rely for a living on the favor of any one group among his neighbors, including those who wielded political power, a colonial printer by custom labored to serve diverse interests in his community. Unlike London, where large profits were sometimes to be had by making partisan commitments to one well-financed faction or another, colonial America was a place for printers to be studiously impartial.[24]

Upon occasion they explained and justified this trade strategy in elevated terms, professing devotion to 'liberty of the press,' as they chose to understand that phrase.[25] A press was 'free,' in this formulation, only if it was 'open to all parties.' A printer, in other words, should offer everyone the 'liberty' of his press, without favoring one set of opinions over the rest. Whatever the social utility may have been of equalizing access to every colonial press, printers were attracted to the principle because it suited their business interests to serve all customers. Often they frankly admitted as much, in language that ignored the traditional learned pretensions of the English trade; at times, indeed, they sought to take rhetorical advantage of their conventional social standing as mechanics.

---

[23] *Autobiography of Franklin*, pp. 195–96.

[24] See Cranfield, *Development of the Provincial Newspaper*, p. 118; Wiles, *Freshest Advices*, pp. 33–34, 292. The London pattern is illustrated in Sale, *Samuel Richardson*, pp. 54–59, and treated more generally in Laurence Hanson, *Government and the Press, 1695–1763* (London, 1936).

[25] The literature on liberty of expression in the colonies is vast but mainly tangential to the point here, since most of what has been written does not take into account the perspectives of printers. A useful overview of some general issues raised by the secondary literature may be found in Leonard W. Levy's preface to the paperback edition of his *Legacy of Suppression*, published as *Freedom of Speech and Press in Early American History: Legacy of Suppression* (New York, 1963). For a view that differs from what follows, see Lawrence H. Leder, *Liberty and Authority in Early American Political Ideology, 1689–1763* (Chicago, 1968), chap. 1.

'Governour, it is my imploy, my trade and calling,' Pennsylvania's first printer had argued in 1689, finding himself in trouble for printing an unauthorized edition of the colony's charter, 'and that by wch I get my living, to print; and if I may not print such things as come to my hand, which are innocent, I cannot live.' Printing, he insisted, was 'a manufacture of the nation,' not an instrument of faith or ideology.[26]

By far the best known and most sustained colonial argument for an impartial press was Franklin's 'Apology for Printers,' first published in a 1731 issue of the *Pennsylvania Gazette*, after the wording of an advertising handbill produced in his shop had given offense to the local clergy. 'Printers are educated in the Belief,' Franklin insisted, 'that when Men differ in Opinion, both Sides ought equally to have the Advantage of being heard by the Publick.' Here was a principle consistent with advanced eighteenth-century doctrines of the public good, defined in terms of free competition by individuals or interests, but Franklin was quick to ground such considerations in business pragmatism. Printers 'chearfully serve all contending Writers that pay them well' he explained, 'without regarding on which Side they are of the Question in Dispute.'[27] This was precisely the modest, self-denying role—so exclusively 'mechanical'—that some members of the trade in London found disagreeable. Although literary craft traditions seemingly accorded more with reality in the colonies than in the mother country, Franklin's 'Apology' offered on behalf of printers a formulation of principles usefully congruent with the trade strategies required by an underdeveloped economy. One man's right to be heard might be another man's employment.

The chief difficulty, as Franklin knew well, was to persuade one's neighbors to recognize the legitimacy of this strategy. It might be acceptable enough in normal circumstances, but in times of bitter contro-

[26] John William Wallace, *An Address Delivered at the Celebration . . . of the Two Hundredth Birth Day of Mr. William Bradford* (Albany, N.Y., 1863), pp. 49–52.

[27] *Pennsylvania Gazette*, June 10, 1731. Whether or how a newspaper contributor was expected to pay is unclear, but the possibility was certainly contemplated in the well-known 'Stage Coach' metaphor to which Franklin referred in his autobiography. (Anyone willing to pay had 'a Right to a Place.' *Autobiography of Franklin*, p. 175.) On the other hand, there is no evidence to suggest that in practice printers of colonial newspapers routinely received payments from contributors or that they gave weight to the prospect of such payments in their business calculations. (Accusations that they did were rarely made before the Revolutionary period.) By accepting or rejecting controversial articles, they figured that they might gain or lose subscribers or—and this was doubtless more important—other kinds of printing business.

versy—when powerful men in the community turned to print to gain advantage in their quarrels with one another—its usefulness became less certain. Because 'the Business of Printing has chiefly to do with Mens Opinions,' Franklin observed, printers had to live with 'the peculiar Unhappiness' of 'being scarce able to do anything in their way of getting a Living, which shall not probably give Offence to some and perhaps to many.'[28] Possibly because disharmony in the public forum was at odds with traditional norms of political behavior, many colonists still held a printer responsible for the sentiments he set in type and seem to have been unprepared to tolerate him if, caught in the middle of intense conflict, he wished to publish both sides.

When attitudes polarized, a printer sometimes had to work for a single faction; otherwise he might antagonize everyone. That this solution might be at least briefly lucrative, as well as unavoidable, is evident from the experience of such printers as John Peter Zenger and Franklin's brother James. Publications like the *New-York Weekly Journal* and the *New-England Courant* reflected temporary calculations by their printers that more was to be gained and little could be lost in periods of political turmoil if they abandoned neutrality and served those who insisted on and were willing to pay for partisanship. In quieter times Zenger or James Franklin might hope to maintain the 'liberty' of their presses to different opinions, but this was a policy that did not always promise to be advantageous for a printer, especially if he were less than fully established in the trade. To pursue it rigorously could subject him to severe and contrary pressures when the political scene became agitated.[29]

To avoid trouble, the potential for which was greatest in the conduct of a newspaper, probably it was best in the long run to abstain from publishing polemics altogether, or as much as possible. Frequently, therefore, printers would qualify their dedication to the principle of an 'open press' not by expressing veiled partiality to any one side but by trying to exclude the more censorious effusions of all parties. The result was not receptivity but even-handed aversion to diverse and forceful opinions. Although in his 'Apology' Franklin wished to persuade people to tolerate

[28] *Pennsylvania Gazette*, June 10, 1731.

[29] See generally Livingston Rutherford, *John Peter Zenger, His Press, His Trial, and a Bibliography of Zenger Imprints* (New York, 1904); Harold Lester Dean, 'The *New-England Courant*, 1721–1726: A Chapter in the History of American Culture' (Ph.D diss., Brown University, 1943).

the publication of polemical matter without blaming its printer, he also affirmed that printers did 'continually discourage the Printing of great Numbers of bad Things, and stifle them in the Birth.' Returning to the subject in his *Autobiography*, he was even more emphatic. 'In the Conduct of my Newspaper,' he recalled, 'I carefully excluded all Libelling and Personal Abuse.'[30]

Pre-Revolutionary trade habits of neutrality, it seems, did not always promote that disputatious 'liberty of the press' advocated by such libertarian authors as Trenchard and Gordon. Instead, sometimes citing Addison, colonial printers repeatedly indicated their reluctance to open their presses—their newspapers especially—wide enough to allow a full range of controversial matter into the public forum.[31] Most commonly, by filling the columns of their papers with anecdotal news of European war and diplomacy, colonial printers tried to avoid becoming embroiled in local struggles. Accordingly, the contents of most colonial papers were unrelievedly bland—'*dull and flat*,' as James Franklin would tacitly concede in a late subdued phase of his career.[32]

If it is true that the political language and thought of pre-Revolutionary America were often curiously unrevealing, highly sensitive perhaps to the shared concerns of local elites but not to the issues that made for divisions among both powerful and common people, the trade strategies of printers may have been partially responsible. Unaccustomed to a politics in which partisan activity was fully legitimate, they acted in such a way as to retard the development of a public forum where conflicts could be thoroughly and continuously articulated. Only during

[30] *Pennsylvania Gazette*, June 10, 1731; *Autobiography of Franklin*, p. 165. From one point of view, James Morton Smith, *William and Mary Quarterly*, 3d ser. 20 (1963): 157–59, is probably correct in arguing that in practice—regardless of prevailing legal doctrine—there was considerable freedom in the American colonies from official coercion of the press. Self-censorship on the basis of business strategy, however, made the colonial press far less 'radical' than Gary B. Nash suggests in 'The Transformation of Urban Politics, 1700–1765,' *Journal of American History* 60 (1973–74): 606, 616–18.

[31] On the influence of political writers like Trenchard and Gordon, see Gary Huxford, 'The English Libertarian Tradition in the Colonial Newspaper,' *Journalism Quarterly* 45 (1968): 677–86, but the argument there ignores an important contrary tradition; see, for example, Elizabeth Christine Cook, *Literary Influences in Colonial Newspapers, 1705–1750* (New York, 1912), p. 125.

[32] The convenience of foreign news has been noted with regard to the provincial English press by Cranfield, *Development of the Provincial Newspaper*, p. 67; the point applies equally well to America. *Rhode-Island Gazette*, Nov. 23, 1732.

the prolonged crisis of the Revolutionary period did printers as a group begin to act in ways that promoted a politics directly expressive of tension and dissent.

3. FRANKLIN AND HIS FRIENDS

In the first major political contest of the Revolutionary years, the controversy over the Stamp Act, colonial printers had a substantial economic interest. David Ramsay was later to suggest that printers, never lacking in 'attention to the profits of their profession,' had united to oppose legislation that 'threatened a great diminution' of their income as well as an abridgement of American liberty.[33] At the time the act was passed, Franklin—serving as a colonial agent in London—realized immediately that it would place a heavy economic burden on his former profession. 'I think it will affect the Printers more than anybody,' he wrote early in 1765 to his managing partner in Philadelphia, 'as a Sterling Halfpenny Stamp on every Half Sheet of a Newspaper, and Two shillings Sterling on every Advertisement, will go near to knock up one Half of both. There is also Fourpence Sterling on every Almanack.'[34]

There was ample precedent in England for taxing printed matter, novel as it was of Parliament to apply such a plan to the empire. For over half a century, a stamp tax had been in force in the mother country, and the system was not generally regarded as intolerable.[35] It had caused occasional distress in the provinces, however, and previous experience with local stamp duties in New York and Massachusetts had suggested that a tax on paper, payable by the printer in advance, might damage the colonial trade. Like their provincial brethren, but unlike

[33] Ramsay's observations were cited approvingly by Arthur M. Schlesinger, *Prelude to Independence: The Newspaper War on Britain, 1764–1776* (New York, 1958), which greatly elaborated on the theme; a more recent discussion along the same lines is provided by Francis G. Walett, 'The Impact of the Stamp Act on the Colonial Press,' in Donovan H. Bond and W. Reynolds McLeod, eds., *Newsletters to Newspapers: Eighteenth-Century Journalism* (Morgantown, W.Va., 1977), pp. 157–69. An abbreviated version of the analysis that follows, through part 5, appeared in Botein, ' "Meer Mechanics" and an Open Press,' pp. 211–25.

[34] Franklin to David Hall, Feb. 14, 1765, *Franklin Papers*, 12: 65–67.

[35] On English experience, which suggested that the 'vent' of newspapers depended less upon price than upon 'circumstances of the times exciting more or less curiosity,' see Frederick S. Siebert, 'Taxes on Publications in England in the Eighteenth Century,' *Journalism Quarterly* 21 (1944): 12–24; Edward Hughes, 'The English Stamp Duties, 1664–1774,' *English Historical Review* 56 (1951): 234–64.

publishers in London, printers in the colonies sold mostly on credit, some of which inevitably turned out to be bad. Understandably, then, they were fearful that much of the new tax could not be passed on to their customers.[36]

The first reaction of David Hall, Franklin's Philadelphia partner, was that it might not be worthwhile to continue the *Pennsylvania Gazette* at all. 'The Case betwixt you and us, with respect to News Papers,' Hall explained to William Strahan in London, 'is very different—your Hawkers are ready to take yours all off, and pay the Ready Money for them.' James Parker, a key Franklin associate in New York, predicted that his days in the trade were numbered, since 'the fatal *Black-Act*' with its 'killing Stamp' would surely turn printing into a business of 'very little Consequence.'[37]

No doubt this was unduly alarmist; both Franklin and Strahan tried to encourage Hall with a variety of optimistic suggestions.[38] But by the beginning of summer it was apparent that the dimensions of the problem had changed. Well before they had the opportunity to formulate business strategies that would minimize the threat of the Stamp Act to their livelihoods, printers in the colonies were faced with the more urgent challenge of coping with unprecedented political turbulence. For some—often 'the more opulent,' as Isaiah Thomas recalled[39]—traditional habits of political caution prevailed; among the hesitant were Franklin's associates in the trade. Such was the magnitude of the trans-

[36] On the problems of printers in provincial England, see Cranfield, *Development of the Provincial Newspaper*, pp. 44–47, 237–40; Wiles, *Freshest Advices*, pp. 98–103. Colonial experience is discussed by Mack Thompson, 'Massachusetts and New York Stamp Acts,' *William and Mary Quarterly*, 3d ser. 26 (1969): 253–58. The distress of printers in Massachusetts is mentioned by Thomas, *History of Printing*, 2: 186n, 232, 238–41. The effects of similar legislation in New York, 'like to a killing Frost,' were vividly described at the time in a printer's broadside; 'James Parker *versus* New York Province,' ed. Beverly McAnear, *New York History* 22 (1941): 321–22, 326–28, 330n. Parker's reaction to the new parliamentary statute, illustrated below, was perhaps predictable.

[37] Hall to Strahan, May 19, 1765, David Hall Papers, American Philosophical Society, Philadelphia; Parker to Franklin, Apr. 25, June 14, 1765, *Franklin Papers*, 12: 111–13, 174–76.

[38] Their basic assumption was that Hall would be able to add the tax to his prices and inaugurate a policy of payment in advance. Franklin to Hall, June 8, 1765, *Franklin Papers*, 12: 170–72; Strahan to Hall, July 8, 1765, David Hall Papers.

[39] Thomas, *History of Printing*, 2: 189.

atlantic crisis, however, that their customary business strategies failed to provide reliable guidelines for behavior.

David Hall, for one, had never been inclined to meddle rashly in controversy; but this instinct, so often useful in the past, seemed inappropriate or even imprudent in the radically altered circumstances. In June 1765, he reported to Franklin with some bewilderment that the *Gazette*'s customers were already 'leaving off fast' in anticipation of the Stamp Act. For the most part, it was not that they lacked the extra shillings; it was a question of principle. Their resolution, Hall said, was 'not to pay any thing towards that Tax they can possibly avoid; and News Papers, they tell me, they can, and will, do without.' Evidently uncertain himself as to the constitutional implications of the new law, Hall perceived the temper of the colonies with apprehension. 'In short,' he observed privately, 'the whole Continent are discontented with the Law, think their Liberties and Privileges, as Englishmen, are lost, and seem, many of them, almost desperate.—What the Consequences will be, God only knows.' Hall's own fear was that there would be 'a great deal of Mischief.'[40]

Unquestionably, considered from the perspective of his trade, the Stamp Act was a 'horrid Law' that would 'knock up' most printers in America. But Hall was in no hurry to oppose it publicly. From the first, he told Franklin, exaggerating somewhat, 'all of the Papers on the Continent, ours excepted, were full of Spirited Papers against the Stamp Law, and . . . because, I did not publish those Papers likewise, I . . . got a great Deal of Ill-will.' Hall had hoped to ride out the storm, but after a while came to realize that he had been 'much mistaken' as to his proper course of action. The *Gazette*'s silence, zealous patriots warned, would injure the cause of the people. 'And, I have been told by many,' Hall explained, 'that our Interest will certainly suffer by it.' It would be best 'to humour them in some Publications, as they seem to insist so much upon it.' Yet he hesitated to rush into the fray, 'the Risk being so great' if he pursued a course of outright defiance.[41] Eventually, like

[40] Hall to Franklin, June 20, 1765, *Franklin Papers*, 12: 188–89; Hall to Strahan, Sept. 6, 1765, David Hall Papers.

[41] Hall to Strahan, Sept. 19, 1765, David Hall Papers. Hall to Franklin, Sept. 6, Oct. 14, 1765, *Franklin Papers*, 12: 255–59, 319–21. See generally Robert D. Harlan, 'David Hall and the Stamp Act,' *Papers of the Bibliographical Society of America* 61 (1967): 13–37.

many of his colonial brethren, he made the most of a disagreeable situation by publishing his paper without his name on it. Uneasily and with circumspection, he became and would remain a patriot—less ardent than his chief business rival, William Bradford III, but forthright enough at least to avoid being accused of Toryism.[42]

Further to the south, Charleston's Peter Timothy was even more circuitous in his response to the issues of the Revolutionary period. Since he was an official in the imperial postal system, his loyalties were suspect from the very beginning of the crisis. Naturally, he abhorred 'Grenville's hellish Idea of the Stamp-Act,' but he was reluctant to join the resistance movement. Acting in concert with most of his southern brethren, he elected to suspend his *Gazette* temporarily rather than to continue publication in overt disregard of the new law. Furthermore, he declined 'to direct, support and engage in the most violent Opposition'—so he later explained to Franklin, a former business associate— and this thoroughly 'exasperated every Body.' The result was that within a short time he found himself reduced from 'the most *popular*' to 'the most *unpopular* Man in the Province.' Especially humiliating was the decision of local patriots to help Charles Crouch, his brother-in-law and once his apprentice, to set up a new *South-Carolina Gazette* that would represent the cause of American liberty more boldly than either Timothy's or the even more timorous *Gazette* of Robert Wells. For a time, Crouch's paper prospered, as its warm criticism of the Stamp Act attracted patriot readers. Having missed his chance, Timothy seemed unable to restore his credit with the more hot-blooded spirits of Charleston. 'Ruduced [*sic*] to this situation,' he advised Franklin in 1768, 'I have not been myself since Nov. 1765. Nor shall I recover, unless I quit the Post-Office when some other Occasion offers to distinguish myself in the Cause of America.'[43]

When opportunity next beckoned, Timothy was somewhat more alert to the perils of hesitation. In 1770 he distinguished himself as the only southern printer to mark the Boston Massacre with black newspaper borders. Just the year before, however, he had printed William Henry Drayton's caustic criticisms of the nonimportation agreement in force

[42] Schlesinger, *Prelude to Independence*, pp. 77–78.

[43] Timothy to Franklin, Sept. 3, 1768, *Franklin Papers*, 15: 199–203; Hennig Cohen, *The South Carolina Gazette, 1732–1775* (Columbia, S.C., 1953), p. 142; Schlesinger, *Prelude to Independence*, pp. 78–79; Thomas, *History of Printing*, 2: 160–61, 370–71.

at Charleston, and as late as 1772 his interest in politics seemed to lapse. He had 'suffered, by never being lukewarm in any Cause,' he told Franklin then, and so—his eyes 'almost worn out'—he was prepared to accept a comfortable retirement post in the British imperial administration. As it happened, nothing was immediately forthcoming, and soon afterward Timothy's patriotic ardor revived, carrying him to the prestigious peak of his lengthy career. In the following years, as he proudly informed Franklin in 1777, he was 'continually in Motion,' as secretary to the second Provincial Congress and a member of various political committees. Briefly imprisoned by the British in 1780, he died two years later, assured of his reputation as a patriot.[44] To reach that point, however, had required a long and somewhat roundabout journey.

For James Parker—temporarily in New Jersey when the Stamp Act passed, having left his New York office under the management of a Virginian named John Holt—even a lukewarm commitment was to be avoided. Much as he loathed the new tax, he could not seriously contemplate resistance. Sometimes, he wrote to Franklin in June 1765, 'the true Old English Spirit of Liberty will rise within me, yet as there is a Necessity to acquiesce in the Chains laid on me, I endeavour at a patient Resignation.' Fortunately, it appeared, he was at a distance from the arena of conflict—'or perhaps the Impetuosity of my Temper would have plunged me deep one way or the other.' Impetuous or not, he plainly had no stomach for popular agitation and disorder. As tensions mounted in the fall of 1765, it seemed to him that the people were 'running Mad,' and would speedily bring 'an End to all Government' by their 'dreadful Commotions.'[45]

---

[44] Cohen, *South Carolina Gazette*, pp. 13, 244–47; Schlesinger, *Prelude to Independence*, pp. 126–27. Timothy to Franklin, Aug. 24, 1772, *Franklin Papers*, 19: 283–85; June 12, 1777, in 'The Correspondence of Peter Timothy, Printer of Charlestown, with Benjamin Franklin,' ed. Douglas C. McMurtrie, *South Carolina Historical and Genealogical Magazine* 35 (1934): 128–29.

[45] Parker to Franklin, June 14, Sept. 22, Oct. 10, Nov. 6, 1765, *Franklin Papers*, 12: 174–76, 274–77, 308–10, 355. Parker's eagerness to avoid trouble may have been heightened as a result of his apparently inadvertent connection with the notorious *Constitutional Courant*, an extraordinary one-issue journal of radical propaganda that William Goddard—then associated with John Holt—seems to have printed on Parker's press at Woodbridge, presumably without Parker's permission. See ibid., pp. 287–88n, and Ward L. Miner, *William Goddard, Newspaperman* (Durham, N.C., 1962), pp. 50–52. Schlesinger, *Prelude to Independence*, p. 111, misleadingly groups Parker with Holt as 'devoted patriots.'

The next year, returning to New York, Parker continued to lament the insubordinate 'Spirit of Independence' that inflamed the populace. He had moved back at the urging of Franklin, who wanted him there to serve more effectively as general comptroller of the colonial post office; as an additional incentive to relocate, Franklin provided a minor customs post in the city. Predictably, like Peter Timothy in Charleston, Parker soon became implicated in the bitter political divisions of the time. The Sons of Liberty, he told Franklin, 'carry all before them.' Their favorite printer, John Holt, was emboldened to harass Parker by refusing to relinquish management of the New York office, although Parker was unquestionably its sole proprietor. Eventually Holt yielded the title of Parker's old paper, the *New-York Gazette*, renaming his own after John Peter Zenger's famed *Journal*, but Parker was still obliged to 'launch into Business' anew, without his former clientele and even some of his office equipment.[46]

Most damaging was the decline that his political reputation had suffered in the course of the previous year. 'Mr. *Holt*,' he noted in a bitter broadside, 'seems to insinuate . . . that in the late Troubles I was no Friend to Liberty.' This was probably unfair of Holt, but Parker's public record was indeed ambiguous. In spite of his antipathy to the Stamp Act, he had done what he could to insure compliance with the law, evidently considering this to be the unavoidable duty of a royal official. One consequence, apparently, was 'a little Sour Looking, and perhaps some Contempt.' More serious was the widespread feeling, nurtured carefully by Holt, that Parker's crown offices—his customs appointment in particular—had compromised his personal integrity. In 1768, the customs job may well have cost him the patronage of the New York Assembly.[47]

Evidently it was difficult for Parker to abandon the old trade ways and plunge into controversy with enough zeal to please the emerging leadership of the patriot movement. John Holt had no trouble outmaneuvering his former employer and business associate. In 1768 Parker's fortunes rose as he began to run the 'American Whig' essays of the

[46] Parker to Franklin, June 11, May 6, Oct. 25, 1766, *Franklin Papers*, 13: 300–312, 262–66, 472–76.

[47] Beverly McAnear, 'James Parker *versus* John Holt,' *Proceedings of the New Jersey Historical Society* 59 (1941): 88–95, 199. Parker to Franklin, Sept. 11, Oct. 11, 1766, *Franklin Papers*, 13: 409–13, 454–59; Jan. 21, 1768, ibid., 15: 27–28.

Livingstonian party in his *Gazette*; within a short time he had gained more than 200 new subscribers, while losing only 70 Anglicans. Holt quickly pirated the series, though, and it became doubtful whether Parker's recently acquired customers would stay with him. Once again, late in 1769, he chose to try his hand at polemical politics by printing an anonymous broadside libel written by Alexander McDougall; then, threatened with a legal proceeding and dismissal from the post office, he backed down and identified the author. Not long afterward Parker died, having made a few last-minute efforts to atone for this treachery by publishing on behalf of McDougall's cause.[48]

Perhaps this indicated where his true sympathies lay; possibly he was in the process of beginning to commit himself aggressively—as Timothy would—to the Revolutionary position. Nevertheless, considered as a whole, Parker's politics in the crucial years after passage of the Stamp Act had been unhappily inconsistent. No American printer had been more vehement in his criticism of colonial stamp duties than Parker, but his perceptions of economic self-interest had not made him into a Son of Liberty. The lasting strength of old trade ways, in spite of new political realities, was revealed in Parker's continuing attempts to shun conflict long after it might have been apparent that this strategy was unwise. By trying to avoid one kind of trouble, Parker invited another.

One reason Hall, Timothy, and Parker were unequipped to deal with the abnormal pressures of a Revolutionary situation was Franklin, their long-time patron and associate in the trade. More than anyone else, even while on assignment as a colonial agent in London, he could claim influence among American printers; over the years, especially south of New England, he had accumulated business connections that to some observers looked dangerously like a transatlantic propaganda network. 'Depend upon my doing every Thing in this Affair for the Printers and Papermakers,' he had promised Hall at the time of the Stamp Act, 'as zealously as if I were still to be concerned in the Business.'[49] Unfortu-

---

[48] Parker to Franklin, April 18, 1768, ibid., 15: 100–102; May 30, 1769, ibid., 16: 137–40. Thomas, *History of Printing*, 2: 479–83; Schlesinger, *Prelude to Independence*, pp. 114–15.

[49] Franklin to Hall, June 8, 1765, *Franklin Papers*, 12: 170–72. The charge that Franklin used his trade connections for political advantage became especially pointed as a result of his role in the Hutchinson letters controversy. *Writings of Franklin*, 6: 286–88, and see more generally *Benjamin Franklin's Letters to the Press*, ed. Verner W. Crane (Chapel Hill, 1950).

nately for those who followed his cues, Franklin's political judgment at the beginning of the Revolutionary crisis was unsure, not least because at some level of consciousness—despite his retirement from active business life—he remained a colonial printer. His practice of imperial politics represented with curious exaggeration the habitual trade policy of neutrality, elevated to the sphere of statecraft. Much has been written of Franklin's passion for conciliation and his extraordinary diplomatic skill; interpretations based on political and even psychoanalytic theory have been suggested. Viewed from a different perspective, however, Franklin's public behavior in London during the period before Independence may be understood as an extension of the business and political strategies that he and his brethren in the colonial trade had followed for decades preceding the Revolutionary crisis.[50]

Thus, as an agent, he tried to act the part not of an advocate but of a reporter—an 'impartial historian of American facts and opinions.' With some of the instinctive distaste for controversy that characterized newspaper publishers in the colonies, Franklin also set out to mute transatlantic political debate. 'At the same time that we Americans wish not to be judged of, in the gross by particular papers written by anonymous scribblers and published in the colonies,' he wrote to his son in 1767, 'it would be well if we could avoid falling into the same mistake in America of judging of ministers here by the libels printed against them.' His self-assigned task was not only to report impartially the arguments of both sides, each to the other, but also to discount all extreme, offensive statements of opinion—'to extenuate matters a little,' as he explained.[51]

If in the past this approach to imperial affairs had worked well, it was ill suited for a period of intense political turmoil. Hoping to please both his colonial employers and British officialdom, Franklin found it difficult to satisfy either side. It 'has often happened to me,' he wrote shortly after his subtle involvement in the Hutchinson letters uproar

---

[50] See, for example, Gerald Stourzh, *Benjamin Franklin and American Foreign Policy* (Chicago, 1954); Richard Bushman, 'On the Uses of Psychology: Conflict and Conciliation in Benjamin Franklin,' *History and Theory* 5 (1966): 227–40. Another interpretation of Franklin's outlook as a printer—which does not take into account the habits of a provincial tradesman—is to be found in Lewis T. Simpson, 'The Printer as a Man of Letters: Franklin and the Symbolism of the Third Realm,' in J. A. Leo Lemay, ed., *The Oldest Revolutionary: Essays on Benjamin Franklin*, (Philadelphia, 1976), pp. 3–20.

[51] *Franklin's Letters to the Press*, p. xxxvii. Benjamin Franklin to William Franklin, Nov. 25, Dec. 29, 1767, *Franklin Papers*, 14: 322–26, 349–51.

had been exposed, 'that while I have been thought here too much of an American, I have in America been deem'd too much of an Englishman.'[52] Both compromised and compromising, Franklin played a role in London—so typical in its essentials of a colonial printer—that diminished his credibility with patriots as well as English officials, and therefore reduced his usefulness to long-time associates like Hall, Timothy, and Parker.

Most troublesome to patriots was the lingering memory of his initial acquiescence in the Stamp Act. With pardonable ambivalence, Hall wrote that he wished his famous partner could have provided daily counsel 'on the Spot' instead of three thousand miles away. Yet, added Hall, 'I should be afraid of your Safety, as the Spirit of the People is so violent against every One, they think has the least concern with the Stamp Law, and they have imbibed the Notion, that you had a Hand, in the framing of it.' Nowhere were the distortions of Franklin's outlook more evident than in the congratulations he conveyed to Hall for trying to exclude criticism of the Stamp Act from the *Pennsylvania Gazette*. 'Nothing has done America more Hurt here,' he explained, 'than those kind of Writings; so that I should have been equally averse to printing them if I had held no Office under the Crown.'[53]

Whether or not Franklin really was 'a dangerous Person,' as John Holt would later complain in private to a fellow printer, it was plain enough—within the trade as well as without—that in the early years of the imperial crisis he lacked his usually shrewd sense of political direction. His decision to abandon the middle ground and espouse the colonial cause was gradual and far from enthusiastic. 'I assure you,' he wrote in 1772 in answer to Peter Timothy's request for a job, 'it is not in my Power to procure you that Post you mention or any other, whatever my Wishes may be for your Prosperity.' His explanation reflected resigna-

---

[52] *Writings of Franklin*, 6: 260. This observation appeared in an apologetic tract of 1774 that went unpublished during his lifetime. To English radicals like Thomas Hollis, too, Franklin was a 'doubtful Character.' See, for example, Franklin to Thomas Brand Hollis, Oct. 5, 1783, ibid., 9: 103–5.

[53] Hall to Franklin, Sept. 6, 1765, *Franklin Papers*, 12: 255–59; Franklin to Hall, Sept. 14, 1765, ibid., 12: 267–68. Indeed, Franklin's custom of publishing softened versions of his opinions in London—which were then reprinted in colonial newspapers—was especially damaging to his reputation at home; see ibid., p. 207n. Of course, his position at the head of the colonial post office and the political ambitions of his son also complicated his role in London.

tion more than patriot ardor. 'I am now thought here too much an American,' he pointed out, 'to have any Interest of the kind.' Ultimately, like Timothy but on a much grander scale, Franklin emerged from the Revolutionary turmoil with honor, even glory; but this happened at least in part because in 1774 the British ministry moved against him so heavy-handedly for his complicity in the Hutchinson affair.[54] Until then, still the colonial printer, he had persisted in his reluctance to engage in overt partisan politics, continuing perilously late to value the benefits of official British patronage.

4. RELUCTANT PARTISANS

Similar doubts and hesitation were characteristic of other colonial printers, although they were not as close to Franklin as Hall, Timothy, or Parker. Unused to the violently polarizing effects of a Revolutionary conflict, they tried to temporize, often to their eventual regret. Willingly or not, sooner or later most printers in the colonies gave up neutrality to choose sides. More than twice as many, it appears, opted for the patriots as for the Tories. No exact count is possible, however, since some switched parties and others were so tepid in their commitments as to elude meaningful classification.[55] Reluctant to advertise themselves as full-fledged partisans, many printers tried in public to claim the middle of the road, steering one way or another only when obliged.

Some, like Franklin and his associates, managed in the end to establish themselves convincingly as patriots. In North Carolina, for example, James Davis and Adam Boyd were able to take a patriot line while continuing to avoid excessive partisanship, as were James Adams in Delaware and Jonas Green in Maryland.[56] Outside the southern colonies, however, this was less usual, on account of competition from

[54] Miner, *William Goddard*, pp. 163–64; Franklin to Timothy, Nov. 3, 1772, *Franklin Papers*, 19: 362; and see David Freeman Hawke, *Franklin* (New York, 1976), chaps. 29–30.

[55] Sidney Kobre, *The Development of the Colonial Newspaper* (Pittsburgh, 1944), pp. 147–48, lists 39 newspapers as patriot, 18 as Tory—which is probably as useful a ratio as any, since it was mainly by the contents of their papers that colonial printers signalled their loyalties.

[56] Charles Christopher Crittenden, *North Carolina Newspapers before 1790* (Chapel Hill, 1928), pp. 36–38; D. L. Hawkins, 'James Adams, The First Printer of Delaware,' *Papers of the Bibliographical Society of America* 28 (1934): 45–46; David K. Skaggs, 'Editorial Policies of the *Maryland Gazette*, 1765–1783,' *Maryland Historical Magazine* 59 (1964): 346.

more energetically patriot presses. For a patriot printer who wished seriously to persist in the old ways, the most effective solution may have been that adopted by the Fleet brothers, Thomas, Jr., and John, who published Boston's *Evening-Post*. Although it was known that their personal sympathies lay with the American cause, their policy as printers was to maintain at least a semblance of impartiality. According to one querulous Tory, the Fleets restricted comments by pro-American 'Dirt-casters' to 'the Holes and Corners and other private Purlieus' of their paper, whereas 'all the Pages and Columns' of the fiery *Boston Gazette* were filled with inflammatory propaganda against the mother country. As late as the early months of 1775, the Fleet brothers were still promising that the *Evening-Post* would be 'conducted with the utmost Freedom and Impartiality,' and would always, 'as usual, be open for the Insertion of all Pieces that shall tend to amuse or instruct, or to the promoting of useful Knowledge and the general Good of Mankind.' The next month, they published a letter from a self-styled moderate commending their editorial policy, and another—on the duty of obedience—that hailed their 'well known impartiality.' A week later, without prior notice, the last issue of the *Evening-Post* appeared, with a brief note from the printers explaining that they had decided to suspend publication until matters were 'in a more settled State.' Since matters only became more unsettled, the *Evening-Post* never revived. Without sacrificing other printing business, the Fleets were thus able to remain faithful to old trade ways in a stridently patriot community.[57]

More commonly, however, lukewarm Toryism became the only realistic option for a printer determined to stay neutral in the face of strenuous patriot pressures. Georgia's James Johnston, for one, veered inconsistently as he responded to both threats and incentives; eventually, because he was not enough a patriot, he became a Tory, was declared by patriots to be guilty of treason, and was banished. Among other printers who were forced by this logic to back slowly into Toryism were such prominent figures as Robert Wells of Charleston and Boston's Richard Draper. Strict political neutrality, which had never been easy to achieve

[57] Thomas, *History of Printing*, 2: 333–34; Schlesinger, *Prelude to Independence*, p. 93; *Boston Evening-Post*, Mar. 6, Apr. 10, 17, 24, 1775. Mary Ann Yodelis, *Who Paid the Piper? Publishing Economics in Boston, 1763–1775* (Lexington, Ky., 1975), pp. 11–13, indicates that the Fleets' general printing business did not suffer especially before the outbreak of war; it was their newspaper that was vulnerable.

in a time of conflict, became highly implausible during a revolution. In 1775, Philadelphia's James Humphreys, Jr., founded the *Pennsylvania Ledger* with the naively stated intention of keeping it authentically open to all sides. When this proved futile, he became known by default as a Tory. 'The impartiality of the Ledger,' Isaiah Thomas commented laconically, 'did not comport with the temper of the times.'[58]

How Revolutionary pressures within the printing trade could transform an uneasy patriot into an uneasy Tory was revealed painfully in the careers of Daniel and Robert Fowle, in New Hampshire. Perhaps because of his previous unhappy involvement in a 'famous Cause' of New England's political history, Daniel Fowle was disinclined to make a firm commitment in the Revolutionary crisis. Although he associated himself with Wilkes to support the longstanding lawsuit that he had brought after his false imprisonment by the Massachusetts House in 1754, for allegedly printing the notorious *Monster of Monsters*, otherwise his deportment reflected habits of prudence befitting a public printer who also served as a magistrate. His *New-Hampshire Gazette*, which he conducted with his nephew Robert, 'was not remarkable in its political features,' according to Isaiah Thomas. If 'its general complexion was favorable to the cause of the country,' mild patriotism was not enough in time of stress. 'Some zealous whigs,' Thomas recalled, 'who thought the Fowles were too timid in the cause of liberty, or their press too much under the influence of the officers of the crown,' encouraged one Thomas Furber to establish the *Portsmouth Mercury* early in 1765. Although the upstart paper began with a customarily cautious promise 'to print Nothing that may have the least Tendency to subvert Good Order,' it went on to assert that 'neither Opposition, arbitrary Power, or publick Injuries' would be 'screen'd from the Knowledge of the People, whose Liberties are dearer to them than their Lives.'[59]

Furber himself proved so disappointingly prudent that the Fowles were able to outdo him in patriot spirit by the end of the Stamp Act controversy, but in the long run their *Gazette* was still insufficiently partisan. In 1772 Benjamin Edes and John Gill, printers of the *Boston*

---

[58] Alexander A. Lawrence, *James Johnston: Georgia's First Printer* (Savannah, 1956), pp. 10–22; Philip Davidson, *Propaganda and the American Revolution, 1763–1783* (Chapel Hill, 1941), pp. 304–7; Thomas, *History of Printing*, 2: 333–34.

[59] Clyde Augustus Duniway, *The Development of Freedom of the Press in Massachusetts* (New York, 1906), p. 172; Thomas, *History of Printing*, 2: 281–84, 1: 434.

Gazette, accused Robert Fowle of scheming to obtain a customs house appointment—a charge that Fowle merely dismissed as 'premature and founded in a Mistake.' Furthermore, he told his readers, it was 'more honorable to hold any Post under the Government, than to spend his Time in libelling and railing at the Rulers of the People,' as Edes and Gill did. Two years later, following the neutral logic of pre-Revolutionary printers, the *New-Hampshire Gazette* reprinted the opposing views of 'Novanglus' and 'Massachusettensis' in parallel columns, along with advice from the printers that people '*read both Sides with an impartial Mind*.' Daniel Fowle was subsequently reprimanded by the New Hampshire legislature for his willingness to publish an argument against American independence; Robert, less fortunate, came to be known unequivocally as a Tory and was forced to flee, eventually finding consolation as a British pensioner.[60]

Most Tory printers waited as long as they dared before abandoning fully the trade principle of neutrality. This was especially so in Boston, where patriot feeling was a stern discouragement to those interested in printing for the cause of crown and Parliament. Because Richard Draper was insufficiently enthusiastic in his attachment to the mother country, despite his appointment as printer to the governor and king, it was necessary for Thomas Hutchinson and his friends to cast about for more adventurous figures in the trade. To find the right men proved difficult. John Green and Joseph Russell, in business together since 1755 and printers to the Assembly, were apparently prepared to risk the displeasure of patriots and accept the lucrative contract that Governor Bernard secured for them in 1767, to serve the new Board of Customs Commissioners in Boston. It also seems that when John Dickinson's *Farmer's Letters* first attracted local notice, partisans of the mother country privately urged Green and Russell 'by no means to print the same.' Heeding this advice, they promptly fell out of favor with the House of Representatives and most of their former clientele. 'Mind, Green, who will get most at the winding up of Affairs,' Bernard supposedly said by way of cajolery, 'Edes and Gill or you.'[61] This was not

60 Ibid., 2: 283–84; *New-Hampshire Gazette*, Nov. 20, 1772; Schlesinger, *Prelude to Independence*, p. 221; Ralph H. Brown, 'New Hampshire Editors Win the War,' *New England Quarterly* 12 (1939): 35–51.

61 Thomas, *History of Printing*, 1: 347–48; O. M. Dickerson, 'British Control of American Newspapers on the Eve of the Revolution,' *New England Quarterly* 24 (1951): 455–59.

enough to reassure the anxious partners, however, so Massachusetts Tories were forced to seek out other printers.

John Mein and his partner John Fleeming, recent immigrants from Scotland, had been quick to serialize the *Farmer's Letters* in their *Boston Chronicle*, professing eagerness that the paper 'always, when any dispute claims general attention, give both sides of the question, if they can be obtained.' But evidently the prospect of customs patronage persuaded them instead to try specializing in 'the partial Praise of a Party,' as Edes and Gill scornfully explained. Mein, it seems, was altogether too choleric to survive in Boston. After exposing local violators of the non-importation agreement, assaulting John Gill, and drawing a pistol on a hostile mob, he hastily made his way to England, where he became a hack writer for the North ministry. Left behind, his associate Fleeming struggled on for a time, only to be supplanted by a new Tory team consisting of two young printers—John Hicks, formerly an apprentice of Green and Russell, and Nathaniel Mills, who had been trained by Fleeming. Hicks, who originally had been something of a patriot, was said to have been involved creditably in the circumstances of the Boston Massacre. But, observed Isaiah Thomas, 'Interest too often biasses the human mind.' Although his own father was killed by English troops at the very beginning of the Revolutionary War, Hicks became a Tory.[62]

To the south, only New York offered Tories adequate printing facilities. By 1774, according to an indignant out-of-town newspaper reader, Hugh Gaine and James Rivington were brazenly publishing anyone who would 'sneer at, and deduct from the merit of the most ascertained and sacred Patriots.' Nevertheless, both printers persisted in justifying themselves in accordance with traditional trade rhetoric. 'Gaine,' Isaiah Thomas would recall, 'seemed desirous to side with the successful party; but, not knowing which would eventually prevail, he seems to have been unstable in his politics.' Perhaps because of his previous connections with New York's Anglican community, his *Mercury* appeared to be leaning in the direction of Toryism by the early 1770s, but not irrevocably so. Nor was Rivington's bias especially obvi-

[62] Joseph T. Buckingham, *Specimens of Newspaper Literature*, 2 vols. (Boston, 1850), 1: 213; John E. Alden, 'John Mein: Scourge of Patriots,' *Publications of the Colonial Society of Massachusetts* 34 (1937–42): 582–83, and 571–99 in general; 'The Letter-Book of Mills & Hicks,' ed. Robert Earle Moody and Charles Christopher Crittenden, *North Carolina Historical Review* 14 (1937): 39–41; Thomas, *History of Printing*, 1: 389–91.

ous when in 1773 he began to publish his highly successful *Gazetteer*. Promising to avoid 'acrimonious Censures on any Society or Class of Men,' Rivington announced that it was his goal to be 'as generally useful and amusing as possible.' In the circumstances, this would have required remarkable diplomatic talent. 'When so many Persons of a vast Variety of Views and Inclinations are to be satisfied,' the *Gazetteer* conceded in a shrewder vein, 'it must often happen, that what is highly agreeable to some, will be equally disagreeable to others.'[63]

What stamped both Gaine and Rivington as Tory sympathizers by 1774 was not so much their public political sentiments as their apparent determination to maintain the traditional neutrality of the trade. In contrast to Philadelphia's patriot printers, who were said to refuse to publish the Tory viewpoint because of their 'unaccountable delicacy,' Gaine and Rivington claimed to understand what a 'free press' should be. The 'TRUE SONS OF LIBERTY,' Rivington suggested in his *Gazetteer*, were those who printed without showing partiality. A few issues later, he quoted with approval an article from a London newspaper that caustically described the efforts of American patriots to abridge 'freedom of the press' by preventing printers from 'daring to publish on both sides.' Fortunately, noted Rivington, there were some courageous souls who could withstand such pressure. 'The printer of a newspaper,' he declared, 'ought to be neutral in all cases where his own press is employed.' He himself would definitely publish all views in his paper, and also all pamphlets submitted to him, 'whether of the Whig or Tory flavour.'[64]

Privately, too, Rivington did his best to resist a premature commitment to Toryism, despite his own personal and business ties to the mother country, from which he had emigrated a decade earlier. In 1774 he assured Philadelphia's Charles Thomson that he would listen to the latter's 'excellent moral Counsell' against antagonizing patriot colonists, and would be careful to 'give no more offence on the score of

[63] *Pennsylvania Journal*, Oct. 19, 1774. Thomas, *History of Printing*, 2: 300; *The Journals of Hugh Gaine, Printer*, ed. Paul Leicester Ford, 2 vols. (New York, 1902), 1: 51–52; *Rivington's New-York Gazetteer*, Apr. 22, 1773. Rivington's goals may have been quite conventional at the outset. According to Thomas, *History of Printing*, 2: 315–16, no American paper was 'better printed, or more copiously furnished with foreign intelligence' than the *Gazetteer*.

[64] *New-York Gazette; and the Weekly Mercury* (the formal title of Gaine's paper after 1768), July 25, 1774; *Rivington's New-York Gazetteer*, July 14, Aug. 11, Dec. 8, 1774.

Impurity.' Most certainly, he would be happy to publish the opinions of American partisans in Philadelphia—'and I will use every endeavor to please all my patrons.' Through Henry Knox, his Boston correspondent, he also seems to have tried to let John Hancock know that he had meant no harm whatsoever, but had acted merely out of 'a necessity,' in publishing a letter critical of his conduct. Any appropriate reply, he indicated, would be graciously received and promptly put into print.[65]

That this was an untenable strategy to follow in an era of revolution was tacitly conceded by Rivington in a *Gazetteer* of December 1774, which presented a brief poetic summary of the printer's plight:

> Dares the poor man impartial be,
> He's doom'd to want and infamy.

A week later, a correspondent commended Rivington for following the policy of 'a true whig,' by remaining 'open to all doctrines,' but admitted that this could be accomplished 'only at the hazard of your fortune and your Life.' Circumstances were forcing Rivington to become a partisan. Toryism, after all, might bring its own rewards, which Isaiah Thomas considered 'sufficiently apparent' to be left unspecified. Circulating rumors mentioned the sum of £500 as a possible incentive. A boycott was organized against Rivington, and he was hanged in effigy; angry patriots went so far as to threaten his personal safety.[66]

Well into 1775, however, both he and Gaine were still equivocating. Much to the irritation of Lieutenant Governor Colden, Gaine refused to include in his *Mercury* a Tory account of what had happened at Lexington and Concord, and Rivington—who in March had begun to serialize Burke's 'Speech on American Taxation'—published two contradictory narratives. For a time, the latter even seemed to make his

[65] Rivington to Thomson, June 24, 1774, Bradford Papers, Historical Society of Pennsylvania, Philadelphia; Rivington to Knox, Apr. 20, 1774, in 'Henry Knox, Bookseller,' *Proceedings of the Massachusetts Historical Society* 61 (1927–28): 279–81. See generally Leroy Hewlett, 'James Rivington, Loyalist Printer, Publisher, and Bookseller of the American Revolution, 1724–1802' (Ph.D. diss., University of Michigan, 1958), chap. 2.

[66] *Rivington's New-York Gazetteer*, Dec. 8, 15, 1774; Thomas, *History of Printing*, 2: 113; Hewlett, 'James Rivington,' chap. 3. Further information about Rivington, for these and subsequent years, may be found in *Rivington's New York Newspaper: Excerpts from a Loyalist Press, 1773–1783*, Collections of the New-York Historical Society, vol. 84 (New York, 1973), pp. 1–27; Robert M. Ours, 'James Rivington: Another Viewpoint,' in Bond and McLeod, eds., *Newsletters to Newspapers*, pp. 219–33.

peace with some of the local patriots. Agreeing that he had 'given great Offence to the Colonies,' Rivington vowed publicly to make amends, explaining that he had been acting simply in deference to his notions of 'the Liberty of the Press' and his 'duty as a Printer.' Having conformed, he was exonerated by the Provincial Congress, only to lose all of his equipment to a destructive mob, apparently unimpressed by his show of penance. In 1776, he returned to England; Gaine, just before English troops occupied the city, left for Newark.[67]

Both would be back, though. Eventually, war—and the comforting presence of the British army—brought vacillating printers like Gaine and Rivington into the Tory ranks. Once there, they had little choice but to declare their loyalties with a forthrightness that their brethren of an earlier day would have considered most unbusinesslike. Gaine, it seems, deliberated and finally decided that 'the strongest party' was encamped in New York; accordingly, he recrossed the Hudson and resumed trade there. Then, in October 1777, Rivington 'surprised almost every Body,' as Gaine recorded in his journal, by reestablishing himself in the city with new equipment and the title of King's Printer. Plainly, this was bad news for Gaine, although he professed to welcome it; soon he had to take second place to Rivington. Always, Rivington announced in a new version of the *Gazetteer* brought out under the royal arms, he had labored 'to keep up and strengthen our Connection with the Mother Country, and to promote a proper Subordination to the Supreme Authority of the British Empire.' He hoped that 'his former Friends' would recall his services and patronize his office. Having belatedly discovered a firm sense of political principle underlying his previous conduct, Rivington proceeded to make the most of it.[68]

Like Gaine and Rivington, other printers in the colonies moved along the same circuitous route to Toryism, becoming unequivocally one-sided printers as much from military circumstance as from political principle or connection. Such camp followers in the trade included John Howe, the Robertson brothers, Mills and Hicks, and James Humphreys, Jr. Once they had made their decisions, they could not

[67] *Journals of Hugh Gaine*, 1: 52, and see generally Alfred Lawrence Lorenz, *Hugh Gaine: A Colonial Printer-Editor's Odyssey to Loyalism* (Carbondale, Ill., 1972), chaps. 6–10. *Rivington's New-York Gazetteer*, Mar. 16, 23, Apr. 27, June 1, May 4, 1775.

[68] Thomas, *History of Printing*, 2: 103–4; *Journals of Hugh Gaine*, 2: 50; *Rivington's New-York Gazette*, Oct. 13, 1777 (title varied afterward); Hewlett, 'James Rivington,' chap. 4.

easily retrace their steps. No one 'can wish more ardently than myself for a peace with America,' wrote John Hicks from Charleston in 1782, 'but rather than Great Britain should Stoop to acknowledge ye independency of this country I would sacrafice every farthing of my property & then my Person to oppose them.' Having been forced to leave Boston, Hicks had tried his hand at a number of different printing jobs and then—after being reunited with his partner Mills, who had spent two intervening years in England—he had opened a luxury import shop in British-controlled South Carolina. By the close of 1782, as the two men told their London supplier, they could only 'dread' a parliamentary surrender to American demands.[69]

In the end, like several of their fellow craftsmen who had come to favor the cause of the mother country, Mills and Hicks moved to Nova Scotia.[70] Toryism had been a gamble for them, and they had lost. More generally, traditional trade strategies had proven ineffective in Revolutionary conditions, incapable of protecting and sustaining those American printers who had tried to maintain the 'freedom' of their presses to Tory points of view.

5. New Commitments

As the prospects of some colonial printers became uncertain after 1765, with passage of the Stamp Act, those of others looked brighter. Seemingly, what was required was a knack for exploiting the political situation. Benjamin Mecom, Franklin's nephew, was as quick as anyone to see the possibilities of the crisis, although—as always—he lacked the talent to achieve success. Despite the economic burden that the new stamp duties threatened to place on printers, he proposed to establish a newspaper of his own. This was to be a staunchly patriot revival of the *Connecticut Gazette*, aimed at zealous Whigs in New Haven. Rival printers soon moved into town and took away his business by putting out a superior paper, but Mecom had acted in terms of the same strategy followed by Charleston's Charles Crouch and New Hampshire's Thomas Furber, in trying to profit from the partisan fervor of the moment.[71]

---

[69] Schlesinger, *Prelude to Independence*, pp. 291–92. Hicks to Thomas Dickenson, Jr., May 27, 1782, in 'Letter-Book of Mills & Hicks,' p. 62; Mills and Hicks to Champion and Dickenson, Dec. 9, 1782, ibid., pp. 68–69; and see ibid., pp. 41–44.

[70] Schlesinger, *Prelude to Independence*, pp. 257–58.

[71] Ibid., p. 75, and see James Parker to Benjamin Franklin, Dec. 24, 1767, *Franklin*

Especially for a printer of middling prosperity or less, the crisis could be interpreted as an opportunity to get ahead, by riding the waves of political emotion.

Correctly or not, many colonial printers appear to have made optimistic business calculations in response to the political troubles of the 1760s and 1770s, disregarding the economic discouragements first of the Stamp Act and later of the tax on paper included in the Townshend Act.[72] Before war physically disrupted the colonies, the Revolutionary period was a time of expansion in the American printing trade. From 1763 to 1775 the number of master printers at work in colonial America increased from forty-seven to eighty-two, while the number of newspapers that they published doubled, from twenty-one in 1763 to forty-two in 1775.[73] Conditions were such that many men in the trade were ready to try their luck and reach for entrepreneurial success. At least to some, however, it seemed that success was not to be achieved by following traditional routes. The vicissitudes of transatlantic conflict, nonimportation in particular, constricted the profits that printers could expect to derive from such allied enterprises as imported books and stationery. At the same time, newspaper circulation increased markedly, reflecting the heightened polemical temperature of colonial journalism. In the circumstances, it was natural enough for some printers to conclude that partisan commitments might prove advantageous. Although it is unclear whether or to what extent purely political printing grew to become a significant business of its own during the Revolutionary years, it was obvious that the political loyalties of printers could be crucial in determining who would be their customers, or readers, and who would not.[74]

Papers, 14: 345–48. It was a sign of Parker's own political obtuseness that he failed to appreciate Mecom's reasons for undertaking the project.

[72] Schlesinger, *Prelude to Independence*, p. 86, and Wroth, *Colonial Printer*, pp. 142–43, present the paper duties as onerous for the trade, but there is no evidence to suggest that printers perceived a serious economic threat. See, for example, Robert D. Harlan, 'David Hall and the Townshend Acts,' *Papers of the Bibliographical Society of America* 68 (1974): 19–38.

[73] Figures for printers are based on Charles Frederick Heartman, *Checklist of Printers in the United States from Stephen Daye to the Close of the War of Independence* (New York, 1915), which derives from a variety of standard bibliographical sources. As far as possible, Heartman has been corrected in the light of more accurate available information. Figures for newspapers are from Davidson, *Propaganda*, p. 225.

[74] See, for example, Harlan, 'David Hall and the Townshend Acts,' pp. 31–37; Schlesinger, *Prelude to Independence*, appendix A. Peter J. Parker, 'The Philadelphia

Compared with their Tory brethren, many patriot printers saw reason to react to the Revolutionary crisis by making early and relatively unambiguous political moves, accompanied by ardent expressions of high constitutional principle. Their cause, after all, was generally popular—hence likely to be profitable as well. Although some decorated their newspapers with variations on the slogan 'Open to ALL Parties, but Influenced by NONE,' this was now an empty gesture recalling a policy no longer relevant to the realities of American political controversy.[75]

Despite the persistence of conventional rhetoric, there was emerging a rudimentary alternative to the familiar trade understanding of 'liberty of the press.' Some of the inevitable verbal confusion accompanying this shift in meaning was evident in an issue of the *Pennsylvania Journal* that appeared in September 1766. Its printers, William Bradford III and his son Thomas, came forward to answer a harsh attack by the local stamp distributor, John Hughes, provoked by their exposé of his political correspondence. In threatening to start a lawsuit, they claimed, Hughes was trying 'to demolish the liberty of the Press.' But what precisely was that? Although the elder Bradford was a leading Son of Liberty and his paper had firmly opposed the Stamp Act, the Bradfords went on to recite a customary trade refrain. 'We are only the printers of a free and impartial paper,' they argued, 'and we challenge Mr. Hughes and the world, to convict us of partiality in this respect, or of even an inclination to restrain the freedom of the press in any instance.' Then, abruptly, they altered their emphasis. 'We can appeal to North-America not only for our impartiality as printers,' they said, 'but also for the great advantages derived to us very lately from the unrestrained liberty, which every Briton claims of communicating his sentiments to the public thro' the channel of the press. What would have become of the liberties of the British Colonies in North-America, if Mr. Hughes's calls on

---

Printer: A Study of an Eighteenth-Century Businessman,' *Business History Review* 40 (1966): 38; but cf. Yodelis, *Who Paid the Piper?*, pp. 19–23, 42–43, and passim, where it is suggested that the volume of purely political printing business did not become large enough to be the only or decisive consideration. It should be noted, too, that calculations made by patriot printers before 1776 would not necessarily assure them of success in the turbulent years that followed Independence.

[75] Schlesinger, *Prelude to Independence*, pp. 137, 165, gives examples of the old trade rhetoric that may have reflected confusion during a period in which habits were being altered; see also Davidson, *Propaganda*, p. 304.

Great Britain had been heard, to restrain the printers here from publishing, what he is pleased to stile *inflammatory pieces?*' Here was a subtle indication that 'freedom' might become a word without implications of political neutrality. Like Zenger's paper in an earlier day, the *Pennsylvania Journal* could be considered 'free' because it made a stand for 'liberty' against the supposedly tyrannical designs of those in power.[76]

A similar distinction was suggested that same year by developments in Virginia. Alexander Purdie was naturally anxious to reassure readers that his new *Virginia Gazette*—unlike its 'closed' predecessor—would be 'as free as any publick press upon the continent,' ready to publish the views even of those parties at odds with the authorities for whom he was official printer. But impartiality was not what would satisfy 'some of the hot Burgesses,' as Governor Fauquier called them, so William Rind was procured to print a second *Virginia Gazette*. This impressed Thomas Jefferson as truly a 'free paper.' Although its masthead bore a motto making the familiar promise of openness to all sides, Rind's practical understanding of 'freedom' differed from Purdie's. Anticipating in his first issue what would later become more obvious, Rind hinted that he was particularly 'free' from the influence of Tories, and highly receptive to patriot viewpoints. In publishing a piece of propaganda put out by the local Sons of Liberty, he also printed their monitory suggestion that by so doing he would give 'an early Instance' of his determination to conduct his press with due respect for principles of freedom.[77]

One further indication of a new trade ethic came in 1774, when John Holt chose to respond to accusations in Rivington's *Gazetteer* that the fiery partisanship of his *New-York Journal* was 'a flagrant perversion' of 'Liberty of the Press.' Was he a biased printer, 'wholly employed in prosecuting Party Designs'? Holt's reply was not strictly a denial. He was indeed trying 'to make the people in general sensible of their just Rights,' and to warn them of 'the great Danger of losing them.' Had he sold himself to those able to offer the most? The ministry, noted Holt, 'could bid higher than any Body else, nor are they without Mercenaries even more contemptible than myself'—a jab at Rivington. If 'the Pub-

[76] *Pennsylvania Journal*, Sept. 11, 1766, and see John William Wallace, *An Old Philadelphian: Colonel William Bradford, the Patriot Printer of 1776* (Philadelphia, 1884), chap. 13.

[77] Thomas, *History of Printing*, 2: 146; *Virginia Gazette* (Purdie), Mar. 28, Nov. 6, 1766; Schlesinger, *Prelude to Independence*, p. 79; *Virginia Gazette* (Rind), May 16, 1766.

lic in general' was what the words 'highest Bidder' meant, added Holt, then to be sure he was guilty as charged. In fact, just recently his patriot editorial line had brought the *Journal* more than 200 new subscribers. Nevertheless, unwilling to leave the subject on that note of self-interest, Holt proceeded to emphasize a different set of motives; he was himself personally devoted to the American cause. 'In short,' he concluded, 'I have endeavoured to propagate such political Principles . . . as I shall always freely risk my Life to defend.' Disingenuous or not, this was a statement that would have been unthinkable for a colonial printer before the Revolutionary era.[78]

Although the old standards and assumptions of the colonial printing fraternity were losing their force, the process of change was uneven and individuals pursued unclear or contradictory objectives. An instructive case is that of Isaiah Thomas, whose original contribution to the American cause was neither prompt nor enthusiastic. Recalling the first appearance of his *Massachusetts Spy* in 1770, he later explained that he had intended the Boston paper to 'be free to both parties, which then agitated the country, and, impartially, lay before the public their respective communications.' He soon found, however, that 'this ground could not be maintained' in the passionate atmosphere of the period. For a few weeks, in accordance with a policy of 'openness' proclaimed in its masthead, the *Spy* published some opinion favorable to the claims of the mother country, but not enough to satisfy hard-line Tories in the vicinity. As a result, they turned against Thomas, boycotted his paper, and used the powers of imperial officialdom to harass him. Supported by John Hancock, Joseph Greenleaf, and others whose politics were warm, Thomas with reluctance converted the *Spy* into a stridently one-sided organ of opinion. In 'a general commotion of the state,' one of his correspondents observed in 1771, 'there should be *no neuters.*' Though unavoidable and seemingly much to the advantage of the *Spy*, the circulation of which soon exceeded that of any other New England paper, this policy was not altogether to Thomas's liking. The next year, he contemplated abandoning the high road of patriotism in Boston and moving to the West Indies. Because a printer in Boston 'must be either of one party or the other (he cannot please both),' he wrote to an acquaintance in Bermuda, 'he must therefore incur the censure and dis-

[78] *Rivington's New-York Gazetteer*, Aug. 11, 1774; *New-York Journal*, Aug. 18, 1774.

pleasure of the opposite party.' And 'to incur the censure and displeasure of any party or persons, though carressed and encouraged by others,' he added, 'is disagreeable to me.'[79]

Very gradually, despite such uncertainties of purpose and practice, there arose from the Revolutionary experience a revised understanding of what it was to be an American printer. Responding to and perhaps also promoting a new belief that sharply antagonistic opinions might properly be articulated in the public forum, printers in America began to discard their neutral trade rhetoric, in order to behave aggressively and unapologetically as partisans. At the same time, reflecting the more intense ideological content of Revolutionary politics, American printers began to revive the ancient trade refrain of their English forebears. Once again it was insisted that printers were not mere 'mechanics' but men of independent intellect and principle.[80]

That this new understanding agreed with the spirit of the time is apparent from the response of patriot wits to the conduct of printers who sided with the mother country. Whether or not their motives were any more mercenary than those of their patriot brethren, Tory printers could not devise a rationale for their business strategies that drew effectively on the prevailing popular creed of 'liberty.' As one Philadelphian observed in 1774, it was difficult for anyone to print a Tory sentiment without exposing himself to the charge that he had been subsidized by the Treasury in London. Rivington, in particular, was the object of vicious diatribe. He was 'not actuated by any Principles' but worked simply as 'a tool' of officialdom, in implicit contrast to dedi-

[79] Thomas, *History of Printing*, 1: 378–79, 2: 250; Buckingham, *Specimens of Newspaper Literature*, 1: 232–33; William Coolidge Lane, 'The Printer of the Harvard Theses of 1771,' *Publications of the Colonial Society of Massachusetts* 26 (1924–26): 9; Thomas to (Joseph Dill?), Mar. 18, 1772, Isaiah Thomas Papers, American Antiquarian Society, Worcester, Mass.; Clifford K. Shipton, *Isaiah Thomas: Printer, Patriot, and Philanthropist, 1749–1831* (Rochester, N.Y., 1948), chap. 2.

[80] How gradual and uncertain the process of change would be is evident from Dwight L. Teeter, Jr., 'Decent Animadversions: Notes Toward a History of Free Press Theory,' in Bond and McLeod, eds., *Newsletters to Newspapers*, pp. 237–45. Like most Americans for a long time to come, printers were inclined and expected to justify partisanship in terms of the general public interest. It should be understood, of course, that printers were not the only occupational group to show the effects of politicization during the years of Revolutionary crisis; see, for example, Charles S. Olton, *Artisans for Independence: Philadelphia Mechanics and the American Revolution* (Syracuse, N.Y., 1975). As custodians of the press, however, their trade response to Revolutionary conditions had unique impact on the nature of American public discourse.

cated patriot printers. 'I am . . . literally hired'—so went one parody of his position—'to wage open war with Truth, Honour and Justice.' According to a 'MIRROR for a PRINTER,' submitted in 1774 to John Holt's *Journal* by an anonymous local poet, Rivington operated

> Without one grain of *honest* sense,
> One virtuous view, or *just* pretence
> To patriotic flame;
> Without a patriotic heart or mind.[81]

Most vulnerable to such satire were those Tory printers who, loath to go into exile, managed to rehabilitate themselves after their cause had failed. Rivington was perhaps acting as a double-spy by 1781, whereby he may have earned permission to remain in New York and carry on his trade after the war. By means of skillful but less desperate footwork, Hugh Gaine was able to rescue his reputation and stay on. Elsewhere, Georgia's James Johnston and Pennsylvania's Benjamin Towne were also able to negotiate abrupt reversals. Towne's political loyalties were more spectacularly erratic than those of any other colonial printer. Originally associated with Joseph Galloway and his friends, he later became a stout Whig and drove James Humphreys, Jr., from Philadelphia by prematurely branding him a Tory. Once British troops had taken over the city, Towne switched sides—and was promptly attainted as a traitor by the patriots. After Philadelphia had been retaken, he changed his colors again, and succeeded in escaping prosecution.[82]

New York's two outstanding examples of unpunished fickleness inspired Philip Freneau to compose biting doggerel. 'As matters have gone,' he had Hugh Gaine say of his initial decision to join the Tories,

> it was plainly a blunder,
> But *then* I expected the whigs must knock under,
> And I always adhere to the sword that is longest,
> And stick to the party that's like to be strongest.

[81] *Rivington's New-York Gazetteer*, Sept. 2, 1774; 'To the Publick' (New York, Nov. 16, 1774); *Pennsylvania Journal*, Mar. 8, 1775; *New-York Journal*, Sept. 15, 1774.

[82] Charles M. Thomas, 'The Publication of Newspapers during the American Revolution,' *Journalism Quarterly* 9 (1932): 372; Catherine Snell Crary, 'The Tory and the Spy: The Double Life of James Rivington,' *William and Mary Quarterly*, 3d ser. 16 (1959): 61–72; *Journals of Hugh Gaine*, 1: 63–64; Lawrence, *James Johnston*, pp. 24–27; Dwight L. Teeter, Jr., 'Benjamin Towne: The Precarious Career of a Persistent Printer,' *Pennsylvania Magazine of History and Biography* 89 (1965): 316–24.

A comparable calculation underlay Rivington's subsequent desertion of King George:

> On the very same day that his army went hence,
> I ceas'd to tell lies for the sake of his pence;
> And what was the reason—the true one is best;
> I worship no suns that decline to the west;
> In this I resemble a Turk or a Moor,
> The day star ascending I prostrate adore.[83]

Lack of principle, it seems, was the major offense committed by these two men, and the charge itself was a sign that expectations concerning the responsibilities of American printers were being reshaped by the Revolutionary conflict.

This change was revealed strikingly in John Witherspoon's prose satire upon Benjamin Towne's last political conversion. Towne's conduct, according to Witherspoon, was due to nothing more than 'desire for gain,' since he was utterly indifferent to the content of what he published. 'I never was, nor ever pretended to be a man of character, repute or dignity,' conceded Witherspoon's lampoon version of the capricious Philadelphia printer. Echoing a pre-Revolutionary formula of the American trade, Witherspoon had Towne explain that he was 'neither Whig nor Tory, but a printer.'[84] The disarmingly self-deprecatory style of Franklin's 'Apology' had become the stuff of satire.

There would still be printers—New Jersey's Isaac Collins, for one—who continued to follow the traditional strategy, claiming that they hoped to please as many people as possible even during the most heated political struggles. For some, on the other hand, it became almost obligatory to assert their own principles. In 1770, when William Goddard wrote and published a lengthy defense of his stormy partnership with Joseph Galloway and Thomas Wharton, the old role and the new were balanced uneasily. In 1766, soon after printing an emphatically patriot *Constitutional Courant* in Woodbridge, New Jersey, Goddard had showed up in Philadelphia—'on speculation,' as he put it. As it turned out, he was 'misled' by Galloway's promises of support into forming an unnatural alliance with men whom he later came to regard as 'enemies to

---

[83] Freneau's poems are reproduced in Thomas, *History of Printing*, 2: 483–95.
[84] Ibid., pp. 453–58: 'The Humble Confession, Declaration, Recantation, and Apology of Benjamin Towne, Printer in Philadelphia.'

their country.' Explaining his decision to strike out on a more independent path, Goddard relied in part on trade custom. It was his policy, he said, to act 'in the most impartial and just manner' in order to promote his own interest 'without becoming a party in any disputes.' Being implacable party men, Galloway and Wharton would not permit their printer to be true to the traditions of his craft. At the same time, Goddard offered another, less conventional apology for quarreling with his employers. Against Galloway's wishes, he had printed Dickinson's *Farmer's Letters* because he thought 'they deserved the serious attention of all *North-America.*' Apparently this initiative took his partners by surprise. 'Mr. *Galloway,*' Goddard remembered, 'ridiculed my notions about liberty and the rights of mankind.'[85]

Such ridicule was understandable enough. Unlike the European founders of their craft, printers in colonial America had neither professed nor been expected to have notions of any sort; they were supposed to make and sell their product indifferently, to suit this or that customer. During and after the Revolution, expectations came to differ. It was in the war years, for example, that the printer of Hartford's *Courant*, George Goodwin, first explicitly identified himself as an 'editor.' In Massachusetts, glossing over his reluctance to deviate from neutral trade policies, Isaiah Thomas subsequently insisted that he had given the *Spy* 'a fixed character' consistent with his own patriot beliefs.[86]

In 1785, when the state of Massachusetts attempted to raise a revenue for itself by imposing stamp duties, the printing trade was piously indignant. The new tax, it was said, would lead to 'the ruin of a set of artisans' whose exertions in the Revolutionary movement should have guaranteed them 'a more liberal fate.' Thomas's paper registered special outrage. 'Generous Reader,' it made a point of stressing, 'the services rendered by the SPY to the Publick, were not for the sake of sordid gain, but from *Principle.*'[87]

Late in the century, Benjamin Edes—a former Son of Liberty—would

[85] Richard F. Hixson, *Isaac Collins: A Quaker Printer in Eighteenth-Century America* (New Brunswick, N.J., 1968), pp. 97–98; William Goddard, *The Partnership: or the History of the Rise and Progress of the Pennsylvania Chronicle &c* (Philadelphia, 1770), pp. 5, 17, 8–9, 16, and see generally Miner, *William Goddard*, chaps. 4–5, 7.
[86] J. Eugene Smith, *One Hundred Years of Hartford's Courant* (New Haven, 1949), p. 15; Thomas, *History of Printing*, 1: 379.
[87] Duniway, *Development of Freedom of the Press*, p. 136n; Buckingham, *Specimens of Newspaper Literature*, 1: 241–42.

conjure up an image of himself standing forth as 'an undaunted Centinel in those times which "tried men's souls" . . . , when the hope of gain could not be considered as the lure to pretended Patriotism.' However self-serving, his words did reflect the new rhetoric of ideological commitment that had entered the trade during the Revolutionary years. With that commitment went pride. The newspapers of colonial America, John Holt told Samuel Adams in 1776, had first received 'Notice of the tyrannical Designs formed against America,' and generated a response 'sufficient to repel them.'[88]

When Virginia's Governor Dunmore seized the patriot Norfolk press of John Holt's son, in 1775, there was an appropriate echo of the past in the words with which he justified the action. Thus would be suppressed 'the means of poisoning the minds of the people,' and arousing 'the spirit of rebellion and sedition.'[89] More than 100 years had passed since Governor Berkeley had warned of the disastrous consequences that would accompany the introduction of printing into Virginia. Alarmist as Berkeley's reaction had been, it had pointed to a distant future. For much of the eighteenth century American printers had followed business and political strategies that impeded the flow of diverse and dissident opinion into the public forum. But during the Revolutionary years the trade adapted to a new politics of controversy. By so doing, printers seemed assured of recognition as major figures in the political life of the republic. Presiding over a press transformed by the pressures of the Revolution, they would be free to report basic conflicts and disputes as well as remote 'occurrences'; they would be expected not only to register events but to make and modify them.

6. '76 IN RETROSPECT

Long after Independence, as the machinery of the new American party system came to be elaborated at both national and state levels, printers continued to express satisfaction at the expanding importance of the press. Newspapers 'exert a controlling influence on public opinion, and decide almost all questions of a public nature,' boasted one Boston

---

[88] Rollo G. Silver, 'Benjamin Edes, Trumpeter of Sedition,' *Papers of the Bibliographical Society of America* 47 (1953): 265; Holt to Adams, Jan. 29, 1776, in Victor Hugo Paltsits, *John Holt, Printer and Postmaster, Some Facts and Documents Relating to His Career* (New York, 1920), pp. 10–15.

[89] Paltsits, *John Holt*, p. 10.

printer before a gathering of his brethren in the third decade of the new century. Partisan journalism was a well-established feature of American politics.[90]

Undeniably powerful as the press had become, however, this was not to say that nineteenth-century American printers had succeeded in realizing the promise of the role fashioned for them during the Revolutionary years. Gradually, in a sequence of developments that in some respects resembled what had happened to the London trade more than a century before, printers in republican America had to withdraw from entrepreneurial activities previously associated with their craft skills. The trend in American publishing—accelerated by the introduction of costly new technology that opened up larger markets—was toward specialization. A 'publisher' with capital would hire printers and others to produce the goods he wished to sell.[91] An exceptionally enterprising printer like Isaiah Thomas could count himself among the ranks of leading publishers, much as the London printer William Strahan had done in the eighteenth century, by investing capital in copyright and book production. But it soon came to appear that only in the 'yet almost uncorrupted West' could the average printer still realistically plan to build the diversified business and act the prominent part in his community characteristic of the trade in colonial days. So, early in the century, one New Yorker with 'utopian expectations' reportedly resolved to go west 'to give elevation to the art of Printing.' Remaining in the settled sections of the country, a printer might well have to relinquish his hopes of becoming a publisher as well.[92]

From the perspective of most printers, unprepared and unwilling to adjust to such changes, the conditions of the trade had deteriorated

[90] Jefferson Clark, *Address Delivered at the Anniversary Celebration of the Franklin Typographical Society* (Boston, 1826), p. 14. On the development of partisan journalism at the beginning of the nineteenth century, see generally Donald H. Stewart, *The Opposition Press of the Federalist Period* (Albany, N.Y., 1969), chap. 1.

[91] See, for example, Rollo G. Silver, *The American Printer, 1787–1825* (Charlottesville, 1967), pp. 40–62; Milton W. Hamilton, *The Country Printer, New York State, 1785–1830* (New York, 1936), p. 46; Ethelbert Stewart, *A Documentary History of the Early Organizations of Printers* (Indianapolis, 1907), pp. 5–41. Of course, this trend in publishing was one element in a more general process of industrialization that affected other American craftsmen in the first half of the nineteenth century.

[92] Shipton, *Isaiah Thomas*, chap. 4; Stewart, *Documentary History*, p. 134; David Bruce, 'Recollections of New York City' (c. 1810), Miscellaneous Manuscripts, New-York Historical Society, New York, N.Y.

alarmingly. Like other artisans of the period, they turned to verse and song at their fraternal gatherings to share and perhaps alleviate their experiences of hardship. Pervading the folklore of post-Revolutionary American printers, whose 'sorrows, sufferings, cares and strife' followed them 'like their shadows . . . through life,' was a bitter sense of economic ruin. 'Sheriff,' went one seriocomic poem,

> . . . spare that press;
> Touch not a single type;
> Don't put me in distress,
> To stick to me through life.
>
> 'Tis all in all to me;
> If lost, what shall I do?
> Then why not let it be,
> Oh, sheriff, boo hoo hoo.[93]

For journeymen, grievances multiplied early in the century and soon prompted organized protest. Their wages were said to be lagging behind those of other mechanics; new machinery seemed to threaten some jobs, while employers tried to cut costs by hiring foreign or inadequately trained native labor. According to one estimate of 1809, the situation in New York was so bleak that nearly half of those who completed their apprenticeships as printers were forced eventually to abandon their trade altogether and look for other kinds of work. Chief among the villains, as journeymen in Philadelphia viewed matters about the same time, were 'the gang of pettifogging master printers,' whose dedication to the welfare of the trade as a whole was appreciably less heartfelt than their individual desires for gain.[94]

Over time, the intensity of this particular antagonism seems to have subsided, to be replaced by a broader range of complaint with which many employers as well as employees in the trade could sympathize. Again and again, most regularly in the 1830s, public expressions of protest focused not on exploitation of journeymen by master printers but on exploitation of the entire craft by outside entrepreneurs. Such people, 'speculating on the labor of printers,' were out to reduce everyone

[93] Robert S. Coffin, *The Printer and Several Other Poems* (Boston, 1817), p. vii; *A Collection of Songs of the American Press and Other Poems Relating to the Art of Printing*, ed. Charles Munsell (Albany, N.Y., 1868), p. 45.
[94] Stewart, *Documentary History*, pp. 11, 28–29, 43, 21, 14.

in the trade to poverty, according to some contemporaries. Perhaps most damaging to the traditional craft pride of American printers, long accustomed to function as newspaper proprietors, was the appearance of 'professional' or 'hireling' editors, who worked under contract to entrepreneurial publishers. Usually these new editors were lawyers. By midcentury, it had become rare for a printer in an urban center to edit a paper of his own.[95]

Like their English brethren of a previous era, many American printers in the early nineteenth century declined to accept passively the implications of the new economic order. Summoning up legends of learned Europeans in the trade, they began to affirm with an insistence unknown before in America that printers had contributed significantly and uniquely to the progress of western civilization. The art of printing, according to one of its New York practitioners in 1801, 'is the parent of every other'—'an Art, the adoption of which has, in some degree, banished baleful superstition from the world, and in its stead reason and philosophy have found sanctuary in the mind of man.' Another New York printer some years later called it 'an art truly divine,' without which the human intellect forever 'might have slumbered in the lap of ignorance.'[96]

The irony beneath this fulsome oratory, applied specifically to the situation of American printers, was obliquely acknowledged in the wordplay of one printer's song:

> Though I'm not skill'd in Greek or Latin lore,
> Nor ancient Hebrew in days of yore,
> With due submission I inform my betters,
> That I can boast I am a man of *letters*.

But others in the trade were less inclined to admit so humorously the discrepancy between their intellectual aspirations and reality. In the glorious career of Benjamin Franklin, above all, they found inspiration. As one printer in Boston chose to interpret the biographical facts, Franklin had made of printing 'the instrument of his own fame,' rising through his craft to become 'a scholar, statesman, and philosopher.'

[95] Ibid., pp. 59 and n, 131–32; Hamilton, *Country Printer*, pp. 150–51.

[96] John Clough, *An Address . . . before the Franklin Typographical Association* (New York, 1801), pp. 10–11; Adoniram Chandler, *An Oration, Delivered before the New-York Typographical Society* (New York, 1816), p. 9.

Despite discouraging trade conditions, Franklin's successors had only to follow in his footsteps to redeem their fraternal heritage. 'The next in rank,' continued the same Boston printer, '. . . is ISAIAH THOMAS.'[97]

Thomas, indeed, emulated 'learned' European predecessors not only by writing his *History* but by founding the American Antiquarian Society. His natural successor was Boston's Joseph Buckingham, whose career epitomized the post-Revolutionary sensibilities of the trade. Born just a few years after Independence, he had been impressed as a young man with the 'dignity and importance' of printing a newspaper, and so determined to learn the craft. Like Franklin, he read voraciously, stressing grammar in his self-education. 'I foresaw that it would be useful to me, as a printer,' he later explained, 'but indispensable as an editor,—a profession, to which I looked forward as the consummation of my ambition.' From the beginning, he recalled, 'I found it difficult to repress my aspirations to display my intellectual as well as my industrial and mechanical abilities.' Eventually, having satisfied himself by building a reputation as a journalist with a mind of his own, he assumed 'the character and pursuits of a scholar' to edit a sequel to Thomas's *History*, a two-volume historical anthology called *Specimens of Newspaper Literature*, published in 1850.[98]

Other American printers, too, refused to limit their intellectual prerogatives and be demoted to mere mechanics. In 1808, Boston's Society of Printers—of which Buckingham was a leading member—went so far as to change its name to the Faustus Society, because the old name was 'too narrow and confined to embrace the higher branches of our profession, which are not *mechanical*, nor bounded by rules, but which soar to improvements as valuable to science and humanity as those which have immortalized the discovery of Faustus.' The New-York Typographical Society, for its part, included men of recognizable 'intellectual, moral, and social worth,' not least its one-time president Peter Force, later an active antiquarian and editor of historical documents.[99]

[97] *Collection of Songs of the American Press*, p. 113; John Russell, *An Address, Presented to the Members of the Faustus Association* (Boston, 1808), pp. 20–21.

[98] Shipton, *Isaiah Thomas*, chap. 6; Thomas, *History of Printing*, 1: 10, had undertaken his chronicle of the trade despite a feeling that the task might have been better performed by 'some person distinguished for literature.' Joseph T. Buckingham, *Personal Memoirs and Recollections of Editorial Life*, 2 vols. (Boston, 1852), 1: 21, 27–28, 53.

[99] Silver, *American Printer*, p. 88; *Autobiography of Thurlow Weed*, ed. Harriet A. Weed (Boston, 1883), p. 58.

'I have heard old journeymen claim that it was a Profession,' William Dean Howells wrote of printing at the very end of the century, 'and ought to rank with the learned professions.' Himself the son of a printer, Howells remembered well one youth who had entered his father's shop 'with the wish to be a printer because Franklin had been one, and with the intent of making the office his University.' Such purposefulness may not have been uncommon in the nineteenth-century trade. 'Let it not be to any a subject of special wonder,' announced the preface to a mid-century collection of literature written by printers, 'that they who have so often assisted in ushering into the world the productions of others should now in turn venture to originate ideas of their own, and appear before the public in the ambitious character of Authors.' In fact, several of the century's most distinguished American writers—Walt Whitman and Mark Twain as well as Howells among them—had worked as young men in printing shops.[100]

Some notable political personalities, too, began their careers as members of the trade, often entering politics through journalism. 'Printers should never lose sight of the dignity of their profession,' observed a member of the fraternity, 'for the most eminent men have embraced it.' One was the Republican politician Thurlow Weed, who made a point in his memoirs of emphasizing that several of his journeymen acquaintances in the trade had been endowed with 'decided literary taste and acquirements.' Another was Horace Greeley, for whom entry into the trade had marked the beginning of his escape from the *mindless monotonous drudgery* of farming. Governors, legislators, diplomats, mayors—printers were pleased to record that among their brethren were occupants of the highest offices in the land.[101]

These of course were uncommon men, but ordinary printers could and did also claim a place of special importance in public life. Out of

[100] William Dean Howells, *The Country Printer* (Norwood, Mass., 1919), p. 36; *Voices of the Press; A Collection of Sketches, Essays, and Poems, by Practical Printers*, ed. James J. Brenton (New York, 1850), p. iii. The link between printing and authorship remained, of course, journalism; see S. M. Lipset, M. A. Trow, and J. S. Coleman, *Union Democracy: The Internal Politics of the International Typographical Union* (Glencoe, Ill., 1956), pp. 29–30, where the role of printers editing the modern labor press is noted.

[101] Charles Turrell, 'Longevity of American Printers,' in *The Typographical Miscellany*, ed. Joel Munsell (Albany, N.Y., 1850), pp. 82–83; *Autobiography of Thurlow Weed*, p. 44; Horace Greeley, *Recollections of a Busy Life* (New York, 1868), pp. 60–61.

their Revolutionary heritage, they tried to assert a role less prominent but perhaps ultimately more rewarding. 'Among the gloriously congenial effects, produced by the ART OF PRINTING,' declaimed a patriotic speaker in 1802 at the Boston Franklin Association, 'no one is so conspicuous on the roll of fame, as the FOURTH OF JULY, 1776!' Throughout the early decades of the nineteenth century, similar sentiments were repeatedly expressed by printers before assemblages of their brethren. According to the prize-winning ode at a July 4th celebration of the New-York Typographical Society in 1811,

> . . . Heaven decreed
> That Columbia be freed,
> And *Printing* and valour accomplish'd the deed.
> The banner of war was by Justice unfurl'd,
> And Freedom by Printing proclaim'd to the world.[102]

It was in this self-congratulatory spirit that at one banquet of printers a toast was offered to the Declaration of Independence—'From the *Press of Franklin and Company*.' As late as 1834, a grandson of the famed patriot printer William Bradford III could argue feelingly that his father, the printer Thomas Bradford, was entitled to a Revolutionary war pension because publication of the *Pennsylvania Journal* had been '*of more value to the cause of American freedom than if he had for six years commanded a regiment in the field*.' Isaiah Thomas probably did more than anyone else to sustain such affirmations, having labored over his hagiographical *History* to demonstrate as fully as possible that the press 'had a powerful influence in producing the revolution.'[103]

Faithful to the relatively recent political traditions of the trade, it was understandable if a printer in the new republic should want to refer hyperbolically to the press as 'one of the most deadly engines of destruction that can possibly be arrayed against the encroachments of

---

[102] William Burdick, *An Oration on the Nature and Effects of the Art of Printing* (Boston, 1802), p. 20; Asbridge, *Oration*, p. 26. Other groups of mechanics continued to celebrate the Revolution, but without as specific a sense of participation; see Howard B. Rock, 'The American Revolution and the Mechanics of New York City: One Generation Later,' *New York History* 52 (1976): 367–82. The 4th of July, of course, was the favored occasion for expressing such sentiments.

[103] Clark, *Address*, p. 21; Thomas Bradford, Jr., to Samuel McKean, May 7, 1834, Bradford Manuscripts, Historical Society of Pennsylvania, Philadelphia; Thomas, *History of Printing*, 1: 15.

despotic power.' Especially in America, where newspapers were so widespread as to be considered among 'the necessaries of life,' printers had awesome public responsibilities. Since a 'free press' was 'the people's surest safeguard,' it was vitally important for printers to 'support the right, and wrong attack'—and 'tweak the despot's nose.'[104]

As custodians of the public welfare, too, printers could hope to make an unusually forceful case in protesting the very economic conditions that had conspired to diminish their livelihoods and undermine their social standing. The narrow interests of the trade, it seemed, were linked to the well-being of the larger American public. For if printers were the 'natural guardians' of a free press, it was their duty as citizens and the duty of the general citizenry as well to resist usurpation by 'hireling editors,' subservient to combinations of wealthy individuals. To retain control of the press, thereby preserving its integrity, would require of printers much the same degree of 'jealous regard and sleepless vigilance' that had marked their Revolutionary forebears—the generation memorialized by Isaiah Thomas.[105]

Appropriately, 'independence' was a key word in the vocabulary of socioeconomic complaint by printers in early nineteenth-century America. As with other struggling mechanics at the time, *independence* signified desirable conditions of work and unoppressive structures of economic life; most emphatically for printers, the word also brought to mind crucial political experiences of a previous era. In 1826, at the Franklin Typographical Society in Boston, current aspirations and historical memories mingled revealingly in an elaborate toast:

> *Getting under weigh*—the good ship *Typographical*, Captain *Franklin*, with a *true hearted crew, bound on a voyage* of *charity, sailing* in the *current of public opinion*, with *favourable breezes*, and taking the correct *course* of *truth, honesty*, and *sobriety*; keeping out of the *calm latitudes* of *idleness* and *gulph* of *intemperance*; avoiding the *rocks* of *dissipation; steering clear* of the *shoals* of *poverty*, and *touching* at the *port* of *benevolence*, may she *finally arrive* in *safety*, in the *harbour* of INDEPENDENCE.[106]

[104] Asbridge, *Oration*, p. 12; Clark, *Address*, p. 14; *Collection of Songs of the American Press*, p. 21.

[105] Stewart, *Documentary History*, pp. 147–48.

[106] Clark, *Address*, p. 22. On the relationship of the American and Industrial Revolutions, see generally Alan Dawley, *Class and Community: The Industrial Revolution in Lynn* (Cambridge, Mass., 1976).

They have been called 'intellectuals of the working class.' Whatever the merits of that designation, printers in early nineteenth-century Europe joined the ideological vanguard of the first workingmen's movements. That this was so in America as well, despite the bland politics of the eighteenth-century trade, reflected the strong impact of the Revolution upon their occupational identity.[107]

Historical ironies aside, which might have been grimly pleasurable to a loyalist like Peter Oliver, it was peculiarly fitting that in 1856 the 150th anniversary of Benjamin Franklin's birth should have been celebrated in the city of Boston by a huge self-assertive parade of patriotic mechanics, in which the printing fraternity was separated from most other groups of mechanics by being designated one of the 'mechanical professions.'[108] Franklin himself had been more of a mechanic than sometimes he had cared to admit, and less of a Revolutionary; for American printers by the middle of the nineteenth century, the meaning of both experiences had been redefined, and fused symbolically in his name.

---

[107] Lipset et al., *Union Democracy*, p. 30.
[108] *Memorial of the Inauguration of the Statue of Franklin* (Boston, 1857), pp. 146–87.

Freedom of the Press in Revolutionary America: The Evolution of Libertarianism, 1760–1820

RICHARD BUEL, JR.

THERE CAN BE NO DOUBT that the Revolutionary leadership attached great importance to the freedom of the press, at least as they understood it. In 1765, John Adams observed in his *Dissertation on the Canon and Feudal Law* that he knew of no 'means of information . . . more sacred . . . than . . . [a free] press.' In 1768, the Massachusetts House of Representatives refused to act upon the Governor and Council's charge that the *Boston Gazette* had committed libel, because 'the liberty of the press is the great bulwark of the liberty of the people.'[1] And in 1774, in its 'Address to the Inhabitants of Quebec,' the First Continental Congress made the point still more emphatically. This document, aimed at explaining to a largely alien audience the political rights that Americans felt they must defend against ministerial encroachment, set freedom of the press among the five foundation stones of English liberty.[2]

Throughout the imperial controversy, all patriots agreed that without this freedom the colonists could not hope to defeat the ambition of a powerful ministry seeking arbitrary power.[3] Nor did the force of

---

[1] John Adams, 'Dissertation on the Canon and Feudal Law,' in *The Works of John Adams*, ed. Charles Francis Adams (Boston, 1851), 3: 457; Alden Bradford, ed., *Speeches of the Governors of Massachusetts from 1765 to 1775* (Boston, 1818), p. 121.

[2] Worthington C. Ford, ed., *Journals of the Continental Congress 1774–1789* (Washington, 1904–37), 1: 106–13, quote from p. 108; hereafter cited as *JCC.*

[3] Cf. 'A Freeman of Virginia' in *Virginia Gazette* (Purdie and Dixon), Nov. 6, 1766; unsigned in *New-York Journal*, Nov. 27, 1766; unsigned in *Maryland Gazette*, Oct. 29, 1772; 'Centinel' in *Massachusetts Spy*, Nov. 14, 1771; Dec. 14, 1771; Jan. 2, 1772. The list of citations could be extended indefinitely.

their sentiments dwindle when victory had broken the British hold forever. Ten state constitutions, including that of Vermont, explicitly provided that the press should be free. Supporters of the new Federal Constitution felt obliged to apologize for its failure to provide the same assurance.[4] And Congress, to forestall an upheaval that might throw the new government off its delicate balance, soon framed an amendment barring itself from making 'laws . . . abridging the freedom of the press,' an amendment that three-quarters of the state legislatures ratified at once.[5]

Such were the beliefs and the formal statements. In practice, however, these declarations were heavily qualified. Though after 1760 the lower houses in patriot control largely abandoned the practice of punishing printers for breach of privilege, the patriots found new, informal ways of keeping opinions contrary to their own out of print. When John Mein, publisher of the *Boston Chronicle*, offended the patriot faction, a mob attacked him in the street so viciously that he subsequently fled the province.[6] James Rivington and his *Gazetteer*, which clearly did much to deter New York from giving its whole heart to the patriot cause after 1773, suffered a similar fate. In 1774 the patriots began organizing a boycott against Rivington from New Hampshire to South Carolina. In the wake of Concord and Lexington the printer bowed briefly to the pressure brought against him, but in the autumn of 1775 he lapsed into his old ways. In November of that year, an armed band from Connecticut, led by Isaac Sears, invaded the city and destroyed Rivington's types. Importing a new set from Europe took a year and a half, during which time Rivington could not put his views in print.[7] Such incidents as these gave apparent confirmation to the loyalist charge that in suppressing Tory opinion the colonists directly contradicted their professed ideals.[8]

[4] 'Landholder' VI and 'A Citizen of New Haven' II in Paul L. Ford, ed., *Essays on the Constitution of the United States* (Brooklyn, 1892), pp. 164, 239.

[5] Robert A. Rutland, *The Birth of the Bill of Rights 1776–1791* (Chapel Hill, 1955), chap. 9.

[6] Hiller B. Zobel, *The Boston Massacre* (New York, 1970), pp. 154–63.

[7] Arthur M. Schlesinger, *Prelude to Independence: The Newspaper War on Britain, 1764–1776* (New York, 1958), pp. 225–27, 240.

[8] Daniel Leonard, *Massachusettensis* (Boston, 1775), p. 77; Josiah Quincy, Jr., ed., *Reports of Cases Argued and Adjudged in the Superior Court of Judicature . . . Between 1761 and 1772* (Boston, 1865), p. 244, as quoted in Levy, *Legacy of Suppression: Freedom of Speech and Press in Early American History* (Cambridge, Mass., 1960), p. 87; cf. also 'Freeman'

Men in the thick of a revolution may well be forgiven if they sacrifice principles to the needs of a desperate moment. But the events of the late 1790s cannot be so explained. Less than ten years after framing the First Amendment, Congress passed a sedition law making it a federal crime to 'write, print, utter or publish . . . any false, scandalous and malicious writing . . . against the government of the United States.'[9] Armed with this statute, the secretary of state, Timothy Pickering, proceeded to launch a systematic attack on the major opposition presses, clearly with the design of silencing them during the election of 1800. In addition several Republican printers in the states with Federalist-controlled judicial systems were prosecuted under the common law.[10] No one could seriously have doubted that these prosecutions represented a deliberate attempt to muzzle the Republican presses. Nevertheless, Federalists maintained that nothing, either in the sedition law or its administration, was inconsistent with the First Amendment, and that the law actually expanded the freedom of publishers by liberalizing the common law of libels.[11]

The Revolutionaries had an explanation for the apparent conflict between their words and deeds. None had ever denied that the press could abuse its privileges and that such abuse should be restrained. The distinction between freedom and license found its most forceful expression in a resolution published by the Committee of Inspection in Newport, Rhode Island, endorsing a boycott of Rivington. The preamble to the resolution quoted from the 'Address to . . . Quebec' on the virtues of a free press, calling it the duty of 'every friend of Civil Government to protect, and preserve from violation, that . . . great sup-

---

in *Boston Censor*, Jan. 4, 1772. Myles Cooper, *A Friendly Address to All Reasonable Americans* (New York, 1774), p. 50; Thomas Gage to Lord Dartmouth, July 5, 1774 in Peter Force, ed., *American Archives*, 4th ser. (Washington, 1837–53), 1: 514.

[9] *Debates and Proceedings in the Congress of the United States, 1789–1824* (Washington, 1834–56), 5th Congress, pp. 3776–77; hereafter cited as *Annals*.

[10] James Morton Smith, *Freedom's Fetters* (Ithaca, 1956), pp. 159–417.

[11] Cf. *Annals*, 5th Congress, pp. 2112, 2904, 2989; 6th Congress, p. 925; Alexander Addison, *Liberty of Speech and the Press* (Albany, 1798), p. 7 and *Analysis of the Report of the Committee of the Virginia Assembly, on the Proceedings of Sundry of the Other States in Answer to Their Resolutions* (Philadelphia, 1800), p. 49; Charles Lee, *Defense of the Alien and Sedition Laws, Shewing Their Entire Consistency with the Constitution of the United States, and the Principles of Our Government* (Philadelphia, 1798), pp. 30, 36–37; *Observations on the Alien and Sedition Laws of the United States* (Washington, Pa., 1799), p. 42; [Henry Lee], *Plain Truth: Addressed to the People of Virginia* (Richmond, 1799), p. 48.

port of Public Liberty; and to . . . encourage the Press, so long as it shall be employed in promoting these beneficial purposes.' Then it went on:

> But when, instead thereof, a Press is incessantly employed and prostituted to the vilest uses; in publishing the most infamous falsehoods; in partial or false representations of facts; in fomenting jealousies, and exciting discord and disunion among the people; in supporting and applauding the worst of men, and worst of measures; and in vilifying and calumniating the best of characters, and the best of causes; it then behooves every citizen . . . to discountenance and discourage every such licentious, illiberal, prostituted Press.[12]

To us the distinction between use and abuse appears vague, particularly as the Revolutionaries acted upon it: to justify simultaneously the absolute freedom of their own press and the ruthless repression of adversary printers. We would not talk of a 'free press' where this meant freedom to serve the political interests of one faction exclusively. Their apparent lack of consistency on this point has provoked a highly critical assessment of their contributions to our libertarian tradition. According to this view, the Founding Fathers left us not the legacy of a free press but rather one of 'suppression.'[13] The following essay seeks to challenge this judgment by showing that what appears contradictory and meaningless to us was not so to those living in eighteenth-century America. When we set Revolutionary thought and action about the press in the larger historical context, it then becomes clear that though the Revolutionaries did not always act consistently, they made a tremendous stride toward formulating and implementing those libertarian ideals concerning freedom of the press that we embrace today.

I

Perhaps the best way to bridge the gap between our world and theirs is to consider what obstacles existed to their acceptance of our assump-

[12] Force, ed., *American Archives*, 4th ser. 2: 12; similar sentiments pervade such pre-Revolutionary pieces as William Livingston's essay 'Of the Use, Abuse, and Liberty of the Press' in Milton M. Klein, ed., *The Independent Reflector* (Cambridge, Mass., 1963), pp. 336–42.

[13] Leonard W. Levy, *Legacy of Suppression;* cf. also Levy's subsequent books, *Jefferson and Civil Liberties: the Darker Side* (Cambridge, Mass., 1963), chap. 3. In *Freedom of the Press from Zenger to Jefferson* (New York, 1966), Levy altered his assessment of the Jeffersonians somewhat; cf. p. lxxvii.

tion that a legitimate state cannot be assaulted by words alone and therefore is seldom if ever justified in interfering with freedom of speech or the press.[14] The general currency of this liberal idea among all political persuasions in America today owes much to a development in the recent past that has highly illiberal implications for the future: the development of an exotic technology over which the state exercises a monopoly and which no alienated individual or group can hope to match. This has drastically diminished the vulnerability of the fully industrialized state to sedition. Before the advent of printing, the pre-industrial state enjoyed an analogous advantage, at least over the common people. Successful acts of sedition could be mounted by feudal nobles with the power to gather a force that could match that of the crown, but the masses lacked any such power. Since the character of life seldom gave a significant number of them common grievances against the authorities, or, when it did, put obstacles in the way of a concerted response, public opinion became a formidable force only in isolated areas. And the government possessed the means to crush local uprisings easily. Heretical groups suffered similar disadvantages and, as W. K. Jordan has said, 'the Middle Ages provide examples of [their] successful extermination . . . by the concerted action of the civil and ecclesiastical authorities.'[15]

The printing press changed all this. Initially valued mostly as a way to make accurate copies of texts, printing soon began to spread literacy simply by making the written word more available. By the time of the Reformation printing could be used to reach not only the already literate, but also a vast new audience with powerful incentives to achieve literacy in the search for divine truth. As an instrument for shaping public opinion, printing thus became a revolutionary force. By enabling the people to unite in action it made the state vulnerable to sedition as it had not been before. And it helped to bring about more than a century of religious turmoil and the permanent rupture of the Christian world.[16]

It should not surprise us that print could so agitate society. For cen-

[14] Cf. Levy, *Legacy of Suppression*, p. x and passim.

[15] W. K. Jordan, *The Development of Religious Toleration in England* (London, 1932–40), 1: 23.

[16] Ibid.; cf. also Kenneth A. Lockridge, *Literacy in Colonial New England* (New York, 1974), pp. 44–45, 72, 101 for the religious motive in the expansion of literacy.

turies, literacy had belonged largely to the clergy, and the printed word continued to enjoy an aura of scriptural authority that a secular culture bombarded with messages can hardly conceive. This reverence for words could work in two ways, of course. It could destroy a church but it could also make the church whole again, provided only that the presses supported orthodoxy rather than ideas that challenged the singularity of truth. As soon as civil and religious authorities perceived this they instituted control prior to publication with the aim of maintaining doctrinal uniformity, and they did this often with the active cooperation of the printers. In England, for instance, printers welcomed the royal licensing laws of Henry VIII as a way of keeping their business exclusive and discouraging the entrance of competitors. And the course of the Reformation on the continent encouraged a disposition, born of weariness with the religious wars of the sixteenth century, to accept curbs on freedom as the price of peace.[17]

Gradually, however, systems of prior control became less effective. The first unanimity of the English Reformation fell apart with the death of Henry VIII. Mary's attempt to bring back Catholicism led to a violent breach between religious extremes which even Elizabeth's genius could not quite heal.[18] Dissidents met no obstacle when they sought to publish their views unlicensed, there being more printers than authorized presses, a situation that worsened with time.[19] Most fatal of all to censorship, popular demand for literature (both secular and sacred) exploded so that it could not be met by any establishment small enough to allow effective prior control. And though throughout the tumult of the seventeenth century whatever party was in power clung to the idea of prior restraint, those charged with its practice relied more and more on punishment after the offense as their only recourse. Thus the abandonment of prior controls in England in 1696 was in one sense an accommodation to reality rather than a rejection of the idea that words or opinions could endanger society.[20] All Europe, and particularly England, had seen too much turmoil not to regard untrammeled circulation of opinion with doubt and fear.

[17] Frederick S. Siebert, *Freedom of the Press in England 1476–1776* (Urbana, Ill., 1952), pp. 26, 30, 34–38, 42–51.
[18] Ibid., 58–60, 89, 95–100; G. R. Elton, *England under the Tudors* (London, 1955), passim.
[19] Siebert, *Freedom of the Press*, p. 40.
[20] Ibid., pp. 117ff; Levy, *Legacy of Suppression*, p. 104.

In these unpropitious circumstances, modern libertarianism began to take shape. The seed of it lay in the growth of religious toleration throughout the sixteenth and seventeenth centuries. W. K. Jordan has traced this complex process in detail. By 1660, Jordan found, 'the *theory* of religious toleration stood substantially complete . . . and, what is even more important, the sober and responsible thought of the nation stood convinced, in consequence of an extraordinary and complex concatenation of causes, of the necessity of translating into institutional terms the principles which England had accepted after so much travail and bitter historical experience.'[21] Jordan observes, nevertheless, that extremists in the Church of England continued trying to harness the reaction accompanying the Restoration to the service of penalizing dissent. But James II's determination to restore Catholicism encouraged latitudinarianism within the Church of England and drove the Protestant dissenters to support the Glorious Revolution of 1688, for which they were rewarded with the Act of Toleration. Though the act did not alter the disqualification of dissenters from public office, the removal of other penalties previously laid on them showed a growing acceptance of the idea that the state should not regulate religious opinion to achieve orthodoxy. Parliament's refusal to renew the Licensing Act in 1695 also signaled its recognition that the principal rationale for prior control no longer existed.

There remained the need for some means of restraining expressions of opinion, though not prior to publication, in order to protect society against sedition. The slow decline of deadly religious controversies accompanying the rise of toleration did not sufficiently reassure the English people that such a danger was disappearing. With a century and a half of turmoil just behind them, and the Protestant succession after 1715 dependent on an unpopular foreign dynasty, they continued to perceive sedition as a real threat. Moreover, all Europe knew that the city-states of antiquity had fallen victim to purely secular acts of sedition, and still remembered a Neapolitan revolution of the mid-seventeenth century that proved people had not lost their weakness for demagogues. An English account of the episode, probably dating from the mid-eighteenth century, bore the lurid title *The History of the Surprising Rise and Sudden Fall of Masannello, the fisherman of Naples, who in the Space of*

---

[21] Jordan, *Development of Religious Toleration*, 4: 468.

four days raised 150,000 People in arms; and in two days more made himself Governor, or King of Naples. Though the rising took place in 1647, before the religious wars of the continent had ended, this account made clear that it had contained no religious ingredient but had been touched off by oppressive taxation.[22]

The foremost libertarian thinkers of the early eighteenth century could not ignore the danger of sedition. John Trenchard and Thomas Gordon, writing in the *Independent Whig*, argued for total freedom of opinion in religion but acknowledged in a later number that 'Proceedings the most advantageous to the people, may by a malicious representation of them, or even by an unpleasing name given them, be rendered odious to the people. Measures the most mischievous to the people, may, by plausible and false colouring, be made clear and interesting to the people.'[23] Nonetheless, in their famous libertarian papers, *Cato's Letters* (1720–24), they called for a 'True and impartial Liberty' for 'every Man to pursue the natural, reasonable, religious Dictates of his own Mind; to think what he will, and act as he thinks, provided he acts not to the Prejudice of another.'[24] Trenchard and Gordon voiced their confidence that 'Whilst all Opinions are equally indulged, and all Parties equally allowed to speak their Minds, the Truth will come out.'[25]

They based their optimism on a superficial rationalism which relied more on an appeal to results than on epistemological analysis. On the one hand, they argued that if men were 'not permitted . . . to communicate their Opinions or Improvements to one another, the World must soon be overrun with Barbarism, Superstition, Injustice, Tyranny, and the most stupid Ignorance.'[26] On the other hand, they attributed Britain's growing wealth and power—and just about everything else they found commendable—to liberty.[27] John Trenchard best summed it up. In *Cato's Letter* No. 13, he wrote:

[22] *The History of the Surprising Rise* (Oxford, Eng., n.d.). The Library of Congress suggests 1747 as a possible publication date. Cf. also Thomas Paine, *Common Sense and the Crisis*, Dolphin ed. (Garden City, N.Y., n.d.), p. 41.

[23] John Trenchard and Thomas Gordon, *The Independent Whig*, from the 6th London ed. (Hartford, 1816), no. 104, p. 277.

[24] John Trenchard and Thomas Gordon, *Cato's Letters*, 3d ed. (London, 1733), 2: 248.

[25] Ibid., 3: 295.

[26] Ibid., 3: 297.

[27] Ibid., Letters 62–68.

[T]he Difference between Nation and Nation, in Point of Virtue, Sagacity, and Arms, arises not from the different Genius of the People; which, making very small Allowances for the Difference of Climate, would be the same under the same Regulations; but from the different Genius of their political Constitutions; The one perhaps making common Sense dangerous, and Enquires criminal, cowing the Spirits of Men, and rebuking the Sallies of Virtue; while the other, at the same Time, encourages the Improvement of the Understanding, rewards the Discovery of Truth, and Cultivates as a Virtue, the Love of Liberty and of one's Country.[28]

An argument so founded on possible results was premature. Britain had just passed through a financial crisis that should have shaken the confidence of anyone proposing her increasing wealth and power as the cornerstone of an argument for liberty of the press, and shortly afterwards a suspected conspiracy to depose the Hanoverians came to light. Trenchard, replying to an objection that libel could endanger the state at the time of the Atterbury conspiracy, acknowledged 'that libels may sometimes, though very rarely, foment popular and perhaps causeless Discontents, blast and obstruct the best Measures, and now and then promote Insurrection and Rebellions.' But he was unwilling to justify curtailing the liberty of the press, going on to note that

> These latter Mischiefs are much seldomer produced than the former Benefits [of keeping great men in awe]; for Power has so many Advantages, so many Gifts and Allurements to bribe those who bow to it, and so many Terrors to frighten those who oppose it; besides the constant Reverence and Superstition ever paid to Greatness, Splendor, Equipage, and the Show of Wisdom, as well as the natural Desire which all or most Men have to live in Quiet, and the Dread which they have of publick Disturbances, that I think I may safely affirm, that much more is to be feared from flattering Great Men, than detracting from them.[29]

Trenchard and Gordon obviously feared that the ministry would use the Atterbury conspiracy as an excuse to curtail the liberty of the subject. But their theories about the state's advantage over the people must have seemed extreme to the nation at large.

Nonetheless, the libertarianism of thinkers like Trenchard and Gordon came increasingly to influence a substantial minority in and around

[28] Ibid., 1: 82–83.
[29] Ibid., 3: 294.

London as the century progressed. The sophistication of England's economy, the cultural blossoming that accompanied prosperity, and her political stability as shown in the long tenure of Sir Robert Walpole and the collapse of the Jacobite Rebellion in 1745 gave retrospective support to Trenchard's and Gordon's extravagant claim that criticism of government was no longer a threat to the state. And London so dominated the rest of the country that practices that seemed suited to her alone could be imposed on all England without much repercussion. As a consequence of concerted action by the London populace, by certain magistrates, and by the printers of the city—all of whom actively challenged the government's attempt to restrict expression—controls imposed on printers and authors began to loosen in the mid-eighteenth century. Juries showed themselves ever more unwilling to convict for seditious libel,[30] and the press became virtually free from the control of both houses of Parliament, while the courts ruled against the issuance of general warrants to seize evidence in seditious libel cases. Admittedly, most of the gains were more de facto than de jure. For instance, the law did not recognize the right of juries to decide whether or not a publication had printed sedition until Fox's Libel Act of 1792, and Parliament never explicitly renounced the power to punish for breach of privilege. But after 1771 it rarely exercised the power, and excused itself when it did with the pretense that parliamentary debates had been misreported.[31]

II

This pragmatic growth in the freedom of the press in England had many parallels in America. There too the defense of orthodoxy and the precariousness of civil order in the seventeenth century led officialdom to think that it must guard against abuse of the press by attempting to impose controls much like those used in England.[32] In the eighteenth century, however, the controls began to relax and printers found themselves enjoying greater de facto liberty. To some extent, greater freedom of the press kept pace with the increasing acceptance

[30] Cf. Stanley N. Katz, ed., *A Brief Narrative of the Case and Trial of John Peter Zenger* (Cambridge, Mass., 1963), p. 31.

[31] Siebert, *Freedom of the Press*, pp. 5, 356–92.

[32] Clyde A. Duniway, *The Development of Freedom of the Press in Massachusetts* (New York, 1906), pp. 25ff; Levy, *Legacy of Suppression*, pp. 19ff.

of religious dissent and the recognition that the American social order rested on firmer foundations in the eighteenth century than it had before. It also owed something to the influence of English libertarian thinkers like Trenchard and Gordon. One of the *Cato's Letters* on freedom of the press and of speech was reprinted in Zenger's *New-York Journal* before Zenger's famous trial for seditious libel in 1735.[33] And in the late colonial period American writers often paraphrased these ideas. They were plainly echoed in John Dickinson's 'Farmer's Letters' where he emphasized the intimate connection between liberty on the one hand and human happiness, benevolence, and material prosperity on the other.[34] They also influenced Congress's 'Address to the Inhabitants of Quebec' in 1774, which asserted that 'the advancement of truth, science, morality, and arts in general were attributable to the freedom of the press.'[35]

There were, however, more differences than likenesses in the progress of America and England toward free expression. The breakdown of effective control over the press in America owed something to the demand for printed matter and the increase in printers; it owed more to the geographic diffuseness of American society. Though England had her provincial presses, most publishers, up through the seventeenth century, were in London and therefore the more easily controlled.[36] And all presses in England were subject to a common legal system. The colonies lacked both an obvious center for the trade and a common legal system, so that people wishing to publish matter that might offend the authorities in one place could usually find a neighboring jurisdiction which took a more tolerant attitude.[37]

Yet, though the colonists became passionately concerned for the freedom of the press in the late colonial period, the principal cause was not their espousal of libertarian principles. Nowhere is this more evident than in William Livingston's essay 'Of the Use, Abuse and Liberty of the Press' which appeared in the New York *Independent Re-*

[33] David L. Jacobson, ed., *The English Libertarian Heritage* (New York, 1965), pp. li-lii.

[34] Cf. John Dickinson, *The Political Writings of John Dickinson* (Wilmington, 1801), 1: 144, 186, 215.

[35] *JCC*, 1: 108.

[36] Marjorie Plant, *The English Book Trade: An Economic History of the Making and Sale of Books*, 2d ed. (London, 1965), pp. 80–86.

[37] Cf. Duniway, *Development of Freedom of the Press*, pp. 74–75.

flector in 1753. Though Livingston echoed the libertarian sentiments of Trenchard and Gordon in one paragraph, in the next he condemned the English for the 'unbounded Licentiousness' of their press and went on to argue that the phrase '*Liberty of the Press*' did not mean 'an equal Unrestraint in Writing.' Livingston then explained that just as 'no State can permit any Practice detrimental to the public Tranquility, but in direct Opposition to its fundamental Principles,' so 'I lay it down as a Rule, that when the Press is prejudicial to the public Weal, it is abused.' He added, in direct contradiction to Trenchard and Gordon, that 'If . . . we suppose any broader Foundation for the *Liberty of the Press*, it will become more destructive of public Peace, than if it were wholly shut up.' What Livingston meant by the freedom of the press, then, was 'a Liberty of promoting the common Good of Society, and of publishing any Thing else not repugnant thereto.'[38]

The sympathy with which the colonists received this interpretation derived from their unique place in the empire, and their reception of an opposition ideology originating in the mother country. Libertarianism and opposition ideology were not incompatible; indeed, men like Trenchard and Gordon helped to transmit both across the Atlantic. But opposition ideology had deeper roots in English political culture than libertarianism. The Tory Bolingbroke could espouse it as passionately as Trenchard and Gordon because it filled so well the needs of an opposition seeking to justify a role condemned by the official ideology of the post-Revolutionary establishment.[39] And opposition ideology had special appeal for the colonists because they found themselves mostly excluded from the centers of imperial power. It gave them the means of diagnosing and resisting the evils of executive aggrandizement in provincial politics and the threat to English liberty posed by the attempt to centralize the empire after 1763.[40] A free press would be essential to victory in these engagements, though not for the reasons implicit in libertarianism. Commentators who see inconsistency between the ideology and practice of the colonists have not properly understood their ideology in the first place.

[38] Livingston in Klein, ed., *Independent Reflector*, pp. 338–41.
[39] Bernard Bailyn, *The Origins of American Politics* (New York, 1967), pp. 39–45; Isaac Kramnick, *Bolingbroke and His Circle* (Cambridge, Mass., 1968), passim and especially pp. 243–52.
[40] Bailyn, *Origins of American Politics*, chaps. 2–3.

Bernard Bailyn has given the classical exposition of the premises behind opposition ideology in his *Ideological Origins of the American Revolution*. He sees it as a theory of politics postulating that the basic problem in government was how to establish an equilibrium between two forces, one tending to destroy liberty, and the other to defend it, though sometimes at the expense of public order. In the British political system these forces manifested themselves as crown and people, respectively. Equilibrium was continuously threatened by the nature of its components. On the one hand, the crown, whose interest was power, directed its whole restless, aggressive character to the enlargement of its prerogative. On the other hand, the people, whose interest was liberty, suffered from the weakness that, despite the sheer weight of their numbers, their strength tended to melt away in disunity. Opposition ideology stressed the crown's advantage in this struggle. The crown's singlemindedness, its capacity to attract able people of standing and influence in society, and its control of the institutions having legal claim to society's total resources put its power of decisive action far beyond that of a diffuse populace; or so the theory ran.[41]

To maintain a balance between crown and people, the people had to develop institutions by which their scattered powers might be gathered to keep the executive in check. Though ultimately the people might have recourse to revolution, the principal institution they should rely upon was that of representation. Representatives endowed with certain limited powers, such as the power of the purse and the power to discountenance laws proposed by the executive and the upper house, could protect the people by exercising effective restraint over the actions of hereditary or appointed rulers. And periodic elections would ensure that the people could have representatives responsive to their interests.[42] They could also have their say in the execution of the law through the grand and petit juries on which they served.[43]

These institutions were thought of as bringing the popular and prerogative forces into equilibrium. Yet the constitution of the body pol-

[41] Bernard Bailyn, *The Ideological Origins of the American Revolution* (Cambridge, Mass., 1967), chap. 3; Richard Buel, Jr., 'Democracy and the American Revolution: A Frame of Reference,' *William and Mary Quarterly*, 3d ser. 21 (1964): 169–70.

[42] Ibid., 170ff.

[43] Bailyn, *Ideological Origins*, p. 74; Buel, 'Democracy and the American Revolution,' 168n.

71

itic, like the human body, was vulnerable to corruption, particularly as the people did not possess uncontested influence over their representatives. If the executive ministers ever succeeded in winning a majority of the House of Representatives over to their own side rather than the people's, the subject would lose his main defense against arbitrary power. The judicial system at least had built-in protection against executive influence. The procedures for impaneling petit juries generally preserved impartiality, and because the jurors served briefly, giving judgment in only one cause whose trial usually lasted but one day, it was hard to tamper with them.[44] The legislature, on the other hand, held long sessions, allowing the ministry closer contact with the legislators and more opportunity to influence them than the people they served. As the agents of established power, ministers had both a motive for corrupting the people's representatives and the means in their ability to give preferments and pensions. With every expansion of the economy and the bureaucracy, this power increased. Lastly, individuals could never hope to influence more than their own representative, whereas executive officials had the opportunity to influence the whole representative body. Clearly, to check the tendency of power to encroach would require united action on the part of a naturally disunited people.[45]

Colonial Americans viewed the function of the press from the standpoint of these assumptions. Primarily they saw it as an instrument by which the mass of the people might seek to compensate for some of the disadvantages they labored under in their struggle with the executive.[46] Specifically it offered a remedy for the people's most chronic ailment: disunity. Newspapers could play a special part in welding together a united populace by disseminating knowledge of the constitution and of how their ruler's actions related to it. Without such knowledge, subjects would not know when their rights were invaded nor have a com-

[44] I have canvassed some of these features of juries in my 'Studies in the Political Ideas of the American Revolution' (Ph.D. dissertation, Harvard University, 1962), chap. 4, especially p. 132.

[45] Bailyn, *Origins of American Politics*, pp. 44–48; 'Junius Cato' in the *Connecticut Gazette*, Jan. 15, 1773, reprinted in *Massachusetts Spy*, Feb. 4, 1773; cf. also 'Centinel' V in *Massachusetts Spy*, May 30, 1771.

[46] Trenchard and Gordon, *Cato's Letters*, 3: 294; *Massachusetts Spy*, Jan. 2, 1772; Dec. 10, 1772; 'Address to the Inhabitants of Quebec' in *JCC*, 1: 108; cf. also J. L. De-Lolme, *The Constitution of England*, new ed. (London, 1777), pp. 26off.

mon principle on which to act.[47] The press could also rouse the people to action. As John Adams complained in 1765, 'inconsideration' no less than 'ignorance' had brought ruin on mankind.[48] One should not stop at explaining the Constitution and broadcasting violations of it, for 'the people are not persuaded without the utmost difficulty to attend to facts and evidence.'[49]

If, then, the newspapers could educate and exhort the people into making common cause and using their limited powers to maximum effect, the proper balance between rulers and ruled could be maintained in most contingencies. And if a faction bent on seizing power should ever destroy all the people's constitutional weapons, the power of the press would become even more vital to their cause. For when all other defenses against tyranny had collapsed, the people might still beat back injustice with the threat of rebellion, if not with rebellion itself. But they could not do either without some means of bringing everyone to agree on both grievance and redress. Only a united people could by their 'Prudence and Resolution . . . prevent the Committing of . . . Wrongs' by showing their rulers that they would not tolerate acts against 'the general bent of the people's inclination.' Only a united people could intimidate 'oppressive officers' who refused to be otherwise deterred.[50]

Such ideas as these set eighteenth-century America on a different course from that taken by Britain. The power to control the press through the courts diminished more rapidly in the colonies than in the mother country. Colonial juries had more immediate reasons to balk at collaborating with crown officials in convicting printers of seditious

[47] J. Adams, 'Dissertation on the Canon and Feudal Law' in *Works*, 3: 448–50, 462; 'Consideration' in *Massachusetts Spy*, Mar. 7, 1771; 'Centinel' in *Massachusetts Spy*, Mar. 26, 1772; Katz, ed., *Brief Narrative*, p. 81; James Burgh, *Political Disquisitions* (Philadelphia, 1775), 3: 247.

[48] J. Adams, 'Dissertation' in *Works*, 3: 448, 489–90; cf. also William Goddard, *The Partnership: or the History of the Rise and Progress of the Pennsylvania Chronicle* (Philadelphia, 1770), p. 57.

[49] *Boston Gazette*, Feb. 9, 1767; *South-Carolina Gazette* (Timothy), Dec. 3, 1764, Nov. 7, 1768; *Pennsylvania Chronicle*, May 23, June 27, 1768; *Pennsylvania Gazette*, Feb. 1, 1770; *Maryland Gazette*, July 18, 1765, Apr. 8, May 6, 1773.

[50] Katz, ed., *Brief Narrative*, p. 80; *Boston Evening-Post*, Oct. 14, 1765; *Virginia Gazette* (Rind), Dec. 25, 1766; *South-Carolina Gazette* (Timothy), Jan. 19, 1765; 'Crisis' in *Virginia Gazette* (Dixon), May 18, 1776; DeLolme, *Constitution of England*, p. 274; quote from 'Address to the Inhabitants of Quebec,' *JCC*, 1: 108.

libel.[51] Such prosecutions had come to an end in the 1730s with the Zenger case. The publicity given to it by the *Narrative of the Zenger Case* not only drew attention to the claim that the libelousness of a publication should be judged by jurors, not by courts, using truth as their criterion, but also showed that a jury might defy the directions of the court with impunity.[52] Though executive officials would not formally renounce the right to prosecute for libel, they could no longer bend the judicial machinery to their will.[53] In the late colonial period, they only once succeeded in wresting an indictment from a grand jury. And even this victory they owed to a division in the ranks of the local populace which gave a party favorable to the crown some brief control over New York's government. But both the New York House and crown officials soon saw the futility of attempting to convict by unanimous consent of twelve petit jurors, and abandoned this prosecution too.[54] Attempts to circumvent grand juries by having the public prosecutor file an information against an offensive press were open to the same objections.[55]

The lower houses of assembly, however, did not so readily surrender their power. While championing the liberty of the press against royal officials, the colonial assemblies refused to have such a weapon turned against themselves and suppressed dissent without a qualm. After 1738 it was the 'acclaimed bastion of the people's liberties . . . the popularly elected Assembly,' not the executive power, that persecuted the press, imprisoning both authors and publishers for breaches of privilege. And they usually had considerable popular support for their acts.[56] The an-

[51] Cf. Duniway, *Development of Freedom of the Press*, pp. 78–79, 87–88, 91–92.

[52] Katz, ed., *Brief Narrative*, pp. 62ff.

[53] Thomas Hutchinson, *The History of the Colony and Province of Massachusetts-Bay*, L. S. Mayo, ed. (Cambridge, Mass., 1936), 3: 135.

[54] Cf. *No. 3 The Dougliad. On Liberty. Humbly Inscribed to the Grand Jury for the City and County of New York* (New York, 1770), pp. 2–4; Joseph A. Ernst, *Money and Politics in America 1755–1775* (Chapel Hill, 1973), pp. 276–77; Levy, *Legacy of Suppression*, p. 82.

[55] Isaiah Thomas, *The History of Printing in America*, ed. Marcus A. McCorison (Barre, Mass., 1970), p. 167; Schlesinger, *Prelude to Independence*, pp. 140–41. Cf. Livingston R. Schuyler, *The Liberty of the Press in the American Colonies before the Revolutionary War* (New York, 1905), pp. 15, 21.

[56] Levy, *Legacy of Suppression*, p. 20. The one exception to the rule was the New York Assembly's imprisonment of McDougall for breach of privilege after abandoning the effort to prosecute him in the courts. Cf. Alexander McDougall, 'To the Freeholders of the City and Colony of New York,' reprinted in Levy, ed., *Freedom of the Press*, pp. 117–27. Efforts of colonial councils to imprison for breach of privilege were not popular, though; cf. Levy, *Legacy of Suppression*, pp. 76–77.

tagonism between the house and the governor in the colonial legislatures paralleled the competition for local resources between administrators in the mother country and local politicians in each colony. As
England intensified her efforts to bring the colonies under control,
local interests tended to consolidate against her claims. The legislature
seldom exercised its power to punish for breach of privilege. Most
printers had to cater to existing public sentiment if they wanted enough
readers to keep them going, and nothing reflected that sentiment more
faithfully than majority opinion in the legislature. Even papers having
official patrons, as Green and Russell's *Boston Post-Boy and Advertiser*
had the American Board of Customs Commissioners, could find themselves in trouble if they let their patrons deny their readers such popular
items as John Dickinson's 'Farmer's Letters.'[57]

This state of affairs led to anything but a free press in our terms. Yet
the colonists themselves did not see any inconsistency. They equated
structural divisions in their political system with the eternal struggle
between the crown and the people, or between power and liberty. Bernard Bailyn has shown how their penchant for interpreting their experience in terms of seventeenth-century constitutional struggles helped
make their politics unstable, particularly since the royal governors were
all too apt to claim powers long renounced by the crown in England.[58]
No wonder, then, if ideas of parliamentary privilege developed in the
sixteenth and seventeenth centuries to give the Commons some defense
against the crown seemed ever more timely in America as their relevance faded in Britain. How could the legislature defend the people
against executive aggrandizement or ministerial plots against colonial
liberty when it could not preserve its own independence?[59] This line of
thought led to such frank statements as one in the *Maryland Gazette* to
the effect that 'the liberty of the press . . . should . . . be totally at the
devotion of the . . . friends of the people.'[60] The one-sidedness of this

[57] O. M. Dickerson, 'British Control of American Newspapers on the Eve of the
Revolution,' *New England Quarterly* 24 (1951): 456; also, Goddard, *The Partnership*,
pp. 16–18.

[58] Bailyn, *Origins of American Politics*, chaps. 2–3.

[59] Richard Buel, Jr., *Securing the Revolution: Ideology and American Politics, 1789–1815*
(Ithaca, 1972), p. 245.

[60] 'A Customer' in *Maryland Gazette*, Oct. 21, 1773; cf. also Isaiah Thomas's declaration of intent in the *Massachusetts Spy*, Jan. 3–7, 1771.

concept was only evident to those who dissented from patriot opinion, namely the loyalists and occasionally some religious minorities.

III

The colonists' partisan perspective on the freedom of the press took on practical significance during the imperial crisis when they came to feel that they could permit no dissension from the policy of boycotting English commerce if they were to succeed against the Townshend Duties as they had succeeded against the Stamp Act. Denied all other means of redress, the colonists on that occasion had threatened to withhold their trade, much as representatives withheld supplies.[61] When Parliament imposed the Townshend Duties in 1767, the colonists had once again to choose either submission or organized resistance. But this time two new factors complicated matters. The colonists did not gain the kind of support in England that had previously helped them secure repeal of the Stamp Act with minimal commercial disruption. And whereas some royal governors had sanctioned the sending of delegates to the Stamp Act Congress,[62] in 1768 the ministry ordered all governors in effect to dissolve any colonial legislature giving consideration to the circular letter of the Massachusetts House of Representatives advocating commercial measures against Great Britain. The colonists would have to frame a commercial boycott suitable for all the colonies without central direction from their legislatures.[63]

In some ways, working outside existing political institutions had advantages. If the legislatures had actively sponsored what was in effect a conspiracy against trade, England would probably have attempted an immediate remodeling of colonial institutions like that imposed on Massachusetts in 1774, provoking the colonists to a premature rebellion. Having to rely on the initiative of unofficial committees advocating nonimportation and nonconsumption kept them on safer ground, since no law could force people to buy British manufactures. Moreover, the task of building an intercolonial association turned out to be less formidable than they expected. Severe imbalances in the postwar

[61] Cf. John Dickinson, *Works*, 1: 173.

[62] Edmund S. Morgan and Helen M. Morgan, *The Stamp Act Crisis* (Chapel Hill, 1953), p. 104.

[63] The story has been most recently retold by Pauline Maier, *From Resistance to Revolution* (New York, 1972), chap. 5 and p. 170.

economy gave many merchants and consumers a positive interest in nonimportation.[64] When some merchants proved reluctant, as in Philadelphia, the press succeeded in arousing enough popular indignation against the recalcitrants to make them knuckle under.[65] And where whole ports tried to reap the benefits that others had chosen to forego, as did the lesser towns of Newport and Portsmouth, patriots organized boycotts against them too.[66] Indeed, their success in implementing the Association of 1768–70 (everywhere but in New Hampshire) impelled many colonial leaders to see the colonists as a uniquely virtuous people. This, in turn, made republicanism, and ultimately independence, seem a real option.

The trouble with nonimportation lay more in maintaining it than in establishing roughly equitable restrictions, though the exact terms did vary from region to region.[67] Problems arose when the economic imbalance that first made nonimportation attractive began to be replaced by positive incentives to give it up. And one feature of the Association itself helped build up the pressure to abandon it: the first violators to order large shipments of goods from Europe would stand to gain an advantage over those who continued loyal. Here the press played a particularly vital part in keeping the Association together. On the local level, the newspapers could discourage individual violators by holding recreants up to public disgrace and urging that no one do business with them. And more important still, they could keep all the colonies informed and persuaded of each other's continued good faith. Every time a local paper reprinted another's reports of associations entered into and enforced throughout the continent, the merchants there felt reassured that their competitors elsewhere were not taking advantage of their patriot naïveté.

John Mein's *Boston Chronicle* did precisely the opposite. Mein both questioned the wisdom of the Association and charged that 190 import-

[64] C. M. Andrews, 'The Boston Merchants and the Non-Importation Movements,' *Publications of the Colonial Society of Massachusetts* 19 (*Transactions* 1916–1917): 184ff; Maier, *From Resistance to Revolution*, pp. 118–19; G. C. Smith, 'An Era of Non-Importation Associations, 1768–1773,' *William and Mary Quarterly*, 2d ser. 20 (1920): 92–93.

[65] A. M. Schlesinger, 'Politics, Propaganda, and the Philadelphia Press, 1767–1770,' *Pennsylvania Magazine of History and Biography* 60 (1936): 317–18.

[66] Andrews, 'Boston Merchants,' pp. 214, 221, 224, 236–38, 245; Maier, *From Resistance to Revolution*, pp. 137–38; 'A Citizen' in *New-York Journal*, June 21, 1770.

[67] Andrews, 'Boston Merchants,' pp. 201–5, 257.

ers in Boston had violated the agreement during the first six months.[68] The patriot leadership retorted that Mein had padded his list with many who did not live in the town, including 'clergymen, Masters of Vessels and private Persons who only had a single Article for their Family Use,' and by listing partnerships twice. The goods he itemized, they said, included much not forbidden by the terms of the Association.[69] Mein replied in August, denying the claim of the merchants' committee that most Boston merchants had faithfully observed non-importation. To support his charge, he began printing the manifests of vessels that had entered the port of Boston since January 1, 1769. Among them were three vessels owned by John Hancock, suggesting that Hancock had exploited the Association for personal gain.[70] The merchants' committee and Hancock's agent, William Palfrey, promptly denied these charges, alleging that the manifests in Mein's paper had been doctored to make permitted goods look like imports. He also lumped the manifests of nonsigners, transients, and nonresidents together with the manifests of signers.[71] Nonetheless, Mein continued publishing manifests into October. On the night of October 28, an assault on Mein and his partner, John Fleeming, almost ended in violence between the regular troops and the townspeople. Mein retired to a man-of-war, and shortly afterwards took ship for England.[72]

Fleeming, however, remained in Boston and continued to publish the *Chronicle*. In the upper left-hand column of the front page, reserved in other papers for the names of violators of the Association, he printed 'A QUESTION FOR THE "WELL DISPOSED", Who are the "*Committee*" who have entertained the "*base*" design of deceiving the Public by publishing "false" accounts of Importations and of the Importers into this port? Surely the following cannot be of the number.' Beneath this appeared the names of the Boston merchants on the committee to enforce the Association.[73] A week later Fleeming added the following advertisement underneath the committee names: 'Is not the detection

[68] *Boston Chronicle*, June 1, 1769.

[69] *Boston Gazette*, June 12 and July 13, 1769.

[70] *Boston Chronicle*, Aug. 17, 1769, and subsequent issues.

[71] *Boston Gazette*, Aug. 28, Sept. 18, Oct. 9 and 23, 1769. Andrews accepts Mein's charges as being true without taking account of these rebuttals; cf. 'Boston Merchants,' p. 229n.

[72] Hiller B. Zobel, *The Boston Massacre* (New York, 1970), pp. 156–59, 161–63.

[73] Beginning Oct. 23, 1769.

of the "Well Disposed" owing to the Glorious Liberty of the Press?"[74] On December 11 he resumed printing the manifests, and by the beginning of March, fifty-five of them had appeared.[75]

The mob did not attack because a better strategy for silencing the *Chronicle* had suggested itself. Shortly before Mein's flight, his principal London creditor had asked John Hancock to act for him in enforcing collection of Mein's debts. It would take time for Hancock to obtain power of attorney, but he hoped then to silence Fleeming's press by attaching it for debt.[76] Unfortunately, legal proceedings dragged out until the following summer.[77] Though the mob, like Hancock, saw themselves as surrogates for the legislature in bringing abuses of the press to account, after the Boston Massacre they were content to wait for a judicial remedy. Not only had Fleeming discreetly stopped publishing manifests and his provocative advertising of the Boston Committee, but the patriots knew that renewed violence in Boston might lead to Britain's sending more troops.

In the meantime, various forces worked to undermine the unanimity of the colonists on the aims of nonimportation. They had started out in agreement that they would not abandon or modify the Association until they had gained total repeal of all the revenue acts. But pressure began to mount in mercantile centers like New York and Philadelphia for the resumption of commerce with England, and the *Chronicle* had something to do with this. The customs service apparently subsidized the distribution of the published manifests both as individual sheets and in the form of a pamphlet, *A State of the Importations from Great Britain into the Port of Boston, from the Beginning of January 1769 to August 17th 1769.*[78] The violations alleged there received corroboration from British merchants who reported to their American correspondents that large shipments of boycotted goods were going to various North American ports, particularly Boston.[79] At the same time, word came that Parliament definitely intended to repeal the Townshend Duties, at least in part. Merchants in Philadelphia and New York, particularly New York, began to agitate

[74] Beginning Oct. 30, 1769.

[75] Andrews, 'Boston Merchants,' p. 228n.

[76] L. Kinvin Wroth and Hiller B. Zobel, eds., *Legal Papers of John Adams* (Cambridge, Mass., 1965), 1: 200.

[77] Ibid., pp. 202–4.

[78] Zobel, *Boston Massacre*, p. 154.

[79] Andrews, 'Boston Merchants,' pp. 241–42.

for modification of the Association so that the boycott would apply only to dutied goods.

New York had an extra incentive to press for the change, report having reached her that Parliament contemplated a special dispensation from the Currency Act of 1764 permitting her to emit £120,000 in bills of credit having the status of legal tender.[80] In the summer of 1770, New York merchants went ahead on their own and modified the Association, even though the other major ports, including Philadelphia, had vigorously rejected their overture and bitterly censured them for it. The merchants had taken care not to act entirely alone. They took the trouble to collect signatures from the townspeople to a statement favoring alteration of the agreement, again sent it to Boston and Philadelphia, and again received a rebuff. On July 9, after a perfunctory second canvass, they took their own way and, despite strong protests from the local Sons of Liberty, ordered everything but tea from England.[81]

A new pamphlet from Fleeming's press, entitled *A State of the Importation from Great Britain into the Port of Boston*, may have spurred them on. In eighty-five pages, Fleeming itemized the cargoes entering Boston from the mother country during the period January 8 through June 29, 1770, though this time without naming the vessels' owners so that there would be no chance to distinguish nonsigners from signers. The pamphlet bore no name, but everyone knew who had printed it, thanks to the distinctive typeface Mein and Fleeming used. When one of the copies went astray, Fleeming fled to the harbor castle rather than face the people of Boston, thus putting a quicker end to his activities than Hancock's litigation could have done.[82] Customs officials circulated the second edition of the pamphlet in Philadelphia, where impatient merchants used it to beat down popular objection to New York's act by pointing to Boston's culpability.[83]

Given the disadvantages the patriots labored under when they tried to counter British subversion of the Association, they had some reason to think that suppressing the *Chronicle* had nothing to do with violating

[80] Ernst, *Money and Politics*, pp. 276–77.
[81] Andrews, 'Boston Merchants,' pp. 244–45.
[82] Zobel, *Boston Massacre*, p. 232.
[83] Cf. Charles Evans et al., *American Bibliography* (Chicago and Worcester, 1903-61), 4: 240, notation under entry 11744; Andrews, 'Boston Merchants,' pp. 251–53.

the freedom of the press. A free press was supposed to be an instrument of liberty enabling a scattered people to make common cause against oppression, and the patriots would not have it perverted to the uses of power, wisely preferring the substance of liberty to the slogans. The same reasoning spurred the boycott of Rivington's press, and eventually its destruction, as well as the mob's efforts to suppress Charles Inglis's rebuttal of *Common Sense* in March 1776.[84]

The outbreak of the war did nothing to make the patriots more tolerant of opposition. The new state governments did not hesitate to proceed against anyone advocating opinions that might help the enemy. But there were differences. Now, instead of allowing mobs to do their work for them, the states asserted their own right to control abuse. When a Whig Club in Baltimore censured William Goddard for a certain article in the *Maryland Journal*, the club in turn was censured by the Maryland House for usurping the power of government and the governor issued a proclamation against "Bodies of Men associating together and . . . presuming to exercise any power over the persons or property of any Subject of this State."[85] And, as the new governments enacted treason and sedition statutes, jurisdiction over matters of opinion passed from the legislature to the executive and judiciary, though the legislature remained ready to act if problems arose not covered by existing law.[86] Lastly, authors became the targets of action, not printers who did not need the state's guidance to know where public opinion lay.

Congress alone showed restraint in controlling the press during the war. Three times it was asked to act against presses allegedly violating Congress's privileges, and each time invoked the principle of 'freedom of the press' to excuse its inaction.[87] But members seem to have had more on their minds than liberty. The majority recognized the absur-

[84] Robert A. Rutland, *The Newsmongers: Journalism in the Life of the Nation, 1690-1972* (New York, 1973), p.60.

[85] W. Bird Terwilliger, 'William Goddard's Victory for the Freedom of the Press,' *Maryland Historical Magazine* 36 (1941): 139–49, quote from p. 147.

[86] Cf. for instance W. W. Hening, ed., *The Statutes at Large Being a Collection of All the Laws of Virginia 1619–1792* (Richmond, 1809–23), 10: 268–70; Charles J. Hoadley, ed., *The Public Records of the State of Connecticut* (Hartford, 1894–), 1: 4, 377; also Connecticut State Archives, Revolutionary War, 1st ser., XIII, 220, Connecticut State Library, Hartford, Conn.

[87] *JCC*, 12: 1205–6; 14: 588, 589, 592–93, 611, 799–800.

dity of a body without a constitutional authority undertaking to punish for breach of constitutional privilege.[88] What would prevent those arrested from challenging Congress's authority on these constitutional grounds? Behind each appeal for Congress to punish abuses of the press lay a desire to compensate for its powerlessness in dealing with the economic problems of the war. Nevertheless, most people realized that for Congress to take such action would probably be a mistake, since it would dramatize its weakness. And soon after Congress attained the constitutional status that would have given it legitimate power to punish those infringing on its privileges, the need for it to do so faded as the war took a favorable turn. Through the 1780s, the issue of whether or not to restrain the press seldom arose. Even in Massachusetts, torn by a rebellion in 1786, prosecutions for sedition were brought against armed rebels, not printers.

IV

Americans emerged from their Revolution with mixed feelings about freedom of the press. Their success had apparently depended simultaneously on the assertion of freedom from one executive's control while ruthlessly using another's to repress loyalist opinion. But postwar circumstances seemed to suggest that the ambiguity would be resolved in favor of a genuinely free press. For one thing, the end of the imperial relationship restructured government in such a way as to eliminate the irreconcilable tensions between central and local authorities that had existed in the British Empire. Thus the justification for the one-sided freedom Americans had formerly claimed for their presses no longer existed. In any case, the wartime controls had not much affected either the emergence of loyalist opinion or the outcome of the war. The sources of loyalism obviously lay deeper than mere newspaper exhortations, and though loyalist propaganda did affect patriot morale, no one could ever wholly prevent the underground circulation of loyalist newspapers. The politically threatening aspect of such propaganda had to be met by either direct rebuttal or satire,[89] but the patriots

[88] Cf. Edward Langworthy to William Duer, Dec. 8, 1778, in Edmund C. Burnett, ed., *Letters of Members of the Continental Congress* (Washington, 1921–38), 3: 540.

[89] Offers of clemency were most threatening to the Revolutionary leadership. For the way in which they were handled, cf. *Connecticut Courant*, Sept. 15, 1777, May 5, 1778, July 27, 1779.

seldom felt at a disadvantage in this respect and often republished pieces from Rivington's paper. The one postwar pamphlet explicitly discussing freedom of the press concluded that judicial repression had no effect on public opinion 'because the opinion of the publick is in itself a law.'[90] Such skepticism about controls, along with the speedy passage of a constitutional amendment preventing Congress from abridging the freedom of either religion or the press, suggested that unequivocal libertarianism would emerge in the postwar period as the republic recovered its balance.

Unfortunately, the French Revolution and the European war it precipitated arrested what might otherwise have been a spontaneous and orderly development.[91] America's interests would obviously best be served by maintaining neutrality, but this was easier said than done. Since no one power had unchallenged naval superiority, United States shipping became an important strategic asset in the calculations of each combatant. In addition the United States was technically bound to defend France's West India possessions by the Franco-American Treaty of 1778. Though France chose not to invoke the guarantee a domestic obstacle to neutrality remained, namely the hatred of Britain and love for France instilled during the Revolutionary War. In 1793–94, France's transition to a revolutionary republic, coupled with British depredations on American commerce, strengthened feelings to the point where public opinion would have supported provocative measures against Britain if not outright war.

The issue of how the United States should respond to these pressures divided the national leadership into two hostile parties. The Republicans would have preferred to improve the occasion by pressuring Britain into full compliance with the Peace Treaty of 1783 and into giving satisfaction for the commercial spoliations, but they did not control the executive department. The Federalists, doubtful of the republic's stability and determined to avoid war with Britain at all costs, chose instead to negotiate a treaty with her in 1794. The Jay Treaty made major concessions to Britain in the matter of neutral commerce, thereby threatening hardship to France. Most Americans regarded it with disfavor which the French tried to exploit. In 1796, just before

[90] *Candid Consideration on Libels* (Boston, 1789), p. 15.
[91] What follows is a summary of the argument I have previously developed in *Securing the Revolution*, chaps. 3, 5–8.

the electoral college met, Ambassador Adet announced that France meant to break off diplomatic relations over the Jay Treaty. Adet's declaration did not make Jefferson president. But increasing French depredations on American shipping threatened to force the new Federalist administration into an unpopular confrontation with France.

The moment called for negotiation. But negotiations coincided with France's most glorious victories, and the Directory chose to demand in effect that the country buy peace. Their behavior gave the Federalists an immediate advantage at home. By releasing the dispatches of the American envoys they forced the people to recognize that Talleyrand's agents had tried to impose terms that humiliated the United States. The maneuver succeeded, at least momentarily, in purging Americans of sentimental feeling for France, either as their former ally or as a sister republic. But the slightest conciliatory gesture from the Directory would revive it again. Many Federalists longed for a way to disenchant the people with France once and for all, as the Revolutionary War had disenchanted them with Britain. Some began to hope for war with France. They assumed that France would not have a free hand against the United States, that all conflict would take place on the sea, and that the British navy would help the United States, so that the nation would emerge undamaged but with a new, inimical view of France. But how could they get into such a war? The Federalists did not feel they could declare war on France as long as the opposition continued to argue that war was unnecessary and unwise, for the republic would divide even more drastically under the pressure of the ensuing conflict. And France resolutely refused to issue the unambiguous challenge the Federalists needed to rally unanimous public opinion behind them.

In the end, the Federalists settled for attacking Francophilia through the Sedition Act. In principle, the law only forbade printing 'false' and 'malicious' matter, the guilt or innocence of a particular piece to be judged by a jury. But it gave administration authorities the power to hound the opposition press throughout the nation, and, wherever a jury agreed, to punish printers with heavy fines and other penalties. The Federalists could not defend the law by citing Revolutionary precedent for controlling opinion during wartime.[92] So they retreated to a position formerly taken in justifying the assemblies when they punished

[92] *Annals*, 5th Congress, pp. 2161-62; *The Virginia Report of 1799–1800, Together with . . . the Debates and Proceedings Thereon* (Richmond, 1850), p. 50.

84

for breach of privilege: that is, they argued that government could not fulfill its obligation to its constituents unless it possessed such a power. Robert Treat Paine put the point best in a charge to the grand jury of Barnstable County, Massachusetts: 'How can the Congress protect the people, their constituents, if they are not able to protect themselves?' he asked.[93] By means of such analogies, the Federalists proclaimed the Sedition Law 'as essential to the rights and privileges of the people as any law upon our code.'[94]

It soon became clear, though, that the Sedition Law was meant to do more than guard against a dangerous resurgence of 'French influence.' The Federalists so distrusted the popular character of republican government that they felt the administration must possess some power to control opinion if the nation were to survive. James Bayard expressed this view before Congress in February 1799:

> This Government . . . depends for its existence upon the good will of the people. That good will is maintained by their good opinion. But, how is that good opinion to be preserved, if wicked and unprincipled men, men of inordinate and desperate ambition, are allowed to state facts to the people which are not true, which they know at the time to be false, and which are stated with the criminal intention of bringing the Government into disrepute among the people[?] This was falsely and deceitfully stealing the public opinion; it was a felony of the worst and most dangerous nature.[95]

In effect, Bayard was saying that an administration could not survive without the power to punish 'the publication of false, scandalous and malicious matter against the Government.' Most Federalists would have agreed, only adding that popular government stood in the greatest danger in this respect. For if the channels of communication between itself and the people became 'corrupted' by misrepresentation and falsehood, the people so misled might vote a good administration out of office.[96] As Alexander Addison observed, 'To mislead the judgement of

[93] *Independent Chronicle*, June 6, 1799. Here and in notes 94–97, 105–7, and 109 I use material that has already appeared in *Securing the Revolution*, with the permission of the Cornell University Press.

[94] *Annals*, 5th Congress, p. 2892; *Observations on the Alien and Sedition Laws*, pp. 8–9; *The Virginia Report*, pp. 105, 133, 134.

[95] *Annals*, 5th Congress, pp. 2960, 2961; 6th Congress, p. 967.

[96] 'Aristides' in *Middlesex Gazette*, Oct. 3, 1800; *Annals*, 6th Congress, pp. 412, 931, 956, 961.

the people, where they have no power, may produce no mischief. To mislead the judgement of the people, where they have *all* power, must produce the greatest possible mischief.'[97]

The Republicans had seen Federalist attempts to manipulate public opinion before; they easily recognized the Sedition Law as yet another, this time designed to deny the opposition victory in the coming elections. Consequently they attacked it. But the Republicans were not in agreement among themselves. Their most articulate leaders came from widely different social and regional backgrounds, and they differed considerably in their interests. Though their union into one party owed far more to shared ideology than is true of the major political parties today, they responded variously to the Sedition Law. Certain patterns appear, though, in the variations.

The northern Republicans made less of an ideological attack on the law than did the Republicans in the South. James Sullivan, a rising Republican and future governor of Massachusetts, held the office of state attorney general in 1799. During that time, under the common law of libels, he prosecuted the bookkeeper of the Republican *Independent Chronicle*.[98] And Sullivan appears to have acted according to his principles. In 1801, he published a pamphlet entitled *A Dissertation upon the Constitutional Freedom of the Press in the United States of America*, which, while admitting that in a republic citizens had a right to criticize their representatives and acknowledging that the Federalists had misused the Sedition Law, nonetheless concluded that the law itself was a constitutional measure.[99]

Sullivan's readiness to endorse the Sedition Law in principle never produced serious objections to his Republican candidacy,[100] but it might have had he stood for office in the South, where feeling ran high against it. The legislatures of Virginia and Kentucky pronounced the Sedition Law unconstitutional in their Resolutions of 1798, while

[97] Addison, *Analysis of the Report of the Committee*, p. 42.

[98] Smith, *Freedom's Fetters*, pp. 253–54; also Thomas C. Amory, *Life of James Sullivan* (Boston, 1859), 2: 66–68.

[99] Cf. passim, especially p. 31.

[100] Cf. James Sullivan to Henry Dearborn, May 11, 1804, in Amory, *Life of James Sullivan*, 2: 136. Elbridge Gerry, a Republican successor to Sullivan as governor of Massachusetts, also would not disavow the right of the state to curb the licentiousness of the press. Cf. Duniway, p. 154; George A. Billias, *Elbridge Gerry: Founding Father and Republican Statesman* (New York, 1976), pp. 322–23.

even Federalists like John Marshall questioned its propriety and voted against its renewal in 1801.[101] Differing patterns of settlement and commercial development may lie behind the different regional responses to the Sedition Law. The South's diffuse population and relatively undeveloped commercial channels made it harder for newspapers to survive there. At the same time they were more important in keeping the people in touch with one another. If a sedition prosecution silenced an opposition paper in the North, its readers still would not be left in the dark. Some would have access to opposition papers printed elsewhere; others would keep informed through the grapevine until another printer filled the gap. They would not have to wait long, because the high density of population produced a correspondingly high number of printers on the lookout for markets to be served.[102]

Though the southern Republican leadership opposed the Sedition Law unanimously, their opposition took many forms. Protest could focus on the constitutional issue construed in jurisdictional terms, which had an advantage for the elite of not denying that the press could be misused and that misuse should be punished. But the question remained, did the Constitution allow the federal government to deal out the punishment? The First Amendment explicitly barred Congress from abridging the freedom of the press. If the power to abridge this freedom existed anywhere, the Tenth Amendment had bestowed it on the individual states.[103] More than mere legalism inspired this strategy. Behind the constitutional objections to the Sedition Law (and the Alien Act too) lay a real fear of allowing federal power to expand. Part of

[101] Albert J. Beveridge, *The Life of John Marshall*, 2 vols. (Boston, 1916–19), 2: 389, 451.

[102] One crude measure of the comparative indispensability of newspapers in the respective regions is to take the ratio of papers to population in Virginia, Connecticut, and Massachusetts. In 1800 Virginia had approximately one newspaper for every 40,000 inhabitants, Massachusetts including Maine had one for every 21,000 inhabitants, and Connecticut one for every 11,500. Cf. also Homer L. Calkin, 'Pamphlets and Public Opinion During the American Revolution,' *Pennsylvania Magazine of History and Biography* 64 (1940): 28.

[103] The Republican tracts giving the jurisdictional point the greatest emphasis were 'Philodemus,' *An Enquiry Whether the Act of Congress . . . Generally Called the Sedition Bill, is Unconstitutional or Not* (Richmond, 1798); St. George Tucker, *A Letter to a Member of Congress, Respecting the Alien and Sedition Laws* (n.p., 1799); Nathaniel Pope, *A Speech, Delivered . . . the 17th Day of October, 1798* (Richmond, 1800); cf. also *Annals*, 5th Congress, pp. 2142, 2153–54.

this fear sprang from the Virginia leadership's feeling that they faced an administration hostile to them.[104] But there was an ideological dimension as well. A government whose powers exceeded the realm of specific common interests would be strongly tempted to give up the hard task of ruling so large and diverse a country according to republican principles. The continuous pressure to sacrifice one sector's interests to another's might in time create a government of force. In other words, every increase in the power of the central government took the nation one step further away from government by consent.[105]

The Sedition Law invited a broader ideological attack than this, though, and most Republican leaders with eyes on the election of 1800 did not mean to let the opportunity slip. Though writers touched on many peripheral ideological issues, for instance the Federalists' reliance on monarchical precedent in justifying the law,[106] the most telling objection was that it would strike at the heart of republican government by making elections meaningless. Madison put the case in his influential 'Report of the Committee to whom were referred the communications of various States':

> [In] competitions between those who are and those who are not members of the Government, what will be the situations of the competitors? Not equal; because the characters of the former will be covered by the Sedition Act from animadversions exposing them to disrepute among the people, whilst the latter may be exposed to the contempt and hatred of the people without a violation of the act. What will be the situation of the people? Not free; because they will be compelled to make their election between competitors whose pretensions they are not permitted by the act equally to examine, to discuss and to ascertain. And from both these situations will not those in power derive an undue advantage for continuing themselves in it, which, by impairing the right of election, endangers the blessings of the Government founded on it?[107]

[104] Buel, *Securing the Revolution*, pp. 219–20.

[105] Ibid., p. 19; James Madison, 'Report of the Committee to Whom Were Referred the Communications of Various States,' *The Writings of James Madison*, ed. Gaillard Hunt (New York, 1900–1910), 6: 357; John Page, *Address to the Freeholders of Gloucester County* (Richmond, 1799), p. 31.

[106] Buel, *Securing the Revolution*, pp. 248–49.

[107] Madison, 'Report of the Committee,' in *Writings*, ed. Hunt, 6: 397–98; also *Annals*, 5th Congress, pp. 2110, 2144, 2996, 3003, 3006–7, 3014; 6th Congress, pp. 406, 964.

Moreover the jurisdictional and ideological arguments could be used as complements. Madison pointed this out, observing that 'the peculiar magnitude of some of the powers necessarily committed to the Federal Government; the peculiar duration required for the functions of some of its departments; the peculiar distance of the seat of its proceedings from the great body of its constituents; and the peculiar difficulty of circulating an adequate knowledge of them through any other channel' all justified barring the federal government from touching the only means of making it accountable to its constituents.[108]

The Federalists protested that the law would not preclude honest examination of the government's actions. How, they asked, did 'a law to restrain lying' abridge legitimate freedom of the press? The Sedition Law would in fact preserve that freedom by protecting truth and punishing falsehood.[109] Republican spokesmen retorted that political criticism necessarily contained opinion as well as fact, and that no jury could determine the truth or falsehood of an opinion but only 'whether or not it is their own.' Therefore the provision for the jury to decide whether or not the libel was true would not protect free expression. 'No man will be safe, for though he may have formed his opinion as correctly as possible, if twelve men are to sit upon it, and if it should happen not to be their opinion . . . he will be liable to severe fine and imprisonment,' they wrote. Thus the law might punish men for publishing opinions thoughtfully formed and honestly held 'merely because accident, or design, has collected a jury of different sentiments.'[110] And as time went on, the Republicans could point to partisan applications of the law as evidence disproving the Federalist claim that it would help to keep the channels of information pure. As Gallatin said, that would hardly result when 'only certain kinds of libels were punished' while the scandalous misrepresentations by Federalist papers went free.[111]

This critique left one crucial question unanswered. If a government innocent of the charges leveled against it could nevertheless be toppled by those charges, would not the national interest demand that

---

[108] Madison, 'Report of the Committee,' in *Writings*, ed. Hunt, 6: 392–93.

[109] *Annals*, 5th Congress, pp. 2097, 2103, 2112, 2960–61.

[110] Ibid., pp. 2006, 2108, 2113, 2162-64, 2969, 2970, 3005; Pope, *Speech, Delivered*, p. 21; Madison, 'Report of the Committee,' in *Writings*, ed. Hunt, 6: 395–96.

[111] *Annals*, 6th Congress, pp. 93, 922, 952.

there be some power to control abuse of the press? As the Federalists looked about them, they saw little to reassure them that a legitimate government serving the people's best interests had nothing to fear from the uncontrolled circulation of opinion. Events in France since 1789 proved to them beyond a shadow of a doubt that a league of clubs and societies misusing the press could incite the people to destroy the best government they had ever known.[112] If further proof were needed, the Federalists would have found it in their own increasing insecurity, brought about by opposition activities. They had become convinced that abuses of the press posed as real a threat to republican government during the late 1790s as during the Revolution. And they unhesitatingly dismissed the argument of some that the states' power over seditious libel would be sufficient to protect the federal government from injury.[113]

The Republicans had several possible ways of responding. They could say that this was a constitutional issue to which questions of necessity were irrelevant.[114] But most went further to argue that no deserving government could be damaged by abuse from the press. Arguing along the lines of the early eighteenth-century libertarians, they said that though the power of the press could be abused, the forcible suppression of falsehood would carry with it the risk that truth might also suffer. They would prefer to tolerate some abuses 'than, by pruning them away, to injure the vigor of those opinions yielding the proper fruits.'[115] In effect, they assumed what the Federalists denied, that when ideas could compete freely true opinions would always triumph. Despite the insistence of some that no jury could pass on the truth of an opinion, most Republicans did not deny that an opinion could be true or not. But what they meant by 'true' was that an opinion had won general acceptance as a result of free discussion. It followed that good governments would never need protection against wrong opinion, while bad governments did not deserve it.[116]

[112] Ibid., 5th Congress, p. 2098; Alexander Addison, *Liberty of Speech and Press*, pp. 12-13; also 'A.B.' from *Columbian Centinel* in *Gazette of the United States*, Jan. 1, 1798; 'Plain Truth' in ibid., Feb. 5, 1798.

[113] *Observations on the Alien and Sedition Laws*, p. 32; Lee, *Defense of the Alien and Sedition Laws*, p. 23.

[114] Madison, 'Report of the Committee' in *Writings*, ed. Hunt, 6: 392.

[115] Ibid., p. 289; *Annals*, 5th Congress, p. 2140; Page, *Address*, p. 15n.

[116] Cf. [George Hay], *An Essay on the Liberty of the Press . . . by Hortensius* (Philadelphia, 1799), pp. 44, 47–48; *Annals*, 5th Congress, pp. 2133–34; 6th Congress, pp. 921, 963.

Thomas Cooper—the English-born radical and friend of Joseph Priestley, recently arrived in the United States—most fully canvassed the Federalist fear of mistaken opinion in his essay 'On the Propriety and Expediency of Unlimited Enquiry.' Cooper drew heavily on Old Whig, eighteenth-century radical ideology when he wrote that 'the immediate interest of the people is to discover and promote the general good: that of governors to extend their own power, or preserve it by the continuance of the present order of things.' From this it would follow that true perception of the public interest would more probably arise from untrammeled popular discussion than from the theorizing of a small elite. Some people would utter pernicious opinions, no doubt, but to Cooper this did not matter. 'The mass of talents, of knowledge, and of respectability will, in every country, from interest as well as principle, be on the side of good order and morality,' he wrote. 'There can be few who, from ignorance or design, will be tempted publicly to support opinions inimical to the general welfare.' And any government that took care to promote the general interest need not fear the few who did. 'Should false opinions be propagated, is it probable that the majority of the people . . . will be misled by them, and that persons in power only will have the acuteness and discernment to detect their fallacy?,' asked Cooper. 'But were even this the case, surely the friends of the existing establishment, with truth on their side, and the collateral aids of wealth and power, will have no difficulty in confronting them.'[117]

Republican ideologues like Cooper did not stop at arguing that freedom of discussion could not endanger the state. They asserted that denying it would do positive harm. Cooper held that 'restraints imposed on freedom of speech and writing, are evidently calculated to produce the mischief they ostensibly aim to destroy. While one party assumes a right to suppress the opinions of those who differ from them, and the other experiences a degrading and unjustifiable subjection—violence, ill-will, and rancour must subsist.'[118] Cooper blamed the excesses of the French Revolution and the Whiskey Rebellion on the ignorance of the people, best remedied not by coercion but by free discussion. If government allowed opinion to circulate freely and express itself through

[117] Thomas Cooper, 'On the Propriety and Expediency of Unlimited Inquiry,' *Political Essays, by Thomas Cooper, Esq. of Northumberland,* 2d ed. (Philadelphia, 1800), pp. 64–66.

[118] Ibid., p. 67; [Hay], *An Essay,* p. 47.

electoral institutions, and remained responsive to that expression, no clash need ever take place between the two. Even if public opinion and government did collide, 'the convulsions . . . of revolution' could be minimized as during the American Revolution by allowing the free flow of opinion to make 'the nature and necessity of the change proposed . . . understood through the whole society previous to its taking place.'[119]

Cooper spoke from the standpoint of a tradition familiar to most Americans and agreeable to most Republican leaders. There were more radical voices in the Republican coalition. The most important representative of this radicalism, Tunis Wortman, a New York Republican, published *A Treatise Concerning Political Enquiry and the Liberty of the Press* in 1800, which has begun to receive attention from historians.[120] Little is known about the other figure, John Thomson, whose *An Essay Concerning the Liberty and Licentiousness of the Press* was published in New York in 1801. Both spoke from the perspective of the extraordinarily heterogeneous Middle Atlantic states and both were identified with religious dissent.[121] Certainly they were sensitive to the warnings of other Republicans that allowing the Federalists to tamper with the First Amendment in respect to the freedom of speech and of the press would render the guarantee of religious liberty worthless.[122] But what particularly distinguished these writers was the degree to which they drew on the work of the revolutionary anarchist William Godwin.

The second edition of Godwin's *Enquiry Concerning Political Justice and Its Influence on Morals and Happiness* had been republished in Philadelphia in 1796. In it, Godwin had laid the philosophical foundation for the idea that human reason, when freed from injustice and the unequal distribution of property, would lead irresistibly to human perfection.[123]

---

[119] Cooper, 'On the Propriety of Unlimited Inquiry,' pp. 66–67, 84.

[120] Cf. Levy, *Legacy of Suppression*, pp. 283–89; Gordon S. Wood, 'The Democratization of Mind in the American Revolution,' *Leadership in the American Revolution* (Washington, 1974), p. 88.

[121] Cf. Tunis Wortman, *A Solemn Address, to Christians and Patriots* (New York, 1800), pp. 9ff. John Thomson, *An Enquiry Concerning the Liberty and Licentiousness of the Press* (New York, 1801), p. 84.

[122] Madison, 'Report of the Committee,' in *Writings*, ed. Hunt, 6: 389, 399–401.

[123] William Godwin, *Enquiry Concerning Political Justice and Its Influence on Morals and Happiness* from the 2d London ed., 2 vols. (Philadelphia, 1796). The one other confessed disciple of Godwin was the quixotic Scottish pedagogue, James Ogilvie, whose

The American disciples of Godwin did not follow him in everything. The relative equality existing among Americans allowed them to avoid his insistence that mankind would not be free until property had been redistributed. And they could easily substitute republicanism for Godwin's anarchism. But Godwin made it possible for Wortman and Thomson to express a radical confidence in man's capacity for infinite improvement through free expression and discussion of opinion.[124]

V

Despite the many different approaches the Republicans took to criticism of the Sedition Law, Jefferson's victory in 1800 marked a major advance toward true freedom of the press. The strict constructionism which provided the broadest common ground of agreement within the Republican Party ensured that opinion could in fact express itself freely. For, with the power of punishing abuses confined to the states, the total suppression of a political opinion regardless of its unpopularity became unlikely. A printer or author victimized in one state jurisdiction could always take refuge in another.[125] Leonard Levy has pointed out that the Republicans initiated several prosecutions for seditious libel in the state courts with Jefferson's approval. But there is no evidence that Jefferson supported a systematic prosecution like that visited on the Republican press in 1800, or that he ceased to believe unswervingly that the judicial remedy for abuses rested with the state courts.[126] And so long as the national government abjured the power to punish abuses of the press, the actions of state governments could have but limited

---

A Speech Delivered in Essex County (Richmond, 1798) betrays Godwin's influence. In his *Cursory Reflexions on Government, Philosophy and Education* (Alexandria, 1802), vol. 2, Ogilvie compared Godwin favorably with Rousseau, Newton, and Milton. Some measure of Godwin's impact on American thought can be gained from Burton M. Pollin, *Godwin Criticism: A Synoptic Bibliography* (Toronto, 1967). Cf. also John P. Clark, *The Philosophical Anarchism of William Godwin* (Princeton, 1977), especially chap. 8.

[124] Tunis Wortman, *A Treatise Concerning Political Enquiry and the Liberty of the Press* (New York, 1800), passim and especially pp. 121–29, 189; Thomson, *Enquiry*, pp. 78–79. Cooper explicitly dissociated himself from Godwin's doctrines, cf. p. 83, though he, like Wortman and Thomson, and for that matter all libertarians, looked to free discussions to advance human knowledge and happiness.

[125] Buel, *Securing the Revolution*, p. 263.

[126] Levy, *Jefferson and Civil Liberties*, pp. 58–60.

effect. Indeed the threat of local prosecution helped make the Federalists instrumental in establishing the right in several state judicial systems to plead truth as a defense where the alleged libel involved an elected official.[127] This does not appear to have guaranteed the impartial administration of justice, but at least it made conviction more difficult than it had been under the common law.[128]

One group of Republicans, in Connecticut, did institute a series of common law prosecutions for seditious libel in the federal courts in 1806 and 1807. But the evidence suggests that they were defending themselves from the attempts of the local Federalist leadership to wage law against their opponents in the state courts. Only one prosecution ended in conviction, and the judge suspended sentence while in effect inviting the Supreme Court to bar the federal courts from assuming a common law jurisdiction.[129] After 1808 the Republicans gave up all such proceedings, though international pressures again grew great.[130] When the Federalists did their best to subvert the Embargo and to negate all Republican attempts to deal with the international crisis beginning in 1807, they gave their opponents as good reason to control the press as they had ever had. They were trying to force the Republicans either to admit inability to defend the nation, or to declare war. They did not, however, expect the Republicans to choose a war that would have to be fought offensively. This seemed to them unlikely considering that the republic found itself as divided in 1812 as in 1798 and that, to judge from the French experience, conquering Canada might lead to military despotism at home. When the event proved their calculations wrong,

[127] Cf. *Connecticut General Statutes, Acts and Laws 1801–07* (Hartford, 1807), p. 664, where the legislature passed a law to this effect in 1804; in New York the legislature passed a declaratory act in 1805, in response to Hamilton's eloquent defense of the Federalist editor Croswell in 1804, permitting truth as a defense. Cf. Thomas Cooper, *A Treatise on the Law of Libel and the Liberty of the Press* (New York, 1830), pp. 80–82. Massachusetts appears to have established a similar doctrine by the judicial pronouncement of Chief Justice Theophilus Parsons on motion for new trial in *Commonwealth v. Clap* (1807), though Parsons only held 'that publication of truth as to the characters of elective officers, or of candidates for such offices, were not a libel.' Cf. Duniway, *Development of Freedom of the Press*, p. 152.

[128] *Development of Freedom of the Press*, pp. 153–54; Billias, *Elbridge Gerry*, p. 322.

[129] Levy and I disagree on this issue; cf. his *Legacy of Suppression*, pp. 61–66; and Buel, *Securing the Revolution*, pp. 267–71.

[130] What follows is a summary of the argument in my *Securing the Revolution*, pp. 272ff.

94

they then did all they could to fulfill their prophecies of doom by hampering the war effort.

Despite extraordinary provocations, the Republicans never responded as the Federalists had in the analogous circumstances of the late 1790s. In the frustrating years between the repeal of the first embargo and the declaration of war against Britain, the Republicans did not curb the freedom of the Federalist press through the federal courts. Nor did they pass any federal internal security measures comparable to the Sedition Law during the war itself. Yet the Federalists complained bitterly that their opponents were trying to silence their presses. They were referring primarily to a series of mob actions, the worst of which occurred in Baltimore in 1812, just after the declaration of war. The first riot briefly shut down Maryland's leading Federalist paper, the *Federal Republican*, and the second forced it out of Baltimore and resulted in the death of one prominent Federalist and the maiming of others. But public opinion, not the state, was the power behind these acts. Indeed, throughout the war the federal government let the *Federal Republican* flourish right under its nose in Georgetown.[131] The Republican leadership might deplore the way public opinion had expressed itself in Baltimore, but most Jeffersonians would not have said that the press should be immune to it. All Republicans looked to public opinion to sanction their government's actions and condemn treasonous attempts to prostrate the republic for a party's vindication and advancement. And though they abhorred violence, they recognized as a fact that it might occur when the public had been inflamed to rage.[132]

The Republicans fought the War of 1812 without any of the coercive devices hallowed by Revolutionary usage, and which the Federalists in 1798 had seen as the inevitable concomitants of war. The only legal weapon the Republicans employed against dissenters was the charge of treason. But prosecutions for treason could only be brought against those who committed overt acts, and the constitutional requirements for a verdict of guilty, further refined by Marshall in the Burr trial, made conviction virtually impossible.

The Republicans' reluctance to make obstructing the war effort a

[131] Clarence S. Brigham, *History and Bibliography of American Newspapers 1690–1820*, 2 vols. (Worcester, Mass., 1947), 1: 89–90.
[132] This and what follows closely parallels my argument in *Securing the Revolution*, pp. 288ff.

lesser crime proceeded more from necessity than from abstract concern for individual freedom. Like the Revolutionaries, they never doubted the occasional need to sacrifice the forms of liberty to the preservation of its substance. Had circumstances favored it, they would have been as ready to control the press during the War of 1812 as the patriots had been during the Revolutionary War.[133] But in many states public opinion did not have the power to curb Federalist treason. Wherever the Federalists remained in office throughout the war, they used their control of state government to refuse compliance with federal militia requisitions. This, together with more informal methods of discouraging enlistments, was intended to force the government toward that policy of conscription on which the Revolutionary War effort had almost floundered. And Federalist attempts to discourage subscriptions to a federal loan in 1814, clearly designed to bring the war to a halt for lack of money, or to make the government impose unpopular taxes, very nearly succeeded. The Republicans knew, however, that trying to suppress such activities during the war would have added a civil war to the foreign one.

When peace came, the Republicans had their reward in seeing the Federalists disgraced forever. Their obstructionism had had for its sole justification their opinion that the republic was not strong enough to do battle with a powerful monarchy. Yet though they had put the republic to the harshest possible test, it had survived. They had also inadvertently proved the libertarian view that a genuinely popular government had nothing to fear from free expression, no matter how erroneous the opinions vented or how willful the misrepresentation of government measures.[134] Many people, of course, remained unconvinced that a press free of all controls could do no harm, but the future clearly belonged to libertarianism. As the Republican majority expanded into the North and West, and as the aristocratic Virginia leadership gave way to new leaders concerned with the problems of a growing capitalist economy, a democratic view of public opinion as a dynamic, sovereign force became central to popular ideology.[135] Faith

[133] Billias, *Elbridge Gerry*, pp. 322–23.
[134] Wortman had argued in 1800 that such misrepresentations were better destroyed 'by fair argumentative refutation' than 'by the terrible dissuasive of a statute of seditions.' Cf. *Treatise*, pp. 159–60.
[135] Wood, 'Democratization of Mind,' pp. 82–84.

in public opinion grew ever stronger as the economy prospered.[136] But the republic's ability to survive the war without repressing a treacherous opposition had prepared the ground for that faith. It had apparently confirmed in practice what had hitherto been ideological theory, that the state was not endangered by mere words, and therefore was seldom, if ever, justified in curbing the expression of opinion.

[136] Cf. Cooper, *Treatise*, p. xx.

The Role of the Newspaper Press in the Southern Colonies on the Eve of the Revolution: An Interpretation

ROBERT M. WEIR

ᕕ᠍ᕗ ᕕ᠍ᕗ ᕕ᠍ᕗ ᕕ᠍ᕗ ᕕ᠍ᕗ ᕕ᠍ᕗ ᕕ᠍ᕗ ᕕ᠍ᕗ ᕗ᠍ᕕ ᕗ᠍ᕕ ᕗ᠍ᕕ ᕗ᠍ᕕ ᕗ᠍ᕕ ᕗ᠍ᕕ ᕗ᠍ᕕ ᕗ᠍ᕕ

A S DAVID RAMSAY NOTED nearly 200 years ago, 'the pen and the press' presumably 'had merit equal to that of the sword' in achieving American independence, and with few exceptions his intellectual successors in the historical profession as well as contemporary participants on both sides of the Revolutionary controversy have agreed with this assessment. Even Ambrose Serle, who observed the Revolution at close range from British headquarters in New York, claimed that the influence of the newspapers was second only to that of the ministers in raising 'the present Commotion.' Later students of the subject have overwhelmingly concurred, as one of the most distinguished phrased it, in believing that the 'movement [toward independence] could hardly have succeeded without an ever alert and dedicated press.' Such services in behalf of American freedom, these historians have also generally argued, not only instilled 'a newspaper-reading habit which has characterized all succeeding generations' but also firmly established 'the opinion-making function of the press' and thereby contributed substantially to the democratization of Amer-

The author would like to thank Professor Bailyn as well as other friends and colleagues for their many helpful suggestions. In particular, Profs. Calhoun Winton and Stephen Meats called attention to illustrative material about Robert Wells and William Gilmore Simms, while Carol and Suzanne Weir supplied the item from *Peanuts*. Generous support from the Southern Studies Program and the Department of History of the University of South Carolina enabled Lacy Ford, JoAnne McCormick, James Scafidel, and George Terry to provide valuable assistance in collecting numerical data.

ican politics.[1] So pervasive has this interpretation become that it now permeates general accounts of the Revolution as well as histories of the communications media in America.[2]

The present popularity of this point of view results from several factors. One of the most important, certainly, is a belief inherited from the eighteenth century that an enlightened and informed populace will behave wisely in the long run. British authorities like Serle, who established a Tory paper in New York to promulgate the Truth, were therefore virtually compelled to assume that the American people had been misled by the Whig press. Conversely, in seeking aid from the court of France, Silas Deane sought to justify the Revolution by claiming that every American had 'some Education,' and even 'the very poorest' furnished themselves 'with Gazettes & political publications, which they read, observe upon and debate in a Circle of their Neighbors.' Thus, he argued, 'they are not an ignorant unprincipled rabble, heated and led on to the present measures by the artful & ambitious few. . . .' More alert to—or perhaps more willing to discuss—the machinations of the artful few but believing them in this case to have been generally on the side of the angels, the Progressive historians of the early twentieth century could encompass both the Whig and Tory points of view within an ambivalent frame of reference which permitted them to recognize the pre-Revolutionary newspapers as perhaps 'the finest instance of the propagandists' activity' in educating the American public.[3] Although the ease with which this interpretation conforms to our patriotic assumptions and intellectual proclivities

[1] David Ramsay, *The History of the American Revolution*, 2 vols. (1789; reprint ed., New York, 1968), 2: 319; Arthur M. Schlesinger, *Prelude to Independence: The Newspaper War on Britain, 1764–1776* (New York, 1958), pp. 284 (Serle quote), 285, 296. See also Philip Davidson, *Propaganda and the American Revolution, 1763–1783* (Chapel Hill, 1941), pp. 225–45.

[2] John C. Miller, *Origins of the American Revolution*, rev. ed. (Stanford, Calif., 1959), pp. 288–93; Merrill Jensen, *The Founding of a Nation: A History of the American Revolution, 1763–1776* (New York, 1968), p. 128; Frank Luther Mott, *American Journalism: A History, 1690–1960*, 3d ed. (New York, 1962), pp. 107–8; John Tebbel, *The Media in America* (New York, 1974), pp. 34–50.

[3] Schlesinger, *Prelude to Independence*, p. 292; Silas Deane, 'Memoire,' Sept. 24, 1776, in Benjamin F. Stevens, ed., *Facsimiles of Manuscripts in European Archives Relating to America, 1773–1783*, 25 vols. (1889–95; reprint ed., Wilmington, Del., 1970), 6: Document 585, folios 225–26; Davidson, *Propaganda and the American Revolution*, p. 225; Bernard Bailyn, ed., *Pamphlets of the American Revolution, 1750–1776* (Cambridge, Mass., 1965), pp. 8, 17.

should perhaps make us wary of accepting it uncritically, its ability to subsume both Tory and Whig testimony suggests a more valid reason for its continued vitality. In short, despite recent scholarship which indicates that American polemicists were often less interested in 'propagandizing' their audience than in explaining their own positions, the Progressive view of the Revolutionary press was based upon too much evidence to be hastily discarded.

Most of this evidence, however, has been derived from the study of the northern and middle colonies. Close examinations of the situation in the South are scarce, and the contemporary observers so frequently quoted usually had northern ties. Even Ramsay, who wrote in South Carolina, spent most of the pre-Revolutionary period in Pennsylvania and New Jersey. Furthermore, the recent work of some scholars seems to indicate that the press in the eighteenth century was generally more elitist than most historians had hitherto realized; and, though no one has yet worked them out in detail, the implications of this scholarship would appear to have special relevance to the role of the newspapers in the southern colonies.[4] For Deane's idyllic description of an America in which 'Schools and Colleges are more Numerous . . . than perhaps in any other Country' and where the 'Voice of the poorest is equall to that of the richest' in public debate, though doubtless exaggerated, was probably a good deal more descriptive of his native Connecticut than of South Carolina, where public schools were rare and a local college only an abortive dream until the nineteenth century. Although the testimony of a British merchant with economic interests in the area is doubtless as suspect as that of an American minister with a cause to plead, Richard Oswald may have been more accurate than Deane in characterizing the southern provinces when he noted that in the three most important 'a Sort of Aristocracy prevails' by which 'these [leading] Families have a great weight in all the affairs of the Country.' Indeed, their weight was sufficient, a tutor to one of them cautioned an old acquaintance from New Jersey, to make the society so different

[4] Gordon S. Wood, 'The Democratization of Mind in the American Revolution,' in *Leadership in the American Revolution* (Washington, 1974), pp. 65, 67-70; Richard D. Brown, 'Knowledge is Power: Communications and the Structure of Authority in the Early National Period, 1780–1840' (paper delivered at the annual meeting of the American Historical Association, Dec. 28, 1974).

from what he had been accustomed to that he would 'find the tables turned the moment' he entered Virginia.[5]

That such differences in social structure did not differentiate the press in the two areas seems highly unlikely in the light of one of the axioms of modern communications research which holds that 'the structure of social communication reflects the structure and development of society.' Proceeding on the assumption that newspapers are but one aspect of social communication, this paper attempts a preliminary reassessment of their role in the southern colonies on the eve of the Revolution. For the sake of clarity, the ensuing discussion will be organized along Harold Lasswell's classic paradigm for the study of communications: who says what to whom with what effect?[6]

I

To ask 'who says' is to inquire, ultimately, who controls the press. Although the immediate answer would seem to be the printers who compiled the newspapers, the question is complicated by pressures upon the men who decided what and what not to print. At times, especially in the earlier colonial period, material might be sufficiently scarce to preclude much choice, and printers printed virtually everything available. But increased trade, better communications, and the intensifying pre-Revolutionary debate permitted—in fact, demanded—greater selectivity and by the 1760s printers were regularly postponing or excluding items on the basis of length, character, or political priorities.[7] Ironically, the increased freedom of choice involving sensitive mate-

[5] Deane, 'Memoire,' Sept. 24, 1776, in Stevens, ed., *Facsimiles*, 6: Document 585, folio 225; Richard Oswald, 'Plan submitted for breaking up the American Confederacy by detaching one of the Southern Provinces,' enclosed in Oswald to Lord Dartmouth, Feb. 9, 1775, ibid., 24: Document 2032, p. 2; Philip Fithian to John Peck, Aug. 12, 1774, in *Journal and Letters of Philip Vickers Fithian, 1773-1774: A Plantation Tutor of the Old Dominion*, ed. Hunter Farish (Charlottesville, 1968), p. 161.

[6] Wilbur Schramm, 'Communication Development and the Development Process,' in Lucian W. Pye, ed., *Communications and Political Development* (Princeton, 1963), p. 34. Sidney Kobre, whose *Development of the Colonial Newspaper* (Pittsburgh, 1944) was a pioneering attempt to treat the subject in its social context, limited his coverage to Baltimore northward after 1750. For a recent attempt to evaluate and elaborate Lasswell's format, see Daniel Lerner, 'Notes on Communication and the Nation State,' *Public Opinion Quarterly* 37 (1973-74): 546-47.

[7] Mott, *American Journalism*, pp. 55-56; Alexander A. Lawrence, *James Johnston, Georgia's First Printer* (Savannah, 1956), pp. 9-10; Ronald Hoffman, *A Spirit of Dissension: Economics, Politics, and the Revolution in Maryland* (Baltimore, 1973), p. 56.

rials imposed constraints of its own. Like Linus in the comic strip 'Peanuts,' many printers learned that 'life is full of choices, but you never get any.' Referring to himself in the third person, Andrew Steuart, who published the *North-Carolina Gazette* at Wilmington, expressed the essence of the resulting dilemma when he asked, 'What Part is he now to act? . . . Continue to keep his Press open and free and be in Danger of Corporal Punishment, or block it up, and run the risque of having his Brains knocked out? Sad Alternative. . . .' Not always quite so unacceptable, the alternatives—such as they were—nevertheless often dictated such a narrow course that Adam Boyd preferred to operate the *Cape-Fear Mercury* alone. 'The Times are very critical,' he explained to a would-be partner, '& at all Times the Director of a printing office is liable to Censure & . . . you would like as little to bear Censure for Me as I would for you.'[8]

Ironically, once again, navigating the tricky political waters between Scylla and Charybdis was usually most difficult for men whose monopoly of local printing would superficially appear to have placed them in a strong position. In actuality, however, their rare skills could subject them to especially intense pressure. Thus, in Georgia, where a parliamentary subsidy assisted an unusually effective governor in contesting the power of the lower house of the legislature, the relative equilibrium dictated neutrality. 'I have endeavoured,' James Johnston could therefore honestly say in 1775, 'to conduct myself, in the Publication of my Paper, as impartially as I co[ul]d,' and his paper continued to contain polemics reflecting both sides of the controversy until it ceased publication early in 1776. Undoubtedly, Johnston then fled because the pressure had become too great for him after the local Council of Safety searched his print shop for anything 'that might endanger the public safety.' Contrary to what has sometimes been implied, though, Georgia patriots did not close Johnston's press—in fact, they even promised to guarantee his safety if he would continue to operate it.[9]

Lacking an effective guarantee of his safety, Robert Wells would

[8] Steuart quoted in Charles C. Crittenden, 'North Carolina Newspapers before 1790,' *James Sprunt Studies in History and Political Science* 20, no. 1 (1928): 37; Boyd quoted in Douglas C. McMurtrie, *A History of Printing in the United States*, vol. 2, *Middle and South Atlantic States* (New York, 1936), p. 350.

[9] Lawrence, *James Johnston*, pp. 9–18.

probably have been unable to maintain his paper had he not been in Charleston where special circumstances permitted greater latitude than most printers enjoyed. Coming to South Carolina from Scotland in 1752, Wells discovered a prosperous urban market that enabled him to establish a lucrative trade in books and stationery well before the pre-Revolutionary controversy erupted; and by the end of the colonial period his 'Great Stationery and Book-Store on the Bay'—which supplied customers from North Carolina to the Floridas—appears to have been the largest establishment of the kind south of Philadelphia. Furthermore, he enjoyed the patronage of royal officials. Accordingly, in 1766 his shop printed the regimental order book for the Ninth British Regiment, while he himself served as marshal of the local vice-admiralty court and public auctioneer. In addition, Wells was a close friend and business agent of John Stuart, the superintendent of Indian affairs for the southern district of North America.[10] What his exact relationship with the royal governors was is not so clear, but it may have been more than coincidental that his first newspaper, the *South-Carolina Weekly Gazette*, commenced publication not long after William Henry Lyttelton and the local Commons House quarreled over the quartering of British troops. Certainly its successor, the *South-Carolina and American General Gazette*, was unusual in praising British regulars for their good order, sobriety, and piety! Be that as it may, Wells was equally singular among local printers for his approval of the Stamp Act which imposed a substantial tax on American newspapers. Perhaps he could afford it; later he was to estimate his combined income at well over £2,285 sterling per year.[11] In short, royal patronage and a dominant position

[10] Evidence by Robert Wells, Mar. 25, 1784, and Nov. 24, 1787, Examinations in London: Memorials, Schedules of Losses, and Evidences, South Carolina Claimants, American Loyalists, Audit Office Transcripts, 56:539, 542, New York Public Library; hereafter cited as Loyalists' Transcripts. Calhoun Winton, 'The Colonial South Carolina Book Trade,' *Proof: The Yearbook of American Bibliographical and Textual Studies* 2 (1972): 81–82; Winton, 'English Books and American Readers in Early Florida' in Samuel Proctor, ed., *Eighteenth-Century Florida and the Revolutionary South* (Gainesville, 1978), pp. 110–21; Aug. 17, 1771, South Carolina Council Journals, 36: 170, South Carolina Department of Archives and History, Columbia, S.C. For further indications of Wells's early book trade on Elliott Street prior to establishment of the *American General Gazette*, see his ad in the *South-Carolina Gazette*, July 1, 1756, and Christopher Gould, 'Robert Wells, Colonial Charleston Printer,' *South Carolina Historical Magazine* 79 (1978): 23–49.

[11] Clarence S. Brigham, *History and Bibliography of American Newspapers, 1690-1820*, 2

in the book trade enabled Wells to continue publishing the *Gazette* despite the 'great deal of ill will' which, a royal official testified, he thereby incurred. Nevertheless, in May of 1775 when rumor proclaimed that his friend Stuart was attempting to organize the Cherokee Indians for an attack upon local Whigs, both men sought safety in flight. Robert's son John, who took over the *Gazette*, then not only sought to make it more pleasing to patriot leaders, but also sold cartridge supplies and military training manuals. Although John pursued an equivocal course which included service in the American militia as well as later publication of the *Royal Gazette*, he eventually became a loyalist.[12] Like James Johnston, he may have been as much buffeted by circumstance as guided by principle. Robert Wells, on the other hand, was clearly unwilling to equivocate, and his readiness to incur substantial economic loss as a loyalist appears to testify to his political commitment.

The situation of the Whig printers, who backed the winning cause and hence had no need to explain the pressures of circumstance, was less clear-cut. The case of Peter Timothy, perhaps the most famous of southern printers, was especially ambiguous. In South Carolina 'the Opposition to Tyranny was raised by a single inconsiderable Man here, under all the Discouragements imaginable, even [Christopher] Gadsden doubting whether it could be attempted,' Timothy boasted in recounting his exploits: 'I was both a Member of and Secretary to the Congresses, General Committee, Charles-Town Committee; Chairman (and did all the Business) of the Committee of Observation and Inspection . . . and also Secretary to the Councils of Safety.' These activities may have been the result of a reasoned commitment to the patriot cause, and they most certainly were not crude attempts to ad-

---

vols. (Worcester, Mass., 1947), 2: 1041; M. Eugene Sirmans, *Colonial South Carolina: A Political History, 1663–1763* (Chapel Hill, 1966), pp. 320–24; *South Carolina and American General Gazette*, Jan. 9, 1769; Robert Wells to [?], Aug. 13, 1765, South Carolina Miscellaneous, Box 1, New York Public Library; Wells, Loyalists' Transcripts, 56: 539.

[12] Wells, Loyalists' Transcripts, 56: 542, 553; John R. Alden, *John Stuart and the Southern Colonial Frontier* (1944; reprint ed., New York, 1966), p. 170; Henry Laurens to John Laurens, Sept. 26, 1775, in 'Letters From Hon. Henry Laurens to His Son John, 1773–1776,' *South Carolina Historical and Genealogical Magazine* 5 (1904): 75; *South Carolina and American General Gazette*, Aug. 4, Sept. 8, 1775; Isaiah Thomas, *The History of Printing in America, with a Biography of Printers*, 2d ed., 2 vols. (1874; reprint ed., New York, n.d.), 1: 344, 351.

vance his economic position. Indeed, they usurped most of the time that he had hitherto given to the printing business, and he abandoned the *South-Carolina Gazette* late in 1775.[13] Nevertheless, Timothy kept his options open for quite a while, and his choice clearly reveals his awareness of political realities.

The son of its founder, Timothy had been printing the *South-Carolina Gazette* for twenty-five years by 1764 when he temporarily suspended publication to reorganize finances. Upon resuming the newspaper later the same year, he turned it into what Lieutenant Governor William Bull, Jr., later would call the 'conduit Pipe' for 'principles . . . imbibed & propagated from Boston & Rhode Island.' On the day before the Stamp Act was to go into effect Timothy issued an oversized number, its columns bordered in funereal black, and announced that because his subscribers refused to purchase newspapers printed on stamped paper, he was suspending publication. His own words best describe the sequel: 'By taking upon me a Place in the Post. [*sic*] Office at the Time of the Stamp Act, discontinuing Printing, while its Operation was in Suspense; and declining to directly support and engage in the most violent Opposition' he was transformed 'from the most *popular* . . . [in]to the most *unpopular* Man in the Province. . . .' His actions, he later believed, 'so exasperated every Body' that they took 'every Step to injure, and set up Crouch (a worthless Fellow) against me, whom they support with their utmost Zeal and Interest.' Thereafter, though one ostensible correspondent claimed that he did not deserve the '*coolness which you unfortunately labour under*,' Timothy was convinced that he would remain suspect until he had another opportunity to 'distinguish' himself 'in the Cause of America.'[14] During the controversy over the Townshend Duties he attempted to do so with only partial success. In

[13] Timothy to Benjamin Franklin, June 12, 1777, in Douglas C. McMurtrie, 'The Correspondence of Peter Timothy, Printer of Charlestown, with Benjamin Franklin,' *South Carolina Historical and Genealogical Magazine* 35 (1934): 128–29; Edward C. Lathem, comp., *Chronological Tables of American Newspapers, 1690–1820* (Barre, Mass., 1972), p. 13.

[14] *South-Carolina Gazette*, Mar. 10, 1764, Oct. 31, 1765, Oct. 3, 1768; Bull to Lord Dartmouth, Mar. 10, 1774, and to Board of Trade, Nov. 3, 1765, Transcripts of Records in the British Public Record Office Relating to South Carolina, 34: 18, and 30: 281–82, South Carolina Department of Archives and History (hereafter cited as Transcripts of Records in the BPRO Relating to S.C.); Timothy to Benjamin Franklin, Sept. 3, 1768, in 'Four Letters from Peter Timothy, 1755, 1768, 1771,' ed. Hennig Cohen, *South Carolina Historical Magazine* 55 (1954): 162.

1772, having resolved to retire from the printing business, he turned active management of the *Gazette* over to two new partners, while he sought a crown appointment as naval officer in the port of Charleston. But he failed to obtain the position; one of his partners died, and the other, Thomas Powell, ran afoul of the placemen in the royal council by printing some of its proceedings without official authorization. Jailed for contempt, Powell eventually dropped out of sight after being released on a writ of habeas corpus issued by two justices of the peace who, like most of their colleagues in the lower house, claimed that the council was not an upper house of the legislature and therefore lacked the power of commitment. Benefiting from a simultaneous resolution of the Commons, Timothy then resumed publication of the *South-Carolina Gazette* under the proud banner '*Printed by* PETER TIMOTHY, *Printer to the Honourable the* COMMONS HOUSE *of* ASSEMBLY.'[15] Evidently, he had at last found the cause in which he could distinguish himself, and the cloud of suspicion departed.

'Crouch,' however, did not. Charles was his first name, and he had once been Timothy's apprentice. Though a competent individual, he appears to have had a fondness for gambling, strong drink, and other diversions, so Timothy discharged him in 1754. His subsequent obscurity, his willingness to defy the Stamp Act (a trait that a Whig who knew him implied was most characteristic of printers who had little to risk), and Timothy's statement that he was 'set up' all suggest that Crouch found men who were willing to invest in a new enterprise. Precisely who they were remains obscure, but members of the Commons House were probably among them.[16] At least there is every rea-

[15] Hennig Cohen, *The South Carolina Gazette, 1732–1775* (Columbia, S.C., 1953), p. 4; Timothy to Franklin, Aug. 24, 1772, in *Letters of Peter Timothy, Printer of Charleston, South Carolina, to Benjamin Franklin,* ed. Douglas C. McMurtrie (Chicago, 1935), p. 15; Jack P. Greene, ed., *The Nature of Colony Constitutions: Two Pamphlets on the Wilkes Fund Controversy in South Carolina By Sir Egerton Leigh and Arthur Lee* (Columbia, S.C., 1970), pp. 31–33; *South-Carolina Gazette,* Nov. 8, 1773.

[16] Timothy to Franklin, June 14, 1754, in *Letters of Peter Timothy to Benjamin Franklin,* ed. McMurtrie, p. 13; Thomas, *History of Printing in America,* 2: 10. That Crouch borrowed money from John Paul Grimke one year to the day after the appearance of his first issue does not necessarily indicate the termination of an earlier loan, but that Peter Manigault (speaker of the Commons, 1765–72) later loaned money to Thomas Powell of the *South-Carolina Gazette* is certain. Court of Common Pleas, Judgment Rolls, 002, 076B, 0080A (1768), S.C. Dept. of Archives and Hist.; Inventory of Peter Manigault's Estate, & (1772–76), p. 413, S.C. Dept. of Archives and Hist. For an in-

son to believe that Crouch's paper, the *South-Carolina Gazette and Country Journal*, was initially designed to be the voice of the House. Thus the first issue, which appeared on December 17, 1765, carried the resolves against the Stamp Act which the Commons had ordered published so 'that a just Sense of Liberty, and a firm Sentiments [*sic*] of the Loyalty, of the Representatives of the People of this Province, may be known to their Constituents, and transmitted to Posterity.' Although he failed to retain a monopoly of the public business, Crouch continued his newspaper, which appears to have been a financial success, almost until his death in 1775.[17]

Meanwhile, in North Carolina the lower house also clarified its relationship with the local printer. Both houses of the legislature and the governor having joined in appropriating a salary for the public printer in 1751, James Davis accepted the appointment and established a newspaper at New Bern which appeared rather irregularly under different names until 1778. Early in the 1760s, however, doubts that he had fulfilled the terms of his contract, questions about the proper location of the public printer, and rivalry among public authorities complicated the picture when Andrew Steuart, an Irishman recruited in Pennsylvania by a committee from North Carolina, established a press at Wilmington. There, backed by the governor and council, he printed another *North-Carolina Gazette* while Davis, supported by a majority of the lower house, continued as public printer at New Bern. Whereupon the governor, Arthur Dobbs (another Irishman), appointed Steuart 'printer to his Majesty in this Province.' Deeming the appointment to be 'of a new and unusual nature, truly unknown either to our Laws or constitution,' the lower house refused to sanction it, and for the next two years both printers claimed to be the public printer. In 1766, however, Steuart lost his commission from the governor for printing material against the Stamp Act and discontinued the paper. Thus his types appear to have been idle until 1769 when he, like both Crouch and Timothy at later dates, drowned. Although such a fate could hardly be considered

---

teresting physical description of Crouch at about 18 years of age, see Timothy's ad for his runaway apprentice. *South-Carolina Gazette*, Feb. 5, 1753.

[17] Nov. 29, 1765, South Carolina Commons Journals, 37: 31, S.C. Dept. of Archives and Hist.; McMurtrie, *History of Printing in the U.S.*, p. 331; Thomas, *History of Printing in America*, 1: 345. The first two issues of Crouch's paper were entitled the *South-Carolina Gazetteer and Country Journal*.

an occupational hazard, nonpayment was, and the lower house successfully asserted its authority over the public printer by denying Steuart all but token compensation while persuading the council to approve full payment to Davis. After Steuart's death Adam Boyd, a local figure without training as a printer, took over his equipment and established the *Cape-Fear Mercury* which he published intermittently through most of 1775. During the last year of its existence this paper was supported by the Revolutionary Wilmington Committee of Safety.[18]

Ties between government and the press were equally close in Virginia where the *Virginia Gazette*, established thirty years earlier, was the only paper published in Williamsburg as late as 1766. Within the next decade, however, political exigencies combined with intricate family relationships among printers to more than triple the number of newspapers. Late in 1765 Joseph Royle transferred active management of the *Gazette* to Alexander Purdie, who suspended it for several months during the Stamp Act crisis. Soon after resuming publication, Purdie joined John Dixon (who had recently married Royle's widow) in a partnership which lasted until 1775 when the former established his own *Virginia Gazette*, while the latter took William Hunter, Jr., as his partner. Hunter, who eventually became a loyalist, had inherited his interest from his father who had managed the *Gazette* in the 1750s. Meanwhile, a third *Gazette* also entered the field in May 1766. Its printer, William Rind, had come to Williamsburg at the invitation of Thomas Jefferson and some other leading local men. Perhaps Rind attracted their attention by his willingness to print the resolutions of the House of Burgesses against the Stamp Act in the *Maryland Gazette* in which he was then the junior partner of Jonas Green. At any rate, Rind soon became the public printer in Virginia. After his death in 1773, his widow, Clementina, succeeded to the post and continued the newspaper for another year until she followed her husband to the grave and John Pinkney took over. Not long thereafter, however, a leading Revolutionary patriot from North Carolina, Willie Jones, helped to bring Pinkney southward to replace Davis as the public printer at Halifax, but Jones's loan proved to be a bad investment when Pinkney died in 1777.[19]

[18] McMurtrie, *History of Printing in the U.S.*, pp. 338–44, 349, 351; Jack P. Greene, *The Quest for Power: The Lower Houses of Assembly in the Southern Royal Colonies, 1689–1776* (Chapel Hill, 1963), pp. 292–94; Thomas, *History of Printing in America*, 1: 339.
[19] McMurtrie, *History of Printing in the U.S.*, pp. 284, 288, 290–91, 344, 457; Ed-

In Maryland, as in Virginia, there was only one paper during much of the period under consideration. Benefiting from government largess, Green in 1745 established the *Maryland Gazette* which he continued to publish until his death twenty-two years later. Thereafter, it was printed first by his widow, Anne Catherine (until 1775), and then by their son Frederick. A wit as well as a Whig, Jonas Green suspended publication of the *Gazette* in response to the Stamp Act, but on December 10 issued a sheet called 'AN APPARITION of the *MARY-LAND* GAZETTE, Which is not Dead, but only Sleepeth.' Using a skull and crossbones to depict the revenue stamps, Green also lamented that 'the Times' were 'Dismal, Doleful, Dolorous, Dollar-less.' In 1773, however, a man less noted for his sense of humor established a competitor to the *Maryland Gazette*. He was the publisher of the *Pennsylvania Chronicle*, William Goddard, who soon turned management of the *Maryland Journal and Baltimore Advertiser* over to his sister while he sought to set up a continental postal system. Two years later, John Dunlap, who also printed a paper in Philadelphia, the *Pennsylvania Packet*, established the *Maryland Gazette; or the Baltimore General Advertiser* under the management of James Hayes, Jr.[20]

Even more than the short-lived *Virginia Gazette or, Norfolk Intelligencer* (June 1774 to September 1775), which was silenced when Lord Dunmore seized its press, the *Baltimore Advertiser* presaged a new era of journalism which would prove to be less characteristic of the south than of other areas. 'Advertisers' not 'gazettes,' these newspapers, like those of similar name founded after the war, were designed to facilitate commerce more than government.[21] In the case of the other papers under consideration the situation was reversed. Nothing illustrates the role that even the printers themselves expected to play more clearly than a brief report carried by Timothy's *Gazette* in 1765: 'We hear that a patent for a council and assembly, for the government of . . . Nova Scotia, is ordered to be made out and registered, and their

mund S. and Helen M. Morgan, *The Stamp Act Crisis: Prologue to Revolution*, rev. ed. (New York, 1963), p. 128; Greene, *Quest for Power*, p. 290.

[20] McMurtrie, *History of Printing in the U.S.*, pp. 23, 115–17, 120, 125; Thomas, *History of Printing in America*, 2: 156; Aubrey C. Land, *The Dulanys of Maryland* (Baltimore, 1968), p. 268; *Maryland Gazette*, Sept. 19, Oct. 10, 1765.

[21] McMurtrie, *History of Printing in the U.S.*, p. 292; Allan R. Pred, *Urban Growth and the Circulation of Information: The United States System of Cities, 1790–1840* (Cambridge, Mass., 1973), pp. 20–26.

meeting appointed to be held at Halifax, where types and other implements for printing will soon be sent.' Like the *London Gazette*, which for a hundred years had been the official organ of government, these southern weeklies remained adjuncts of the state. Almost all were founded by printers who enjoyed public subsidies, and most of them continued to benefit from government support in one way or another. In fact, Timothy received more than £500 sterling in 1764 from public printing, and the owners of the *Virginia Gazette* seem to have been only slightly less dependent on the government.[22]

That many of these newspapers could have survived without subsidies is doubtful. In rural areas personal contact provided the fabric of local economic life, and none of the papers published outside of Charleston carried a great deal of advertising. Most of that in the *North-Carolina Gazette* advertised the printer's own wares, while the provincial government supplied nearly one-fifth of the advertisements in the *Georgia Gazette*.[23] Only in Charleston, which was the busiest seaport south of Philadelphia, could ads generate a substantial amount of revenue. There in the 1760s the *South-Carolina Gazette*, for example, averaged approximately eighty-eight items per issue. If each advertiser paid the customary rate of £1 (South Carolina currency) for three insertions, advertisements would have brought in slightly over

---

[22] *South-Carolina Gazette*, Apr. 6, 1765; Solomon Lutnick, *The American Revolution and the British Press, 1775–1783* (Columbia, Mo., 1967), appendix; Thomas Cooper and David McCord, eds., *The Statutes at Large of South Carolina*, 10 vols. (Columbia, S.C., 1836–41), 4: 199; Stephen Botein, ' "Meer Mechanics" and an Open Press: The Business and Political Strategies of Colonial American Printers,' *Perspectives in American History* 9 (1975): 143; Richard Beale Davis, *Intellectual Life in the Colonial South, 1585–1763*, 3 vols. (Knoxville, 1978), 2: 595.

[23] Estimates based on a numerical count of advertisements in 1 randomly selected issue per year—cross-checked against column inches in 3 other similarly chosen issues—indicate that the *Maryland Gazette* carried approximately 42 advertisements per issue between 1763 and 1775; the *Virginia Gazette* (Royle, Purdie and Dixon, Dixon and Hunter), 55; the *Virginia Gazette* (Rind and, later, Pinkney), 42 (computed on an adjusted basis, 1766–75); and the *Georgia Gazette*, 32. The comparable figure for all North Carolina newspapers—calculated from Wesley H. Wallace, 'Advertising in Early North Carolina Newspapers, 1751–1778' (M.A. thesis, University of North Carolina, 1954), pp. 20, 26—was 7. Next to the *Georgia Gazette* in which approximately 17 percent of the advertisements were government notices, the *South-Carolina and American General Gazette* carried the highest proportion of administrative notices (roughly 8 percent). See also Ronald Hoffman, 'The Press in Mercantile Maryland: a Question of Utility,' *Journalism Quarterly* 46 (1969): 536–44.

£29 per week. Converting currency to sterling and assuming that the *Gazette* appeared weekly, we find that annual income from advertisements was probably close to £215.[24]

How this sum compared to the revenue derived from subscriptions is more difficult to estimate. Ads generated only about one-third of the amount derived from sales of the *Pennsylvania Gazette*. But the figures are less certain for other newspapers. In most cases comparable records are lacking, and Timothy's claim that the circulation of his *Gazette* was 'as extensive . . . as any in America' suggests that printers may have deliberately concealed low circulation rates. Furthermore, there was probably a good deal of promotionalism hidden in notices like the one demanding payment from more than 1,000 subscribers to the *Virginia Gazette*.[25] Thus even such explicit statements need to be treated with caution. In theory, however, they might be checked by indirect methods. For example, one could compute the total output by knowing when an issue went to press, the maximum capacity of the press per hour, and the time when the paper appeared. The average output of a colonial press was between 80 and 120 copies an hour; Timothy wanted ads submitted before noon Saturday; and his paper was supposed to appear on Monday. But the attempt to calculate the maximum press run possible under these conditions fails because the amount of type set before the deadline remains unknown and some colonial papers—including the *South-Carolina Gazette*—seldom appeared on the day they were dated.[26] Consequently, convincing estimates of circulation figures are rare. Few English provincial papers printed

[24] During 1767–68, fairly 'normal' years in South Carolina, the *Country Journal* carried approximately 97 ads per issue, and the *American General Gazette* 76. Jacob M. Price, 'Economic Function and the Growth of American Port Towns in the Eighteenth Century,' *Perspectives in American History* 8 (1974): 157, 162–63; Cohen, *South-Carolina Gazette*, p. 9. Normally, after 1725, the rate of exchange between South Carolina currency and sterling was approximately 7 to 1. Henry Laurens to John Knight, Aug. 24, 1764, *The Papers of Henry Laurens* 4, Sept. 1, 1763 – August 31, 1765, ed. George C. Rogers, Jr. (Columbia, S.C., 1974), p. 380, and John J. McCusker, *Money and Exchange in Europe and America, 1600–1775: A Handbook* (Chapel Hill, 1978), pp. 223–24. It should be noted that the *Gazette* often failed to appear as scheduled.

[25] Botein, ' "Meer Mechanics" and an Open Press,' p. 148; *South-Carolina Gazette*, Aug. 25, 1764; Schlesinger, *Prelude to Independence*, p. 304.

[26] Lawrence C. Wroth, *The Colonial Printer* (1938; reprint ed., Charlottesville, 1964), pp. 80, 234; Kobre, *Development of the Colonial Newspaper*, p. 27; *South-Carolina Gazette*, Aug. 25, 1764; Thomas, *History of Printing in America*, 2: 170.

much more than 1,000 copies before 1760; and the *Virginia Gazette* may have had only 800 subscribers as late as 1765. Carl Bridenbaugh's average of 1,550 is therefore probably too high for most southern colonial newspapers. Yet if he is correct for the *South-Carolina Gazette*, subscriptions at £3 currency per year would have yielded £664 sterling,[27] and Timothy—like Franklin—would have found the newspaper itself nearly three times as remunerative as the sale of advertising space.

Yet neither of these items appears to have been the major source of a printer's income. Only newspaers that operated on a shoestring, such as the *North-Carolina Gazette*, required quarterly payment. Others frequently contained notices demanding remittances from tardy subscribers who may have continued to receive their papers for as long as eight years without payment. However reluctant printers may have been to alienate customers, few would have been so lax in collecting had they not possessed more important sources of revenue from the sale of books, stationery, and other goods. Such sales provided at least fifty percent of the income received by the printers of the *Virginia Gazette* in 1764, and Wells's book store obviously accounted for most of his business.[28]

Not government printing alone but a combination of activities— which often involved retail trade, publishing a newspaper, and job printing—provided the key to economic success. Significantly, however, the combination often depended on a single set of customers. For, by and large, those who sought a printer's skills, news, or goods were men of property. Where books and stationery were expensive, where the discretionary income of most individuals was limited, and where a year's subscription to a newspaper might cost more than a week's wages for a laborer, the paying customers at least usually came from the upper levels of society.[29] Only where a printer's competitive posi-

[27] G. A. Cranfield, *The Development of the Provincial Newspaper, 1700–1760* (London, 1962), p. 176; Botein, ' "Meer Mechanics" and an Open Press,' p. 150, n. 47; Carl Bridenbaugh, *Cities in Revolt: Urban Life in America, 1743–1776* (London, 1971), p. 388; Cohen, *South Carolina Gazette*, p. 7. See also Schlesinger, *Prelude to Independence*, pp. 303–4.

[28] *North-Carolina Gazette*, Nov. 15, 1751; Cohen, *South Carolina Gazette*, p. 8; Botein, ' "Meer Mechanics" and an Open Press,' p. 143.

[29] Gov. Arthur Dobbs to Board of Trade, Jan. 4, 1755, in Edgar W. Knight, ed., *A Documentary History of Education in the South before 1860*, vol. 1, *European Inheritances* (Chapel Hill, 1949), p. 706; Crittenden, 'North Carolina Newspapers before 1790,' pp. 17, 21.

tion was exceptionally strong or local leaders unusually divided could he afford to alienate a substantial portion of them.

Moreover, few printers felt compelled to do so. As Franklin's well-known career should remind us, most printers sought to be—and some actually were—men of wealth and influence. By almost any standard, Jonas Green was one of the first citizens of Annapolis. Not long after founding the *Maryland Gazette*, he joined the Tuesday Club, which included local clergymen, professionals, officials, and members of the assembly. Green himself eventually became an alderman of the city, a local vestryman, postmaster, clerk of the races, and secretary of the masonic society. James Davis was postmaster of New Bern, sheriff of Craven County, and a member of the local assembly. Timothy's offices, in addition to those enumerated above, included a seat in the Commons House. Without belaboring the point, one finds evidence in these examples that the printers frequently rose to be at least marginal members of the local establishment. Like many such upwardly mobile men, or those who aspire to become upwardly mobile, they usually subscribed to the values of the group that they sought to enter.[30] Furthermore, being immigrants, many found it especially important to demonstrate that they did in fact share these values.

Although such considerations alone would undoubtedly have predisposed printers to become zealous champions of the local leadership, other circumstances helped to insure that most in fact became spokesmen of the lower houses of assembly. In the first place, men of property dominated these bodies, and Alexander Purdie's ambiguous reference to '*the Publick, for whose Favour I am a Candidate*'—by which he could have meant the legislature as well as the public at large—neatly reflects the economic and political realities of a society in which most of the Burgesses were members of that 'great tangled cousinry' constituting the Virginia gentry. In the second place, with the possible exception of Georgia, the lower houses were the most powerful branch of local government by the 1760s. Thus, as we have so clearly seen in

---

[30] Richard Beale Davis, *Literature and Society in Early Virginia, 1608–1840* (Baton Rouge, 1973), p. 162; J. A. Leo Lemay, *Men of Letters in Colonial Maryland* (Knoxville, 1972), pp. 202, 209, 211, 245–46; McMurtrie, *History of Printing in the U. S.*, pp. 116, 346; Walter B. Edgar, ed., *Biographical Directory of the South Carolina House of Representatives*, vol. 1, Session Lists, 1692–1973 (Columbia, S.C., 1974), p. 109; Robert B. Zajonc, 'Conformity,' *International Encyclopedia of the Social Sciences* 3: 258.

the case of North Carolina, they were in a crucial position to control public patronage. Moreover, they possessed the most effective legal restraint on the press. To be sure, printers could be charged with libel, and most sought to minimize the risk by refusing to print a polemic unless they knew the author's identity. More cautious yet, Anne Green even asked some of her more vehement correspondents to post bond to indemnify her in the event of a suit. Nevertheless, such suits were rare by the eve of the Revolution, and, as the futile attempt to imprison Powell suggests, the upper houses were seldom in a position to chastise printers. The representatives of the people, on the other hand, clearly possessed the power to punish for contempt of their authority, and printers were usually most circumspect in dealing with them.[31] Thus Royle's unwillingness to print the Stamp Act resolves of the Virginia House of Burgesses may have been partly due to lack of a specific authorization by the House itself. Being in Maryland made it much easier for Green and Rind to ignore such technicalities. That in 1774 both *Virginia Gazette*s printed the proceedings of the Burgesses protesting the Boston Port Act does not necessarily indicate much greater boldness. This time they were authorized to do so. Furthermore, neither paper commented upon the official resolve, though Purdie and Dixon explicitly praised the unofficial actions of the Burgesses after the House was dissolved by the governor.[32] Moreover, a certain ideological affinity also helped to align printers with the representatives of the people. For the traditional political motto of the press, 'Open to ALL PARTIES but Influenced by NONE,' corresponded to the politicians' equally traditional credo eschewing partisanship. Only where a party was clearly committed to the public welfare—as in the case of its op-

[31] *Virginia Gazette* (Purdie), Feb. 3, 1775; Bernard Bailyn, 'Politics and Social Structure in Virginia,' in James M. Smith, ed., *Seventeenth-Century America: Essays in Colonial History* (Chapel Hill, 1959), p. 111; Greene, *Quest for Power*, pp. 4–7; David C. Skaggs, 'Editorial Policies of the *Maryland Gazette*, 1765–1783,' *Maryland Historical Magazine* 59 (1964): 345, 346; *South-Carolina Gazette*, July 20, 1769; *Virginia Gazette* (Pinkney), Feb. 2, 1775; *South-Carolina and American General Gazette*, Aug. 25, 1775; Leonard W. Levy, *Freedom of Speech and Press in Early American History: Legacy of Suppression*, paperback ed. (New York, 1963), pp. 74–76. See also Harold L. Nelson, 'Seditious Libel in Colonial America,' *American Journal of Legal History* 3 (1959): 163–64, 172.

[32] May 29–30, 1765, *Journals of the House of Burgesses of Virginia, 1761–1765*, ed. John P. Kennedy (Richmond, 1907), pp. 356–60; May 24, 1774, *Journals of the House of Burgesses of Virginia, 1773–1776*, p. 124; *Virginia Gazette* (Purdie & Dixon), May 26, 1774; *Virginia Gazette* (Rind), May 26, 1774.

position to tyranny—could such behavior be condoned, and then, as Lord Bolingbroke observed, the party became not a party but the united voice of the country. And that was increasingly the role in which most members of the lower houses saw themselves. Fortunately, English libertarian thought also defined a free press not merely as one open to all persuasions but, more important, as one that could be counted upon to keep a watchful eye on the encroachments of executive power.[33] Thus it appeared that the press and the lower houses had complementary roles to play.

This did not mean, however, that they were equal partners in the enterprise. The printers had started out as the voice of the whole government; prudence and ideology combined to dictate patriotism and align most of them with the most powerful branch. Doubtless, the evolution was a natural one which would have occurred in any event, but the Stamp Act crisis greatly accelerated the process. Aware of the hardships experienced by English printers because of similar taxes imposed in 1712 and 1757, American printers almost to a man opposed the Stamp Act. But equally aware that the penalties for violations were substantial, many in the southern colonies suspended their newspapers. That action, however, tended to make the individuals whom they sought to emulate and upon whom they were most dependent doubt their commitment to the 'right principles.' Nothing, one suspects, would have been more apt to make the printers cooperative in the future. Thus, contrary to a recent assertion, it is a mistake to try 'to relate the situation of the colonial press before the Revolution to our own times' by imagining 'that the student radicals of the late sixties had gained control of the nation's leading newspapers, and were using them to attack the establishment.'[34]

Printers were the voice of the local political establishment. Like the

[33] *Virginia Gazette* (Rind), Apr. 14, 1768; Quentin Skinner, 'The Principles and Practice of Opposition: The Case of Bolingbroke Versus Walpole,' in Neil McKendrick, ed., *Historical Perspectives: Studies in English Thought and Society in Honour of J.H. Plumb* (London, 1974), p. 108; 'A Dissertation upon Parties,' in *The Works of Lord Bolingbroke*, 4 vols. (Philadelphia, 1841), 2: 48; *South-Carolina Gazette and Country Journal*, Dec. 31, 1765; Botein, ' "Meer Mechanics" and an Open Press,' pp. 200–25; Clark Rivera, 'Ideals, Interests and Civil Liberty: The Colonial Press and Freedom, 1735–1776,' *Journalism Quarterly* 55 (1978): 50.

[34] Cranfield, *Development of the Provincial Newspaper*, pp. 42–47; Mott, *American Journalism*, pp. 71–72; Morgan, *Stamp Act Crisis*, pp. 241–42; Tebbel, *Media in America*, pp. 35–36.

colonial agents in London (who had also been one of the prizes in the struggle for power between different branches of the governments) they became the spokesmen of colonial leaders. While the agents spoke to imperial officials, the press addressed American constituents. Unfortunately, however, the more accurately the agents reflected the views of the colonial assemblies the less chance for compromise there was as the incompatibility of British and American constitutional positions became increasingly obvious. Better communications among Americans, on the other hand, unified and strengthened their opposition to imperial policies. Moreover, once resistance had destroyed royal government in the colonies, the creation of efficient substitutes required the assistance of the press. Consequently, the *Maryland Gazette* became, as one historian has noted, 'an organ of the Anne Arundel committee of correspondence'; thus after Johnston fled, the Council of Safety in Savannah frantically begged their compatriots in Charleston to send them a printer. And thus, the 'semiofficial role assigned the press by the First Continental Congress' was the logical outgrowth of its previous relationship with the lower houses. No wonder that a loyalist traveling through Virginia soon discovered that 'Freedom of speech . . . is now a stranger in the Land. The boasted liberty of the press is as a tale that was told.'[35]

II

Being the medium of the leadership, colonial newspapers normally contained what its members wanted said. And this, it appears, was a very mixed bag indeed. Advertisements, literary essays, political polemics, and news filled pages studded with everything from an account of violence in Britain over a 'buxom country wench,' to a locally composed elegy on the death of a favorite cat, to the proceedings of the Continental Congresses. Such a 'superabundance of jumbled, dispa-

---

[35] Greene, *Quest for Power*, pp. 266–96; Michael G. Kammen, *A Rope of Sand: The Colonial Agents, British Politics, and the American Revolution* (Ithaca, N.Y., 1968), pp. 314–15; Skaggs, 'Editorial Policies of the *Maryland Gazette*,' p. 348; Georgia Council of Safety to South Carolina Council of Safety, Mar. 8, 1776, Sparks Collection, 59: 506–7, Houghton Library, Harvard University, Cambridge, Mass.; Schlesinger, *Prelude to Independence*, p. 208; entry of July 19, 1777, *The Journal of Nicholas Cresswell, 1774–1777* (New York, 1924), p. 262. See also Rollo G. Silver, 'Aprons Instead of Uniforms: The Practice of Printing, 1776–1787,' *Proceedings of the American Antiquarian Society* 87 (1977): 111–94.

rate and mainly trivial details,' as Allan Nevins once remarked, imposes 'on the writer a burden of assortment and synthesis under which most men break down.' Worse yet, successful attempts at assortment frequently confront a historian with one of the central dilemmas of a craft that sometimes seems to demand rational explanations for the effects of chance. And there is reason to believe that the vagaries of wind and weather possessed an especially potent influence in determining the contents of colonial newspapers which, like their provincial English counterparts, contained much material reprinted from the London gazettes. Unlike their counterparts in England, though, American printers often failed to credit the specific source of their materials, and the most obvious explanation for the difference in practice would seem to be the greater effect of unforeseen contingencies on the longer communications route. Compiling colonial newspapers, one therefore suspects, was such a haphazard process that American printers doubtless felt that any regular attempt to identify even major London sources would prove more bewildering than enlightening to readers over the long run. Accordingly, systematic classification of the contents of these newspapers tends to be inherently misleading.[36]

Nevertheless, because there is virtually no other way to cope with this miscellaneous information, scholars have usually sought to isolate and study specific aspects of it. Most recently, they have found advertisements for runaway slaves to be a rich source of otherwise elusive data about the black population; more traditionally, students of colonial literature have derived much of our current knowledge about the subject from the newspapers.[37] That the same has been true with re-

[36] *Virginia Gazette* (Purdie & Dixon), Sept. 3, 1767; *Maryland Gazette*, Apr. 16, 1772; *South-Carolina Gazette and Country Journal*, Nov. 15, 1774; Allan Nevins, 'American Journalism and Its Historical Treatment,' *Journalism Quarterly* 36 (1959): 413; R.M. Wiles, *Freshest Advices: Early Provincial Newspapers in England* (Columbus, Ohio, 1965), p. 199; Botein, ' "Meer Mechanics" and an Open Press,' p. 196, n. 66.

[37] Darold D. Wax, 'The Image of the Negro in the *Maryland Gazette*, 1745–1775,' *Journalism Quarterly* 46 (1969): 73–80, 86; Gerald W. Mullin, *Flight and Rebellion: Slave Resistance in Eighteenth-Century Virginia* (London, 1972), pp. 39–40; Daniel E. Meaders, 'South Carolina Fugitives as Viewed through Local Colonial Newspapers with Emphasis on Runaway Notices, 1732–1801,' *Journal of Negro History* 60 (1975): 288–319; Lemay, *Men of Letters in Colonial Maryland;* Davis, *Literature and Society in Early Virginia.* See also Gillian B. Anderson, *Freedom's Voice in Poetry and Song* (Wilmington, Del., 1977), for an inventory of 'political and patriotic lyrics' in colonial newspapers, 1773–83, which will greatly facilitate future research.

gard to political developments scarcely needs to be pointed out. To be sure, no one has yet done for the newspapers what Bernard Bailyn recently did for the political pamphlets of the period. But for the moment at least indications are that his work makes a full-scale analysis of the rhetoric and ideology of the newspaper essays superfluous. This is of course not to claim that specific investigations of selected aspects might not prove fruitful; rather it is to suggest that, given the nature of the press in the southern colonies, there is little reason to expect to find great differences in the content—or even in the expression—of political ideas embodied in different formats, though each possessed unique advantages.[38] As George Mason observed in thanking a friend for some pamphlets which had previously appeared 'in detach'd Peices [*sic*] in the public papers . . . there is no judging of such Performances by Scraps,' and pamphlets were obviously better for developing extended arguments. But as Mason's comment also indicates, newspapers usually provided a quicker means of wide geographic distribution, and later pamphlets embodying the same material sometimes proved to be a drug on a saturated market.[39] Nevertheless, the two forms of publication were frequently employed interchangeably; published first in the newspapers, Arthur Lee's 'Monitor's Letters' were later collected in a pamphlet; reversing the sequence, Jefferson's pamphlet *A Summary View of the Rights of British America* was later carried by the newspapers.[40]

For present purposes it is therefore necessary to mention only two features of these essays that may have been especially characteristic of the southern press. One is the relative prominence of Henry St. John, Viscount Bolingbroke; the other is the virulent hatred of Scots-

[38] Bailyn, ed., *Pamphlets of the American Revolution*. But for the contention that different literary styles were sometimes associated with different formats, see Schlesinger, *Prelude to Independence*, p. 46; Davidson, *Propaganda and the American Revolution*, p. 210; and Jensen, *Founding of a Nation*, p. 128.

[39] Mason to [George Brent?], Dec. 6, 1770, in *The Papers of George Mason, 1725–1792*, ed. Robert A. Rutland, 3 vols. (Chapel Hill, 1970), 1: 127; Clinton Rossiter, *Seedtime of the Republic: The Origin of the American Tradition of Political Liberty* (New York, 1953), p. 329; Gadsden to Thomas and William Bradford, Mar. 28, 1775, in *The Writings of Christopher Gadsden*, ed. Richard Walsh (Columbia, S.C. 1966), pp. 101–2.

[40] Rossiter, *Seedtime of the Republic*, p. 329; Davidson, *Propaganda and the American Revolution*, p. 241; Schlesinger, *Prelude to Independence*, p. 125. For Arthur Lee's [?] dedicatory address 'To the King' prefacing the London editions of Jefferson's *Summary View*, see also the *North-Carolina Gazette*, Mar. 24, 1775, and *The Papers of Thomas Jefferson*, vol. 1, 1760–1776, ed. Julian P. Boyd et al. (Princeton, 1950), pp. 673–75.

men. Scholars have long known that in attacking the English ministry under Sir Robert Walpole (1721–42) Bolingbroke and his associates—who included the most popular poet of the eighteenth century, Alexander Pope—contributed to the body of opposition thought termed 'country ideology' which, as we have recently recognized, permeated the political culture of the colonies. But students of the subject have hitherto usually assumed that two less highly placed popularizers, John Trenchard and Thomas Gordon, were the most frequently quoted source of libertarian ideas.[41] It therefore comes as something of a surprise to discover that—at least in Virginia and South Carolina during the late colonial period—more explicit use was made of Bolingbroke's works. Furthermore, his ideas and phrases were almost certainly subject to more silent plagiarism.[42] For the works of Trenchard and Gordon were sufficiently respected—at least in New England—for Josiah Quincy, Jr., to list them along with those of Bacon, Locke, and Al-

[41] Isaac Kramnick, *Bolingbroke and His Circle: The Politics of Nostalgia in the Age of Walpole* (Cambridge, Mass, 1968), p. 11; Agnes M. Sibley, *Alexander Pope's Prestige in America, 1725–1835* (New York, 1949), p. 1; Jack P. Greene, 'Changing Interpretations of Early American Politics,' in Ray A. Billington, ed., *The Reinterpretation of Early American History: Essays in Honor of John Edwin Pomfret* (San Marino, Calif., 1966), pp. 172–75; Bernard Bailyn, *The Ideological Origins of the American Revolution* (Cambridge, Mass., 1967), pp. 35–39; Rossiter, *Seedtime of the Republic*, p. 141; Gary Huxford, 'The English Libertarian Tradition in the Colonial Newspaper,' *Journalism Quarterly* 45 (1968): 677–86.

[42] Perhaps a less wealthy colonial gentry and the relatively fresh memory of Bolingbroke's misdeeds limited references to him prior to his death in 1751; thereafter, increasing prosperity (at least in South Carolina), waning awareness of his career, and the increased availability of his writings resulting from the several collected editions published in London after 1752 partially account for his increased prominence. Thus the works of Trenchard and Gordon figure in the issues of the *South-Carolina Gazette* of June 12, 1736, July 16, 29, Aug. 8, 1748, Mar. 20, 1749, Oct. 17, 1754, and the *Country Journal*, Oct. 19, 1773; whereas explicit reference to Bolingbroke appears in the *South-Carolina Gazette* issues of Mar. 26, 1763, Aug. 20, 1770, and the *Virginia Gazette* (Dixon), Feb. 18, 1775. Plagiarism of *Cato's Letters* occurs in the *South-Carolina Gazette* of Sept. 14, 1769 (cf. 'The Important Duty of Attendance in Parliament recommended to the Members'), whereas covert borrowings from Bolingbroke occur in the *Virginia Gazette* (Rind), July 12, 1770, and *South-Carolina Gazette*, Sept. 7, 14, 1769, and June 13, 1774 (cf. *Freeholder's Political Catechism*, 'Dissertation Upon Parties' : Dedication to Robert Walpole and Letter XVII).

Without doubt, the use of Trenchard and Gordon, as well as Bolingbroke, was far more frequent than these examples indicate. My point is merely that a reasonably careful search reveals that after midcentury the latter had probably replaced the former as the most quotable authority in these newspapers.

gernon Sidney in a bequest to his son upon whom, his father hoped, 'the spirit of liberty [might] rest. . . .' Bolingbroke, on the other hand, was widely known to have been a man of shady reputation and unorthodox religious views. Thus a few years after his death an English reviewer, whose comments were reprinted in the *Virginia Gazette*, claimed that Bolingbroke's posthumously published works had excited more attention than they deserved. For having expended the 'Vigor of his Youth in every Species of Riot and Debauchery . . . , he became the Partisan of a Cause [the Jacobite] which he condemned, and which could not be supported without deluging his Country in Blood, merely that he might gratify the Vices of a Man. In his Life, indeed,' the reviewer continued, 'there is no less Absurdity than in his Writings; nor was there any Difference between his Life and his Death, but that the Folly of Vice was then complicated with the Horrors of Impiety.'[43] As a Jacobite and a libertine, he was a somewhat tarnished champion of liberty.

Nevertheless, he was also a master stylist, and his eminently quotable writings embodied ideas about the abuse of political power that appeared especially relevant to Americans during the pre-Revolutionary controversy. It is therefore perhaps understandable that the note in Rind's *Virginia Gazette* of July 12, 1770, introducing more than a full page of extracts from Bolingbroke's *Freeholder's Political Catechism*, which was described as containing '*a short but judicious Summary of the Duty, as well as Rights, of every English Freeholder,*' attributed the work to the earl of Bath. Doubtless much more common than such erroneous attributions camouflaging the extent of Bolingbroke's contribution to the ideas expressed in these newspapers was the entire omission of his name. Crediting only 'a celebrated Politician' for a few words, a leading South Carolina planter, John Mackenzie, quietly borrowed extensive passages from Bolingbroke in the course of advocating the nonimportation association. Furthermore, though difficult to identify with certainty unless they are as conspicuous as the Americanized versions of Bolingbroke's stirring declaration that 'the friends of liberty' would 'rather choose, no doubt, to die the last of British freemen, than bear to live the first of British slaves,' the phrasing of common beliefs often

---

[43] H. Trevor Colbourn, *The Lamp of Experience: Whig History and the Intellectual Origins of the American Revolution* (Chapel Hill, 1965), p. 78; *Maryland Gazette,* July 4, 1754; *Virginia Gazette,* Apr. 4, 1755.

seems briefly to echo Bolingbroke. Thus it is impossible to be sure that a South Carolinian signing himself 'THE CRAFTSMAN' intended to adopt the title of Bolingbroke's famous journal for his pseudonym. But that he did not call himself a 'mechanic' or 'tradesman'—terms then much more common in the area—suggests that he was not an artisan. Furthermore, if his magisterial advice to vote for a planter in the pending election does not positively confirm this inference, it indicates that his ideas at least were remarkably similar to Bolingbroke's, for they both believed that independent men of landed property were the most reliable guardians of freedom. And this notion, with its special appeal to the planting classes of the southern colonies, was a fundamental element in the political culture of the region.[44]

Ironically, therefore, a man whose support of the Stuart Pretender involved him in the Scottish Rebellion of 1715 may have indirectly contributed to an equally conspicuous feature of these political essays —that is, a hatred of Scotsmen in general and Scotch merchants and politicians in particular. For his Tory misgivings about the political effects of financial intrigue and mercantile manipulation fused easily in the colonial environment with later Whiggish denunciations of the presumed insidious influence at court of John Stuart, Earl of Bute, and his Scottish cohorts.[45] No doubt the desire to keep abreast of London fashions partly accounts for the occasional appearance of this invective even in papers owned by Scotsmen; and it is worth noting that '*May*

[44] David Lundberg and Henry F. May, 'The Enlightened Reader in America,' *American Quarterly* 28 (1976): 271ff. For the quotations and their sources, see note 42, above, under the *South-Carolina Gazette*, Sept. 7, 14, 1769, and June 13, 1774.

'THE CRAFTSMAN' appeared in the *South-Carolina Gazette* of Apr. 4, 1774, while more remote echoes of Bolingbroke may also appear in the *South-Carolina Gazette* of Sept. 14, 1769 (cf. 'Dissertation upon Parties,' concluding paragraph), Oct. 26, 1769 (cf. ibid., Letters III and VIII on 'passive obedience and non-resistance'), Dec. 12, 1774, and Sept. 7, 1775 (cf. ibid., Letter XVII). For the contrary supposition that 'The Craftsman' was an artisan, see Richard Walsh, *Charleston's Sons of Liberty: A Study of the Artisans, 1763–1789* (Columbia, S.C., 1959), p. 27.

Jack P. Greene, 'The Growth of Political Stability: An Interpretation of Political Development in the Anglo-American Colonies, 1660–1760,' in John Parker and Carol Urness, eds., *The American Revolution: A Heritage of Change* (Minneapolis, 1975), p. 47.

[45] For anti-Scottish prejudices in British politics, see John Clive and Bernard Bailyn, 'England's Cultural Provinces: Scotland and America,' *William and Mary Quarterly*, 3d ser. 11 (1954): 212; M. Dorothy George, *English Political Caricature to 1792: A Study of Opinion and Propaganda* (Oxford, Eng., 1959), pp. 119–40; and John Brooke, *King George III* (New York, 1972), p. 145.

the light of Liberty never be put out by a Scotch *Extinguisher!*' was, according to the *North-Carolina Gazette*, a toast common 'in the most polite companies' among the supporters of John Wilkes. Nevertheless, increasing Scottish domination of the Chesapeake tobacco trade, as well as the prominence of Scotch placemen farther south, made the southern colonies fertile ground for the growth of prejudice. The riots in 1769 against the Scotch merchants of Norfolk, Virginia, are therefore perhaps the most accurate indication of the emotion underlying these diatribes.[46]

Manifestations of the widespread hatred and fear took many forms. '*Irish impudence* is of the downright, genuine, and unadulterated sort,' Pinkney's *Virginia Gazette* declared. But 'a *Scotchman*, when he first is admitted into a house, is so humble that he will sit upon the lowest step of the staircase. By degrees he gets into the kitchen, and from thence, by the most submissive behaviour, is advanced to the parlour. If he gets into the diningroom, as ten to one but he will, the master of the house must take care of himself; for in all probability he will turn him out of doors, and, by the assistance of his *countrymen*, keep possession forever.' Again and again, the same themes reappeared. Timothy's hostility to the combination of Wells and Stuart, which often forced him to reprint news about Indian affairs from the *South-Carolina and American General Gazette*, made him especially sensitive to the '*Scratch me, Countryman!—and I'll scratch thee*' syndrome reputed to be common among Scots, but their supposed clannishness was a proverbial lament.[47] So too was their corrupting influence which, paraphrasing Pope, Arthur Lee later described as spreading as insidiously and pervasively as 'a low-born mist, a Scottish mist.' Accordingly, 'THE CRAFTSMAN' warned fellow South Carolinians, 'You are soon, my Countrymen, to

[46] *Georgia Gazette*, May 9, 1770; *Virginia Gazette* (Purdie), Oct. 6, 1775; *North-Carolina Gazette*, June 24, 1768; J. H. Soltow, 'Scottish Traders in Virginia, 1750–1775,' *Economic History Review* 12 (1959): 83–98; Robert M. Weir, 'Who Shall Rule at Home: The American Revolution as a Crisis of Legitimacy for the Colonial Elite,' *Journal of Interdisciplinary History* 6 (1976): 689; William M. Dabney, 'Letters from Norfolk: Scottish Merchants View the Revolutionary Crisis,' in Darrett B. Rutman, ed., *The Old Dominion: Essays for Thomas Perkins Abernethy* (Charlottesville, 1964), p. 111.

[47] *Virginia Gazette* (Pinkney), Oct. 20, 1774, conveniently available in 'Trivia,' *William and Mary Quarterly*, 3d ser. 11 (1954): 291; J. Ralph Randolph, 'The End of Impartiality: *South-Carolina Gazette*, 1763–75,' *Journalism Quarterly* 49 (1972): 706–9, 720; *South-Carolina Gazette*, May 30, 1774. For an attempt to counter some of this prejudice, see *Virginia Gazette* (Pinkney), Dec. 30, 1775.

have a *Scot* Governor. If you have a *Scot* Assembly . . . the Lord have Mercy on you!' The outcome, he declared, 'would be worse for this Province than it was for Sodom and Gomorrah.' Equally alarmed, Christopher Gadsden thought he detected an unusually elaborate conspiracy. 'Dear *Charley* [the Young Pretender] is THEIR object,' he told readers of the *South-Carolina Gazette*. Scotsmen, he claimed, promoted oppressive measures in order to provoke a rebellion against the House of Hanover. Posing as a champion of the oppressed in England as well as in America, the Stuart Pretender would then appear to come to the rescue. But after he was firmly seated on the throne, Americans could, Gadsden once privately prophesied, bid 'good (or rather bad) night to the English liberties. . . .' Although this scenario elicited a 'Great God!' from someone with a less fevered imagination, Gadsden was only one of many who believed that Scotsmen were at the bottom of a conspiracy against American liberty. And some polemicists, at least, were certain that they saw further proof of it in the supposedly pusillanimous and self-serving conduct of Scottish merchants during the crises over the Stamp Act and Townshend Duties.[48]

Thus, as those who bore the brunt of these attacks would have been quick to point out, historians might do well to view these newspapers as organs of the local establishments and to view their contents with commensurate skepticism. Although not always readily identifiable, omissions were frequently significant. 'No Newspapers the last week,' a Tory in Virginia shrewdly observed in 1776, 'I suppose the rascals have had bad luck of late and are afraid it should be known.' Reports of slave insurrections appear to have been regularly suppressed until the danger was apparently over.[49] And potential insurgents, such as

[48] Arthur Lee to Chairman of Committee for Foreign Correspondence, Nov. 30, 1777, in Richard Henry Lee, *Life of Arthur Lee, Ll. D.*, 2 vols. (1829; reprint ed., Freeport, N.Y., 1969), 2: 30; *Pope, Poetical Works*, ed. Herbert Davis (London, 1966), p. 306; *South-Carolina Gazette*, June 1, 22, July 13, 1769, Apr. 4, 1774; Gadsden to William S. Johnson, Apr. 16, 1766, in *Writings of Christopher Gadsden*, ed. Walsh, pp. 73–74.

[49] Entry of Oct. 9, 1776, *Journal of Nicholas Cresswell*, p. 163. For reports of insurrection scares that did not appear in the *Country Journal*, see Henry Laurens to John L. Gervais, Jan. 29, 1766, *The Papers of Henry Laurens*, vol. 5, Sept. 1, 1765–July 31, 1768, ed. George C. Rogers, Jr. and David R. Chesnutt (Columbia, S.C., 1976), pp. 53–54; and 'Extracts from the Journal of Mrs. Ann Manigault, 1754–1781,' ed. Mabel L. Webber, *South Carolina Historical and Genealogical Magazine* 20 (1919): 209. See also Winthrop D. Jordan, *White Over Black: American Attitudes Toward the Negro, 1550–1812* (Chapel Hill, 1968), p. 395; and *North-Carolina Gazette*, May 12, 1775.

the Regulators of South Carolina, often found the press 'shut against them.' According to their spokesman, Charles Woodmason, 'the Printers said, *They dar'd not*[,] being (as supposed) inhibited and afraid to affront the Commons House.' Less blatant but no less real was the censorship of public opinion that apparently prompted an Anglican clergyman in Maryland, Thomas Bacon, to abandon a political allegory that he feared would be too moderate for the tastes of his 'Dear Fellow Planters and Country-men' to whom it was addressed.[50]

Evidence of such stillborn items also raises questions about much of the material actually printed. A careful study of the *Virginia Gazette*s published in 1773 and 1774 found that 'about 9% of all political articles were manifestly erroneous or significantly distorted' in favor of the Whigs. Particularly dubious are the numerous accounts that depict popular protests as decorous demonstrations. According to the *Virginia Gazette*, the exercise of force in North Carolina was so well organized in 1766 that 'few instances can be produced of such a number of men being together so long, and behaving so well; not the least noise or disturbance . . . neither was there an injury offered to any person, but the whole affair [was] conducted with decency and spirit, worthy the imitation of all the Sons of Liberty throughout the Continent.' Although this report may have been more accurate than many, the *South-Carolina Gazette* described activities in Charleston, which unquestionably included looting, in remarkably similar terms.[51] In short, because they reflect a desire to make the American cause appear righteous and irresistible by emphasizing its orderliness and unanimity, these reports can seldom be read literally.

Faced with such often misleading and intractable materials, scholars have recently turned to the computer in the hope of providing a solid statistical basis for inferences that would otherwise remain impressionistic. The results, however, have been rather uneven. Among the most successful, Richard Merritt's work has revealed an enormous growth in 'the amount of intercolonial news carried by the newspapers' which,

[50] Richard J. Hooker, ed., *The Carolina Backcountry on the Eve of the Revolution: The Journal and Other Writings of Charles Woodmason, Anglican Itinerant* (Chapel Hill, 1953), p. 210; Lemay, *Men of Letters in Colonial Maryland*, pp. 341–42.

[51] Willard C. Frank, Jr., 'Error, Distortion and Bias in the *Virginia Gazettes*, 1773–74,' *Journalism Quarterly* 49 (1972): 739; *Virginia Gazette* (Purdie & Dixon), Mar. 21, 1766; *South-Carolina Gazette*, Oct. 31, 1765; Oct. 19, 21, 1765, S.C. Council Journals, 32: 628–30, S.C. Dept. of Archives and Hist.

he found, 'increased sixfold and more from the late 1730s to the early 1770s.' Certainly such findings are illuminating enough for many purposes to warrant application of similar techniques to the contents of the more important newspapers omitted from Merritt's study. Nevertheless, problems arise in interpreting the data. Merritt's discovery that the *South-Carolina Gazette* gave an unusually large amount of attention to local attitudes may reveal more about Timothy's competitive position vis-à-vis Wells, whose ties to royal officialdom frequently gave him priority in acquiring imperial news, than about the interests of subscribers who probably read both papers. Valid generalizations about the attention patterns of individuals in any area served by more than one newspaper would therefore require an examination of all the papers involved. But even then the meaning of the findings would not necessarily be clear because, as Stephen Botein has recently pointed out, increasing coverage of American affairs might merely have reflected changes in the British press from which American printers borrowed. It is therefore quite conceivable that in some cases more frequent use of 'American symbols' indicated not a growing sense of American community but the continuation of unusually close ties to Britain. After all, imperial officials were the first to refer consistently to America in a collective sense, and a Tory, Wells, was the only southern printer to use the term on the masthead of his newspaper. Furthermore, even if Merritt is correct in concluding that changes in symbol usage did in fact 'suggest aroused expectations about group membership in a distinctly American political community,' the reason for the change (as he was the first to admit) remains elusive.[52]

Given these considerations and our present interest in understanding the role of the newspapers in the social context of the southern colonies, how can one usefully examine their contents? Perhaps the question can best be answered by inquiring what contemporaries considered the special function of the newspaper to be. That some were named after Mercury, the speedy messenger of the gods, and many bore some variant

[52] Richard L. Merritt, *Symbols of American Community, 1735–1775* (New Haven, 1966), pp. 56, 97, 131, 180. For indications of the printers' competitive positions, see *South-Carolina Gazette*, May 4, 1765, June 22, 1767, Aug. 1, 1768, Aug. 17, 1769; *South Carolina and American General Gazette*, July 8, Dec. 30, 1774. Botein, ' "Meer Mechanics" and an Open Press,' p. 196, n. 66; Oliver M. Dickerson, 'England's Most Fateful Decision,' *New England Quarterly* 22 (1949): 388–94.

of the motto 'Containing the freshest Advices, Foreign and Domestick' suggests the answer. Their special purview was the prompt reporting of news. Furthermore, several recent studies have demonstrated that the speed with which news travels possesses important social and political consequences. In particular, I. K. Steele has explored some of the relationships between community cohesiveness and the speed of communications within the empire at the beginning of the eighteenth century; and Allan Pred has shown a connection between the flow of information in antebellum America and the ability of the largest metropolitan centers to maintain their dominant positions.[53] Because similar effects were doubtless even more pronounced during the Revolutionary crisis when the prompt knowledge of events was especially important, we err if we overlook significant variations in times that perhaps now seem to have been almost equally sidereal.

An examination of the speed with which southern colonial newspapers delivered the news is therefore in order. First, a word about the composition of the sample. Practical considerations limited it to approximately 200 issues selected by randomly drawing one item per quarter from the newspapers published in each of the southern colonies between 1763 and 1775. The importance of Virginia and the large gaps in the extant files led us to draw from the gazettes of all publishers. In North Carolina, on the other hand, Davis's greater professionalism and established contacts dictated the choice of his *North-Carolina Gazette*. For South Carolina, Crouch's *Country Journal* proved preferable because it was the only local paper regularly published on the nominal date of issue.[54] The last point suggests a caveat. Some

---

[53] Thomas, *History of Printing in America*, 2: 157, 163, 166, 169, 173; I. K. Steele, 'Time, Communications and Society: The English Atlantic, 1702,' *Journal of American Studies* 8 (1974): 1–21; Pred, *Urban Growth and the Circulation of Information*, p. 3 and passim. For some earlier, unsystematic attempts to deal with speed in this period, see Crittenden, 'North Carolina Newspapers before 1790,' pp. 26–27; and Schlesinger, *Prelude to Independence*, p. 283.

[54] Lathem, comp., *Chronological Tables of American Newspapers*, pp. 9, 13; Crittenden, 'North Carolina Newspapers before 1790,' p. 20; Thomas, *History of Printing in America*, 2: 168, 170, 172, 173. In the Dec. 25, 1770, issue Crouch apologized for failing to put out the *Country Journal* on the day it was dated—the first such failure, he claimed, in its history. Even though the other printers were not as punctual in publishing, trial samples of the *South-Carolina Gazette* and the *South-Carolina and American General Gazette* suggest that there was little difference in the speed with which each of the Charleston papers delivered the news.

news circulated for days before being confirmed by the weekly press, while the practice of predating delayed issues gives a misleadingly foreshortened impression of elapsed time. Although these two sources of distortion tend to cancel each other out, their net effect may make the average transit times given here a bit high. Furthermore, despite the possibility of seasonal and perhaps long-term variations, no regular pattern emerged for either. Perhaps enough of the news from Britain arrived via the regular monthly packet service to camouflage seasonal irregularities, and the lack of technological innovation during the period certainly precluded much acceleration except under unusual circumstances. Finally, because in a few cases (e.g., North Carolina items in the *Georgia Gazette*) the sample yielded only one or two usable datelines, some of the figures should be regarded as being very tentative.

TABLE I
The Comparative Speed (in Elapsed Days) with Which Leading Southern Colonial Newspapers Reported the News[55]

News from:	Md. Gaz.	Va. Gaz. (Royal, P&D, D&H)	Va. Gaz. (Rind, Pinkney)	Va. Gaz. (Purdie)	NC Gaz.	SC Gaz. & CJ	Ga. Gaz.
British Isles	84	80	78	77	83	71	69
Mass.	21	22	22	24	27	26	31
R.I.	22	18	30	X	16	24	X
N.Y.	16	21	19	15	28	23	40
Pa.	12	19	15	16	23	23	28
Md.	—	X	14	X	X	24	X
Va.	19	—	—	—	19	33	15
N.C.	49	30	4	X	—	20	11
S.C.	43	35	44	X	25	—	15
Ga.	48	65	X	X	X	13	—

[55] The figures in Table I are numerical averages, rounded off to the nearest day, derived from the items which appear to have been treated as current news. X indicates that the sample yielded no reports permitting computation of elapsed time. For the range of times involved and a complete tabulation of the number of items in each category, consult the Appendix.

Nevertheless, despite limitations imposed by the preliminary nature of the present sample and the elusiveness of much of the data, analysis of the nearly 600 datelines reflected in Table I clearly reveals several points. Most striking is the magnitude of the difference between the speeds with which news arrived from North America and Great Britain. On the average, news from even the remote corners of New England was published in all of the southern colonies in less than a third of the time required for that from London. In fact, the latter often took more than ten to twelve weeks, whereas items from New York and Philadelphia normally arrived in two to three. Equally significant, these two cities obviously served as important distributing centers for news originating elsewhere. Although indirect transmission was probably considerably more common than the datelines indicated, nearly a tenth of the items permitted positive identification of the routes involved; and, as Table II indicates, approximately two-thirds of these were through Philadelphia and New York.

TABLE II
INDIRECT ROUTING OF NEWS ITEMS IN LEADING SOUTHERN COLONIAL NEWSPAPERS[56]

Via:	Md. Gaz.	Va. Gazettes	N.C. Gaz.	S.C. Gaz. & C.J.	Ga. Gaz.	Total
Mass.	4 Brit.	1 Brit. 1 N.Y. 1 S.C.				7
R.I.	1 Mass.	2 Mass. 1 N.Y.	2 Mass.			6
N.Y.	5 Brit. 1 Mass. 1 Pa.	1 Brit. 1 Mass. 2 S.C.	1 Brit.	1 Mass. 1 Pa. 1 Va.	2 Pa. 1 S.C.	18
Philadelphia	2 Brit. 1 Mass. 1 N.Y. 1 S.C.	6 Brit. 1 N.Y.	1 Brit. 2 Mass.	1 N.Y.	1 N.Y.	17
N.C.	1 Va.	1 N.Y.				2
S.C.		1 Ga.			1 Va.	2

[56] Of the 584 datelines in the sample, 52 (or 9 percent) indicate indirect routing.

Being both the western terminus of a transatlantic packet line and the headquarters of the British army in America, New York was in an especially favorable position to relay news from Canada and the military outposts in the Mississippi Valley as well as from Britain itself.[57] Proximity to New York, strong ties with the west, and good trade connections with the southern colonies meant that Philadelphia was nearly as well situated. Moreover, both of these cities appear to have been quite efficient distributors of the news, and the fastest route from London to Annapolis and Williamsburg was frequently by way of Philadelphia or New York.[58] But if links between the northern and southern colonies appear to have been surprisingly strong, ties among the southern towns seem to have been quite weak. Thus the frequency as well as the speed of reports indicates that Charleston was connected more closely to New York than Wilmington, North Carolina, was to Savannah, Georgia. Furthermore, Savannah seems to have been unusually close to London and relatively isolated from everything north of Charleston. Elsewhere in the southern colonies communications appear to have been mediocre at best. Even between towns as close as Savannah and Charleston trading information usually took two weeks.

Although the significance of these figures will become more apparent after we discover who read the newspapers, some observations can be made at this point. First, because the datelines indicated a positive correlation between the amount of news and speed in transit, it seems reasonable to suppose that both were partly a function of the volume of trade between the areas concerned. This, however, is not to say that relatively weak economic links might not have been associated with good communications or vice versa. Thus, the regular coastal trade between the middle and southern colonies could have been more im-

[57] William Smith, 'The Colonial Post-Office,' *American Historical Review* 21 (1916): 271–72; John Shy, *Toward Lexington: The Role of the British Army in the Coming of the American Revolution* (Princeton, 1965), pp. 96, 158, 268. For interesting examples of items routed through New York, see *Maryland Gazette*, June 30, 1763, Mar. 1, 1764, June 27, 1765, Mar. 13, 1766, Mar. 5, 1767, Sept. 13, 1770, Apr. 13, 1775; *Virginia Gazette* (Purdie & Dixon), May 21, 1767; and *Georgia Gazette*, June 2, 1763, Feb. 7, 1765.

[58] Joseph A. Ernst and H. Roy Merrens, 'The South Carolina Economy of the Middle Eighteenth Century: A View from Philadelphia,' *West Georgia College Studies in the Social Sciences* 12 (1973): 16–29. Thus, on Nov. 5, 1772, for example, the *Maryland Gazette* reported an item from London by way of Philadelphia in only 67 days, or 20 percent less than the average time.

portant in some respects than the larger but seasonal transatlantic commerce in manufactured goods and agricultural staples.[59] But to conclude that such was in fact the case requires knowing that contemporaries considered the quality of communications to have been important. That someone was careful to indicate that an item published in the *Maryland Gazette* arrived via the packet service from Britain to New York, that Adam Boyd planned to use express riders to distribute the *Cape-Fear Mercury*, and that Rind began his *Virginia Gazette* by observing, 'a well conducted NEWS:PAPER *would, at any Time, be important, but most especially at a Crisis, which makes a quick Circulation of Intelligence particularly interesting to all the* AMERICAN COLONIES,' all suggest that printers believed their readers did indeed want the 'freshest Advices.' And that some citizens in South Carolina privately supported a rider who presumably made regular runs from Charleston to Pocataligo reveals that the printers understood their customers.[60]

III

Like the men who employed the '*Pocataligo Private Rider*,' most of those who were exposed to the colonial press will doubtless never be known with certainty. Nevertheless, they can be divided into two categories. One, containing the individuals who had direct access to the newspapers, was doubtless quite small; the other, composed of men and women who received their news from members of the first group, was probably much larger. Furthermore, despite the bias inherent in the survival of such records, there is considerable evidence to indicate that social class played a large part in determining how an individual re-

[59] David Klingaman, 'The Development of the Coastwise Trade of Virginia in the Late Colonial Period,' *Virginia Magazine of History and Biography* 77 (1969): 29, 32, 38; Klingaman, 'The Coastwise Trade of Colonial Massachusetts,' *Essex Institute Historical Collections* 108 (1972): 217–34; Francis C. Huntley, 'The Seaborne Trade of Virginia in Mid-Eighteenth Century: Port Hampton,' *Virginia Magazine of History and Biography* 59 (1951): 298, 302; Walter F. Crawford, 'The Commerce of Rhode Island with the Southern Continental Colonies in the Eighteenth Century,' *Rhode Island Historical Society Collections* 14 (1921): 99–130; James F. Shepherd and Gary M. Walton, *Shipping, Maritime Trade, and the Economic Development of Colonial North America* (London, 1972), passim.

[60] *Maryland Gazette*, Mar. 1, 1764; Boyd to 'Sir,' Nov. 16, 1772, in W. L. Saunders, ed., *The Colonial Records of North Carolina, 1662–1776*, 10 vols. (Raleigh, 1886–90), 9: 356; *Virginia Gazette* (Rind), May 16, 1766; *South-Carolina and American General Gazette*, May 22, 1776.

ceived information. Almost all of the surviving testimony indicating readership comes from members of the upper classes.[61] Subscription agents for both the *South-Carolina Gazette* and the *Cape-Fear Mercury* were among the most prominent men in their areas;[62] and the same was clearly true of subscribers to the *Virginia Gazettes*.[63] In addition, published personal polemics, like duels, seem to have sometimes been governed by rules of honor which would have required that they be conducted only with and before peers. Stylistic characteristics also confirm that these bouts were usually intended to be in-group affairs. The common, but by no means invariable, use of pseudonyms seldom concealed the identity of writers who were often immediately known to their intended audiences; the abundant use of satire depended on common knowledge and assumptions; and the Latin quotations would have been unintelligible to anyone without at least a rudimentary classical education.[64] Furthermore, frequent mention of the 'vulgar,' the

[61] R. H. Lee to William Lee, June 19, 1771, in *The Letters of Richard Henry Lee*, ed. James C. Ballagh, 2 vols. (New York, 1911), 1: 58; Knight, ed., *Documentary History of Education in the South*, p. 565; Lemay, *Men of Letters in Colonial Maryland*, p. 233; Land, *Dulanys of Maryland*, p. 190; *Journal and Letters of Philip Fithian*, ed. Farish, p. 64; H. Laurens to J. Laurens, Sept. 26, 1775, in 'Letters from Hon. Henry Laurens to His Son John, 1773–1776,' *South Carolina Historical and Genealogical Magazine* 5 (1904): 75.

[62] The *South-Carolina Gazette*, Aug. 25, 1764, listed 3 subscription agents in the Floridas, 17 in Georgia, 5 in North Carolina, and 122 in South Carolina. Among the latter, 28 can be identified as public officials, 9 as militia officers, 9 as professional men, 10 as merchants, and 23 as prominent planters. Of the others, 16 were also sufficiently important to receive miscellaneous mention in standard sources, while 27 cannot be readily identified. The 11 subscription agents listed in the *Cape-Fear Mercury*, Sept. 22, 1773, included 8 public officials, 1 militia officer, 1 prominent South Carolina merchant, and 1 who proved unidentifiable. (Men occupying more than 1 category were counted under the first mentioned here.)

[63] A sample of 40 customers taken from *The Virginia Gazette Daybooks, 1750–1752 & 1764–1766*, Microfilm Publication 5, University of Virginia Library (Charlottesville, 1967), yielded 15 public officials, 1 militia officer, and 5 professional men; 10 others may have fallen into one of these categories but could not be positively identified; 9 could not be traced through Swem's *Virginia Historical Index*. The *North-Carolina Gazette*, July 18, 1777, listed 24 subscribers to the *Virginia Gazettes* presumably resident in North Carolina. Of these, 10 were public officials, 2 were militia officers, 1 a merchant; 4 received miscellaneous mention in the *Colonial* and *State Records of North Carolina*, and 7 cannot be readily identified.

[64] Entry of Feb. 12, 1774, *Journal and Letters of Philip Fithian*, ed. Farish, p. 65; Land, *Dulanys of Maryland*, p. 302; *South-Carolina Gazette*, Sept. 21, Oct. 26, 1769; Drayton, 'To the Public,' in [William Henry Drayton et al.], *The Letters of Freeman, Etc.* (London, 1771), ed. Robert M. Weir (Columbia, S.C., 1977), p. 3; Jack P. Greene, 'The

'lower Class,' and so forth indicates that the authors addressed themselves mainly to a restricted audience. Although such public displays
of arrogance sometimes proved to be mistakes, it is clear that newspaper polemics tended to remain the sport of the relatively wealthy and
prominent.[65]

How much wider the readership was is uncertain. News and information were the commodities conveyed; consumers needed physical
access, the resources, and the motivation to take advantage of them.
In the towns, inns and public houses might have solved the problem of
access while perhaps complicating that of motivation. Though out of
the financial reach of many individuals, newspapers were almost certainly available in many taverns where it seems that they were sometimes used by men learning to spell. But such activity required the
necessary leisure. That few men possessed it is suggested by Isaiah
Thomas's attempt to change the traditional format when he began the
Massachusetts Spy. Smaller amounts of information, more frequently
published, would, he believed, reach a new audience of 'mechanics,
and other classes of people who had not much time to spare from business.' That he believed that he was thereby innovating illuminates the
situation in the southern colonies as well as in Massachusetts, for
Thomas had worked in Charleston and knew the southern papers.[66]
Nevertheless, men from the north often considered southerners dil-
atory, if not lazy, and it is possible that even the working classes took
life easier there than farther north. The existence of more than 100
retail liquor outlets in Charleston (then a city of about 1,300 houses)
seems to confirm reports of a good deal of conviviality among all classes.
And, though this conviviality unquestionably helped to disseminate the

---

Gadsden Election Controversy and the Revolutionary Movement in South Carolina,'
Mississippi Valley Historical Review 46 (1959): 482; Wood, 'The Democratization of
Mind in the American Revolution,' in *Leadership in the American Revolution*, pp. 65, 68–70.

[65] *Virginia Gazette* (Purdie & Dixon), Jan. 20, 1774; *South-Carolina Gazette*, Sept. 21,
1769. For an apparent and certainly delightful exception to the general rule, see the
letter in which some mechanics of Charleston suggested that William Henry Drayton,
who had termed them the '*profanum Vulgus*,' suffered from having had 'his upper works'
damaged at birth. *South-Carolina Gazette*, Oct. 5, 1769.

[66] Charles Shepheard, for example, intended to make the latest newspapers available at his coffeehouse. *South-Carolina Gazette*, May 16, 1743. Alice M. Earle, *Stage-
Coach and Tavern Days* (1900; reprint ed., New York, 1969), pp. 91–92; Thomas, *History of Printing in America*, 1: xxvii–xli; 2: 61.

news, it doubtless also militated against serious reading. So did poor lighting, crude spectacles if any, and cramped pages frequently printed with worn type. The reading aloud and discussion of important items, such as resolutions of the Continental Congress, occurred in taverns; much silent reading is more doubtful.[67]

Outside of the relatively few towns, physical access to the newspapers also presented a formidable problem to all but those wealthy enough to subscribe. Stores and taverns were normally located on the main roads, usually a day's ride apart; militia musters were infrequent and often irregular; and church congregations were doubtless far larger than the number of subscribing members.[68] Nevertheless, multiple readership is still most common in rural areas, and some newspapers obviously circulated beyond the original recipient. For example, John Harrower, who tutored the family of Col. William Daingerfield of Belvidera, near Fredericksburg, Virginia, borrowed old copies from his employer. But their relationship was a close one, and many subscribers were doubtless unwilling to make indiscriminate loans of relatively fragile items that they often regarded as permanent records.[69] Furthermore, had they been willing to lend or give newspapers to acquaintances, distance would have remained an obstacle to potential readers. Even if one grants the unlikely assumption that per capita circulation was the same in the northern and southern colonies, geo-

[67] 'Diary of Timothy Ford, 1785–1786,' ed. Joseph W. Barnwell, *South Carolina Historical and Genealogical Magazine* 13 (1912): 142–43; H. Roy Merrens, 'A View of Coastal South Carolina in 1778: The Journal of Ebenezer Hazard,' *South Carolina Historical Magazine* 73 (1972): 186; Bridenbaugh, *Cities in Revolt*, p. 358; Bull to Hillsborough, Nov. 30, 1770, Transcripts of Records in the BPRO Relating to S.C., 32: 388; Wroth, *The Colonial Printer*, p. 66; entry of Nov. 1, 1774, *Journal of Nicholas Cresswell*, p. 45.

[68] In fact, as late as the 1820s stores and taverns were often still as much as 10 to 20 miles apart. See Robert Mills, *Atlas of the State of South Carolina* (1825; reprint ed., Columbia, S.C., 1938). Don Higginbotham, *The War of American Independence: Military Attitudes, Policies, and Practice, 1763–1789* (New York, 1971), p. 10; Presentments of the Grand Jury, in *South-Carolina Gazette*, Feb. 7, 1771.

[69] Richard L. Merritt, 'Public Opinion in Colonial America: Content-Analyzing the Colonial Press,' *Public Opinion Quarterly* 27 (1963): 363, n. 17; Harrower to his wife, June 14, 1774, *The Journal of John Harrower*, ed. Edward M. Riley (Williamsburg, 1963), p. 56; Davis, *Literature and Society in Early Virginia*, pp. 220–21; Lemay, *Men of Letters in Colonial Maryland*, p. 233; Jensen, *Founding of a Nation*, p. 360; Cranfield, *Development of the Provincial Newspaper*, p. 259; Nov. 29, 1765, S.C. Commons House Journals, 37: 31, S.C. Dept. of Archives and Hist.

graphic distribution, and therefore the possibility of physical access, was far different. Population density in Massachusetts, not including Maine, was approximately thirty-five per square mile at the end of the colonial period; that of Rhode Island about forty-five. Virginia and Maryland, which were the most heavily populated southern colonies, averaged only about half the latter figure; and the area in South Carolina most thickly settled by whites contained less than eight persons per square mile as late as 1790. The only substantial concentrations of population were at Baltimore, Norfolk, and Charleston; Williamsburg and the other cities were scarcely more than villages. The majority of the populace was therefore sparsely scattered over an immense area. So too of course were the newspapers; Timothy's subscription agents for the *South-Carolina Gazette* stretched from Brunswick, North Carolina, to Mobile, West Florida, while the *Virginia* and *North-Carolina Gazette*s penetrated the interior of their own and neighboring provinces.[70] But given prevailing methods of transportation, it is unlikely that most individuals were within personal reach of a copy.

Furthermore, access to the newspapers would not necessarily have implied the ability to read them. Literacy in the colonial period is currently the focus of some scholarly interest if not agreement; and it is impossible to be very positive about its level. But by using signatures on recorded wills as an index, Kenneth Lockridge has recently estimated that about eighty-five percent of the adult males in Massachusetts were literate by the end of the colonial period; the comparable figure in Virginia was approximately sixty-six percent. Although the latter seems to be a bit low in view of a longstanding guess (based on evidence drawn from land records) that would 'place illiteracy between ten and twenty percent' in the interior of South Carolina, it is compatible with the findings of some of Lockridge's critics who have questioned other aspects of his work. However debatable his contention that perhaps no more than fifty percent of the men among the poorer classes in Virginia were literate, Lockridge is almost certainly correct in arguing that the correlation between literacy and relatively

---

[70] Stella H. Sutherland, *Population Distribution in Colonial America* (New York, 1936), p. 37; Bridenbaugh, *Myths and Realities*, p. 3; Julian J. Petty, *The Growth and Distribution of Population in South Carolina* (Columbia, S.C., 1943), p. 69; Bridenbaugh, *Cities in Revolt*, pp. 216–17, 416; *South-Carolina Gazette*, Aug. 25, 1764; *North-Carolina Gazette*, July 18, 1777; Crittenden, 'North Carolina Newspapers Before 1790,' p. 20.

high social status remained much greater in Virginia than in New England, if only because the more complex urbanized economies of the north demanded a higher level of skill from the average man than the relatively traditional rural and agrarian patterns of the south.[71]

But all of this is not to imply that the press failed to influence individuals who neither received nor read the newspapers. For their wide geographic distribution among militia officers, ministers, and other leading men facilitated the verbal dissemination of newspaper content, while the pre-Revolutionary controversy increased the demand for news among all elements of the population. Henry Laurens was not an average man, but his changing interests probably represented a fairly typical pattern. 'I am,' he claimed in 1764, 'never very eager in the pursuite of newes unless it be in my proper way of business & then my duty requires me to be both watchfull & vigilant to learn what is going forward & to improve upon the earlyest intelligence.' By 1775 the erstwhile merchant, who had become president of the South Carolina Council of Safety, observed that he regularly spent Saturday nights 'conning' the only gazette still regularly published in Charleston for a considerably wider range of information. Although the Revolution failed to augment the duties of everyone so dramatically, individuals in all walks of life found the news to be increasingly relevant to their own affairs. Ironically, however, the exigencies of the era may have 'escalated the demands' upon individuals to the point where, as Lockridge has suggested, most were 'relatively less literate than ever before.' Under the circumstances, they naturally turned to leading men not only for the news itself but also for assistance in interpreting it. In the 1740s an educated woman like Eliza Lucas Pinckney drafted wills for her neighbors. More than a century later William Gilmore Simms provided a fictional but essentially accurate description of what had doubtless been a common occurrence: 'Stephen,' one

[71] Kenneth A. Lockridge, *Literacy in Colonial New England: An Enquiry into the Social Context of Literacy in the Early Modern West* (New York, 1974), pp. 21, 73, 78; Robert L. Meriwether, *The Expansion of South Carolina, 1729–1765* (Kingsport, Tenn., 1940), p. 177; Kevin P. Kelly's review of Lockridge, *Literacy in Colonial New England*, in *William and Mary Quarterly*, 3d ser. 32 (1975): 638–40. It seems reasonable to assume that prevailing economic and demographic conditions offset the tendency of Scotch-Irish immigrants, who were probably more literate than less geographically mobile individuals of similar social status, to raise the overall rate of literacy. See Lockridge, *Literacy in Colonial New England*, pp. 46, 78–83.

backcountry man addressed a more informed associate, 'every body knows you to be a mighty smart man, with a head chock full of books, . . . and I want you to tell me something to . . . set my mind at ease, and put me in the reason and the right of every thing in this quarrel [with Great Britain].'[72]

In these semi-traditional societies prominent men were expected to be teachers, and neither Stephen nor his counterparts in real life could have discharged their responsibilities without the aid of the newspapers. Furthermore, Revolutionary leaders appear to have been especially conscious of their role in the communications system. 'It is our Duty to inform you,' the committee of intelligence wrote to district committeemen in South Carolina, 'and through you, the Public at large. . . .' A few months later John Rutledge emphasized the point in addressing members of the South Carolina legislature who were about to return to their constituencies: 'If any persons therein are still strangers to the nature and merits of the dispute between Great Britain and the Colonies, . . . explain it to them fully and teach them, if they are so unfortunate as not to know, their inherent rights.' And so, as Edmund Pendleton later recalled, 'By a free communication between those of more information on political subjects, and the classes who have not otherwise an opportunity of acquiring that knowledge, all were instructed in their *rights* and *duties* as freemen, and taught to respect them.'[73]

[72] H. Laurens to Richard Baker, Jan. 25, 1764, *Papers of Henry Laurens*, ed. Rogers, 4: 146–47; H. Laurens to J. Laurens, Sept. 26, 1775, in 'Letters from Hon. Henry Laurens to His Son John,' *South Carolina Historical and Genealogical Magazine*, p. 75; Lockridge, *Literacy in Colonial New England*, p. 87; E. L. Pinckney to Miss Bartlett, [c. June 1742], *The Letterbook of Eliza Lucas Pinckney, 1739–1762*, ed. Elise Pinckney and Marvin R. Zahniser (Chapel Hill, 1972), p. 41; *The Writings of William Gilmore Simms*, vol. 16, *Joscelyn, A Tale of the Revolution*, intro. and notes by Stephen E. Meats (Columbia, S.C., 1975), p. 34.

[73] *South-Carolina Gazette*, Sept. 7, 1775; Apr. 11, 1776, *Journals of the General Assembly and House of Representatives, 1776–1780*, ed. William E. Hemphill, Wylma Wates, and R. Nicholas Olsberg (Columbia, S.C., 1970), p. 53; 'Address to the Citizens of Caroline,' in *The Letters and Papers of Edmund Pendleton, 1734–1803*, ed. David J. Mays, 2 vols. (Charlottesville, 1967), 2: 650. Interestingly enough, recent studies indicate that those whose prestige depends most directly upon their ability to interpret information for constituents and subordinates still tend to be the most avid readers of organizational newsletters. See Elisabeth Noelle-Neumann, 'Mass Communication Media and Public Opinion,' *Journalism Quarterly* 36 (1959): 408–9; and Frederick Williams and Howard Lindsay, 'Ethnic and Social Class Differences in Communication Habits and Attitudes,' *Journalism Quarterly* 48 (1971): 678.

IV

Because the influence of the southern colonial newspapers extended far beyond their readers, questions about the nature of their impact supersede questions about the character of the primary audience. Thus, having considered who said what to whom, we now turn to inquire with what effects under the prevailing social conditions.

First, let us deal with the case of the initial readership composed primarily of men of property. These individuals were not always in complete agreement among themselves, and it is possible to exaggerate the political homogeneity of newspaper content. Yet, as Richard Oswald observed, in most of the southern colonies, 'Government has no Party. Being left to themselves, they are all of a Side.' Thus with the exception of the *South-Carolina and American General Gazette* and (to a lesser extent) the *Georgia Gazette*, the political news and views were biased in favor of the Whigs. As a result, there can be little doubt that standard interpretations of the role of the press in the coming of the Revolution are substantially accurate in describing its effect on members of the upper classes to which it was initially addressed. Like the pamphlets of the period, the newspapers embodied a heritage of English libertarian thought that predisposed Americans to perceive a conspiracy against liberty in the actions of the British ministry. In fact, the discovery that Bolingbroke may have been a more important source of this thought for leaders in the southern colonies than had hitherto been realized demonstrates once again how widespread and deeply rooted this ideological pattern was. For if Bolingbroke and his associates popularized a form of country ideology which possessed special appeal to the landed gentry of the area, their basic ideas about the inherently expansive nature of political power and the proper means of checking it differed little from those of Trenchard and Gordon.[74]

[74] Oswald, 'Plan,' enclosed in Oswald to Dartmouth, Feb. 9, 1775, in Stevens, ed., *Facsimiles*, 24: Document 2032, p. 2; Bailyn, ed., *Pamphlets of the American Revolution*, pp. 32, 60–89. What the long-term effects of the agrarian version of country ideology in the southern colonies may have been is a question for further research. But for indications of its possible influence, see Lance Banning, *The Jeffersonian Persuasion: Evolution of a Party Ideology* (Ithaca, 1978), pp. 199–201; William D. Liddle, ' "A Patriot King, or None": Lord Bolingbroke and the American Renunciation of George III,' *Journal of American History* 65 (1979): 951–70; Forrest McDonald, *The Presidency of Thomas Jefferson* (Lawrence, Kans., 1976), pp. 19–20, 53–54, 161–63; J. G. A. Pocock, *The Machiavellian Moment: Florentine Political Thought and the Atlantic Republican Tradition*

Furthermore, it is clear that reports of measures taken in one colony stimulated emulation in others. William Henry Drayton's contention that South Carolina patriots hesitated 'till in the Northern hemisphere, a *light* appeared, to shew the political course we were to steer' was therefore accurate enough to rankle. In addition, George Grenville was probably correct in attributing some American protests to factious speeches of the Opposition at home. For the invective of British politics, as well as the violence of the London mob, caused Americans to overestimate their support in England while the apparent contrast in behavior reinforced a belief in their own moderation and reasonableness. Thus when British authorities proved impervious to argument and the Opposition failed them, the disillusionment of Americans was correspondingly complete. Many therefore came to believe with George Mason—and Junius—that corruption was indeed rampant in Britain and 'North America' was 'the only great nursery of freemen now left upon the face of the earth.' Given the premise, the conclusion was almost inevitable: 'Let us cherish the sacred deposit.'[75] In sum, the content of colonial newspapers helped to unify American leaders and to estrange them from Britain.

What is equally probable, though more difficult to demonstrate, is that the speed with which this content was transmitted accelerated and reinforced these developments. Correlation does not imply causation, but it is worth observing that allegiance and relatively good communications accompanied each other. In both respects, it seems, Georgians remained comparatively close to London while other southerners increasingly turned toward Philadelphia and New York, which would eventually become the first two capitals of the new nation. Exploring this line of reasoning a bit further, we find that the classic picture of

---

(Princeton, 1975), p. 531; and Robert M. Weir, review of *Bolingbroke and His Circle: the Politics of Nostalgia in the Age of Walpole* by Isaac Kramnick in *South Carolina Historical Magazine* 70 (1969): 267–73.

[75] *South-Carolina Gazette*, June 16, 1766, Dec. 28, 1769; Brooke, *King George III*, pp. 148–50; Ian R. Christie and Benjamin W. Labaree, *Empire or Independence, 1760–1776; A British–American Dialogue on the Coming of the American Revolution* (New York, 1976), p. 281; Mason, 'Remarks on Annual Elections for the Fairfax Independent Company,' c. April 17–26, 1775, in *Papers of George Mason*, ed. Rutland, 1: 231–32. For experimental confirmation that manipulating the ends of the political spectrum can change the perception of the midpoint, see Eleanor L. Norris, 'Perspective as a Determinant of Attitude Formation and Change,' *Journalism Quarterly* 50 (1973): 11–16.

the British Empire as a rimless wheel with London at the hub holds true only in part for the volume of communication; when the map is redrawn to depict elapsed time, the hub for North America becomes the middle colonies, and a rudimentary rim even connects New England with the South. The possible significance of these findings depends partly on the plausible assumption that American leaders, being accustomed to dominating affairs in their own provinces, would, like citizens in modern democracies, tend to identify more closely with communities in which they felt able to influence the course of public events. Furthermore, though by no means entirely dependent on the speed of communications, their political effectiveness was partly related to it. Given the tempo of life in the eighteenth century, reports from Philadelphia or New York arriving in Williamsburg or Charleston within a few days permitted a response, and even these relatively speedy times could be shortened to meet emergencies.[76] Given the nature of British politics and the pre-Revolutionary debate in which, as one colonial agent observed, 'the Ground of yesterday is no longer tomorrow[']s,' prompt news from Britain was even more important. But because oceans rolled and months elapsed before reports arrived from London, neither speed nor much flexibility was possible. That the ship chartered by London merchants to rush news of the repeal of the Stamp Act foundered off the bar at Charleston more than two months later, whereas express riders were able to speed reports of the battles of Lexington and Concord to Williamsburg in just over a week are therefore facts of some importance.[77] And doubtless frustrated American politicians were conscious of the reason for their significance every time they read the local newspapers.

To find that the communications and political systems of the em-

[76] Cletis Pride, 'Content Analysis of Seven Commonwealth Newspapers,' *Journalism Quarterly* 49 (1972): 753; Gabriel A. Almond and Sidney Verba, *The Civic Culture: Political Attitudes and Democracy in Five Nations* (Princeton, 1963), pp. 230–57; Arthur H. Cole, 'The Tempo of Mercantile Life in Colonial America,' *Business History Review* 33 (1959): 277–99.

[77] Charles Garth to South Carolina Committee of Correspondence, Aug. 14, 1768, Garth Letterbook, p. 61, S.C. Dept. of Archives and Hist.; Garth to Committee of Correspondence, Jan. 19, 1766, in Joseph W. Barnwell, 'Hon. Charles Garth, M.P., The Last Colonial Agent of South Carolina in England, and Some of His Work,' *South Carolina Historical and Genealogical Magazine* 26 (1925): 92; Frank Luther Mott, 'The Newspaper Coverage of Lexington and Concord,' *New England Quarterly* 17 (1944): 502.

bryonic nation were developing while those of the empire were deteriorating should perhaps not be very surprising in view of the recent examples of the rise of modern nationalism under the aegis of better communications.[78] But some other aspects of the contribution made by the press to the development of the new nation may not be so immediately obvious. Take the matter of the Scots. Because national groups normally identify themselves by rejecting others, the presence of a hostile outgroup facilitates the development of internal solidarity. Until the end of the Seven Years' War Frenchmen served as the most important outgroup for both Englishmen and Americans. Later, as the United States came to be defined as a white man's country, Winthrop Jordan's work implies, blacks were the most relevant negative reference group. During the Revolutionary era, however, Englishmen would seem to have been the logical candidates for the position. Nevertheless, a wholesale rejection of British cultural traditions would have been painful for most Americans, and perhaps impossible for members of the southern upper classes. To be sure, the belief that they remained more English in character is part mythical, but the notion was common among contemporaries, and at least one historian has found that the southern colonial newspapers appeared to reflect less hatred of the British than their northern counterparts. Were it not for the Scots, southerners would therefore have faced a particularly acute problem of self-definition during the Revolution.[79]

But the economic and political power of the numerous Scotch merchants and placemen made them especially unpopular in the southern colonies. In fact, a Carolina planter went so far as to stipulate that his daughter would inherit less in the event that she married a Scotsman,

[78] Karl W. Deutsch, *Nationalism and Social Communication: An Inquiry into the Foundations of Nationality*, 2d ed. (Cambridge, Mass., 1966).

[79] Leonard W. Doob, *Patriotism and Nationalism: Their Psychological Foundations* (New Haven, 1964), p. 259; Paul A. Varg, 'The Advent of Nationalism, 1758–1776,' *American Quarterly* 16 (1964): 170–71; Jordan, *White over Black*, pp. 579, 581 and passim; Bridenbaugh, *Myths and Realities*, pp. 94–95; 'Journal of Lord Adam Gordon,' in Newton D. Mereness, ed., *Travels in the American Colonies* (New York, 1916), pp. 397–98; Paul Smith, *Loyalists and Redcoats: A Study in British Revolutionary Policy* (Chapel Hill, 1964), pp. 18–19; Davidson, *Propaganda and the American Revolution*, p. 143. This is not to imply that residents in the northern colonies did not share the hostility to Scots, but merely to suggest that it was probably more intense in the southern colonies. See, for example, John J. Waters, Jr., *The Otis Family in Provincial and Revolutionary Massachusetts* (Chapel Hill, 1968), p. 177.

and Fithian heard one of the young Lees fulminate 'that if he ever Shall have a Daughter, if She marries a Scotchman he shoots her dead at once!' Such exclusion from the ties of family suggests that Scots, like blacks, appeared to embody culturally proscribed traits. Thus when the newspapers depicted them as fawning, miserly, devious, and slavish tools of the ministry, the press was helping to construct an anti-image against which Americans could define themselves as brave, generous, open, honest, free, and virtuous. Unattached to the American soil but addicted to trade, Scotsmen seemed to constitute a subversive group in the colonies and an insidious influence in London. Consequently, as Douglass Adair was one of the first to observe, the 'theme of "Scotch influence" ' linked tyranny at home and abroad.[80] And for southerners, especially, this meant that the Scots provided an explanation of events, as well as a means of defining oneself as an American, that enabled them to retain allegiance to their British political heritage while separating from the British nation itself. From this perspective, neither the willingness of southern patriots to educate children in England during the Revolution nor the rather sudden appearance of a pronounced disdain for the merchant's calling appear quite so puzzling.[81] Insofar as the upper classes are concerned, it is therefore clear that the newspapers helped to make Scotsmen the unwitting midwives of a distinctive brand of American nationalism in the southern colonies.

At first glance, the impact of the newspapers upon men beyond their immediate reach would appear to have been weaker. Yet, the restricted circulation of the newspapers may have actually had the para-

[80] Will of Adam Daniel, proved Feb. 6, 1767, Charleston County Wills, 11 (1767–1771): 130, Works Progress Administration Transcripts, S.C. Dept. of Archives and Hist.; *Journal and Letters of Philip Fithian*, ed. Farish, p. 179; Bertram Wyatt-Brown, 'The Ideal Typology and Ante-Bellum Southern History: A Testing of a New Approach,' *Societas* 5 (1975): 28; John W. Blassingame, 'American Nationalism and Other Loyalties in the Southern Colonies, 1763–1775,' *Journal of Southern History* 34 (1968): 66; Douglass Adair, 'The Stamp Act in Contemporary English Cartoons,' *William and Mary Quarterly*, 3d ser. 10 (1953): 538.

[81] George C. Rogers, Jr., *The Evolution of a Federalist: William Loughton Smith of Charleston, 1758–1812* (Columbia, S.C., 1962), pp. 79, 90–92; Rosser H. Taylor, 'The Gentry of Ante-Bellum South Carolina,' *North Carolina Historical Review* 17 (1940): 116–18; Edmund S. Morgan, 'The Puritan Ethic and the American Revolution,' *William and Mary Quarterly*, 3d ser. 24 (1967): 5; Pred, *Urban Growth and the Circulation of Information*, p. 278. See also George C. Rogers, Jr., *Charleston in the Age of the Pinckneys* (Norman, Okla., 1969), pp. 52–53.

doxical effect of increasing their influence upon the population at large. Even in modern societies, students of the communications process have found a phenomenon known as the 'two-step flow' of information whereby individuals in contact with the mass media gather and relay items of importance to their acquaintances. Especially intriguing is the discovery that the interpersonal contact involved in the second phase of transmission may be more effective in influencing attitudes and behavior than the direct transmission of information by impersonal means. Although explanations of this experimental finding differ, students of the subject seem to agree that it depends in part on the relative social status and presumed expertise of the individuals involved. Thus in traditional societies the impact of news and information is often directly proportional to the authority of the man who transmits it. One scholar has therefore plausibly concluded that the two-step flow is perhaps most common and most effective in developing societies where those first reached by the 'mass' media tend to be the established leaders.[82]

Clues to how the indirect dissemination of newspaper content augmented its impact in the southern colonies appear in Edmund Randolph's almost classic description of the two-step flow. 'Many circumstances,' he observed, 'existed favorable to the propagating of a contagion of free opinion, although every class of men cannot be supposed to have been aided by extensive literary views.' Among these he enumerated two of special relevance to the present discussion. In the 'convivial circles' of the gentry, he seemed to imply, 'a certain fluency of speech, which marked the character' of hospitable Virginians, 'pushed into motion many adventurous doctrines, which in a different situation of affairs might have lain dormant much longer and might have been limited to a much narrowed sphere.' Furthermore, he continued, the

---

[82] Morris Janowitz, 'The Study of Mass Communication,' *International Encyclopedia of the Social Sciences*, 3: 50–51; Elihu Katz, 'Diffusion: Interpersonal Influence,' ibid., 4: 179–82; Katz, 'The Two-Step Flow of Communication: An Up-to-Date Report on the Hypothesis,' *Public Opinion Quarterly* 21 (1957): 61–78; William J. McGuire, 'The Nature of Attitudes and Attitude Change,' in Gardner Lindzey and Elliot Aronson, eds., *Handbook of Social Psychology*, 2d ed., 5 vols. (Reading, Mass., 1968–69), 3: 179, 226; Ithiel de Sola Pool, 'The Mass Media and Politics in the Modernization Process,' in Pye, ed., *Communications and Political Development*, p. 242; Lloyd R. Bostian, 'The Two-Step Flow Theory: Cross-Cultural Implications,' *Journalism Quarterly* 47 (1970): 109–17.

process also operated across class lines for 'even if the fancied division into something like ranks, not actually coalescing with each other, had been really formed,'—which he was reluctant to admit—'the opinions of every denomination or cast would have diffused themselves on every side by means of the professions of priest, lawyer, and physician, who visited the houses of the ostentatious as well as the cottages of the planters.'[83]

Equally idyllic, this picture provides a significant contrast to Deane's description of well-read Americans of all social classes discussing politics as equals. For, idealized as it was, Randolph's account nevertheless reflected the realities of a social setting especially conducive to augmenting the effects of the two-step flow. Because 'People of fortune' were, as Fithian remarked, 'the pattern of all behaviour' in the southern colonies, a leading local figure added his prestige and presumed expertise while passing along news to less prominent associates. Furthermore, if Benjamin Harrison's recall was accurate, an incident in which he was involved indicates that the incremental effect could reach proportions astonishing to even the most patriotic of modern Americans. When the Virginia delegation was about to depart for Philadelphia and the Continental Congress, it seems that some 'respectable but uninformed inhabitants' called upon Harrison and his colleagues, saying: 'You assert that there is a fixed intention to invade our rights and privileges; we own that we do not see this clearly, but since you assure us that it is so, we believe it. We are about to take a very dangerous step, but we have confidence in you and will do anything you think proper.'[84]

By reminding us that superior knowledge usually sanctions leadership, this story also suggests that the press bolstered the local political establishments in subtle as well as obvious ways. Like the possession of a radio which in the twentieth century might confer additional prestige on the headman of a remote village in a developing nation, receipt of the newspapers was itself doubtless a badge of social distinction.

[83] Edmund Randolph, *History of Virginia*, ed. Arthur H. Shaffer (Charlottesville, 1970), pp. 193–94.

[84] Fithian to Rev. Enoch Green, Dec. 1, 1773, *Journal and Letters of Philip Fithian*, ed. Farish, p. 27; entry of April 26, 1782, in *Travels in North America in the Years 1780, 1781 and 1782 by the Marquis de Chastellux*, ed. Howard C. Rice, Jr., 2 vols. (Chapel Hill, 1963), 2: 429. For a similar assessment of the influence of the wealthy, see Gadsden in the *South-Carolina Gazette*, Nov. 9, 1769.

Equally important, greater access to the relatively restricted channels of communication from the outside world contributed to presumptions about the possession of knowledge that even the most arcane information would support. Thus the apparently irrelevant accounts of European royalty, etc., which filled much of the colonial papers were not entirely unrelated to local politics. This of course is not to say that the resolves published by 'the Representatives of the People' to demonstrate their 'just Sense of Liberty' were not more relevant, and it seems fair to assume that messages reflecting favorably on the communicator were the most apt to be disseminated. Virtual control of the press therefore paid multiple dividends to patriot leaders who could thereby sanction their own measures, document the inequities of their opponents, and lend credibility to the leadership of the American cause at all levels. How the process worked in areas where a large part of the populace had direct access to the newspapers is perhaps clear enough merely from Peter Oliver's bitter observation that 'the Press . . . groaned with all the Falsities that seditious Brains could invent, which were crammed down the Credulity of the Vulgar.' But in other areas, like the southern colonies, where newspapers circulated among the relatively few the mechanism was more complex. How it operated there appears perhaps most plainly in the words of Richard Furman. In addressing himself to a number of politically doubting Thomases in the South Carolina backcountry, Furman, who was a Baptist minister as well as a Whig, invoked the 'public Gazettes' which, he noted, 'may be seen' to support what his audience had already been told by patriot leaders. Although he referred to British as well as to American newspapers, his argumentative technique clearly reveals that print could be —and was—used to reinforce the authority of the speaker as well as of the spoken word.[85] Obviously, men with a relative monopoly of the latest information and the ability to interpret it were therefore in a key position to maintain their own influence.

To make this observation is not to claim that receipt of the newspapers always gave leading men the first or even the best report of

[85] Schramm, 'Communication Development and the Development Process,' in Pye, ed., *Communications and Political Development*, p. 53; *Peter Oliver's Origin & Progress of the American Rebellion: A Tory View*, ed. Douglass Adair and John A. Schutz (Stanford, Calif., 1961), p. 105; Furman to 'Gentlemen,' Nov. 1775, Furman Family Papers, Baptist Historical Collection, Furman University, Greenville, S.C.

events; it is, however, to contend that in the long run the press provided them with the most timely and accurate accounts then consistently available. Important news still often travels fastest by word of mouth, and Colonel Daingerfield of Belvidera first learned that the Declaration of Independence had been adopted by sending an overseer to investigate sounds of distant celebration. Errors, too, are not unknown to the modern press, and earlier printers sometimes admitted their guilt with a humorous twist. 'It is well known,' the *South-Carolina Gazette* noted in 1772, 'that Printers are not INFALLIBLE, and are often misinformed.' But, significantly, the advertisement continued, if the present publishers should ever be 'found guilty of marrying Persons contrary to their Inclinations, no *Pope* shall be more indulgent, for a Divorce shall be instantly granted.'[86] Furthermore, leaders, such as Henry Laurens (who received more than one local paper) and Edmund Pendleton (who requested that friends send him gazettes from other areas), were in the best position to verify or correct reports. Thus, greater access to information about current affairs elsewhere complemented more active involvement in local politics to make men of property the most effective interpreters of contemporary events. Consequently, for those who sought to acquire, maintain, and discharge the responsibilities of leadership the current history furnished by the provincial papers was as important as the ancient history provided by their education. For if, as Edmund Morgan has argued, the American Revolution was 'an intellectual movement' in which politics replaced religion as the chief concern of the colonial intelligentsia, newspapers became the equivalent of secular Bibles.[87] No wonder that in the southern provinces the local political establishments often appear to have constituted a revitalized priesthood whose members became the special custodians of the Word.

[86] Karl Erik Rosengren, 'News Diffusion: An Overview,' *Journalism Quarterly* 50 (1973): 90; entry of July 10, 1776, *Journal of John Harrower*, ed. Riley, p. 158; *South-Carolina Gazette*, May 7, 1772.

[87] Laurens to Peter Timothy, July 6, 1768, *Papers of Henry Laurens*, ed. Rogers and Chesnutt, 5: 730; Henry Laurens, Account Book, 1766–1773, pp. 44, 184, 294, Robert Scott Small Library, College of Charleston, Charleston, S.C.; Pendleton to William Woodford, June 6, 1778, in *Letters and Papers of Edmund Pendleton*, ed. Mays, 1: 257; R. H. Lee to Samuel Adams, Feb. 4, 1773, in *Letters of Richard Henry Lee*, ed. Ballagh, 1: 82; Edmund S. Morgan, 'The American Revolution Considered as an Intellectual Movement,' in Arthur M. Schlesinger, Jr., and Morton White, eds., *Paths of American Thought*, paperback ed. (Boston, 1970), pp. 11–33.

The similarity between this development and the temporary strengthening of customary lines of authority that sometimes occurs with the advent of mass communications in the developing societies of the twentieth century suggests that it might have been an ephemeral phenomenon.[88] Yet, the traditional structure of authority appears to have remained remarkably intact in the southern states well into the nineteenth century. To be sure, as Rhys Isaac has observed, the evangelical movement in eighteenth-century Virginia involved an element of rebellion against the literary culture of the gentry, and backcountry men in South Carolina often doubted that anyone from the coast could tell the truth. 'Democratic Gentle-Touch' and others in urban areas like Charleston also attacked the traditional system of politics in general and specific members of the old political establishment in particular during the 1780s.[89] But the political position of the wealthy in South Carolina, like that of the gentry in Virginia, was probably more secure a decade after the war than before it. And, in fact, similar men of property, though occasionally challenged, maintained control throughout most of the South during the entire antebellum period.[90]

[88] See, for example, James N. Mosel, 'Communication Patterns and Political Socialization in Transitional Thailand,' in Pye, ed., *Communications and Political Development*, p. 228; and J. Mayone Stycos, 'Patterns of Communication in a Rural Greek Village,' *Public Opinion Quarterly* 16 (1952): 59, 60, 70.

[89] Rhys Isaac, 'Preachers and Patriots: Popular Culture and the Revolution in Virginia,' in Alfred F. Young, ed., *The American Revolution: Explorations in the History of American Radicalism* (DeKalb, Ill., 1976), p. 139; 'Fragment of a Journal Kept by the Rev. William Tennent Describing his Journey, in 1775, to Upper South Carolina . . . ,' *City of Charleston, S.C., Year Book, 1894*, p. 299; [Unknown] to 'Sir,' n.d., filed first in Nov. – Dec. 1775 box, Clinton Papers, William L. Clements Library, Ann Arbor, Mich.; Furman to 'Gentlemen,' Nov. 1775, Furman Family Papers, Baptist Historical Collection, Furman University, Greenville, S.C.; Pauline Maier, 'The Charleston Mob and the Evolution of Popular Politics in Revolutionary South Carolina, 1765–1784,' *Perspectives in American History* 4 (1970): 192–93. For further discussion of the relationship between an 'elitist typographic culture' and more popular oral cultures, see Rhys Isaac, 'Dramatizing the Ideology of Revolution: Popular Mobilization in Virginia, 1774 to 1776,' *William and Mary Quarterly*, 3d ser. 33 (1976): 357–85; and Harry S. Stout, 'Religion, Communications, and the Ideological Origins of the American Revolution,' *William and Mary Quarterly*, 3d ser. 34 (1977): 519–41.

[90] George C. Rogers, Jr., 'South Carolina Federalists and the Origins of the Nullification Movement,' *South Carolina Historical Magazine* 71 (1970): 17–32; Gordon S. Wood, 'Rhetoric and Reality in the American Revolution,' *William and Mary Quarterly* 23 (1966): 27–30; Richard Buel, Jr., *Securing the Revolution: Ideology in American Politics, 1789–1815* (Ithaca, N.Y., 1972), pp. 79–82; Weir, 'Who Shall Rule at Home,' pp.

A full-scale attempt to account for the resiliency of this pattern would obviously go well beyond the confines of the present topic, but the most relevant elements can be quickly sketched. In the long run, of course, mass communications undermine traditional leaders by short-circuiting the hierarchical flow of information. In the South, however, such short circuits appear to have been relatively rare; and the antebellum press, like its primary audience, remained strikingly similar to its colonial counterpart. As late as 1850 the combined per capita circulation of periodicals and newspapers among whites in the South was only eight copies per year—a figure less than one-third that of the North. Accordingly, the newspapers continued to be organs of the upper classes, and 'the great economic prize for editors,' as Clement Eaton has observed, remained the post of government printer. Hence, a British correspondent visiting the South on the eve of the Civil War discovered neither much enthusiasm for freedom of the press nor the 'dread of its power' which prevailed further north. Newspapers, it seems, were still performing many of the same functions in behalf of the local establishments as they had during the late colonial period.[91]

Although one would prefer to believe that the southern press reverted to a captive position under the pressures of the sectional controversy, there are reasons for doubting that it ever fully escaped dependency. Much of the population in the area remained poorly educated and sparsely distributed, and publishers therefore continued to be responsive to a restricted market. Ironically, too, the Revolution itself may have helped to perpetuate some of these conditions. For if the heightened relevance of political events increased the importance of the newspapers, the disruptions of the war reduced their availability and thereby placed leading men with access to rare copies in an even more strategic position than before. Thus, at least as long as hostilities continued, the press tended to reinforce rather than undermine the position of local leaders. Furthermore, at the end of the war conscious attempts were made to maintain or reestablish the old relation-

---

679–700; David M. Potter, *The Impending Crisis, 1848–1861*, ed. Don E. Fehrenbacher (New York, 1976), pp. 31 n. 16, 455–57.

[91] Clement Eaton, *The Freedom-of-Thought Struggle in the Old South* (1940; reprint ed., New York, 1964), p. 78; Eaton, *The Growth of Southern Civilization, 1790–1860* (New York, 1961), p. 266; William H. Russell, *My Diary North and South*, 2 vols. (London, 1863), 1: 147.

ship between government and the press. Fully understanding his past role (which included publication of the *Royal Georgia Gazette* under British authority during the occupation of Savannah), members of the Georgia legislature reappointed James Johnston as the public printer in 1783. In like manner, some of the shrewdest individuals in public life south of Virginia—John Rutledge, John Matthews, and Nathanael Greene, respectively successive governors of South Carolina and commander of the Continental Army in the South—cooperated with the newly reconstituted state legislature to foster newspapers published at Jacksonborough and Parker's Ferry while British forces still held Charleston.[92]

Consequently, postwar stability and the renaissance of institutional legitimacy depended in part upon the reestablishment of the old symbiotic relationship between the press and the personal influence of leading men which, Greene believed, 'must supply the defects of civil constitution' in the war-torn land. Perhaps the best testimony to his success and to the durability of the relationship can be found nearly 100 years later in the words of a Union officer from Connecticut stationed in South Carolina. 'Every community,' he observed, 'has its great man, or at least its little great man, around whom his fellow citizens gather when they want information, and to whose monologues they listen with a respect akin to humility.' A press that not only helped to carry the southern colonies successfully through the Revolution but also contributed to the perpetuation of social patterns that would characterize the region for decades to come was indeed as mighty as the sword.[93]

---

[92] Lawrence, *James Johnston*, pp. 19, 25–26; John Rutledge to General Marion, Aug. 13, 1781, and John Matthews to General Marion, July 19, 1782, in R. W. Gibbes, ed., *Documentary History of the American Revolution*, 3 vols. (1853–57; reprint ed., Spartanburg, S.C., 1972), 3: 126, and 2: 201; Jan. 26, 1782, *Journal of the House of Representatives of South Carolina, January 8, 1782 to February 26, 1782*, ed. A. S. Salley, Jr. (Columbia, S.C., 1916), p. 27. Jacksonborough Imprints, South Caroliniana Library: Speech of John Rutledge to the General Assembly, Jan. 18, 1782, and the addresses of the House and Senate in reply, n.d.; List of Laws Passed by the Legislature, printed by David Rogers, Mar. 1, 1782; Proclamation of John Mathews [*sic*], Mar. 14, 1782; *South-Carolina Gazette* (Parker's Ferry), May 15, 1782, printed by Benjamin F. Dunlap. Account of Dunlap, Accounts Audited, Stub Entries, W238, S.C. Dept. of Archives and Hist.

[93] Theodore Thayer, *Nathanael Greene, Strategist of the American Revolution* (New York, 1960), p. 289; John William De Forest, *A Union Officer in the Reconstruction*, ed. James H. Croushore and David M. Potter (New Haven, 1948), p. 195.

Appendix

In the table below, N¹ represents the total number of datelines in the sample; N² the number providing sufficient information for calculating transit time; and R the range in days between the slowest and fastest reports.

News from:	Md. Gaz.	Va. Gaz. (Royle, P&D, D&H)	Va. Gaz. (Rind, Pinkney)	Va. Gaz. (Purdie)	NC Gaz.	SC Gaz. & CJ	Ga. Gaz.
British Isles							
N¹/N²	65/63	71/68	17/15	3/2	28/28	55/55	22/22
R	55–321	53–142	63–108	69–85	54–124	59–137	46–134
Mass.							
N¹/N²	20/17	19/19	18/16	2/1	15/10	20/20	10/8
R	14–179	14–52	13–76	24–24	20–51	19–90	23–116
R.I.							
N¹/N²	5/3	3/3	2/2	0	3/3	7/7	0
R	18–27	18–54	26–33		13–35	19–49	
N.Y.							
N¹/N²	14/11	10/9	6/5	2/1	6/6	17/17	5/5
R	10–36	11–40	15–24	15–15	21–43	15–64	28–57
Pa.							
N¹/N²	12/8	10/9	6/5	3/2	9/8	12/12	11/11
R	8–32	8–38	10–21	11–21	18–60	14–77	14–186
Md.							
N¹/N²	—	0	1/1	0	0	4/4	0
R			14–14			24–58	
Va.							
N¹/N²	4/3	—	—	—	9/8	4/4	1/1
R	13–34				13–49	24–49	15–15
N.C.							
N¹/N²	2/1	4/3	1/1	0	—	8/8	1/1
R	49–49	23–41	4–4			12–82	11–11
S.C.							
N¹/N²	5/4	6/5	4/2	0	1/1	—	8/7
R	38–52	25–65	38–49		25–25		12–45
Ga.							
N¹/N²	2/2	2/2	0	0	0	9/9	—
R	44–51	64–66				6–34	

The Colonial German-language Press
and the American Revolution

WILLI PAUL ADAMS

ᏋᏬ ᏋᏬ ᏋᏬ ᏋᏬ ᏋᏬ ᏋᏬ ᏋᏬ ᏋᏬ ᏋᏬ ᏋᏬ ᏋᏬ ᏋᏬ ᏋᏬ ᏋᏬ ᏋᏬ ᏋᏬ

Whether you are Englishmen, Germans, Low-Germans or Swedes, whether you are of the High Church, Presbyterians, Quakers, or of another denomination, by your living here and by the law of the land you are free men, not slaves. You have a right to all liberties of a native-born Englishman, and you have a share in the fundamental laws of the land.

—Christopher Sower, Jr., 1764

AN INHABITANT OF THE BRITISH COLONIES IN NORTH AMERICA did not have to be a reader of English in order to follow and participate in the great public debate accompanying the struggle for colonial rights and, eventually, independence. Any reader of the German-language newspapers, pamphlets, and broadsides printed in Philadelphia and Germantown between 1763 and 1780 would have been able to learn almost as much about what was being said and done in London, Boston, and Philadelphia as a reader of the English-

I wish to express my gratitude for support that greatly aided my endeavors to the American Council of Learned Societies, which granted an American Studies Fellowship in 1975–76, and to the Charles Warren Center for Studies in American History of Harvard University, which, under the directorship of Donald Fleming, permitted me to lead the sheltered, if brief, life of a research fellow. During an intensive week at Worcester, I received the professional help of Marcus A. McCorison, John B. Hench, and their efficient and ever friendly staff at the American Antiquarian Society. In less pastoral a setting but equally professional a spirit, the Historical Society of Pennsylvania in Philadelphia provided what surprisingly little material remains of the Sowers' and Henry Miller's journalistic activities in that city. Kathleen Neils Conzen and Enrique Otte critically read an earlier version of this paper. Joan Regensburger, Heidi Hampton, and Heide Westhusen typed the successive versions. Angela Meurer Adams spent two weeks in the artificial world of the basement of Widener Library in front of a microfilm reader. To all, I acknowledge my gratitude.—W.P.A.

language press. This is a surprising fact, especially in light of the traditional notion of the eighteenth-century German immigrants as an intensely religious and withdrawn group, disinterested in and incapable of comprehending the political principles and institutions of the new nation taking shape around them. One wonders, in fact, what words a German sectarian, who had grown up as the subject of some petty autocrat, might have had available in his language even to name the wrongs British subjects were suffering from the crown and Parliament. How was he to know what British liberties meant and what Whig principles demanded? In short, how could a group as alien to Anglo-American political culture as the Germans are said to have been have taken part in the supreme manifestations of the Anglo-American spirit of liberty, the justification of English constitutional and natural rights, and eventually, of independence and republican government?

German-American historians of two or three generations ago, motivated by the desire to prove the patriotism of their ethnic group by enumerating its contributions to the American success story, desperately fought for a role in the story of the nation's founding. Baron von Steuben, they knew, would never suffice as a patron saint: the general had not been raised in Lancaster County, and he had more to do with drill than with democracy. So they pointed to the high proportion of German-Americans in Washington's armies. Albert Faust did not fail to quote George Bancroft's finding: 'While the Germans in the colonies constituted but one twelfth of the population, yet they formed one eighth of the Continental Army.'[1] Since Germans were also marching on the other side, under the king's banner, the question might reasonably be raised whether the Germans knew what they were fighting for.

In response, the chroniclers of German-American achievements have long held up the front page of Henry Miller's weekly *Der Philadelphische Staatsbote* of July 9, 1776. What more striking proof could anyone desire than this beautifully printed page with the complete text, in translation, of the Declaration of Independence? And it was noted that the *Staatsbote* of July 5 was the first newspaper to announce the existence of the Declaration. Still, did this immigrant printer really know what he was translating, and if he did, did his language permit him to express what he comprehended?

[1] Albert Faust, *The German Element in the United States*, 2 vols. (New York, 1927), 2: 368.

How well the German leaders, and especially the printers, understood the meaning of these documents and how fully they participated in the ideological struggle of the time, emerges only from close investigation of the German-language press in the 1760s and 70s. The German-language press, like its English-language counterpart, made possible rational discourse on questions of statecraft and social betterment beyond the limited circles of the political elite, among a population too spread out and too large to assemble in one city's market place.[2] Further, it helped create a 'new forum' of public opinion essential for the growth of a shared sense of legitimacy. Finally, like the English-language press, the German-language press was an integrating force, essential to the process of nation-building. If 'communication' was a crucial element in the development of Europe's relatively unified regions into modern nation-states, it must have been all the more so for the widely dispersed colonial settlements from New Hampshire to Georgia with their heterogeneous populations and diverging regional interests.[3] Once the War for Independence had begun, public persuasion, information, and propaganda became even more important for the colonists.

The German-language press shared in all of these functions. The standard history of American journalism is emphatically wrong in characterizing the most successful German newspapers of the Revolutionary period, Christopher Sower's *Germantowner Zeitung* and Henry Miller's *Staatsbote*, as 'strongly religious in tone.'[4] At least from the 1760s on, both newspapers were thoroughly secular in tone, though not indifferent to religion. By no means were they sectarian sheets printed only for a tightly

[2] Jürgen Habermas, *Strukturwandel der Öffentlichkeit* (Neuwied, 1962), p. 69. On the significance of public debate for social change in the eighteenth century see also Louis Gottschalk and Donald Lach, *Toward the French Revolution: Europe and America in the Eighteenth-Century World* (New York, 1973), chap. 4, especially pp. 112–13. Hans Speier in his useful summary noted: 'Public opinion is a phenomenon of middle-class civilization. . . . Gains in economic power of the middle class and the gradual spread of literacy are merely two aspects of this process [i.e., the rise of public opinion].' 'Historical Development of Public Opinion,' *American Journal of Sociology* 55 (1950): 379–80.

[3] Karl W. Deutsch, *Nationalism and Social Communication: An Inquiry into the Social Foundations of Nationality*, 2d ed. (Cambridge, Mass., 1966). Only English-language newspapers are analyzed by Richard L. Merritt, *Symbols of American Community, 1735–1775* (New Haven, 1966).

[4] Frank Luther Mott, *American Journalism, A History: 1690–1960*, 3d ed. (New York, 1962), p. 29.

153

knit group of true believers. Written and published for all German readers in the colonies without regard to church membership, these newspapers, broadsides, almanacs, and pamphlets were part of the intensive, this-worldly communication among the Germans in America and between them and the majority culture.[5] They were not part of the cultural baggage brought over from Germany, for no press of this sort existed in Germany at the time.[6]

THE FOUNDERS

Christopher Sower, Father and Son

The first two attempts at German-language periodical publication failed in 1731 and 1732. Andrew Bradford's German almanac and Benjamin Franklin's weekly *Philadelphische Zeitung*, probably planned as a translation of his English newspaper, did not attract enough customers to survive.[7]

The man who succeeded where Franklin had failed was Christopher Sower (1693–1758), not a professional printer but no less skillful a craftsman, no less shrewd a businessman, and probably more forthright a character.[8] He succeeded because of his devotion to the task and the support he received from coreligionists on both sides of the Atlantic. He had come

[5] See Appendix A for a list of the German-language publications with political content between 1764 and 1783.

[6] Margot Lindemann, *Die deutsche Presse bis 1815* (Berlin, 1969).

[7] *Der Teutsche Pilgrim: Mitbringende einen Sitten - Calender*, 1731, last published probably in 1733. Judging from the grammatically impossible 'mitbringende' in the title, the English publisher operated without the benefit of a literate German editor. In his prospectus, which was numbered as the first issue, Franklin announced that he would wait for 300 subscriptions at 10 shillings for the year before he would begin regular publication. Six weeks later only 50 subscriptions had been taken out, and after a second sample issue Franklin and Louis Timothée, a recent immigrant from Holland whom Franklin had hired as a journeyman printer and editor, gave up. *Philadelphische Zeitung*, no. 1, May 6, 1732, no. 2, June 24, 1732; *The Papers of Benjamin Franklin*, ed. Leonard W. Labaree (New Haven, 1959), 1: 230–32, 233–34.

[8] The Sowers used three variations in spelling their name. In 1738 Christopher signed his name to a letter back to Germany as 'J.Chr.Sauer.' See 'Two Germantown Letters of 1738,' trans. with an introduction by Waldemar Westergaard, *Pennsylvania Magazine of History and Biography* 56 (1932): 11. In the masthead of the almanac and newspaper the editors spelled their name 'Saur' from the beginning. The issue of Mar. 12, 1777, was 'herausgegeben von Christoph Saur, junr. und Peter Saur'; the same issue contains the notice, 'All ADVERTISEMENTS to be inserted in this Paper by Christopher Sower, junr. and Peter Sower, Publishers hereof.' When addressing English readers they thus anglicized both their Christian name and their surname.

over with a group of German Baptists, the Dunkers, in 1724 at the age of twenty-nine. He did not, however, become a member of their close-knit religious community but remained to the end of his life a member of one of the more aloof pietist groups, the Separatists.[9] Sower's success is not explicable, however, in terms of a hired printer, or 'court printer,' of the Ephrata or any other pietist sect. On the contrary, he explicitly rejected persistent attempts to win him over to the cloistered community of Ephrata.[10] He rejected the narrow-mindedness of those of his comigrants who 'have barricaded themselves into sects and groups,' among them the Dunkers, who 'have erected a fence around themselves; they admit and expel, and are jealous and quarrelsome with others.'[11] The same traits in his personality that led him to Separatism in religious life, led him to a skeptical view of secular claims of authority and institutions. This skepticism, based on an individualistic type of fundamentalism combined with the ability to acquire an economic basis for his independence, made Sower much more of a publisher and journalist in the modern sense than has usually been assumed. The image of Sower the pietist, the pacifist prayer book printer, needs to be revised. Sower was a journalist who used the modern instrument of the press to influence social conditions and to hold accountable those in positions of authority.

The development of the Sower printing house in Germantown has been fully documented.[12] His almanac, which, published from 1738 on,

---

[9] Years later, the Separatists were characterized as follows: 'The Separatists live here like birds sitting in the midst of seeds. Whoever is punished for something or other by the members of his denomination . . . becomes a Separatist immediately, and if anybody starts talking about religion or salvation it is their common confession to mock at preachers and denominations.' Christopher Schultze to Ehrenfried Hentze, 1768, trans. from the German original in the Kriebel Letter Book, Schwenkfelder Library, Pennsburg, Pa., by Dietmar Rothermund, 'The German Problem of Colonial Pennsylvania,' *Pennsylvania Magazine of History and Biography* 84 (1960): 21. See also Donald F. Durnbaugh, 'Was Christopher Sauer a Dunker?,' *Pennsylvania Magazine of History and Biography* 93 (1969): 383–91. In his article 'Christopher Sauer, Pennsylvania German Printer: His Youth in Germany and Later Relations with Europe,' *Pennsylvania Magazine of History and Biography* 82 (1958): 316–40, Durnbaugh established Jan. or Feb. 1, 1695, as the date and Ladenburg, formerly Laudenburg, on the Neckar as the place of Sower's birth. The biographical sketch in the *Dictionary of American Biography* s.v. 'Sower, Christopher,' is outdated.

[10] Durnbaugh, 'Was Christopher Sauer a Dunker?,' p. 387.

[11] Ibid., p. 388.

[12] Edward W. Hocker, 'The Sower Printing House of Colonial Times,' *Proceedings and Addresses of the Pennsylvania German Society* 53 (1948).

became an institution, contained more interesting matter than the usual calender and quotations from scripture.[13] Another early and successful venture of his was the printing of over 1,000 copies of Luther's translation of the Bible from 1740 to 1743.[14] According to Isaiah Thomas, this was 'the largest work that had issued from any press in that colony, and it was not equalled for many years after.' Priced at twenty shillings per copy, the edition did not sell out until 1758.[15]

As a Separatist and a publisher, Sower remained for two decades an effective and often irritating voice in the public debate accompanying the religious and political conflicts in Pennsylvania. He did not limit himself to printing religious materials. A checklist of his publications from 1738 to his death in 1758 that includes even broadsides and leaflets, though probably incomplete, enumerates 151 items, 18 of them in English. There were 120 imprints whose contents were religious (that is, doctrinal, devotional, and relating to church affairs); 14 were of a political-historical nature, including government publications; 13 of practical instruction, including grammar and spelling; and 4 of entertainment in the form of stories and Indian captivity narratives.[16] As unsatisfactory as this rough breakdown is (a broadside with an inspirational poem counting for as much as a 36-page pamphlet on a conference with Indians or the 1,270 pages of the Bible), it clearly establishes the fact of early diversification of the German-language press. Even in its first decade it was more than what today we would call a 'religious' press, although of course the mainstay of the German printers' business, just as that of their English colleagues all over the colonies, was the printing of sermons, psalters, songbooks, and other inspirational literature.[17]

[13] *Der Hoch-Deutsch Americanische Calender für das Jahr 1739.*
[14] *Biblia, Das ist: Die Heilige Schrift Altes und Neues Testaments, nach der deutschen Uebersetzung D. Martin Luthers, mit jedes Capitels kurtzen Summarien, auch beygefugten vielen und richtigen Parallelen; nebst dem gewöhnlichen Anhang des dritten und vierten Buchs Esra und des dritten Buchs der Maccabäer* (Germantown, 1743). (Evans 5127, and 5128.)
[15] Isaiah Thomas, *The History of Printing in America, with a Biography of Printers and an Account of Newspapers,* ed. Marcus A. McCorison (Barre, Mass., 1970), pp. 407-8; Hocker, 'Sower Printing House,' pp. 37-44.
[16] Hocker, 'Sower Printing House,' pp. 45-57. The annual almanac and the newspaper are not counted. Sower advertised English books with the argument that they were especially good for 'those who want to learn the English language but do not wish to read vain things.' Advertisement for John Joachim Zubly, *The Real Christian's Hope* (1756), in *Pennsylvanische Berichte,* Jan. 8, 1757.
[17] See Mary Ann Yodelis, 'Boston's Second Major Paper War: Economics, Politics,

Even before he printed the Bible, Sower started a newspaper. On August 20, 1739, the first issue of the quarterly *Der Hoch-Deutsch Pennsylvanische Geschichts-Schreiber* appeared. It became a monthly in 1741, a biweekly in 1756, and finally a weekly in 1775.[18] The subtitle from 1745 to 1776 did contain the word 'Kirchen-Reich,' but clearly in a subordinate place: *Collection of Credible News, from the Realm of Nature and the Churches; and also Useful Knowledge for the Common Good.* 'Nature' came first, 'churches' second; and the reference to 'the common good' and 'useful knowledge' announced this-worldly, Franklinian themes rather than other-worldly ones. Sower also asserted his critical editorship from the beginning. In the advertisement of the newspaper in 1739 he announced a 'collection of useful and notable stories and events, partly from the realm of nature (for example, what we learn of wars and the threat of wars in Europe and other parts of the world insofar as we receive reliable news) and well-founded news from the realm of church life, as much as one considers useful.'[19] He alone, and not the politicians or preachers, was to judge credibility and the 'useful' amount of church news. Nor did he hesitate to express his opinion on secular matters by selection of the news and by direct comment. He spoke out against slavery, although he accepted advertisements for runaway slaves, and he took sides in favor of the Indians, in whose behavior he recognized more brotherly love than in that of many

---

and the Theory and Practice of Political Expression in the Press, 1763–1775,' Ph.D. diss., University of Wisconsin, 1971.

[18] The title was changed in 1746 to *Pennsylvanische Berichte*, and in 1763 to *Die Germantowner Zeitung*. The succession of the titles and present-day archival holdings are listed in Karl J. R. Arndt and May E. Olson, comps., *German-American Newspapers and Periodicals, 1732–1955* (Heidelberg, 1961) pp. 523–24. The data given there need to be corrected as follows: the third title, *Pennsylvanische Berichte, oder Sammlung Wichtiger Nachrichten aus dem Natur- und Kirchenreich* was used from Jan. 1746 through 1763. The fourth title, *Die Germantowner Zeitung, Oder Sammlung Wahrscheinlicher Nachrichten aus dem Natur- und Kirchen-Reich* is used from no. 301, Dec. 15, 1763, on. The sixth title, *Die Germantowner Zeitung*, is used from no. 634, Jan. 3, 1776, on. No. 633, Dec. 28, 1775, under the title *Germantowner Wochen-Blat*, can be found in the Historical Society of Pennsylvania. In order to save letters, Sower often did not use double consonants in words like *wenn*, *denn* and *pennsylvanisch*. Since this usage can cause confusion, it is silently corrected throughout, including the title of the newspaper.

[19] *Der Hoch-Deutsch Americanische Calender auf das Jahr 1740.*

fellow Christians.[20] He gave detailed accounts of Pennsylvania politics and of the Seven Years' War.[21]

Sower also presented information about social conditions in England and in Germany and commented on them forcefully. For instance, when he received accounts of the severe winter of 1754–55, the coldest in Germany within living memory, he added, in brackets, an editorial remark to the news item: 'Poor Germany! How your poor are suffering. Only last year the cattle died in an epidemic, those who survived had to feed on straw from the roofs and died in the spring. The poor had no bread, but heavy feudal dues had to be paid. How many will wish they were in America.'[22]

It was no problem at all for Sower to present basic concepts of English constitutional law to his readers. When, for instance, he wanted to contribute to the public justification of Pennsylvania's new Militia Act of 1755, which had been attacked as too weak because it respected conscientious objection to military service, Sower printed a translation of the didactic dialogue that Franklin (who had drafted the bill) had written for this purpose and published in his own *Pennsylvania Gazette*.[23] In an introductory paragraph, Sower told his readers exactly where the text came from and that he supported the bill. The constitutional argument concerned the procedure of having three potential officers elected by the militia company, only one of whom would then be commissioned by the governor. Franklin's original explication of the issue reads:

[20] For example, in *Pennsylvanische Berichte*, June 24, 1758; also in *Der Hoch-Deutsch Americanische Calender* for the years 1742 and 1749. He also published Anthony Benezet, *Observations on Enslaving, Importing and Purchasing Negroes* (Germantown, 1759), (Evans 8298) and reports of conferences with Indian tribes, *Die Beschreibung von dem Friedensschluß* (1757) (Evans 7844) and *Der Inhalt von Verschiedenen Conferentzen* (1757), (Evans 7922).

[21] For example, Sower's account of the struggle between assembly and governor in 1755 about the printing of paper money and the taxation of the Penn family's immense estate. *Pennsylvanische Berichte*, Sept. 1, 1755. The issue of May 1, 1755 lists the warships in Portsmouth and contains detailed news about war preparations all over Europe.

[22] *Pennsylvanische Berichte*, May 1, 1755. Similar accounts of hunger and misery in Germany in the issues of Dec. 10, 1757, and the *Germantowner Zeitung* of Nov. 7, 1771.

[23] *Pennsylvanische Berichte*, Jan. 16, 1756. Text of the Militia Act in *Papers of Franklin*, ed. Labaree, 6: 266–73. Text of Franklin's original in the *Pennsylvania Gazette*, Dec. 18, 1755, and in *Papers of Franklin*, ed. Labaree, 6: 295–306. For a comment on social conditions in England in 1757 see *Pennsylvanische Berichte*, Nov. 12, 1757.

Y. But is it agreeable to the English Constitution?

X. Considered in this Light, I think it is; British Subjects, by removing into America, cultivating a Wilderness, extending the Dominion, and increasing the Wealth, Commerce and Power of their Mother Country, at the Hazard of their Lives and Fortunes, ought not, and in Fact do not thereby lose their native Rights. There is a Power in the Crown to grant a Continuance of those Rights to such Subjects, in any Part of the World, and to their Posterity born in such a new Country; and for the farther Encouragement and Reward of such Merit, to grant *additional* Liberties and Privileges, not used in England, but suited to the different Circumstances of different Colonies.

Sower translated:

Einwurff. Kommts aber auch mit der Engl. Verfassung überein? Antw. ja! dann die Brittanische Unterthanen, so sich in diesen Americanischen Welt-Theil nieder gelassen, verliehren ihr emfangenes englisches Recht alhier nicht, die Crone von Engelland mag solchen und den Eingebohrnen Nachkommen alhier nicht nur dasselbe Recht, sondern auch (um das Land noch mehr in Aufnahm zu bringen), noch einige Zugabs-Freyheiten vergönnen, welche eben nicht in Engelland üblich sind, nach den verschiedenen Umständen dieser oder einer jeden Colonie, wie es mit ihrer Verfassung am besten überein kommt.

Constitutional guarantees and legislative acts were to be clearly differentiated: no militia law, Franklin argued, could force the Quakers into military service because 'they are exempted by the Charter and fundamental Laws of the Province.' Sower translated 'dann sie sind durch den Freyheits-Brief [Charter] und durch die Grund-Gesetze dieser Provintz davon ausgenommen und frey gesprochen.' Sower's translation is not elegant, but it is exact, clear, and forceful; his style reminds one of the coarse woodcut he used on the cover of the almanac. Rendering political concepts presented no special difficulty: 'constitution' is 'Verfassung'; 'charter' is 'Freyheits-Brief'; 'liberties' are 'Freyheiten.' The meaning of 'Zugabs-Freyheiten' ('additional liberties'), possibly a Sower coinage, is quite clear at first sight. 'Rights' are 'Rechte' and 'fundamental laws' are 'Grund-Gesetze.' (Two hundred years later the West German constitution was officially called 'Grundgesetz.') Why, after all, should the basics of British constitutional law be incomprehensible to speakers of German? Europe's *anciens régimes* differed but they were not so different as to be mutually inexplicable in the vernacular. The struggle to guard subjects' rights was a common feature, and conscientious objection was an issue well known across the continent. Sower was publishing a German-language newspaper in a British colony for the very reason that he and many others had been unwilling to live their lives without the enjoyment of certain rights. Pennsylvania's lime soil was not the only reason that he and his readers were where they were.

When Sower died in 1758, a well-established enterprise passed to the hands of his only son, Christopher Sower, Jr. (1721–1784), who was then thirty-seven years old and had spent all his adult life in the shadow of his father. The binding of the books had been his responsibility, and because he wrote English he had also been in charge of the English-language publications. *The Pennsylvania Town and Country-Man's Almanack*, published from 1755 on, bore his imprint. In contrast to his father, he had joined the Dunker congregation at Germantown and now was one of their bishops. Faithfully, and successfully, he continued for twenty years the business his father had built.[24] But the founder's critical spirit was gone. The second Sower divided his energies between pursuing the callings of a printer and a pastor. As an active and beloved Dunker bishop, he viewed the concerns of the larger society with more detachment and less concern than his Separatist father. It may at least partly have been in reaction to this attitude, which included strict pacifism, that his sons Christopher (1754–1799) and Peter (1759–1785) would become active Tory publicists.

Unsuccessful Competitors

For all the critical reaction the elder Sower provoked, it was not until 1762 that a serious competitor was able to establish himself. In 1743, and for three or four years thereafter, a second German weekly was published in Philadelphia by Joseph Crellius, a German recently come from South Carolina.[25] A third attempt, in 1748, by Gotthard Armbruster failed in 1749.[26] Franklin tried a second time to enter the field and bought Arm-

[24] On the second Sower see Thomas, *History of Printing*, pp. 408–17; Hocker, 'Sower Printing House,' pp. 66–110; and Donald F. Durnbaugh, ed., *The Brethren in Colonial America: A Source Book* (Elgin, Ill., 1967), pp. 377–405.

[25] *Das Hoch-Deutsche Pennsylvanische Journal.* No issues have been located, Arndt and Olson, *German-American Newspapers*, p. 560. On Crellius see the editorial note in *Papers of Franklin*, ed. Labaree, 4: 77, n. 2 and Thomas, *History of Printing*, pp. 379, 442.

[26] *Die Zeitung.* No issue has been located. On Gotthard and Anton Armbruster, natives of Mannheim, who had come to the colonies in 1743, see Thomas, *History of Printing*, pp. 380–84, and the editorial note in *Papers of Franklin*, ed. Labaree, 5: 421, n.4.

bruster's equipment. He placed Johann Böhm, a recently arrived copperplate printer, in charge of the operation.[27] When Böhm died in 1751, Franklin tried something new and put out the first bilingual newspaper in North America, the biweekly *Die Hoch-Teutsche und Englische Zeitung/ The High-Dutch and English Gazette.* The English and the German texts were arranged in parallel columns adapted to the 'Convenience of such as incline to learn *either.*' After thirteen issues, in 1752, Franklin broke off the experiment and referred his subscribers to another new bilingual biweekly just begun, with his support, at Lancaster.[28] He had, it was later explained, 'at great expense set up another German Press, in order to rescue the Germans out of Sauer's Hands,' but the rescue operation failed 'for Want of a German Printer with sufficient Skill and Correspondence, and a proper Interest made to support Mr. Franklin's undertaking.'[29]

Whatever his losses, Franklin continued his attempts to break Sower's monopoly, not merely for profit but also for political reasons. Franklin must have believed in the influence of the press on the behavior of at least a sizeable segment of the German colonists from the 1740s on, and, together with other critics of the proprietary Quaker party, he disapproved of Sower's Quaker-oriented, pro-proprietary point of view. He set up two former journeymen printers of his, Samuel Holland and Henry Miller, with a press and German type to start *Die Lancastersche Zeitung/ The Lancaster Gazette.* Publication, however, ceased in 1753.[30] Of Holland nothing more is known; Miller was to become the younger Sower's great rival in the 1760s and '70s.

In 1754, Franklin tried a third and last time to counter Sower's influence by lending his support to the Society for the Relief and Instruction of Poor Germans, the first Americanization society in the history of American immigration. But the society's biweekly, *Philadelphische Zeitung,*

[27] *Philadelphier Teutsche Fama.* No issue has been located. Böhm was probably the 'Behm' mentioned in Thomas, *History of Printing,* p. 443. *Papers of Franklin,* ed. Labaree, 4: 259.

[28] Holdings of *Die Hoch Teutsche und Englische Zeitung* listed in Arndt and Olson, *German-American Newspapers,* pp. 560–61; 'Notice to Subscribers' announcing the demise in *Papers of Franklin,* ed. Labaree, 4: 259–60; editorial notes in ibid., 5: 259–60.

[29] Henry Melchior Mühlenberg to Franklin, Aug. 3, 1754, as abstracted in the minutes of the trustees of the Society for the Relief and Instruction of Poor Germans on Aug. 10, 1754, *Papers of Franklin,* ed., Labaree, 5: 419.

[30] Holdings in Arndt and Olson, *German-American Newspapers,* p. 540. *Papers of Franklin,* ed. Labaree, 4: 260, 506–8; 5: 260 n. 3.

printed by Anthony Armbruster, lasted only from 1755 to 1757. According to one estimate, it never had more than 400 subscribers.[31]

Henry Miller

On January 18, 1762, a new German weekly made its appearance in Philadelphia: *Der Wöchentliche Philadelphische Staatsbote*.[32] It was to be published continuously until 1779 and to become the herald of the Revolution for the Germans. It assumed the active role of the opinion-maker which, after the Stamp Act crisis, the younger Sower abdicated in favor of the function of the passive observer and chronicler. In that sense its editor and printer, Henry Miller (1702–1782), fulfilled a function in the 1760s and '70s that the elder Sower had performed in the '40s and '50s.

Miller was a man of principles without strong regional loyalties. Before he settled in Philadelphia in 1760 at the age of fifty-eight, his extremely mobile life as a journeyman printer had taken him all over Europe. He had been born in 1702 in Rhoden, a small town in the principality of Waldeck near Kassel, where he spent the first twelve years of his life.[33]

[31] On the society and its anglicization program, see Whitfield J. Bell, Jr., 'Benjamin Franklin and the German Charity Schools,' *Proceedings of the American Philosophical Society*, 99 (1955): 381–87; Dietmar Rothermund, 'German Problem in Colonial Pennsylvania,' pp. 11–16; and Lawrence A. Cremin, *American Education: The Colonial Experience, 1607–1783* (New York, 1970), pp. 261–63. On their newspaper see *Papers of Franklin*, ed. Labaree, 5: 418–21 and editorial note pp. 421–22 n. 4, and Arndt and Olson, *German-American Newspapers*, p. 579.

[32] In 1768 the title was changed to *Der Wöchentliche Pennsylvanische Staatsbote*, and in 1775 to *Henrich Millers Pennsylvanischer Staatsbote*. Holdings and full titles in Arndt and Olson, *German-American Newspapers*, pp. 567–68. Many more issues of Miller's newspaper than of the Sowers's have survived. It is available on microcards published by Readex Microprint Corporation and the American Antiquarian Society. Little is known about *Die Pennsylvanische Fama*, also started in 1762. It was edited by Anthony Armbruster, probably for 2 years. No issues have been located. See Arndt and Olson, *German-American Newspapers*, p. 567.

[33] He was baptized Johann Heinrich Möller, but when addressing English readers he used the shortened and anglicized version of his name, Henry Miller, which usage I follow. In the masthead of the *Staatsbote* he is Henrich Miller. The following biographical information is derived from the account of Miller's life in the Moravian congregation's Diarium, vol. 33 for the years 1780–82, entry of Mar. 30, 1782, Moravian Library, Bethlehem, Pa., reprinted in Charles Frederick Dapp, 'Johann Heinrich Miller,' *German-American Annals* 14 (1916): 128–38. The first part of it copies an account written by Miller himself. The Diarium gives 'Rheden im Waldeckischen' as his place of birth and the *Dictionary of American Biography* repeats this. The spelling should, however, be 'Rhoden.' The extant records of the Protestant church of Rhoden, today part of Diemelstadt, show that on Nov. 19, 1690, journeyman mason Hen-

He was raised a Lutheran. His Swiss father, a stonemason, took the family back to his hometown, Altstätten near Zürich, in 1715, and young Miller served a five-year apprenticeship in Basel at Johann Ludwig Brandmüller's printing shop. He repeatedly considered crossing the Atlantic, not as an emigrant with the intention to settle but as a wandering journeyman printer. After a year in London, he arrived in New York in 1741; a week later he was in Philadelphia, and Franklin immediately hired the experienced hand.

During the crossing Miller had been in the company of Moravians, including Count Zinzendorf himself, and in the following year he formally accepted their faith. In 1742 he returned to Europe to take on the task of establishing a printing shop at the Moravian center at The Hague. In 1747 he again went to London, taking jobs in several towns in England, Scotland, and Ireland, until in 1751 he once more joined a group of Moravian emigrants on their way to Pennsylvania. He did not stay to work for them at Bethlehem, but went to Philadelphia and then moved on to Lancaster, to publish the *Lancastersche Zeitung*. But in 1754 Miller once more returned to Europe probably with the intention of acquiring a press for his own shop; he did not want to be one of Franklin's clients for the rest of his life, a fate Armbruster was unable to escape. In 1756 he was hired to publish a semiweekly German newspaper for the 14,000 Hanoverian and Hessian troops encamped in England and awaiting orders for their part in the war against France.[34] By 1758, he had acquired a complete printing outfit for English and German and was running his own printing office in London. He kept in contact with Franklin, and in 1758 Franklin knew of Miller's intention to establish himself in Philadelphia as soon as the war was over and he could safely cross the Atlantic with his equipment.[35] Given his longtime concern with countering the Sowers' influence, we may assume that Franklin expected this addition to the Philadelphia printing trade to be in his interest.

---

rich Möller from Altstätten, Switzerland, was married to Anna Maria Faust, and that on Mar. 12, 1702, their son Johann Henrich was baptized. I thank Pastor C. Sixt for this information.

[34] Not mentioned in the Diarium but in Miller's farewell to his readers, *Staatsbote*, May 26, 1779. There he also says that for almost 50 years he has had 'to do with newspapers, first in Switzerland and Germany.' This vague expression could include any activity from setting type to editing.

[35] Benjamin Franklin to David Hall, June 10, 1758, *Papers of Franklin*, ed. Labaree, 8: 99.

In September 1760 Miller landed in Philadelphia for the third and last time. That his worldly concerns in the past decade had led him away from the Moravian brotherhood is demonstrated by the tenacious efforts of former brothers to win him back, which were successful only in 1773.[36]

Miller knew that the younger Sower, as a printer and journalist, was of lesser calibre than his father, and he did not hesitate to ridicule in public Sower's fear of the new competitor. When the *Staatsbote* was only a few months old, Miller printed a fable about an old eagle who had come to Pennsylvania and caused a young partridge, who had also been hatched in Germany, to fear that he would lose food and some of the feathers he was collecting to further soften the 'wonderful nest which he had inherited from his father, who was of a better sort.'[37] In fairness to the younger Sower, it should be said that the eagle's success derived in part from changes in the German-speaking population. A large number of recent immigrants were no longer sectarians but Lutheran, Reformed, or Moravian, who, given a choice, naturally subscribed to the newspaper whose editor was not as closely associated with a rival, sectarian religious group as was a Dunker bishop.[38]

By 1763, the printing of German texts had become a regular branch of the colonial publishing trade. Sower in Germantown and Miller and Armbruster in Philadelphia had three shops specializing in German printing. Printing in Dutch was negligible, the annual production in New York being limited to an almanac and an occasional official broadside, and French printing was not to start until the Continental Congress began addressing the inhabitants of Quebec;[39] English and Ger-

[36] 'Inhalt eines Briefes,' *Staatsbote*, Jan. 31, 1775; the anonymous letter to the editor identifies Miller with 'the damned Moravian sect.'

[37] 'Der Adler und das Rebhuhn,' *Staatsbote*, Aug. 16, 1762, Beylage.

[38] James Owen Knauss, 'Social Conditions among the Pennsylvania Germans in the Eighteenth Century, as Revealed in German Newspapers Published in America,' *Proceedings and Addresses of the Pennsylvania German Society* 29 (1922): 11.

[39] The index of Charles Evans's *American Bibliography* enumerates foreign-language publications. Examples of Dutch printing in the 1760s and 1770s are Evans 10029, an almanac continued through the 1760s, and 15470, an address of 1777 by the Provincial Congress of New York to the inhabitants. Cf. Hendrick Edelman, *Dutch-American Bibliography, 1693–1794: A Descriptive Catalogue of Dutch-language Books, Pamphlets and Almanacs Printed in America* (Nieuwkoop, 1974). Early French publications on the territory of the future United States are Evans 10032, 12421, 13740, and 14029. The first French newspaper was the army journal *Gazette française*, published in Newport, 'De l'imprimerie royale de l'escadre.' Bristol's supplement to Evans reports 8 numbers published between Nov. 17, 1780 and Jan. 2, 1781 (Evans 44275). The first civilian

man thus were, for all practical purposes, the only two languages in which inhabitants of the thirteen colonies carried on public debate in the decades before independence.

Business Matters

The number of German readers in the 1760s and '70s remains a question for speculation. We can do little better than follow contemporary estimates which say that Pennsylvania's inhabitants were almost equally divided between those of English, German, and Scotch-Irish descent. For 1760 that would mean a German population of about 60,000. Outside Pennsylvania, Germans had concentrated in the Mohawk and Schoharie regions of New York and in the Shenandoah Valley. A recent mapping of German settlements in 1775 shows an almost uninterrupted series of clusters of settlements along the colonial hinterland from New York to South Carolina. In all colonies together, the Germans in 1775 numbered over 200,000 persons—a substantial minority comprising about ten percent of the total population.[40]

Literacy

How many of the Germans could read is not known. Many were farmers with little education. But a large number of them were artisans for whom reading was a basic skill, and most of them shared a religious culture centered around the individual's confrontation with texts. Literacy must, therefore, have been their first educational goal.[41] The absence of lamentation about illiteracy in the German newspapers indicates that it was no public issue. When Christopher Sower announced the publication of his newspaper in 1739, he promised plain prose for everybody to

---

newspaper, the semiweekly *Courier de l'Amérique*, published in Philadelphia, did not appear until 1784. Clarence S. Brigham, *History and Bibliography of American Newspapers, 1690–1820*, 2 vols. (Worcester, Mass., 1947), 2: 898.

[40] Lester J. Cappon, ed., *Atlas of Early American History: The Revolutionary Era, 1760–1790* (Princeton, 1976), pp. 24, 98. By 1770 Pennsylvania's population had grown to 240,000, in 1780 to 327,000. In 1790 the German element of Pennsylvania is estimated to have been 33 percent, and the German percentage of the total future territory of the United States at 8.7 percent. U.S. Bureau of the Census, *Historical Statistics of the United States, Colonial Times to 1970* (Washington, 1976), part 2, p. 1168, series Z 11.

[41] Herbert Schöffler, *Protestantismus und Literatur: Neue Wege zur englischen Literatur des 18. Jahrhunderts* (Leipzig, 1922; repr. Göttingen, 1958). See also Rolf Engelsing, *Analphabetentum und Lektüre: Zur Sozialgeschichte des Lesens in Deutschland zwischen feudaler und industrieller Gesellschaft* (Stuttgart, 1973).

understand. He rejoiced in the fact that the majority of his audience were 'Acker- und Handwercks-Leute' and that there were few 'Gelehrte'; he obviously took it for granted that farmers and artisans could read. And when he published his successful English textbook for Germans (it was published in four editions from 1751 to 1792), he claimed in the subtitle that it was devised especially for 'Land- und Handwercks-Leute.'[42] Similarly, Henry Miller's essay of 1774 on the usefulness of newspapers for everybody did not in any way mention illiteracy as a problem but silently assumed that every farmer and artisan knew how to read.[43] The finding that between sixty and seventy-five percent of the adult male Germans in Pennsylvania could read in the middle of the eighteenth century thus seems quite plausible.[44]

Circulation

Compared to the circulation of the English-language newspapers, the two successful German papers were extraordinarily successful. The average circulation of New England newspapers around 1750 has been estimated at 600 copies, and Hall's *Pennsylvania Gazette*, possibly the largest English-language newspaper on the continent, is thought to have been circulated in editions of 2,500 copies in the early 1760s and over 3,000 in the latter half of the decade.[45] Sower in 1751, at the end of the period of his virtual monopoly, spoke of his readership as a group of 4,000 people. His political opponents in 1754 alleged that his paper was 'universally

[42] *Der Hoch-Deutsch Americanische Calender auf das Jahr 1740* (Germantown, 1739), no pagination. *Eine nützliche Anweisung oder Beyhülfe vor die Teutschen um Englisch zu lernen: Wie es vor Neu-Ankommende und andere im Land gebohrne Land- und Handwercks-Leute, welche der englischen Sprache erfahrene und geübte Schulmeister und Preceptores ermangelen, vor das bequemste erachtet worden; mit ihrer gewöhnlichen Arbeit und Werkzeug erläutert. Nebst einer Grammatic. Vor diejenigen, welche in andern Sprachen und deren Fundamenten erfahren sind* (Germantown, 1751) (Evans 6777). A first edition, published the previous year, did not bear the descriptive subtitle; see Evans 6455. Carl Wittke, *The German-Language Press* (Lexington, Ky., 1957), p. 11, says that the rate of illiteracy was 'high,' but he cites no evidence.

[43] *Staatsbote*, May 31, 1774. Complete text in Appendix B, below.

[44] Alan Tully, 'Literacy Levels and Educational Development in Rural Pennsylvania, 1729–1775,' *Pennsylvania History* 39 (1972): 301–12.

[45] Stephen Botein, ' "Meer Mechanics" and an Open Press: the Business and Political Strategies of Colonial American Printers,' *Perspectives in American History* 9 (1975): 148–49. Lester J. Cappon, ed., *The Atlas of Early American History: The Revolutionary Era, 1760–1790* (Princeton, 1976), p. 35, considers William Bradford's *Pennsylvania Journal* as probably the largest with its circulation of 2,300 copies in 1775.

read by the Germans' all over Pennsylvania and in the neighboring colonies.[46] After the Franklin-Mühlenberg group had been helping Armbruster put out the rival *Philadelphische Zeitung* for two years, Sower still claimed a circulation of 2,600. Fully half of the subscribers, he said in August 1757, still owed him the year's subscription.[47]

One reason for the high circulation figures was the fact that the German press was not yet as regionalized as it became after the Revolution. Sower and Miller aimed at continental distribution, and delivery, therefore, was a main problem for them.[48] The German printers built up a network of agents who accepted subscriptions and advertisements, and acted as distributors. Storekeepers and innkeepers, in addition to certain artisans, and sometimes even clergymen, served as agents. In 1763, the most distant agents in Miller's distribution system were in Halifax, Nova Scotia; Ebenezer, Georgia; and Charleston, South Carolina. In Maryland, he had an agent at Fredericktown; in New Jersey at Pilesgrove, Amwell, New Germantown (now Oldwick), and Paulins Kill; and in New York, in addition to the city, at Albany, Conyschocheny (Canajoharie?) and Stone Arabia. His Pennsylvania agents were located in Ger-

---

[46] *Pennsylvanische Berichte*, Nov. 1, 1751. The figure of 4,000 has been misinterpreted as referring to the number of subscriptions. Sower was reacting to an attack on him 'in der letzten Phil. Zeitung' and said: 'Dieses und Voriges . . . zu beantworten ist in der Zeitung kein Platz, zumal dabey 4000 Menschen nicht wissen was etwa in 150 Stücken zu lesen war.' The newspaper referred to was probably Franklin's *Hoch Deutsche und Englische Zeitung*, of which no issue from Oct. 1751 has been located. Mühlenberg to Franklin, Aug. 3, 1754, *Papers of Franklin*, ed. Labaree, 5: 419.

[47] *Pennsylvanische Berichte*, Aug. 20, 1757. Sower's words in the admonition to the subscribers are: 'Die Hälffte von 2600 hat noch niemals etwas bezahlt.' The 'niemals' is ambiguous. In modern German it would imply that they also had not paid in previous years. If that is what Sower meant, he, in effect, had 1,300 genuine subscribers in 1757 but chose to continue to accommodate 1,300 more free of charge. We do not have conclusive figures on the circulation of Miller's newspaper. In the issue of Nov. 5, 1776, however, Miller announced a new subscription policy. He now required the sum for the whole year paid in advance, and he threatened to have the outstanding debts collected. 'Es ist besser,' he added, '1000 Zeitungen für richtige Bezahler zu drucken als 2000 für solche denen die Bezahlung nicht einfällt.' This may be read to mean that at the time Miller was printing 2,000 copies but was getting paid for only 1,000. At a time of increasing shortage of paper the gratis distribution of 1,000 copies would seem to have overtaxed even Henry Miller's patriotism. His circulation in 1776 was probably closer to 1,000 than to 2,000.

[48] On the problems with private delivery see *Pennsylvanische Berichte*, Dec. 11, 1756, and *Germantowner Zeitung*, Jan. 3, 1776. In the *Staatsbote* of Aug. 27, 1764, Miller suggested that subscribers make private arrangements with post riders since newspapers were not yet officially accepted as mail.

mantown, Lancaster, and Yorktown, and all over Philadelphia County (New Hanover, Douglas, New Providence, Chestnut Hill, Guschehoppen, Skippack, Hatfield, Bernhill), in Berks County (Tulpehocken, Reading, Heidelberg, Maxatawny), and in Northampton County (Easton, Macungie, Sackonum [Saucon?], Arndt's Mill, Williams, Bethlehem, and Nazareth).[49]

Sower, in the same year of 1763, seems to have been less enterprising. He had agents only in Philadelphia, Lancaster, Yorktown, Reading, and Fredericktown in Maryland, and in the city of New York.[50] The ideal of intercolonial circulation was clearly expressed by the Reverend Mr. Mühlenberg when, in 1754, he offered his services to the Society for Relief and Instruction of Poor Germans to oversee publication of a German newspaper. As a special qualification for this task he mentioned his 'large Correspondence with pious German Ministers and Congregations in Pennsylvania, New York, New England, Jersey, Maryland, Virginia, Carolina and Georgia.'[51]

Regionalization of the German-language press began only after the Revolution, when instead of employing agents, printers set up shop at Fredericktown, Maryland (1785),[52] Baltimore (1786),[53] Lancaster (1787),[54] Reading (1789),[55] Winchester, Virginia (1789),[56] Chestnut-

---

[49] *Staatsbote*, May 9, 1763. The spelling of place names follows that in Cappon, ed., *Atlas of Early American History*.

[50] *Pennsylvanische Berichte*, Dec. 15, 1763.

[51] Mühlenberg to Franklin, Aug. 3, 1754, *Papers of Franklin*, ed. Labaree, 5: 420. The ideal distribution network seems to have been achieved by John Dunlap for his German almanac. He advertised that it could be bought 'bey allen Krämern' (at all general stores) in Pennsylvania, New-Jersey, Maryland, and Virginia. *Die Pennsylvanische Gazette*, Feb. 3, 1779.

[52] *Bärtgis' Maryländische Zeitung*, a biweekly published by Matthias Bärtgis from 1785 to 1789. In 1793 Bärtgis started anew with *Der General Staats-Bothe*. Arndt and Olson, *German-American Newspapers*, p. 199.

[53] Weekly, title unknown, published by Henry Dulheuer. From 1795 to 1798 Samuel Sower published *Der Neue Unpartheyische Baltimore Bothe* in the city. Arndt and Olson, *German-American Newspapers*, pp. 185, 195.

[54] *Neue Unpartheyische Lancäster Zeitung*, a weekly published from 1787 to 1797 by Johann Albrecht, Jacob Lahn, and Anthony Stiemer. In 1798 Albrecht and Lahn continued under the title *Der Deutsche Porcupein*. In the same year their competitor became *Des Landmanns Wochenblatt*, published by William Hamilton and Conrad Wortmann, which in 1799 was followed by *Das Lancaster Wochenblatt* under the same management and, after a few months, *Der Lancaster Correspondent*, published by Christian Jacob Hütter. Arndt and Olson, *German-American Newspapers*, pp. 535–39.

[55] *Neue Unpartheyische Readinger Zeitung*, a weekly published from 1789 to 1802 by

hill, Pennsylvania (1790),[57] Easton, Pennsylvania (1793),[58] Hagerstown, Maryland (1795),[59] York, Pennsylvania (1796),[60] Hanover, Pennsylvania (1797),[61] and Harrisburg, Pennsylvania (1799).[62] The metropolis itself also saw a multiplication of German weeklies and semiweeklies from the 1780s on.[63]

Price

The price of the newspapers was low enough to make them available to households with a middle-class income. Annual subscriptions were the rule; no price for individual issues was given. The Sowers charged three shillings for their biweekly of four pages and adhered to this rate even when they published weekly in 1775. Miller, who put out his four pages every week from the beginning, charged six shillings per year and increased the price to eight shillings in 1777 and to three dollars in 1779.

Benjamin Johnson, Thomas Barton, Gottlob Jungmann, Johann Gruber, and Karl Brückmann. A second weekly, *Der Unpartheyische Reading Adler*, was started in 1797 by Jacob Schneider. It continued under various titles until 1913. Arndt and Olson, *German-American Newspapers*, pp. 592–93, 587–88.

[56] *Virginische Zeitung*, published also by Matthias Bärtgis for the Germans in the Shenandoah Valley, for how long is not known. Arndt and Olson, *German-American Newspapers*, pp. 641–42.

[57] *Die Chestnuthiller Wochenschrift*, a weekly published by Samuel Sower from 1790 to 1794. Arndt and Olson, *German-American Newspapers*, p. 514.

[58] *Neuer Unpartheyischer Eastoner Bothe und Northamptoner Kundschafter*, a weekly published by Jacob Weygandt and his son from 1793 to 1805. Arndt and Olson, *German-American Newspapers*, p. 517.

[59] *Die Westliche Correspondenz und Hägerstauner Wochenschrift*, a weekly published by Johann Gruber and Daniel May until 1830. Arndt and Olson, *German-American Newspapers*, p. 201.

[60] *Die Unpartheyische York Gazette*, a weekly published by Salomon Mayer and Christian Schlichting until 1804. The competing *Der Volks-Berichter* was published by Andreas Billmeyer from 1799 to 1803. Arndt and Olson, *German-American Newspapers*, p. 605.

[61] *Die Pennsylvanische Wochenschrift*, published by William Daniel Lepper and Samuel Stettinius until 1802. Arndt and Olson, *German-American Newspapers*, p. 527.

[62] *Unpartheyische Härrisburg Morgenröthe Zeitung*, a weekly started by Benjamin Mayer and Conrad Fahnestock and continued until 1840. Arndt and Olson, *German-American Newspapers*, p. 530.

[63] *Die Pennsylvanische Gazette* (1779), *Gemeinnützige Philadelphische Correspondenz* (1781–90), *Die Germantauner Zeitung* (1785–99), *Der General-Postbothe an die Deutsche Nation in America* (1790), *Neue Philadelphische Correspondenz* (1790–1812), *Das Philadelphische Wochenblatt* (1794), *Die Pensylvanische Correspondenz* (1797–1800). Publication data and holdings listed in Arndt and Olson, *German-American Newspapers*, pp. 559–77.

What did six shillings mean? In wholesale prices of 1770 it meant eighteen pounds of pork, or thirty-three pounds of rice, or forty pounds of medium quality flour, or fifty pounds of ship bread, or a bushel of wheat.[64] Since the average daily wage for a laborer was about two shillings, it may also be considered as the wages for three days.[65] In other words, in the 1760s a laborer had the choice of working a little over a day for a pound of Scottish snuff or a year's issues of Sower's newspaper; or he might save the wages of eleven days for a Sower Bible.[66] Since Sower and Miller were aiming at mass circulation, it would have been self-defeating to price themselves out of the market with a price they knew only a few wealthy merchants could afford to pay.

Advertising

In the 1740s Sower had inserted notices from subscribers gratis. But to counterbalance the tardiness of subscription payments, he took on advertising as a cash business. In 1755 Sower asked five shillings for a 'private advertisement, not too large.'[67] Advertisements appealed to the immigrants' special interests without regard to ethnic barriers. There were long lists of wares 'recently arrived from Germany'; ranging from Ulm scythes to Marburg songbooks; there also was the occasional job opening specifically for a German, and there was the advertisement for a German night school, and the advertisement of a voyager back to Germany who took parcels and letters for a fee.[68] But a quantitative analysis would probably confirm that at least as many English-speaking merchants as German retailers advertised in Sower's and Miller's newspapers. The numerous real estate advertisements from sellers as well as buyers were more concerned with quality of soil and certainty of title than with the cultural identity of the potential partners in business.

The men who overcame the language barrier in advertisements as in

[64] Calculated from Ann Bezanson, *Prices and Inflation during the American Revolution: Pennsylvania, 1770–1790* (Philadelphia, 1951), p. 332.

[65] G. B. Warden, 'Inequality and Instability in Eighteenth-Century Boston: A Reappraisal,' *Journal of Interdisciplinary History* 6 (1976): 590 n. 9.

[66] In the *Staatsbote*, Jan. 25, 1762, 1 pound of Scottish snuff is advertised for 2 shillings and 6 pence.

[67] *Pennsylvanische Berichte*, May 1, 1755. Cash payment is required in *Germantowner Zeitung*, Dec. 15, 1763.

[68] *Staatsbote*, Mar. 22, and Aug. 9, 1762. The job is for a sawmiller. The nightschool is advertised in *Staatsbote*, June 14, 1762, a voyage in *Staatsbote*, April 12, 1762.

the rest of the contents of the newspaper were of course the editors, who also were the printers. They translated advertisements free of charge. From 1765 on, Miller ran as a permanent part of the German masthead the English sentence: 'All Advertisements of any Length to be inserted in this Paper, or printed single by Henry Miller, publisher hereof, are by him translated gratis.' The general effectiveness of advertising is indicated by the fact that the printers themselves advertised new books and pamphlets in their competitors' newspapers.[69]

Candidates for elective offices such as sheriff and representatives in the assembly also found it worthwhile to advertise their candidacy and formally solicit votes.[70] When the heat of a contest led from announcement to denunciation, separate election broadsides were printed. Thus John Morin Scott, candidate for the New York assembly in 1769, found it necessary to publicly refute the charge that he had called the Germans in the city of New York 'feuer braende.' He solicited their votes in behalf of a ticket that included two Livingstons and himself. His opponent, John Cruger, running together with two De Lanceys, was not slow in appealing 'to all High Germans in the City of New York' to defeat the Livingston party.[71]

The printers may have inserted announcements of public notices free of charge as a community service and as an added attraction of the newspaper. When, for instance, Sower received inquiries from Germany concerning the whereabouts of lost relatives or heirs, he put notices in his newspaper and asked the persons sought to come to the printing shop.[72] For letters from Germany that were sent in care of Sower and whose arrival he announced in the newspaper he charged his own rates, until in

[69] See the *Germantowner Zeitung* of Feb. 25, 1773, for an advertisement of Miller's publication of the votes of the Pennsylvania House of Representatives. Professional cooperation among printers in the advertising business as well as its trans-ethnic quality is illustrated by Miller's notice that he does not mind printing an advertisement that will also be carried by other newspapers, German or English. In such a case, he promised, he would get the manuscript to the other printers in time. *Staatsbote*, June 18, 1764.

[70] Examples in *Pennsylvanische Berichte*, Sept. 17, 1757, and *Staatsbote*, Aug. 15, 1763.

[71] The German broadsides are Evans 11455 and 11390. A third one is Evans 11389. For a programmatic election statement by Die Patriotische Gesellschaft, see *Staatsbote*, Aug. 25, 1772.

[72] *Germantowner Zeitung*, Dec. 15, 1763. Sower may, of course, also have been paid for this service from Germany.

1764 the postal service took over and forbade this branch of Sower's and Miller's businesses.[73]

Bookstore and Other Activities

Sower's and Miller's printing shops were no different from the others of the time in that they also sold other paper and household wares and books they had not printed themselves. The thirty-two page catalogue that Miller published in 1769 listed over 700 titles he had in stock, most of them imported from Germany.[74]

To enhance his economic independence, the younger Sower in 1771 or 1772 established his own papermill on the Schuylkill. He also began founding his own type and was even able to supply other printers.[75] An issue of *Geistliches Magazien* of 1772 proudly announced that it was 'Printed with the first type ever cast in America.'[76]

The Sower Fortune

By 1778, the Sower printing house had expanded from one to four presses. The enterprise, with its own papermill and ink-making and type-founding facilities, was the largest printing shop in the colonies.[77] Its success demonstrated more clearly than Miller's smaller operation the growing economic potential of the printing trade in the colonies. When in 1785 the third Christopher Sower submitted the family's losses to the loyalist claims commission in London he estimated the Sower fortune to have amounted to £3,173 worth in real estate, £6,433 in personal prop-

[73] Examples in *Pennsylvanische Berichte*, Dec. 26, 1756, Sept. 17, 1757. Miller's announcement that he was no longer allowed to have letters from Germany picked up at the printing office in *Staatsbote*, Aug. 27, 1764.

[74] *Catalogus von mehr als 700 meist Deutschen Büchern* (Philadelphia, 1769). This aspect of transatlantic cultural relations, or immigrant culture, has hardly been explored. Economic diversification, including bookselling, was no peculiarity of the German printers. See Peter J. Parker, 'The Philadelphia Printer: A Study of an Eighteenth-Century Businessman,' *Business History Review* 40 (1966): 24–46.

[75] Hocker, 'Sower Printing House,' pp. 84–86. The type was cast for Sower by Jacob Bay and Justus Fox.

[76] *Ein Geistliches Magazien* 2, no. 12 (1772), after the poem by Alexander Mack. The Americanness of the achievement has been modified with the observation: 'Though the type was cast in the colonies, this effort may be considered only partially American since the mold and matrices were imported.' Elizabeth Carroll Reilly, *A Dictionary of Colonial American Printers' Ornaments and Illustrations* (Worcester, Mass., 1975), p. xiv.

[77] Hocker, 'Sower Printing House,' p. 85.

erty, and £596 worth of unsold books and outstanding debts lost to the rebels.[78]

Whether it was mainly the printing business that had made the Sowers wealthy is difficult to determine. Good judgment in the Germantown real estate market may have been just as important to the family fortune.[79] But we know that profits from the 1763 edition of the Bible (consisting of 2,000 copies selling at twenty-one shillings per unbound copy) embarrassed Sower. To put his profit to appropriate use he began publishing *Ein Geistliches Magazien* in 1764, the first purely religious periodical in the colonies, which he distributed free of charge.[80] The acquisition of a fortune of £7,000 in two generations was an exceptional achievement among the immigrant artisans of the colonial period. An enterprising spirit, a market for the products of the printing press, and the ability to handle real estate as well as print had made possible the Sowers' unusual commercial success.

POLITICAL CONTENT OF THE GERMAN-LANGUAGE PRESS AT THE EVE OF THE REVOLUTION

By the end of the Seven Years' War, Sower's *Germantowner Zeitung* and Miller's *Staatsbote* were well-established newspapers, serving the needs of a substantial ethnic minority by publishing information and opinions about Europe, the British Empire, and Pennsylvania, and by providing a forum for public debate about secular as well as religious issues of concern to George III's German subjects in North America. The Revolutionary events of the following decade thus could easily be reported to readers of German from Nova Scotia to Georgia. The liberties of a Brit-

[78] 'American Loyalists: Transcript of the Manuscript Books and Papers of the Commission of Inquiry into the Losses and Services of the American Loyalists held . . . 1783–1790,' 49: 446–81, New York Public Library; cited here as computed in James O. Knauss, 'Christopher Saur the Third,' *Proceedings of the American Antiquarian Society* 41 (1931): 241–43. The listing of the property (though without values) is borne out by the second Sower's will of 1777. Dieter Cunz, ed., 'Two Christopher Sower Documents,' *Pennsylvania Magazine of History and Biography* 69 (1945): 60–66. The will was written in English and signed in the anglicized version of the name.

[79] Oswald Seidensticker, *Bilder aus der Deutsch-pennsylvanischen Geschichte*, 2d ed. (New York, 1886), p. 157.

[80] 5,000 copies are said to have been printed per issue; 65 issues were published at irregular intervals from 1764 to 1770. Hocker, 'Sower Printing House,' p. 74. Publication data of *Ein Geistliches Magazien* in Arndt and Olson, *German-American Newspapers*, p. 522.

ish subject were no new concept to them anymore; a good number of German immigrants had probably sacrificed more than many a Yankee to be able to enjoy them. By 1763 the instruments of their further acculturation to Anglo-American life included two politically active newspapers, at a time when no such institutions existed in Germany.

In the address to his readers on the first page of the first issue of the *Staatsbote* on January 18, 1762, Henry Miller tried to counter the obvious initial prejudice against him as an outsider. He addressed his readers as 'meine Landsleute' and declared it to be his particular interest to 'serve the Germans in this part of the world, so far removed from their fatherland.' He felt it necessary to explain that a newspaper could enhance 'not only the common good but also the glory of God' by extolling 'Christian as well as civil [*bürgerliche*] virtues.' He promised to be '*unpartheyisch*' and to avoid 'falsehood and irresponsible writing which contributes to disharmony and divisiveness.' A newspaper, he said, can contribute to God's glory in that 'it makes us understand the signs of the times and tell us of the Lord's judgments and punishments. It also strengthens our faith and confidence in God by considering events showing his goodness and mercy and the growth of his kingdom on earth.' The clear distinction between secular and church-related news also found expression in the full title: 'The Weekly Philadelphia State Messenger: With the Newest Foreign and Local Political ('einheimischpolitischen') News, including the Remarkable Events Occurring from Time to Time in the Church and the World of Learning.'[81]

Miller was aware of the special needs of the Germans as an immigrant group, but he did not publish an emigré gazette full of news about home or a newsletter to inform the various German groups in North America, from Georgia to New York, about each other's activities. He addressed his readers primarily as inhabitants of a British colony, very much as Franklin, Bradford, and the other editors of English-language newspapers addressed their readers. They all thought of their readers as subjects of the British crown whose daily lives, curiosity, and interests were determined by the fact that they lived in a colony in America.

The first issues of the *Staatsbote* in 1762 illustrate the point. They give a complete translation of George III's address to both houses of Parliament, the Lords' congratulatory address on the king's wedding and the

---

[81] *Staatsbote*, Jan. 18, 1762.

monarch's response, an address of the Commons to the king, an address of the English Quakers to the king, the king's declaration of war against Spain, and an episode from George III's coronation ceremony.[82] Information about Pennsylvania politics was equally prominent. The laws enacted by the previous session of the Assembly were listed on the front page. A new road bill was translated in full. The newly elected members of the Assembly were enumerated. Gov. John Penn's proclamation accompanying the king's proclamation of October 1763 that established the four new colonies of Quebec, East Florida, West Florida, and Grenada, and the western boundary line for white settlers completely filled a front page and a second page.[83]

In addition to translating official documents, Miller occasionally explained English political terms such as 'bill,' 'Whig,' and 'Tory' in footnotes, or in relative clauses added in brackets after the word, or in brief independent items. In a footnote to a news item containing the English word 'bill,' Miller explained concisely and correctly: 'In English lands a bill in this sense is the written form of a law made by a parliament or assembly, before it has been agreed to by his Royal Majesty in England, or by the Vice king ('Vicekönig') in Ireland, or by the respective governor in the colonies.'[84] In the news section headed 'London,' Miller reported: 'The obsolete names Whig and Tory have been resurrected and are being employed with the same bitterness as in the year 1680, when the struggle against the so-called court party was initiated, until both parties called each other by smear names.'[85] Christopher Sower, as we have seen, also translated and explained English political language to his readers.[86]

Miller tempered his general interest in information about British imperial government and its relationship to Pennsylvania, and other colo-

---

[82] *Staatsbote*, Jan. 18, Feb. 8 and 15, Mar. 8, and Apr. 5, 1762.

[83] *Staatsbote*, Mar. 1, 15, Oct. 25, 1762, Dec. 12, 1763.

[84] *Staatsbote*, Mar. 15, 1762: 'Eine Bill heißt in diesem Sinn in den Englischen Landen die schriftliche Verfassung eines Gesetzes, so von einem Parlament oder einer Landsversammlung gemacht worden, ehe es in England von Königlicher Majestät, in Irrland von dem Vicekönig, und in den Colonien von den resp. Herren Guvernörs durch deren Zustimmung bekräftiget wird.'

[85] *Staatsbote*, Mar. 28, 1763: 'Die veralteten namen Whig und Tory sind nun mit eben solcher bitterkeit wieder aufgelebt als im Jahr 1680, da die feindseligkeit der zu selbiger zeit sogenannten Hof-parthey entzündet wurde, bis beyde partheyen einander mit schimpfnamen belegten.'

[86] See text following n. 22, above.

nial events, with occasional appeals to ethnic identification, even in advertising.[87] Occasionally the editor, in the news columns, appealed to ethnic pride by printing a story involving Germans, such as the one that Algerian pirates had escaped from under the fifty cannons of a Portuguese man-of-war because the Portuguese crew had fled the main deck in terror while only a lieutenant, a German, stayed at his post. Miller commented: 'This report by the Portuguese captain is a dishonor to his nation and honors the Germans. No German born abroad of German parents and living abroad need be ashamed of his origins. The German people have never been inferior to any other in braveness or any other qualities.'[88]

Miller also shared the high regard of dissenting Protestants for Frederick the Great, of whom a popular biography and a portrait on handkerchiefs were being sold in Philadelphia.[89] Sower praised the Prussian king's enlightened toleration of religious variety and published a German translation of S. H. Dilworth's volume-length biography of Frederick II.[90] At the same time, Miller, like Sower, printed news items about famines and other miseries in Germany and England.[91]

As the conflicts over colonial self-government developed into a full-blown crisis, the two bilingual editors stood ready to report. As it turned out, one of them, Miller, took the part of the Whig activist, while Sower, from the summer of 1775 on, assumed the role of the passive neutral, the two probably representing fairly well the division of opinion among their readership.

The Peace of 1763

The peace settlements that ended the Seven Years' War were duly reported to German readers. Miller published the full text of the treaty of Paris in May 1763.[92] Sower welcomed the Proclamation Line (limiting western settlement at the Appalachians) with special approval because

[87] An anthology of sermons was advertised as designed to wake 'das Deutsche Volk in Pennsylvanien' from its spiritual slumber. *Staatsbote*, Jan. 25, 1762.

[88] *Staatsbote*, Mar. 22, 1762.

[89] Advertisement in *Staatsbote*, Jan. 25, 1762. Laudatory article on Frederick as 'Vater des Vaterlandes' in *Staatsbote*, June 21, 1762.

[90] W. H. Dilworth, *Das Leben und heroische Thaten des Königs von Preuszen* (Germantown, 1761).

[91] *Staatsbote*, June 4, 1764, June 28, 1762.

[92] *Staatsbote*, May 16 and 26, 1763.

it agreed with his own convictions about a paternalistic and protective Indian policy. In an editorial comment following the complete text of the proclamation, Sower hailed the crown's councillors who had not followed the aggressive course of Pennsylvania's Indian-haters, and added a critical remark about a structural deficiency in monarchical government. The court surrounding the king, he wrote, makes it difficult for the people to reach even a well-intentioned monarch's ear. Evil men who strive for personal gain conceal the truth from him so that 'even the best and most just of kings and princes know so little about the needs and distress of their subjects.'[93] The remoteness of the monarch, as compared to the immediate personal interest of a proprietor in his colony, was one of the standard arguments against the change from proprietary to royal government in Pennsylvania. Sower saw no reason to give up his opposition to that scheme only because of one agreeable proclamation from the throne.

The news about the peace treaties was mingled with forebodings of further changes in imperial policy that Miller from the beginning perceived as a threat to the autonomy the colonists had been able to assert within the empire. Thus, in June 1763 Miller presented without explanation or comment the brief notice from a London newspaper: 'It is reported that the plan to bring all our provinces in North America under one military government has been put aside.'[94] A month later he reported that letters had arrived from London that were said to prove Parliament's intention 'to take into consideration the constitution of the various governments in America.' The new 'form of government will rectify past and foreseeable future difficulties and bring the colonies into convenient concordance in all matters concerning the common good.'[95] In the same ominous tone Miller reported three months later that Gen. Jeffrey Amherst, who commanded 16,000 troops in Canada, was demanding three more regiments to secure his hold on Quebec. The result would be a standing army ('stehende Armee') and, Miller added, would contribute to making

---

[93] *Germantowner Zeitung*, Dec. 15, 1763.

[94] *Staatsbote*, June 6, 1763.

[95] *Staatsbote*, July 25, 1763. The final phrase of the last sentence reads, ' . . . sie verbinden, in allen aufs allgemeine beste abzielenden Sachen hübsch einträchtig zu sein.' 'Verbinden' is very vague as to the degree of force employed, 'hübsch' introduces a slight note of defiance, and 'einträchtig' may denote harmony and uniformity among the colonies or absence of disagreement with the mother country.

North America 'eventually the Fifth Monarchy.'[96] Miller disapproved of the continued presence in the colonies of military power; as soon as the war was over, a professional army was considered a burden and a threat to civil government. (Miller's approval of the Prussian king's policies obviously did not extend to his militarism.)

Wilkes

Trust in the British system of government, which had been celebrated by the enlightened in Europe for its regard for the civil rights of subjects, was weakened by Parliament's treatment of the notorious and popular John Wilkes, and Miller kept his readers informed of the whole episode. He published a complete translation of Wilkes's essay vehemently criticizing the Tory policies of Lord Bute, the ensuing charge of libel, and three articles from London newspapers critical of Wilkes.[97] Although Miller rejected Wilkes's writing as 'the howling of a devil' and as the expression of 'licentiousness, not liberty,' he seems to have disapproved of impending restrictions on the liberty of the printing press ('die freyheit der Buchdrucker-Presse') that the London newspapers were speaking of in the summer of 1764.[98]

The Pennsylvania Election of 1764

Although major issues of English politics occupied Sower and Miller in 1764, a controversy closer to home concerned them even more. The election campaign for seats in the Pennsylvania Assembly was accompanied by an unprecedented war of words, drew more Germans than ever before into the electoral process, split the Germans as a voting bloc, and led to the election of the first German to the Assembly. The issue was whether the colony would fare better if proprietary government were replaced by government directly under the crown. Since petitions for the change had already been sent to the king, the question at hand was whether to step up or to discontinue these efforts.[99] The proprietor, no

[96] *Staatsbote*, Oct. 31, 1763. The item is presented under the headline 'London, den 7 August.'

[97] *Staatsbote*, July 18, 1763, gives the complete text of no. 45 of the *North Briton* (published on Apr. 23, 1763). On Feb. 13, 1764, Miller referred to his publication of the text with the comment: 'No one will conclude from the publication that the editor is in sympathy with scribbling of this sort which only causes discord.'

[98] *Staatsbote*, July 2, 1764. See also Jan. 2, 1764. On Wilkes see also n. 164, below.

[99] On the election campaign see J. Philip Gleason, 'A Scurrilous Colonial Election

longer a Quaker, had succeeded in forming a coalition of Anglicans, Presbyterians, German Lutherans, and German Reformed, that proved more numerous than the English and German Quakers, the Moravians, Mennonites, and Schwenkfelders with whom Franklin had aligned himself. A regional factor was involved in that many Lutherans, Reformed, and Presbyterians lived in the west and felt the threat of Indian raids. They expected more help from the proprietor than from a royal governor who depended on an Assembly dominated by pacifist sectarians.[100]

The sympathies of the German printers were divided. Sower, because of his longtime, staunch support of proprietary government and his equally long distrust of Franklin, this time found himself in the company of the Church people. It was probably Sower who in August 1764 printed the brief anonymous pamphlet that reminded the German voters of the bad name Franklin had given them in England and even in all of Europe. The allegation was substantiated by a slightly distorted translation of a paragraph in *The Gentleman's Magazine* of November 1755 in which Franklin had argued for more immigrants from England: 'Why should the Palatine Boors be suffered to swarm into our Settlements, and by herding together establish their Language and Manners to the Exclusion of ours? Why should Pennsylvania, founded by the English, become a Colony of *Aliens*, who will shortly be so numerous as to Germanize us instead of our Anglifying them, and will never adopt our Language or Customs, any more than they can acquire our Complexion.'[101]

Sower's two-page pamphlet appealed to ethnic pride: 'Now let us ask every German subject of the English crown, who feels yet a single drop of blood of his nation in him: . . . does Mr. Franklin merit the vote of a single German in the coming election?' Sower's campaign was effective, a year later a friend of Franklin's was still speaking of the great damage which 'the harmless Word Boor' had done.[102] Sower also addressed the

---

and Franklin's Reputation,' *William and Mary Quarterly*, 3d ser. 18 (1961): 68–84; on the part of the Germans Arthur D. Graeff, *The Relations between the Pennsylvania Germans and the British Authorities, 1750–1776* (Norristown, Pa., 1939), chap. 12.

[100] James H. Hutson, *Pennsylvania Politics, 1746–1770: The Movement for Royal Government and Its Consequences* (Princeton, 1972), pp. 162–63, 173–74.

[101] *An die Freyhalter und Einwohner der Stadt und County Philadelphia, deutscher Nation* (n. p., 1764) (Evans 9575). The text (not the title-page) is datelined 'Philadelphia, den 27sten August, 1764.' Franklin's text from 'Observations Concerning the Increase of Mankind' is in *Papers of Franklin*, ed. Labaree, 4: 234.

[102] Samuel Wharton to Franklin, Oct. 13, 1765, *Papers of Franklin*, ed. Labaree, 12: 317.

free inhabitants of Pennsylvania shortly before election day in another tightly packed two-page broadside in German.[103] He espoused the basic principle of Whig political theory: the necessity of preserving the rights of the subject by limiting the powers of government through institutional checks. Eliminating the proprietor would mean eliminating one check:

> Our mixed form of government, in which the power of the governing and of the governed are balanced so wisely, would be lost, and all semblance and substance of liberty would be extinct. Liberty, my dear compatriots, is our natural right, a right, which the God of nature and of virtue demands you to assert and which he will help you to preserve. Those who govern you have power in order to protect you, not to suppress you. Your form of government is such that you are one half of the process of making laws and regulations. From nature and through the basic rules of the law of the land you have the whole property-right as regards your purse and all else you own. You alone are the great counterweight and have the power to oppose the other part of the government and make it stay within its limits. Whenever it extends over its limits it is your own fault. It is you who through your assembly-men (whose duty and purpose it is) can call to account the tools of suppression and punish them.

Sower's text, in effect, was Locke. The idea of the social contract met the needs of immigrants, as well as of the settled colonists, in a particularly adequate way. It allowed new members of society to become equal members as paternalistic theories of society would not have done. Sower closed with an appeal to transcend ethnic interests in order to preserve the liberties of all British subjects. 'Whether you are Englishmen, Germans, Low-Germans or Swedes, whether you are of the High Church, Presbyterians, Quakers, or of another denomination, by your living here and by the law of the land you are free men, not slaves. You have a right to all liberties of a native-born Englishman, and you have a share in the fundamental laws of the land.'

In short, the concepts that within a year were to be used to justify opposition to the Stamp Act—the combination of natural and constitutional rights of English subjects—and the rhetorical contrasting of 'liberty' and 'slavery' were fully developed and put to political use by Sower in 1764.[104]

---

[103] *Eine zu dieser Zeit höchstnöthige Warnung und Erinnerung an die freye Einwohner der Provintz Pennsylvanien*, broadside, undated and unsigned (Evans 9828).

[104] On election day an anonymous 2-page broadside, probably also printed by

Henry Miller was not as politically committed in this controversy as Sower was; he published pamphlets for both sides.[105] In the *Staatsbote* he printed a four-page supplement, translated from the English, in favor of Franklin. It argued that the cooperation of Pennsylvania's three major ethnic groups would be easier under a royal governor.[106] A third printer, Anthony Armbruster, financially dependent on Franklin, published three pamphlets in German and one in English in favor of the change to royal government.[107]

The public debate caused by the attempt to change Pennsylvania's constitutional status first demonstrated the existence of a German-speaking public that was not only politically aware, articulate, and effective, but Whiggish in terms that were completely identified with the more liberal aspects of Anglo-American political culture.

THE STAMP ACT CRISIS

Given this background, it would have been surprising if German readers had not been fully informed of the even more momentous constitutional issues that concerned all British colonies from 1764 on. Miller and Sower were equally opposed to increased direct rule from London. And since, in the absence of more modern forms of newsgathering, it was customary for one newspaper editor to lift whatever item he chose from any other newspaper, the two bilingual editors had as good an access to news from London, Amsterdam, and Paris as Bradford and the rest. In addition to news, they translated anonymous articles of opinion and even letters to the printers of English-language newspapers, so that in the literal as well

Sower, again strongly attacked the Franklin–Galloway ticket and supported the slate of 6 'English' and 2 'German' candidates, among them Heinrich Keppele, who was indeed to be elected. It also contained the allegation that Franklin hoped to become the first royal governor of Pennsylvania. *Höret ihr deutsche Bürger in Philadelphia, daß euch Gott auch höre.* Photostat in German Broadsides, Historical Society of Pennsylvania; original in Royal Swedish Academy of Science.

[105] Many of the broadsides and pamphlets of the 1764 campaign do not give the printer's name. I rely on the authority of Charles Evans in attributing to Miller the pamphlets in favor of Franklin and the change to royal government: Evans 9673, 9713; and against Franklin and for continuing proprietary government: Evans 9643, 9803, 9865.

[106] *Staatsbote*, Apr. 30, 1764.

[107] *Papers of Franklin*, ed. Labaree, 10: 289 n. 4. The English-language pamphlet is *An Address to the Freeholders and Inhabitants of the Province of Pennsylvania. In Answer to a Paper Called the Plain Dealer* (Philadelphia, 1764) (Evans 9561); for the German pamphlets see Appendix A, under 1764.

as in a figurative sense their newspapers can largely be considered as com-
posites, or anthologies in translation, of English newspapers. All immigrants live in more than one culture, and no doubt various aspects of the
Germans' culture in America were dominated by transplanted German
habits; but their political culture, as reflected in their press, was Anglo-
American, if only because there were no German models to be transplanted that had any relevance to life in British America.

The week-by-week reporting of events and the continuous recording
of opinion can be followed especially well in Miller's *Staatsbote* since a
copy of almost every issue of the newspaper has survived. Sower's publication record is more difficult to reconstruct; for the whole period 1764–
78 only eighteen issues of the *Germantowner Zeitung* survive, and several
of them consist of only two pages instead of the full four. From the num-
bering we know that about 450 issues were printed in this period, so one
must work with the meager sample of one out of twenty-five issues.

News of the Sugar Act arrived in the midst of the internal controversy
over the continuance of proprietary government, and it met with instant
rejection. On May 21, 1764, Miller published the translation of a full
account of the resolves of the House of Commons concerning the new rev-
enues to be raised in America. The translator and printer himself added
an astute editorial comment: 'The Briton who recommended the above
to the government of Britain cannot be a friend of his country. He does
not seem to care whether the American provinces that have been conquered at the price of many thousand lives and millions of pounds will
remain occupied and kept to the advantage of the nation. When this news
will spread in Europe (which it certainly will), it will hardly attract foreigners to come and settle in America. It may even become a means to
drive people away.'

Miller kept hoping for a revision of the bill, following the protestations
of interested merchants in England and a joint petition by the colonies.
'If all North American colonies followed this praiseworthy example,' he
commented on the Rhode Island Assembly's rejection of the Sugar Act,
'and together as one group applied to his Majesty and his Council,
through patriotic men who are thoroughly acquainted with the circumstances of these parts, then there could be no doubt about a happy outcome.'[108] Later in August 1764 Miller translated an essay from Brad-

---

[108] *Staatsbote*, Aug. 20, 1764.

ford's *Pennsylvania Journal* that deplored the new restrictions on trade and explained that they were brought about through the influence of the West Indian planters in Parliament. To counter the new regulations, the article argued, Pennsylvanians should do without expensive imported goods such as West Indian sugar and rum, English cheese, beer, and cloth. For the first time, homespun and colonial resistance were clearly linked.[109] Miller also captured the combination of ridicule and defiance that the new laws aroused when he translated from a London newspaper the proposal of 'A Philadelphian': 'May I humbly request permission to ask the merchants of Great Britain whether it would not be of great advantage to the English nation to force the Americans to have their tea, coffee and chocolate brought over from England ready made with sugar and milk, not to forget buttered warm rolls.'[110]

By 1764 Miller was using the proper nouns central to the development of American national identity: 'die Americaner,' 'die Americanischen Colonien' and 'unsere Americanischen Sachen,' in the sense of 'our American cause.' He also saw no inconsistency in translating literally patriotic phrases from the English-language journals such as 'our honorable forefathers, the first cultivators of this wilderness' and in so doing practically forcing his German readers to adopt Puritan great-grandfathers.[111] Indeed, in all of his faithful translations from the majority-culture political language Miller was intensifying the integrating process by which an alien people came to identify themselves with the British American world.

From April 1765 on, news concerning the stamp tax could be found in almost every number of the *Staatsbote*, and Miller was able to add his own considerations, drawn from his earlier experience. As a journeyman printer, Miller explained, he had seen at first hand the taxes that burdened the sale of products of the printing press in several European countries. In England and Scotland, imprints of less than one and one-half sheets and all almanacs had to be printed on stamped paper, and a tax was added to their price, for example, one penny for a newspaper and two pennies for an almanac; and all legal documents had to be written on stamped paper. In Germany and Denmark the laws were similar. Only

[109] *Staatsbote*, Aug. 27, 1764.
[110] *Staatsbote*, Oct. 29, 1764.
[111] Examples in *Staatsbote*, May 21 and 28, 1764.

Ireland, Miller reported, had no stamped paper.[112] In the next issue of the *Staatsbote* Miller printed a summary of the resolves of the House of Commons that contained most of the provisions of the future stamp tax, including the discriminatory double tax on printed material in any language other than English. Miller added sarcastically: 'If these provisions become law, will they not be considered by European princes and statesmen as either facetious, or else as measures of unfathomable wisdom for peopling a new Empire and making it great?'[113] Miller believed it was greatly in Britain's interest to continue to attract colonists from continental Europe, and he could not imagine how a colonial policy contrary to this aim would endure.

Anglo-American political news continued to figure prominently in the *Staatsbote*. Soon Miller added a special note of alarm for Pennsylvanians with the rumor from a London newspaper that Parliament would soon consider 'whether all proprietary colonies were to be bought by the crown and become royal colonies.'[114] In May 1765 Miller reported fully on the speeches for and against the bill in the Commons.[115] News of the Quartering Act was published early in June and was accompanied by the translation of a letter to the editor of the London *Evening Post* that warned against the dangers of standing armies in general, rejected the quartering of soldiers at the cost of the communities as a form of illegal taxation, and called for 'legal and constitutional' ('gesetz- und landesverfassungsmäßig') resistance against the measure.[116]

At the beginning of the public debate about the Stamp Act in the colonies, Miller, drawing on John Holt's *New-York Gazette*, provided his readers with a list of misconceptions about America in newspapers and pamphlets recently published in the mother country. As with similar texts, translation posed no serious problems. The anonymous author deplored the idea that English readers were being misled into believing 'That the colonies cost them money, that they are dangerous competitors in trade and at the same time more contemptible and submissive than the people of England; that they are rebellious, hostile to the English

[112] *Staatsbote*, Apr. 8, 1765.
[113] *Staatsbote*, Apr. 15, 1765.
[114] *Staatsbote*, Apr. 22, 1765.
[115] *Staatsbote*, May 13, 1765. Excerpts from Colonel Barré's speech against the act are in the issue of June 10, 1765.
[116] *Staatsbote*, June 3, 1765.

constitution and government, and aspire to independence; that they are a burden on England, because they request protection but are not prepared to pay part of the expenses.' The author called upon all 'friends of the natural rights of mankind, on which the English constitution is founded' to help correct these falsehoods.[117]

The custom of copying or translating freely from other newspapers gave a printer ample opportunity not only to bring anything he chose to his readers' attention but also to create a multiple-echo effect. He could, for instance, echo the news of the arrival of the Stamp Act a dozen times over by publishing in translation the respective reports from Portsmouth to Savannah. In this way Miller's newspaper in fact provided full coverage of reactions to the Stamp Act up and down the coast, ranging from formal protests to ponderous essays and human interest stories, such as one from New London, Connecticut, according to which an inhabitant of Windham refused to follow the town's summons for communal road repair because 'a stamp tax will be levied in the colony.'[118]

In August 1765 Miller reported that the boxes of stamped paper and parchment were ready to be sent over. He printed a complete list of the nineteen stamp agents whom the secretary of the treasury had appointed, and he related the latest activities of the 'Söhne der Freiheit' in Providence and the demolition by a Boston mob of the Massachusetts stamp agent's house. 'Would it not be better if all stamp agents took out insurance on their houses?,' he asked.[119] In September he reported more protests and mob violence in New Haven, Newport, Providence, Annapolis, and Boston, where Governor Hutchinson's house was destroyed.[120]

Miller also printed the complete text of formal responses of public bodies such as the Virginia Resolutions of May 1765, the instructions of the town meeting of Providence to its representatives in the Rhode Island Assembly, the circular letter of the Massachusetts Assembly that called for an intercolonial congress to meet in New York, and the Pennsylvania Assembly's refutation of the Stamp Act.[121] The observations and opinions of individual correspondents were no less important. A report from

[117] *Staatsbote*, May 20, 1765.
[118] *Staatsbote*, June 17, 1765.
[119] *Staatsbote*, Aug. 19 and 26, 1765.
[120] *Staatsbote*, Sept. 2, 9, and 16, 1765.
[121] *Staatsbote*, July 22, Sept. 2, 9, and 30, 1765. Similar resolves in *Staatsbote*, Jan. 13, 1766 (New London, Conn.).

Boston, for instance, painted the economic consequences of the new laws in the gloomiest colors: 'Our commerce is in a dismal state, fewer than a fifth of the vessels which used to go to the West Indies are now doing so. Our money will be gone even before the Stamp Act and the Post-Office Act will become effective. Bankruptcies become more frequent.'[122]

The high indebtedness of colonists to British merchants and its foresee-able increase through the new regulations were bitterly resented and led to calls for boycotting European and West Indian imports and keeping what little money was left inside the continental colonies.[123] Perhaps most disquieting of all was the general loss of power of the colonial assemblies. Their reduction to executors of parliamentary fiats caused a fear of yet unseen but impending dangers; 'Trojan horse' and 'opening wedge' were the metaphors for the Stamp Act that Miller himself used to express this anxiety.[124] The demotion of the fondly regarded provincial parliaments was perceived as an uncalled-for breach of the hitherto accepted consti-tutional arrangement; it was, in short, 'unlandsverfassungsmäßig'—un-constitutional.[125] Since the conflict was of such a basic nature, it was not surprising that even the issue of independence was raised openly. In a piece that he took from the London *Evening Post*, Miller presented a refu-tation of the view, allegedly held by many in England, that 'the Ameri-cans' were about to renounce their allegiance to the British crown. A change in the form of government, the unknown author argued, was such a grave matter that it presupposed very serious grievances. Abolishing colonial assemblies would, however, constitute such a cause.[126] As the protest resolutions kept repeating that the new laws violated the exclusive and sacred privilege of the assemblies to levy taxes, the threat was unmis-takable.

The question of the ultimate arbiter, military power, was spelled out

[122] *Staatsbote*, June 17, and Aug. 26, 1765.

[123] *Staatsbote*, July 8, 1765, letter by 'A.T.,' trans. from Bradford's *Pennsylvania Jour-nal*.

[124] *Staatsbote*, Sept. 9, 1765.

[125] *Staatsbote*, Oct. 7, 1765.

[126] *Staatsbote*, Dec. 16, 1765. Further American and English analyses of the conflict that Miller published in the winter of 1765–66 were John Dickinson's *The Regulations Respecting the British Colonies . . . Considered*, in *Staatsbote*, Dec. 23, 1765 (this number is not extant but Miller refers to it in the issue of Feb. 22, 1766); 'Freymann,' 'Freyheit, Eigenthümlichkeit, und keine Stämpeley,' *Staatsbote*, Dec. 30, 1765; letter from a Lon-don merchant to a Lord, *Staatsbote*, Feb. 3, 1766; 'John Hampden an William Pym,' *Staatsbote*, Feb. 10, 1766; 'Phileleuterus,' *Staatsbote*, Feb. 17, 1766.

just as clearly in Miller's *Staatsbote*. The way the Stamp Act was enforced or resisted in the winter of 1765–66 across the far-flung British Empire taught the German readers in the continental colonies a valuable lesson. They heard of the stamped paper being distributed within reach of the navy's cannons in Jamaica, Grenada, Barbados, and Antigua as well as in occupied Quebec, Montreal, and Nova Scotia.[127] After this experience, the quartering of more soldiers south of Canada could only be seen as a clear indication of the government's most pernicious intentions and had to be resisted no less fiercely than the new taxation policy. As a result, the political and military measures constituted a fatal combination, each stimulating more resistance to the other.

The old issue of proprietary or royal government for Pennsylvania and the new issue of parliamentary authority in the colonies overlapped in the election campaign of 1765, and in this episode we have clear evidence of Sower's political activity. Shortly before election day Sower put out a signed two-page broadside in which, among other things, he revealed that he felt an obligation to raise his voice 'as a printer,' and to advise his readers on how to vote.[128] He repeated his argument in favor of proprietary government and against 'Mr. Franklin's followers.' He also censored the Assembly for having been slow in sending delegates to the Stamp Act Congress in New York in order to petition the crown 'to free us of the heavy, unbearable burden of the Stamp Act.' 'Who would have thought,' Sower added, 'that a single member of our Assembly would oppose this proper measure?' With a majority of one vote, a delegation was finally dispatched. Sower published the complete roll call.

Within seven days the reprimanded assemblymen responded with a broadside, printed by Miller, which explained that the Assembly had divided only over a question of procedure: the representatives of Bucks County had favored a petition by the Assembly of Pennsylvania alone, instead of jointly with the other colonies through the congress meeting at New York.[129] With the publication of the roll call, Sower had obviously touched a sensitive nerve. As soon as the Assembly had passed a set of strongly worded resolutions condemning the Stamp Act, the admiralty

---

[127] *Staatsbote*, Jan. 13, 1766.

[128] *Wertheste Landes-Leute, Sonderlich in Philadelphia, Bucks- und Berks-Caunty*, signed 'Germantown, den 18ten September, 1765. Christoph Saur' (Evans 10162).

[129] *An die Deutschen, vornemlich die zum Wählen berechtigten, in Philadelphia- Bucks- und Berks Caunty*, dated Sept. 25, 1765 (Evans 9902).

courts, and any attempts to infringe their rights as Englishmen, Miller received a copy for translation and publication as a broadside. It accused Sower of having printed 'a mish-mash of falsehood and truth,' without, however, challenging a single name in the roll call.[130] Since Miller seems to have delighted in taking issue with Sower, he explained his role as intermediary, insisting that members of the Assembly had seen Sower's piece only when they were already in the middle of passing their resolutions. Miller also questioned as exaggerated Sower's sense of duty 'as a printer.' He did so with a polemical reference to conditions in Germany: 'Does he [Sower] not count on the ignorance of those Germans to whom he thus offers his advice, when he makes them believe that a printer as such and because of his profession is entitled to meddle with matters of state? We all know how limited the printers and the printing trade are in Germany. And in which country in the whole world does a printer, as printer, enjoy such privilege?'[131] Since Miller was as active an opinion-maker as his competitor, he could not have meant to deny the legitimacy of what both of them were doing; he only seems to have felt provoked by Sower's apologetic attempt to hide his ambition as a journalist behind the role of involuntary adviser.

Despite their competition and differences of opinion, the printers of newspapers in Pennsylvania—German and English alike—closed ranks as November 1, the day on which the Stamp Act was to go into effect, drew near. 'We Printers of News Papers here, Dutch and English,' the editor of the *Pennsylvania Gazette* wrote to Franklin, 'have been proposing to take the Advice of the ablest Council, how far we may, or may not, be safe in carrying on our Papers without the Stamps.'[132] Because of this pre-

---

[130] *Weil am 18ten jetztlaufenden Septembers in Germantown eine Schrift herausgekommen ist* . . . , broadside, American Antiquarian Society (Evans suppl. 41581). The resolutions were passed on Sept. 21, 1765.

[131] *Staatsbote*, Oct. 14, 1765. Sower carried his campaign against a new charter for Pennsylvania over into 1766. See the exchanges between 'A.B.' and Ludwig Weiss in *Staatsbote*, Mar. 3 and 24, May 11, and June 23, 1766. The controversy spilled over into the allegation that Franklin and Joseph Galloway had been among the originators of the Stamp Act. Galloway refuted the charge in the supplement to *Staatsbote*, Sept. 30, 1766. Miller also published as a pamphlet of 43 pages Franklin's interrogation by the House of Commons, *Die Verhörung Doctor Benjamin Franklins vor der Hohen Versammlung des Hauses der Gemeinen von Gross-brittannien, die Stämpel-Act, etc. betreffend* (Philadelphia: H. Miller, 1766).

[132] David Hall to Benjamin Franklin, Oct. 14, 1765, *Papers of Franklin*, ed. Labaree, 12: 320.

caution, the defiant special numbers and succeeding issues on unstamped paper reflected probably less heroism than the skulls and crossbones on the front pages might lead one to believe. On October 28, 1765, Miller announced the discontinuation of the *Staatsbote* because 'the most unconstitutional law these colonies have ever seen . . . places too heavy a burden on the editor.' In the same issue he reported that in London coffeehouses bets were being made about the repeal of the act. A few days later he put out a special issue in which he repeated, in English, that he would not publish the paper 'for a While,' but would carry on stamp-free printing and translating work. Three columns of the special issue were taken up by excerpts from the speech to the freeholders of Connecticut that John Holt's *New-York Gazette* had carried as a supplement. It contained an extensive refutation of the new colonial policy, including the concept of 'virtual representation.' The rejection of this idea was clear and simple: 'I cannot imagine a representative whom we have not elected.' Again, a key concept of English political language was correctly translated into clear, plain German: 'wesentlich, obwohl nicht förmlich [i.e., virtually] im Parlament vorgestellet.'[133]

After less than three weeks Miller was back with a regular issue that contained the text of the nonimportation resolves of over 400 Philadelphia merchants.[134] A week later, he commented on the flood of reports about protests against the Stamp Act. Instead of filling several sheets with nothing else, he decided to simply list important items he had seen in the English-language newspapers and refer his readers to them.[135] The fact

---

[133] *Staatsbote*, Oct. 31, 1765. 'Die Mietlinge des Staatsamts schwatzen uns zwar vor, wir seyen wesentlich, obwohl nicht förmlich (i.e., virtually) im Parlament vorgestellet. Dis ist eine geheimnißvolle vorstellung, und von höchst ungewisser bedeutung. Ob wir deswegen wesentlich vorgestellet sind, weil das Brittannische Parlament eine versammlung von menschen ist und einerley geschlechts mit uns, oder weil sie Engländer sind wie wir auch, oder weil selbiges die Nazion vorstellet von welcher wir abstammen, oder weil wir unter Einem Könige stehen, oder in was für einer andern absicht, das ist alles ungewiß. In ein- oder der andern von diesen absichten aber sind die groß und kleinen städte in England eben so wesentlich in unsern allgemeinen Landrathsversammlungen (oder Assemblies) vorgestellet, als die Colonien im Parlament wesentlich vorgestellet sind. Und eine versammlung der Jüdischen Rabbiner in Ungarn würde all durch die ganze welt zerstreuete Juden eben so wesentlich und gut vorstellen. Ich kan mir keinen begriff machen von einem Repräsentanten den wir nicht selbst gewählet, oder nicht hätten wählen dörfen, ja den der Allmächtige nicht einmal für uns hätte wählen mögen.'
[134] *Staatsbote*, Nov. 18, 1765.
[135] *Staatsbote*, Dec. 9, 1765.

that Miller saw sense in doing this suggests once again that he was editing his newspaper not for barely literate farmers but for men of essentially his own cultural level who had some access, perhaps in an inn, to English-language newspapers.

In other instances, handling the proliferation of newsworthy events that Miller did not want to go unnoticed was to summarize newsworthy events in his own words, instead of translating the complete items. An example read:

Of the Sons of Liberty
They continue to pass resolutions
—At Lyme, in the County of New London, in New England, where they passed eleven of them. They say that, as their name indicates, they defend their liberty and will resist stamping with all their might.
—At Wallingford, in New Haven county, they have passed four resolutions which say that they will resist stamping to the last, if necessary even with arms.[136]

Lest anyone misunderstand, Miller added that the dominant spirit of these resolves was one of 'loyalty to the King and a burning eagerness to defend the liberties of the people.'[137]

In February 1766 Sower, in the only surviving issue of his newspaper from the time of the debate over the Stamp Act, also carried news of protest activities in several colonies, and under his own dateline 'Germantown den 24. Februar' reported that repeal of the act was still uncertain and that when the question had recently been put in Parliament whether the Americans were 'rebels,' the majority had answered in the negative. Sower commented: 'From this we may conclude that the majority of the Members of Parliament do not harbor ill feelings against us and will, I hope, seek our best and free us from the unbearable burden which the Stamp Act is.'[138]

From the end of March 1766, false and half-true reports about the repeal of the Stamp Act were published in the colonies and caused confusion and more comments. The *Staatsbote* of April 28, 1766, consisted of

[136] *Staatsbote*, Feb. 10, 1766. Similar summaries in issues of Mar. 3, 10, and 17, 1766.
[137] *Staatsbote*, Mar. 31, 1766.
[138] *Wahre und Wahrscheinliche Begebenheiten auf ungestempeltem Papier, weil kein gestempeltes zu haben ist*, Feb. 24, 1766. Sower published several issues under this temporary title. Arndt and Olson, *German-American Newspapers*, p. 524.

little else than quotations from the debate between Pitt and Grenville in Parliament on January 14. On May 5, Miller reported the positive result of the first reading of the repeal bill in the Commons on February 22; on May 12 he presented Grenville's entire speech in defense of the Stamp Act as a supplement—'irrefutable proof of the impartiality of the editor.' Finally, on May 19, 1766, he announced in 'A Glorious Supplement' of beautiful, large lettering that in the morning a brigantine had arrived from England after an eight-week sail with the news that on March 18 the king had assented to the repeal bill and that the Stamp Act had expired on May 1. Reports about celebrations followed. Especially appropriate, Miller thought, was the release of several Bostonians from debtors' prison.[139] Another printer, possibly Armbruster, distributed an exuberant German broadside in Philadelphia to hail the good news. 'When I came to the coffee house,' the unknown author said, 'I finally saw with my own eyes the long-awaited Act of Parliament which totally repealed the Stamp Act.' The two broad columns of print were crowned by a copperplate engraving showing the resurrection of 'Freyheit' from a coffin and the sun fully risen over the globe that showed 'America.'[140]

At the end of the year, the epoch-making quality of the Stamp Act crisis was also registered in the German almanacs for 1767. Almanacs at this time customarily included a synopsis of world history that placed the current year in historical perspective by enumerating memorable events in the history of mankind, beginning with the creation of the world in 4000 B.C. At the bottom of the list, the editor added the most recent incisive event. Sower and Miller made use of this device to interpret American history. Sower added at the bottom of the list in the 1767 almanac: 'From the repeal of the unbearable burden of the Stamp Act, on May 1, 1 year.'[141]

Even in the midst of the protestations against the Stamp Act the editors had proudly asserted the effectiveness of their newspapers. The editor of the *New-York Journal* had proudly printed, and Miller had eagerly translated, a letter that credited the printers with overcoming the paralyzing feeling of powerlessness after the first petitions had been disre-

---

[139] *Staatsbote*, June 2, 1766.

[140] Dated May 19, 1766, original in German Broadsides, Historical Society of Pennsylvania.

[141] *Der Hoch-Deutsch Americanische Calender auf das Jahr . . . 1767* (Germantown, 1766), no pagination.

garded or dismissed in England. At first, the unknown author claimed,

> even our printing presses almost ceased to speak the language of liberty. But
> finally we began to recollect our disquieted minds, and the spirit of liberty
> seized the press. One or two convincing essays showed our liberties in a
> shining light, and as soon as this was seen and understood, they were being
> asserted and defended. The spark of patriotism ['vaterländischen Sinnes']
> struck every breast, and spoke through every tongue, pen and press and
> soon reached every part of the British provinces in America. It unified us
> all, we seemed to be inspired by one spirit, and that was the spirit of free-
> dom.[142]

A few years later, when Miller looked back on the conflict, there would
be no doubt in his mind about his and his colleagues' role in the outcome:
'The spirit of resistance [in New England and Virginia] spread through
the public newspapers like a brush fire, not only through all colonies in
North America but also to the West Indies, and the whole people soon
was united in one spirit and of one opinion.'[143]

The press had played an important, possibly a crucial, role in bringing
about the repeal. For the first time the major part of the continental
colonies had joined in thwarting an imperial regulation by combining
patiently reasoned statements about representative institutions with
mob violence. The ultimate success of both depended on publicity, on
being supported by a public. The creation of the new forum of public
opinion, on the other hand, depended on the existence of interest-arous-
ing messages to be carried. Both needs were now fulfilled in a process of
mutual reinforcement, so that by the end of the Stamp Act crisis, in the
spring of 1766, an intercolonial, American public had taken shape. The
German-language phase of it was an integral part of the larger whole,
and Miller's pride in the new importance of the printing profession was
justified.

The German-speaking British subjects in the colonies, it was clear,
supported two newspapers that, far from being inward-looking sectarian
sheets, had presented as much news about the Stamp Act crisis as any
other colonial newspaper. In politics, it was equally clear the language
barrier could be overcome, the German language could express English
constitutional concepts, no matter whether such terms were being pub-

[142] *Staatsbote*, Nov. 25, 1765.
[143] *Staatsbote*, Jan. 5, 1768.

licly used in Germany or not. German, after all, was a living language, capable of being adapted to the American environment.

ACTIONS AND ATTITUDES, 1766–1774

In order not to lessen the triumph of 1766, journalists and pamphleteers ignored the Declaratory Act, which despite the repeal of the Stamp Act reasserted Parliament's authority to legislate for the colonies 'in all cases whatsoever.' An abstract principle of this kind was an insufficient target for popular wrath. Dramatic action, villains, heroes, and martyrs were needed to arouse public opinion. All this the following years supplied in a loose succession of incidents until, with the Tea Party, the Boston leaders triggered the chain of events that finally led to war and independence. The pattern of resistance against the Townshend duties, the Quartering Act, the admiralty courts, the new customs commissioners, and the Tea Act followed the successful pattern of 1765–66: the assemblies and other public and private groups passed resolutions, well-led mobs committed violence, and newspapers and pamphlets spread the news and expressed and created opinion.

Henry Miller took part in these developments as fully as he had done during the campaign against the Stamp Act. He unfailingly reported all the events and published all the documents that have become the mosaic stones of today's standard textbook account of the Revolution. And he contributed to the continuing expansion of the colonists' public articulation of political opinion. From 1766 on, Miller was ever mindful of the active role the press had played in getting the Stamp Act repealed. At the height of the agitation against the Townshend Acts, in January 1768, he reminded his readers of the past success by printing a letter to the editor of the *Boston Gazette* that extolled the bravery of Bostonians and Virginians and the role of the newspapers as 'defenders of liberty.' Miller underscored the point by adding his own interpretation:

The resolution to halt the importation of English goods was unanimously taken by all, and appropriate petitions were sent to England. Together, all this happily led to the repeal of the Stamp Act. It was, with divine blessing, largely the result of the freedom of the press. Now that Parliament has seen fit to impose new taxes on many goods, the inhabitants of the city of Boston to their great merit have resolved to import and consume no more superfluous European goods. In order not to be ruined by the debts which they, as well as other colonists, would incur, they will increase the production of their own manufactures and encourage industry and frugality. These laudable resolutions of the city of Boston are not only a model for the other New England colonies, as the public newspapers are telling us every week; we may hope that this news, when it is seen, will eventually inspire all colonies to follow, out of self-interest, the noble example of New England. When this is achieved, the public newspapers will undoubtedly have contributed greatly to it.[144]

Not long after, when he reported that restrictions on the press were being demanded by powerful men in London, Miller repeated: 'All rights and liberties the people still enjoy, they owe to the freedom of the press.'[145]

Actions

Miller reminded his readers of the effectiveness of nonimportation by reporting the revival of the movement in Boston in the summer and fall of 1767. He presented, in the form of letters by James Otis to the *Boston Gazette*, the Boston town meeting resolves in favor of nonimportation, an account of the meeting itself, and an essay from the *Boston Evening-Post* that called for increased substitution of home-grown American products for European imports.[146] The students at Harvard, Miller wanted his readers to know, had decided to wear only American-made clothing at the commencement exercises in 1768.[147] In April 1768 he published the Massachusetts Circular Letter with its ringing defense of colonial rights, and followed it with the letters that the Massachusetts Assembly had sent to parliamentary leaders in England.[148] When he reported the repercussions and responses from other colonies, he commented: 'The colonies should follow the motto of the Dutch: "Eendracht maakt macht"' ['Unity makes for power'].[149] The seizure of John Hancock's smuggling vessel and the ensuing mass meeting in the Old South meeting house organized by the Sons of Liberty was described in great detail.[150]

From the scanty evidence we have of Christopher Sower's attitude in

[144] Ibid.
[145] *Staatsbote*, Apr. 24, 1770.
[146] *Staatsbote*, Sept. 14 and 21, Nov. 16 and 30, Dec. 14, 1767.
[147] *Staatsbote*, Feb. 2, 1768.
[148] *Statesbote*, Apr. 5, 12, and 19, 1768.
[149] *Staatsbote*, July 12, 1768. Dozens of further reports about the nonimportation campaign in the several colonies were given by Miller throughout 1769.
[150] *Staatsbote*, July 5, 1768.

1768 it is clear that he shared Miller's belief in the appropriateness of nonimportation and his disapproval of the tardiness with which the Philadelphia merchants followed the Boston example. When he reported in his *Germantowner Zeitung* that several of the German principalities were planning to stop importing English goods if the British government did not pay the debts it had incurred during the last war, Sower commented: 'It seems as if the German princes learned from the Americans that this is the best and only way to bring England to reason; it is remarkable that our merchants do not recognize this, especially since America's freedom depends on it.'[151]

The arrival of the two infantry regiments in Boston and their quartering in town added a new element to the scene of conflict and many items to the pages of the *Staatsbote*.[152] Also, the clashes between troops and mobs in New York in 1769 and the resistance to the Quartering Act were presented with as many details and resolutions as Miller could find in the New York papers.[153] He dealt with the Boston Massacre in the same thorough way.[154]

The partial repeal of the Townshend duties in April 1770 and the expiration of the Quartering Act at the same time went strangely unheralded. There was no celebrating, by special supplements or otherwise, that could be described as joyful, as the reaction to the news of the repeal of the Stamp Act had been.[155] Instead, when after repeal the nonimportation agreements were discarded in many places, Miller kept reporting the 'laudable' activities of those who decided to continue the battle.[156] In September 1770 a committee of Philadelphia merchants resolved to resume importation of tax-free goods from England. Miller extensively reported the condemnation of this step by the grand jury of the city and county of Philadelphia. He printed their call for continuing nonimportation: the tea duty was meant to be 'ein exempel,' because it symbolized the unconstitutional authority that Parliament claimed over the colonies; it symbolized the fundamental insecurity of property in the colonies; the same principle lay behind the admiralty courts, the customs

[151] *Germantowner Zeitung*, Dec. 8, 1768.
[152] *Staatsbote*, Oct. 18 and 25, Nov. 1, Dec. 27, 1768.
[153] *Staatsbote*, Feb. 6, 20, and 27, Mar. 6, 1769.
[154] *Staatsbote*, Mar. 27, Apr. 10, July 3, 1770.
[155] *Staatsbote*, May 8, June 26, July 17, 1770.
[156] *Staatsbote*, Aug. 28, and Sept. 4, 1770.

commissioners, and the keeping of a standing army in the colonies. All four measures had to be ended before America would be free.[157]

In 1771 and 1772, with the decrease of dramatic events in the colonies and London, the proportion of general European news in the *Staatsbote* increased noticeably. This situation changed again in 1773 when the final round of the Anglo-American conflict began. In March 1773 Miller reported in full the resolves of the Massachusetts Assembly that explicitly, if belatedly, rejected the claim of the Declaratory Act that Parliament could legislate for the colonies 'in all cases whatsoever.' In May and June 1773 he noticed the institution of committees of correspondence in Virginia and other colonies.[158] In July and August 1773 he published items about the situation of the East India Company and the Tea Act of May 1773.[159] The intention of Bostonians not to allow taxed tea to be landed Miller published on December 21, and reports on the Tea Party followed a week later. Miller seems not to have shared the Bostonian sense of humor, and omitted the Indian costumes from his rendering. In his version 'the people' marched to Griffin's Wharf. Miller refrained from a comment of his own, but a week later, on January 4, 1774, he presented a four-column summary of anti-tea activities in Philadelphia since October. A new crisis was at hand.

Attitudes

Since the few political pamphlets that were published in German in the decade before 1776 compared in no way to the number of this genre published in English, in the mother country as well as in the colonies, there was a special function for the German newspapers to perform, which to a certain degree they did. The more theoretical pieces Miller printed allowed his readers to follow the publicly expressed attitudes and arguments as well as the pattern of resistance from the time of the Stamp Act to that of the Declaration of Independence.

One of the recurring themes was the imperial administrators' lack of response to rational arguments concerning concrete proposals, such as one that would permit the colonies to print paper money in order to alle-

---

[157] *Staatsbote*, Oct. 2, 1770.

[158] *Staatsbote*, Mar. 23, May 25, June 22, 1773.

[159] *Staatsbote*, July 13, and Aug. 17, 1773. On Jan. 25, 1774, Miller published a letter on the development of the East India Company.

viate their chronic shortage of currency.[160] Similarly, it was pointed out that concrete figures about profits from the colonists' consumption of untaxed English imports made no impression. (One writer claimed that the colonists bought £500,000 worth of manufactured goods each year and thereby kept 7,780 English manufactures in business.[161]) Long-standing grievances, such as the deportation of criminals and prostitutes to the colonies, could also have been dealt with in London with a minimum of effort and at little cost.[162]

More important than disappointment over any single measure was the general disenchantment with the inefficiency and lack of moral authority of the British government. The readers of the *Staatsbote* were shown an inept system operated by incompetent and corrupt men. The fact that Miller translated many of the critical articles from London newspapers could hardly have made them less credible in the colonies. One of the exposed weaknesses was the venality of members of Parliament, their electors, and the king's ministers.[163] The career of John Wilkes seems to have fascinated Miller as a test case for a system in decline. He reported every step of Wilkes's odyssey, abhorring his blasphemies but praising his courageous probing of the state of civil liberties in Britain.[164]

The decline of liberty in England and its colonies was all the more alarming, and the need to resist it seemed all the more urgent, because Miller saw it as part of the almost universal struggle between the forces of oppression and liberty that, he declared, was surging all over Europe. When, in December 1768, he composed the customary single-sheet New Year's poem that the *Staatsbote*'s newsboys handed out to subscribers, he mentioned the following as noteworthy events of the previous year: the suppression of religious dissent in Poland; the conquest of 'the free people of Corsica' by the House of Bourbon; the expulsion of the Jesuits even from Catholic countries; the fear in England of another war in Europe; 'the suffering of Boston'; and the scarcity of money.[165] During the year,

---

[160] Miller published the complete text of Franklin's memorandum on paper money of February 1764 as a supplement on Aug. 17, 1767.

[161] *Staatsbote*, Feb. 21, 1769.

[162] *Staatsbote*, Apr. 12, 1768, contains a sarcastic item on London prostitutes working as servant girls in the colonies.

[163] *Staatsbote*, June 22, 1767, June 14, 1768.

[164] Reports on Wilkes in the *Staatsbote* during this period on June 3 and 14, 1768; Feb. 28, Mar. 28, Apr. 4, June 27, Aug. 22, 1769; June 12, Aug. 21, 1770.

[165] *Des Herumträgers des Staatsboten Neujahrs-Wunsch, bey seine resp. Geehrten Kundleuten*

Miller had repeatedly reported on the brave struggle of 'the sons of liberty of Corsica' under the leadership of the 'famed hero Paoli.'[166]

The only surviving number of Sower's newspapers after 1768 also contains news about Boston and about Corsica; Sower too saw the similarity. 'Let us hope,' he wrote in commenting on the news that the French troops heavily outnumbered the Corsicans, 'that in the interest of the preservation of freedom and the suppression of tyranny all over the world the bravery of the inhabitants will punish the tyrant as severely as this irresponsible intervention makes him deserve.' In the same issue, Sower printed an abstract of a speech General Paoli was supposed to have given to arouse the youth of Corsica to defend their liberty. His rhetoric of liberty was interchangeable with Sam Adams's: 'If to preserve liberty demanded nothing more than to wish for it, then the whole world would enjoy it. But this precious jewel can be won only by a virtue and a braveness that surmount all obstacles. . . . We have reached a most critical juncture; if we do not resist the danger now, we will lose our honor as well as our liberty.'[167]

Obviously, neither Miller nor Sower limited their interest in European news to Germany. They perceived Europe as a whole, and surveyed the continent-wide struggle for civil liberties against the absolute power of monarchs. In the struggle, they identified their own interests with the forces of enlightenment and liberty, and, needless to say, with America. America had long since captured the imagination of Europeans who often, for lack of information and for reasons of their own, had idealized the New World, as Voltaire had done in his famous panegyrics on life in Pennsylvania, which Miller republished. It does not seem to have been in a satirical mood that the great skeptic celebrated the free and happy Pennsylvanian who 'thinks what he will and speaks what he thinks without fear of the consequences,' who does not know 'the arbitrariness of an unlimited ruler and the burden of ever increasing taxation,' and who is free of 'the servile fear of an overlord' and the capriciousness of petty officials. Only when Voltaire claimed that vice was unknown in Philadelphia did Miller object: 'Wish it were so!,' he added in brackets.[168]

abgelegt den 3 ten Jenner, 1769. Technically these Herumträger broadsides are independent publications, but some can conveniently be found in the microcard editon of the Staatsbote, which includes them in the place of a Beylage.

[166] Staatsbote, Sept. 30, and Oct. 11, 1768.
[167] Germantowner Zeitung, Dec. 8, 1768.
[168] Questions sur l'Encyclopédie (1772), excerpts in Staatsbote, Apr. 27, 1773.

A standard argument among enlightened Europeans against absolute monarchy was the apparent success of Britain's limited monarchy. The colonists made use of the libertarian reputation of the English constitution by warning against its corruption and declaring themselves a test case of its validity. Praising the English constitution thus became a way of asserting colonial rights. Glorification of the constitution found expression in the *Staatsbote* in such harmless pieces as the one signed 'Constitution,' which called for a few unselfish statesmen to rescue a suppressed people out of the hands of rapacious ministers and caballing officeholders.[169] Another article, which covered more than a whole page of the same issue in reporting the likelihood of a repeal of the Townshend Acts, deplored the fact that 'implacable enemies of the constitution of our kingdom have been entrusted with the public offices.' It called upon the king to dismiss his unfaithful servants and to refrain from meddling with elections to the House of Commons.[170]

But there were also more bitter and threatening attacks on the governmental authorities of Britain, including the crown. Miller devoted all four pages of a supplement and most of a front page to presenting two of the Junius letters and a reply. 'The letters of Junius,' he explained to his readers, 'received much attention in England and in the English newspapers.' Written in a fervent language that Miller masterfully translated, they appealed to George III to change his advisors and to make Parliament do its duty. The conclusion reminded the king that his ancestors had succeeded to the throne only because, at the time, their establishment in power had seemed an expedient way of securing civil and religious liberty in England: 'A prince who takes his right to the crown for granted should not forget that it was acquired through a revolution, and that another revolution could take it away.'[171] Miller also presented, as 'the most daring piece ever published in America,' a vehement attack on the governor of Massachusetts which he translated from Isaiah Thomas's *Massachusetts Spy*.[172] The daring quality of the brief essay derived from

[169] *Staatsbote*, Dec. 7, 1767.

[170] *Staatsbote*, Jan. 20, 1770. Miller translated the article from the *London Chronicle* of Aug. 19, 1769. It purports to be a reprint of a letter to the king first published in 1692.

[171] *Staatsbote*, Mar. 13, and Apr. 3, 1770. The text was taken from the *London Evening Post*, Dec. 19 and 26, 1769.

[172] 'Mucius Scaevola' in *Staatsbote*, Dec. 10, 1771, taken from the *Massachusetts Spy*

its radical application of the contract theory to the relationship between the executive branch of a government (Governor Hutchinson) and 'the people' (of Massachusetts). The governor, it was argued, had forfeited the right to his office by breaking his side of the contract, specifically, by attempting to make himself independent of the annual decision of the Assembly over his salary by having the crown pay him, a goal he achieved nonetheless in 1772. The governor was seen as analogous to the king: 'A ruler independent of the people would be a dangerous beast, and that is what Mr. Hutchinson is; and that is what George III would be, if he were ever to become independent of the people of Great Britain.' The charter of Massachusetts was regarded as a contract between the crown and the colonists, and the king could, therefore, not alter the terms unilaterally by paying the governor a salary.

Subversion of 'the liberty and happy constitution' of the colonies remained a constant accusation in the various struggles of colonial assemblies with their governors. The Hutchinson and Oliver letters, one of which Miller published in the summer of 1773, provided further proof of the extent of this danger.[173]

Insistence on preserving the old constitutional arrangement was combined with the assertion that the assemblies had always been for their respective colonies what Parliament was for the mother country. They owed allegiance and were subordinate to the crown, not to the Parliament of Britain. An essay taken from *The Gentleman's Magazine* of 1768 explained the constitutional situation thus:

The British nation or the British Empire consists of different islands and distant countries, clearly separated from each other and in different parts of the globe. But all are united and connected by their allegiance to One Sovereign, and the Common Law, with the exception of Scotland, which had already become part of the old provinces or the mother country before the colonies or the new provinces were formed. The Sovereign together with an

---

of Nov. 4, 1771. On the reaction of Governor Hutchinson, see Thomas, *History of Printing in America*, pp. 165–68.

[173] *Staatsbote*, July 27, 1773 (with Hutchinson's letter of Dec. 12, 1767), quotation from Miller's paraphrase of the resolutions of the Massachusetts Assembly on the letters. On Mar. 8, 1774, Miller published the condemnation of Chief Justice Oliver for accepting a salary from the crown and becoming 'an enemy to the constitution of this colony.' On Mar. 15, 1774, Miller printed the letter in which Franklin confessed being responsible for having the letters sent to Boston.

elected parliament or assembly constitute the legislative power within and for each respective province.[174]

The opposing view, held by the monarch and the majority in both houses of Parliament, was ridiculed and taken to the point of absurdity. Since the colonists were considered subjects without rights, an essay in 1767 warned, they and the Irish could be ceded by the crown to another European monarch; the proceeds could be used to solve the problem of Britain's staggering public debt with one stroke.[175] Another piece of agitation consisted of a mock edict of the King of Prussia that forbade the inhabitants of the British Isles to make hats, establish iron mills, transport wool from one district to another, etc., because all commercial activity had to be organized to the advantage of the fatherland. Why? Because under the leadership of Hengist and Horsa, Hella and Uffa, subjects of a predecessor of Frederick's had migrated to these islands, and its population was, therefore, still subject to his royal will.[176]

By the spring of 1774 the *Staatsbote*, faithfully reflecting the English-language press, had not yet reported arguments or activities openly in favor of independence and republicanism. But the dangers of dependence, of subordination to a Parliament that lacked representativeness and moral authority, and the fear of administration by corrupt crown officials, had been presented as extensively as in the other organs of colonial public opinion. German readers were thus no less prepared than the other colonists for the complete break with the mother country.

INDEPENDENCE

Shortly after the beginning of the Revolutionary War in April 1775, the editors of both German newspapers decided that the speed of events demanded more frequent publication. Sower changed from biweekly to weekly publication, Miller from weekly to semiweekly. 'Since these critical times necessarily make every reader of newspapers desirous of learning the latest news,' Miller explained to his readers, 'the editor decided

---

[174] *Staatsbote*, May 10, 1768. The piece from *The Gentleman's Magazine* of Jan. 1768 was signed 'A.B.' and entitled 'A Defense of the Americans.'

[175] *Staatsbote*, Aug. 3, 1767.

[176] *Staatsbote*, Dec. 21, 1773. In the same mood, Miller covered 2 pages of the Dec. 28, 1773, issue with the essay on 'How to Make a Large Empire into a Small One,' from *The Gentleman's Magazine* of Sept. 1773.

to publish his newspaper twice a week, Tuesdays and Fridays, half a folio each, for the old price of six shillings a year.'[177] He could keep the old price because the output of printed pages remained the same.

Both German printers sided with the colonial opposition to the Coercive Acts. The five issues of Christopher Sower's newspaper that survive from the years 1774 and 1775 indicate that he as well as Miller reported all the major steps in the conflict, including items favorable to the colonists' cause. The later behavior of the third Christopher Sower (1754–1799) and his father's neutrality after the Declaration of Independence have led to the false impression that the Sowers were consistent Tories from the beginning.

In April 1774 Sower printed an alleged letter from a British officer stationed in New York to a friend in London that described the enthusiasm with which New Yorkers, Bostonians, and Philadelphians opposed the landing of East India Company tea. Two columns of detailed news from London included reports on John Wilkes's fight for his seat in the House of Commons, Franklin's activities as colonial agent, and an unnamed London newspaper's assessment of American affairs as 'more serious and alarming than ever.' After noting that in London it was said that Parliament would soon authorize the shipping of seven more regiments to America, abolish the colonial assemblies, and invite the colonists to elect representatives to the House of Commons, Sower himself commented, 'then our liberties would be gone.'[178] In September 1774 Sower printed in full the resolves of the North Carolina convention of August 25, which announced the nonimportation agreement and other measures of resistance. The same issue contained accounts of the late developments in Massachusetts, Connecticut, Rhode Island, and New York. In the report on mob action against the Mandamus Councillors the technical term was neither translated nor explained. Sower also printed the opinion of a correspondent from Massachusetts who claimed, 'The spirit of the people has never been higher here. For a hundred miles around Boston the inhabitants are prepared and willing to die or be free.[179]

Nor does the issue of June 1775 read like a Tory sheet. It contained the complete text of several declarations of the Continental Congress and

[177] The earliest extant of Sower's *Germantowner Wochen-Blat* is that of June 22, 1775, no. 606. Miller's note in *Staatsbote*, May 16, 1775.

[178] *Germantowner Zeitung*, Apr. 21, 1774.

[179] *Germantowner Zeitung*, Sept. 22, 1774.

other items that supported resistance: 'If the Americans continue to be as united as they have been so far,' a piece taken from a London newspaper said, 'the power of this island over them will be as a drop in the ocean. If they are firm in their non-importation association, our merchants and manufacturers will soon find themselves in a sad state.'[180] The same was true of the December 1775 issue, which reported that thirty-four British officers had returned their patents to General Gage because their duty as officers would be incompatible with their feelings as human beings in this civil war.[181] Compared to Miller's *Staatsbote*, however, Sower's *Germantowner Wochen-Blat*, as it was now called, was a rather detached recorder of events and opinions. Miller, in contrast, tried to make opinion and influence events.

For Miller, now in his seventies, the last two years before independence was the high point of a distinguished career as a crusading printer and editor. He became totally partisan to the American cause. When James Rivington's printing shop in New York was vandalized because of the printer's alleged loyalist sympathies, Miller printed not a word of warning against further encroachments on the liberty of the press. And when he reported acts of mob violence in Massachusetts, including barely averted lynchings, he moralized: 'These are, dear reader, the effects of a government the people do not trust any longer. Let those who pretend that they fear disorder and confusion in society realize that the only effective measure to preserve them is to join in the effort of placing the administration of government into the hands of men whom the people honor and love.'[182] In all his reports on crowds preventing the landing of tea and on other acts of violence, Miller consistently accepted the classic revolutionary rhetoric that 'the people' had acted.[183]

The amount of general European news in the *Staatsbote* decreased noticeably in favor of information about the conflict between the colonies and the mother country. Beginning with the issue of May 17, 1774, it became increasingly clear that crown and Parliament would retaliate

---

[180] *Germantowner Wochen-Blat*, June 22, 1775.

[181] *Germantowner Wochen-Blat*, Dec. 28, 1775. Another item from London on the drastic decline of trade and riots in its wake even asked, 'Who can say that none of these events will shake the throne?'

[182] On Rivington, *Staatsbote*, Nov. 28, 1775. 'Eine Geschichte.' *Staatsbote*, Apr. 12, 1774, a fable with the message that Governor Hutchinson 'ought to be hanged because he is responsible for all disorders of the last years.' Quote from *Staatsbote*, Feb. 15, 1774.

[183] E.g., *Staatsbote*, May 3, 1774, under the dateline 'Neuyork, den 21. April 1774.'

and punish Boston severely. Miller commented by comparing the American struggle to that of the Netherlands against Spain: 'What Parliament can do to Boston it can do to any town in America. The motto of the United Netherlands is "Unity makes for Power." This the colonies should never forget under the present circumstances.' Following the established pattern, Miller published as many gubernatorial proclamations as he could find in the English-language newspapers, as well as resolutions of assemblies, congresses, committees of correspondence, county committees, town meetings, mass meetings, and committees of merchants and artisans relating to the resistance against the Coercive Acts in all colonies. As a special supplement to the *Staatsbote* he published the extensive refutation of the Coercive Acts in the 'Phocion' letters. The anonymous author reminded the king of the wise moderation with which he had reacted in 1770 to the insult of the British flag by Spain when it took over the Falkland Islands. 'Phocion,' who took his pseudonym from the Athenian general who had successfully negotiated a peace between Athens and the Antipaters, warned, 'When princes fail to do their duty as rulers, the subjects are free of their allegiance to them; the relationship is reciprocal.'[184]

Needless to say, the activities of the First Continental Congress were fully covered in the *Staatsbote*, from the thirty-two toasts drunk at the welcoming reception of the city of Philadelphia for the delegates, to daily summaries of what was said to have been debated during the sessions, to the recommendation for the convening of a second Congress in May 1775.[185] Shortly after the Congress adjourned, Miller published a booklet of ninety-six pages that contained all the resolutions, petitions, and addresses of the Congress in German. The advertisement stated that he translated and printed the pamphlet 'by order of the Congress.'[186] The Second Continental Congress received the same extensive coverage.[187]

This sort of publicity was not a side effect of the actual transfer of power

[184] *Staatsbote*, Sept. 20, 1774.

[185] *Staatsbote*, Sept. 20 – Nov. 8, 1774.

[186] Advertisement in *Staatsbote*, Nov. 29, 1774. *Auszüge aus den Stimmungen und Verhandlungen des Americanischen Congresses vom Vesten Lande, gehalten zu Philadelphia, den 5ten September 1774* (Philadelphia, 1774) (Evans 13735). In 1775 Miller published a second enlarged edition (Evans 42957).

[187] The major resolutions and addresses of the first months appeared in the *Staatsbote* of June 16, July 11, 14, 25, and 28, 1775. On Dec. 15 and 19, Miller printed excerpts from the journal of the Congress.

but a vital part of it. Without it the new center of power could hardly have established its authority over the country as easily as it did. The de facto government by provincial congresses and committees that developed from the summer of 1774 on, could not have functioned as well as it did without the press as connecting link between the population and the decision-makers. This fact is illustrated by the great number of detailed ordinances on matters like sheep raising, nailmaking, and bread prices, as well as by such announcements as 'The members of the Committee of the County of Philadelphia are requested to meet at the Germantown schoolhouse on Thursday, February 16, punctually at eleven o'clock.'[188]

Miller published the first news of Lexington and Concord on April 25. Its significance as a starting signal was clear from the beginning. He emphasized the authenticity of the first account with the concluding remark, 'A true copy of the original, by the order of the Committee of Correspondence of Worcester; witnessed to and communicated by the Committees of Brookline, Norwich, New London, Lyme, Saybrook, East Guilford, Guilford, Branford, New Haven.' The chain of communication from the event to the editor via the committees of correspondence proved its usefulness. Dozens of depositions of eyewitnesses, also collected and relayed by the Worcester committee, followed in the next issues of the *Staatsbote*.[189] As was to be expected, detailed reports about military preparations and actions from all over the colonies made up a substantial amount of Miller's news thereafter. General European news decreased proportionally. The report of March 8, 1776, that British and French navy vessels had clashed was followed by Miller's comment, 'Perhaps this evil will lead to something good for America, if England and France get in each other's hair.'

The first detailed accounts of mercenaries hired by the crown from the sovereigns of Hessen, Kassel, Braunschweig, Hannover, and Waldeck was commented upon by the editor with the exclamation, 'O George! Are these your messengers of peace?'[190] Closer to home, Miller was instrumental in the debate about the Articles of Association in Pennsylvania

---

[188] Examples in *Staatsbote*, Dec. 20, 1774, Jan. 10, Feb. 7, 1775.
[189] *Staatsbote*, May 2 and 16, 1775.
[190] *Staatsbote*, May 7, 1776.

by which a militia in a permanent state of mobilization (available on a minute's notice) was to be created.[191]

Miller was probably also the printer of three German war songs that were published as broadsides in 1775. The earliest one, entitled 'A Song of the Present Condition of America,' was rhymed in reaction to the Coercive Acts. It was illustrated with a striking woodcut nearly five inches high of a farmer-soldier. A prose translation of five of the fourteen stanzas reads:

> 5. The Act in favor of the Catholics
>   is meant to suppress us.
>   In our North-America
>   the Protestant gospel
>   is to be heard no longer.
>   Idolatry is being established,
>   we are in danger, God help us.
>
> .   .   .   .
>
> 9. And when we have succeeded
>   in fighting the King,
>   who will then be responsible for the ignominy,
>   America or England?
>   Certainly the latter!
>   America will have peace
>   and be free of tyranny.
>
> 10. But what about the other princes
>   who thirst for conquests,
>   will they not disturb our quiet?
>   Each of them is eager
>   to acquire a part of America.
>
> 11. What will France do,
>   and Spain and Portugal,
>   and Holland and Prussia?

[191] Undated anonymous broadside *An die Unter-Officiers und Gemeinen der verschiedenen Companien Associators, die zur Stadt und den Freyheiten von Philadelphia gehören* (Apr. 1776, probably printed by Miller) (Evans 14508). That Evans's dating (1775) is wrong becomes apparent from Peter Force, ed., *American Archives*, 4th ser. 4, cols. 922–23 and 5, cols. 696–713.

They all want part of it,
even if it will cost them thousands of men,
because America is going to pay for it all.

.   .   .   .

13. If the King only listened to us
and not to his false servants in Parliament,
all contention would soon be over,
peace and quiet would return.
His income would increase,
we would be his servants,
without having been subdued in a war.[192]

After Bunker Hill a dirge 'by Oppressed Liberty' was published in the same format, probably also by Miller. The rhythmic, fervent stanzas, foreshadowing nineteenth-century *Vaterlandslyrik*, lamented 'the blood shed at Charlestown,' called America 'the dear fatherland,' and ended with 'dead or free I want to be.'[193]

Beginning in 1774, the idea of independence kept recurring in publications in German. Typical of the early stage of the discussion was the conditional mode of reasoning evident in a speech given before a group of Philadelphia artisans that Miller published. It pleaded for united resistance and recognition of the authority of the Continental Congress but rejected independence as a decoy invented by the administration to scare the British public into acquiescence in its policies. The disclaimer ended on the note, 'If Great Britain, torn by interior strife and emasculated by luxury, like Rome, will no longer be able to maintain its position among the powers of Europe, then its colonies, like those of Rome, will become the prey of a foreign power, unless they seek independence.'[194] Until April 1776 direct and open avowal of a declaration of independence as a

[192] *Ein Lied von dem gegenwärtigen Zustand in America*, German-language Broadsides, American Antiquarian Society, also in Historical Society of Pennsylvania. The woodcut that decorates this broadside is identical with the one entitled 'John, Duke of Argyle,' shown in Elizabeth Carroll Reilly, *A Dictionary of Colonial American Printers' Ornaments and Illustrations* (Worcester, Mass., 1975), p. 381. Of the same format, spirit and period (shortly before Lexington and Concord) is *Ein Lied gegen das unrechte Verfahren des Königs gegen America*, American Antiquarian Society.
[193] *Das Trauer Lied der unterdrückten Freyheit*, German-language Broadsides, American Antiquarian Society.
[194] *Staatsbote*, Sept. 6, 1774, translated from the *Pennsylvania Gazette*, Aug. 31, 1774.

next step to be taken was, however, as noticeably absent from Miller's pages as it was from the whole body of Revolutionary Whig writing.[195]

The spectacular exception, Paine's *Common Sense*, was better advertised in the *Staatsbote* than any previous pamphlet. On January 16 Miller ran an advertisement in English for Robert Bell's edition; on January 23, and several times thereafter, he ran a bilingual advertisement, the German part of which announced, 'Now in press, and to be published by Steiner and Cist in about two weeks, a tract translated from English into German entitled *Gesunde Vernunft*.' The four section headings and a quotation from James Thomson on masters and slaves made up the rest of the advertisement. From February 26 on, Miller had *Gesunde Vernunft* on sale in his bookstore, but he did not print excerpts from it in the *Staatsbote*.[196]

Only in April 1776 did the first explicit expressions of opinion in favor of independence appear in the *Staatsbote*, and even then only in the form of letters from correspondents to English-language newspapers.[197]

Almost no public discussion of the issue of independence took place among the Germans themselves. Several publications in German, however, specifically appealed to German and Swiss immigrants by referring to German and Swiss history. When, for instance, Miller advertised John Dickinson's 1774 pamphlet *An Essay on the Constitutional Power of Great-Britain over the Colonies in America*, he translated, as part of the advertisement, the passage that described the baneful effects of standing armies in Germany and appealed to ethnic pride by reciting the Saxon myth of English constitutional law: 'The Germans may, indeed, be called the fathers of Englishmen. Their ancestors came from Germany, and so did the fundamental principles of their constitution. The Germans, therefore, appear to have a better claim than any other foreigners to the rights

[195] The following articles in the *Staatsbote* urge resistance and indirectly touch on the question of independence, but never plead directly in its favor. 'An die Freyleute von America' by 'Ein Philadelphier,' May 24, 1774; 'An den Drucker der *St. James Chronik*' by 'Cassius,' July 19, 1774; 'Eintracht bringt Macht,' Aug. 2, 1774; 'An Lord North' by 'Ein Soldat,' Aug. 9, 1774; 'An den König' by 'Amor Regentis,' Mar. 7, 1775; 'An Lord Dartmouth' by 'Ein Americaner,' Aug. 8, 1775; 'An den Hochedlen Lord Dartmouth, Staats-Secretär für America' by 'Ein Engländischer Americaner,' Feb. 13, 1776; 'Ihr Deutschen in America, besonders in Pennsylvanien!' by 'Ein Deutscher Freyheits-Freund,' Mar. 19, 1776; 'Ein Mährchen,' Apr. 16, 1776; 'Eine Zweyte Berufung auf die Gerechtigkeit und Vortheile des Volks über die jetzigen America betreffenden Maaßregeln,' May 14, 1776.
[196] Advertisement in *Staatsbote*, Feb. 23, 1776.
[197] *Staatsbote*, Apr. 5 and 23, 1776.

guaranteed by this constitution. To enjoy them in this free country, they came here and now they find themselves persecuted by arbitrary government and a standing army even into these forests.'[198]

Of similar ethnic appeal was John Joachim Zubly's sixteen-page account of how the Swiss fought for their freedom, which Miller published in 1775.[199] With a letter he claimed to be from Germany, Miller in January 1776 conveyed the impression that those who had stayed behind now expected 'our Germans who live in America and enjoy the sweetness of freedom more than they ever could have under our arbitrary and wretched rulers' to fight for liberty. If Germans were to be sent over as mercenaries in the crown's service, the writer consoled his emigrant compatriots, they need not fear. Once in America, they would throw away their weapons and take up the plow.[200] In March 1776 Miller published a stirring piece consisting of a patriotic litany, 'Remember the Stamp Act . . . Remember the Declaratory Act . . . Remember the blood bath of Boston.' To these items, which he had translated from an English-language newspaper, he added, at the request of 'a German friend of liberty,' a vivid reminder of the plight of the common man in feudal Europe:

—Remember—and remind your families—, you came to America, suffering many hardships, in order to escape servitude and enjoy liberty.
—Remember, in Germany serfs ['leibeigene'] may not marry without the consent of their master, . . . they are regarded as little better than black slaves on West Indian islands. . . .
—Remember the forced labor ['Frondienst'] which subjects, especially peasants, must in some places still perform for their overlords. . . .
—Remember the almost unbearable taxes with which the princes burden their subjects. . . .
—Remember, how in many places a farmer is not permitted to shoot the deer which devastates his freshly sown fields. . . .
—Remember, how in times of war soldiers drive the citizen and farmer

[198] *Staatsbote*, Sept. 20, 1774.
[199] *Eine Kurzgefasste Historische Nachricht von den Kämpfen der Schweitzer für die Freyheit* (Philadelphia, 1775). Shortly before, Miller had published John Joachim Zubly's sermon *The Law of Liberty*, which contained the English version of the same account as an appendix. The *Staatsbote*, July 26, 1776, contained Salomon Geßner's didactic idyll 'Das hölzerne Bein,' on the battle of Näfels, in Canton Glarus in 1388.
[200] *Staatsbote*, Jan. 5, 1776. The letter may well be a production of the editor or of one of his Philadelphia friends. On June 28, 1776, Miller printed a similarly doubtful piece which suggested widespread support in Germany for the rebelling colonists.

209

almost out of his house, occupy his best rooms and his beds, and make the owner himself sleep on straw or on a bench.

—Remember that the administration of Britain and its Parliament intends to treat Americans the same way, or worse.[201]

Political agitation based on remembrance of old world experiences, such as this example, was very rare in the German press. It operated on the premise that the British limited monarchy was drifting toward continental absolutism, that Britain's colonies were therefore also threatened by Europeanization, and that the emigrants from Germany knew what that meant.

The only extended public discourse among Germans themselves on the issue of resistance was contained in a formal statement of two organized groups. The council of the Lutheran and the Reformed churches of Philadelphia and the officers of the German Society of Philadelphia joined in an epistle to the German inhabitants of New York and North Carolina that Miller published in August 1775. They acted in response to a request by the Continental Congress, and the bulk of the pamphlet consisted of an appendix with the complete text of all major addresses of the First and Second Continental Congresses.[202] The statement reviewed the development of the conflict since the Stamp Act. It rejected as unconstitutional Parliament's claim to legislative authority over the colonies 'in all cases whatsoever,' and maintained that the colonies possessed the means to resist submission by force if all groups, including the Germans, joined in the effort. The administration, it went on, underestimated the colonists because it forgot that 'there is an important difference between an English peasant who may not carry a loaded gun even on his own land and in his own garden, and an American peasant who has the right to hunt deer and other animals for hundreds of miles.'

The Philadelphia Germans then proceeded to attack the indifference of their compatriots in North Carolina and New York. They blamed the lack of enthusiasm for the colonial cause (the words 'loyalism' or 'Toryism' were avoided) in North Carolina's Tryon County on the lack of information of those living 'far away from the large cities and sea ports,

[201] *Staatsbote*, Mar. 9, 1776.
[202] *Schreiben des Evangelisch-Lutherisch und Reformirten Kirchen-Raths wie auch der Beamten der Teutschen Gesellschaft in der Stadt Philadelphia an die Teutschen Einwohner der Provinzen von Neuyork und Nord-Carolina* (Philadelphia, 1775), pp. 12–40, contains the major addresses of the First and Second Continental Congresses.

where week after week, and sometimes day after day, one can read and hear reliable news of all that is happening in England and the colonies.' The Germans were at an additional disadvantage, they said, because 'when occasionally English-language newspapers find their way into the interior of the province, the Germans cannot read them, and they learn only what their English neighbors choose to tell them.' The loyalism among Germans in New York was explained by their dependent status as tenants of a few large landowners. The Philadelphians did not incite them to revolt, but they did suggest that instead of craving favor with their lord of the manor, they should consider the advantages they would enjoy in the future, once the liberty of the land was secured. They instructed the New York and North Carolina Germans to make a special effort to get hold of German-language newspapers. Any published reaction of those for whom this pamphlet was published does not appear to have survived, and no public debate among the Germans about resistance and independence was begun.

Another example of this kind of one-way communication, this time from opponents of independence, was *The Ancient Testimony* of a committee speaking for the Quakers of Pennsylvania and New Jersey. It was given to Sower and his sons to translate and publish in 2,000 copies; it aroused considerable hostility toward them and led to their reputation as Tory publishers. In obvious reaction to *Common Sense*, the Quakers rejected 'with detestation' the idea of a separation from Britain, and quoted from a 1696 testimony the principle 'that it is God's privilege to make and unmake kings and governments, and that we should have no part in it.'[203]

After the resolutions of the Continental Congress of May 10 and 15, 1776, which constituted a declaration of independence for all practical, domestic purposes, either Miller or Steiner and Cist published a German translation of the brief but incisive pamphlet *The Alarm*.[204] Applying the

---

[203] *Das Alte Zeugniß und die Grund-Sätze des Volks so man Quäker nennet, erneuert, In Ansehung des Königs und der Regierung; und wegen der nunmehr herrschenden Unruhen in diesem und andern Theilen von America. An das Volk überhaupt gerichtet* (Germantown, 1776). The Quaker Monthly Meeting of Sufferings held on June 6, 1778, instructed its treasurer to pay the Sowers 'the sum of forty-four pounds, sixteen shillings and three pence for translating, printing and binding two thousand pamphlets in German.' Durnbaugh, *Brethren in Colonial America*, pp. 396–97.

[204] *The Alarm, or, An Address to the People of Pennsylvania* (n.p., n.d.), pp. 2, 3 (Evans 14642). An 18th-century hand at the end of the copy used for the microcard edition states, 'Distributed on Sunday May 19th 1776 in Philadelphia.' Internal evidence

resolution to the situation in Pennsylvania, it asked the classic revolutionary question, 'What is to be done?' and concluded with the typical American answer, 'We are now arrived at a period from which we are to look forward as *a legal people*. The Resolve of Congress, grounded on the justest foundation, hath recommended it to us, to establish a regular plan of *legal government;* and the means which they have recommended for that purpose are, either by Assemblies or *Conventions*.' The unnamed author, obviously one of Pennsylvania's radical Whigs, argued in favor of a newly elected convention to replace the existing Assembly, which opposed independence.

On July 2 Miller published an essay by 'Republicus,' translated from the *Pennsylvania Evening Post*, that rejected any hope for reconciliation and rejoiced in the proud designation 'The United States of America,' which would soon have to be introduced. The Declaration of Independence was adopted on a Thursday, and since the *Staatsbote* was the only newspaper to be published in Philadelphia on Friday, Miller was given his well-deserved chance to take his place in the annals of American nationalism and German-American patriotism. Before any English-language newspaper did so, the *Staatsbote* announced in conspicuous type: 'Yesterday the Honorable Congress of this continent declared the United Colonies to be free and independent states. The declaration, in English, is now in press; it is dated July 4, 1776, and will be published today or tomorrow.'[205] Over the weekend Miller produced an excellent translation of the complete text, and on Tuesday he published it in the *Staatsbote* on the most imposing title page he ever printed. Beyond the lavish layout, Miller saw no need to comment.[206]

---

supports this dating. The German edition was entitled *Der Alarm, oder, Eine Erweckungs-Zuschrift an das Volk von Pennsylvanien.*

[205] 'Gestern hat der Achtbare Congreß dieses Vesten Landes die Vereinigten Colonien Freye und Unabhängige Staaten erkläret. Die Declaration in Englisch ist jetzt in der Presse; sie ist datiert, den 4ten July, 1776, und wird heut oder morgen im druck erscheinen.' *Staatsbote*, July 5, 1776.

[206] *Staatsbote*, July 9, 1776. The first sentences of the Declaration read: 'Wenn es im Lauf menschlicher Begebenheiten für ein Volk nöthig wird die Politischen Bande, wodurch es mit einem andern verknüpft gewesen, zu trennen, und unter den Mächten der Erden eine abgesonderte und gleiche Stelle einzunehmen, wozu selbiges die Gesetze der Natur und des GOTTES der Natur berechtigen, so erfordern Anstand und Achtung in die Meinungen des menschlichen Geschlechts, daß es die Ursachen anzeige, wodurch es zur Trennung getrieben wird. Wir halten diese Wahrheiten für ausgemacht, daß alle Menschen gleich erschaffen worden, daß sie von ihrem Schöpfer

For the next phase of the development of an American nation-state, the framing of constitutions and the establishment of permanent governmental institutions, the press continued to play as essential a role as it had done in the previous phases of resistance and government by committees. The first reports on newly established constitutions appeared in the *Staatsbote* at the end of April 1776 when it was learned that South Carolina's Provincial Congress had promulgated a new constitution. In June Miller printed the complete text of the Virginia Bill of Rights, in August that of Pennsylvania.[207] In October he announced the adoption of the constitution of Pennsylvania. Only thereafter did public discussion about the controversial provisions of the new fundamental law of the state reach the pages of the *Staatsbote* in the form of translated items from other Pennsylvania newspapers. At first the liberal form of religious affirmations in the oath of office in Article 10 caused debate. One author, whose letter to the *Pennsylvania Evening Post* Miller translated, wanted to see 'Deists, Jews, Mohametans, and other enemies of Christ' excluded from holding public office.[208] More extended and detailed critiques of the new constitution by mass meetings and by individuals, and refutations of these, followed soon. Additional articles and broadsides in German appeared from time to time until 1790, when Pennsylvania's mild 'counter-revolution' brought the experiment with the unicameral legislature to an end.[209] In this conflict Miller reverted to his former role of the liberal edi-

---

mit gewissen unveräusserlichen Rechten begabt worden, worunter sind Leben, Freyheit und das Bestreben nach Glückseligkeit. Daß zur Versicherung dieser Rechte Regierungen unter den Menschen eingeführt worden sind, welche ihre gerechte Gewalt von der Einwilligung derer die regiert werden, herleiten; daß sobald eine Regierungsform diesen Endzwecken verderblich wird, es das Recht des Volks ist sie zu verändern oder abzuschaffen, und eine neue Regierung einzusetzen, die auf solche Grundsätze gegründet, und deren Macht und Gewalt solchergestalt gebildet wird, als ihnen zur Erhaltung ihrer Sicherheit und Glückseligkeit am schicklichsten zu seyn dünket.'

[207] *Staatsbote*, Apr. 30, May 3, June 18, Aug. 27, 1776.

[208] *Staatsbote*, Oct. 1, 1776.

[209] *Staatsbote*, Oct. 29 and Nov. 5, 1776. *An die hochgeehrten Glieder der Assembly des Pennsylvanischen Staats: Das Memorial verschiedener Einwohner der Graffschaft Lancaster* (n.p., 1777?) (Evans 15379). *In der General Assembly von Pennsylvanien, Samstags, den 28sten November, 1778* (Philadelphia, 1778), broadside by Steiner and Cist (Evans 15966). 'Ackermann,' *An das Volk von Pennsylvanien: Erster Brief* (n.p, 1779) (Evans 13113); Evan's dating of the broadside as 1774 is obviously erroneous. 'Sully,' 'Ein politischer Abriß des Staates von Pennsylvanien; *Staatsbote*, Feb. 24, 1779, with the response by 'Tully.' The *Staatsbote*, Apr. 7, 1779, contained the charter of the Constitutional Society of

tor who opened his pages to the contending parties; a role he had decidedly not played in the conflict over the separation from Britain. The stakes, then, had been too momentous; exactly what shape the republican constitution of Pennsylvania would take was of less concern to him.

During the course of the war only a few more German-language texts were published. Some were addressed to the German mercenaries, including a handbill printed for the Continental Congress promising every deserter fifty acres of land.[210] On the loyalist side, Christopher Sower III wrote a pamphlet addressed to the German settlers that pointed out the lack of freedom of speech and press under 'the tyranny of Congress,' reminded them of the deterioration of their paper money and the costs of war, and, as late as November 1780, called for resistance to the rebel governments: no taxes should be paid to the usurpers; Congress's paper money should be refused as currency; the militia should not let itself be drawn into service in the Continental Army; and everybody should talk openly to his neighbors about the hardship and repression suffered under the rebel regime.[211] On the patriot side, a few sermons supporting the war effort and, finally, celebrating victory and peace were printed in German.[212]

DEMISE OF THE PIONEERS

Both veteran German printing houses were caught between the millstones of the Revolution. Beginning in 1775, the third generation of Sowers took increasing control over the family enterprise. Christopher III

Philadelphia. In 1784 the Council of Censors of Pennsylvania ordered 2,500 copies of the text of the constitution and the Council's Report from Steiner and Cist: *Die Regierungsverfassung der Republik Pennsylvanien* (Philadelphia, 1784). The Council's report of 28 pages constitutes a full explanation of Pennsylvania's system of government.

[210] 'Im Congreß, den 14ten August, 1776,' facsimile in Lyman H. Butterfield, 'Psychological Warfare in 1776: The Jefferson–Franklin Plan to Cause Hessian Desertions,' *Proceedings of the American Philosophical Society* 94 (1950), facing p. 239. *An das Publicum. Im Sicherheits-Rath, Philadelphia, den Ersten Jenner, 1777*, broadside (Evans 15521), is an appeal to treat Hessian prisoners of war well, because they were victims of tyrannical petty princes.

[211] [Christopher Sower III], *Zuschrift an die Teutschen in Pennsylvanien, und benachbarten Provinzen* (New York, 1780) (Evans suppl. 43897). A modern translation can be found in Durnbaugh, *Brethren in Colonial America*, pp. 408–19.

[212] Hugh Henry Brackenridge, *Eine Lobrede auf die jenigen tapferen Männer, welche in dem Streit mit Groß-Britannien gefallen, gehalten am Montag, dem 5. Juli 1779* (Philadelphia, 1779). Johann Christoph Kunze, *Eine Aufforderung an das Volk Gottes in America* (Philadelphia, 1784), published by Melchior Steiner.

and his younger brother Peter gave up the cautious course of their father, who had sympathized with the defense of colonial rights until 1775 but in the end had not dared to draw the radical conclusion. In December 1776 the Sowers, father and son, were summoned to appear before the Council of Safety of Pennsylvania. The summons forbade them 'to print in the meantime any political piece whatever, either as a newspaper, or handbill, or disperse any already printed until further orders.'[213] Whether the Sowers appeared before the Council is not known, but the signal was unmistakable. The Sowers were no longer free to publish what they chose. The last extant number of the *Germantowner Zeitung* is that of March 19, 1777. Shortly after British troops occupied Philadelphia in September 1777 the younger Sowers removed the printing presses to Philadelphia and openly espoused the cause of crown and Parliament in their new weekly *Der Pennsylvanische Staats-Courier*. It was probably read mainly by German soldiers stationed in Philadelphia, and it broke off with Howe's departure in June 1778.

In May 1778 the Executive Council of Pennsylvania, in exile at Lancaster, charged seventy-five Pennsylvanians with high treason because they had 'joined the armies of the enemy.' Both Christopher Sowers were among those named. In addition, they had disregarded the Test Act of 1777 which required every adult man to swear an oath of allegiance to the new state of Pennsylvania. (As Brethren, the Sowers refused, for religious reasons, to swear oaths of any kind.)

On May 23, possibly before he had heard of the edict, the fifty-seven-year-old elder Sower returned to Germantown from Philadelphia, where he had gone to live with his children. A whole company of militia came to capture him asleep in his bed, and mistreated and humiliated him before taking him to Washington's camp at Valley Forge. He was released after a few days, but confiscation of the Sower estate seems to have been an inevitable result. Without hearing or trial the elder Sower was forced out of his house on July 30, 1778, his only property the clothes on his back and, as a special favor, the spectacles on his nose. His whole estate, personal and real, was sold at auction. He died in 1784.[214]

---

[213] Durnbaugh, *Brethren in Colonial America*, p. 388.

[214] Detailed documentary accounts of the end of the Sower printing house in Durnbaugh, *Brethren in Colonial America*, chap. 11, 'The Sauer Family,' and Hocker, *Sower Printing House*, pp. 90–110. See also Knauss, 'Christopher Saur the Third,' pp. 235–53. On the value of the estate see pp. 172–73, above.

Christopher III did not deliver himself into the hands of Revolutionary justice but removed with the British troops to New York and continued to be of service to the occupation forces as an informant and translator, printer, and, as we have seen, pamphleteer. At the end of the war he went to Britain and gained indemnification from the claims commission as a certifiable loyalist.[215]

While the Sowers sought refuge in Philadelphia under Howe, Miller fled the city, leaving his press behind. The last *Staatsbote* issued before he departed, dated September 17, 1777, he had to publish without any assistance 'because every honorable man is now occupied with the defense of his country and its freedom.' When he returned in July 1778, after Howe's departure in June, he found his best press and all his type stolen. He told the public in a German broadside, which was translated in the *Pennsylvania Packet*, how Christopher Sower III and an English printer in Howe's service had attempted to 'buy' the press from Miller's housekeeper and, in the end, had carried it off to the waiting ships. The type, Miller claimed, was irreplaceable in the colonies. Behind this act of confiscation he saw a great design 'to deprive the Germans in this country of a knowledge of public affairs ('publike Sachen') so that they might be kept in ignorance and remain dupes to one of the parties, which since the beginning of this contest have done too much mischief in this state.'[216] Within weeks he managed to borrow a press and put together a two-page issue. On August 5, 1778, the *Staatsbote* was back in print.

Finally, with issue number 920, published on May 29, 1779, the seventy-eight-year-old printer, editor, translator, and publisher said farewell to his readers. He retired to spend his last years quietly in the Moravian community at Bethlehem, where he died in 1782. Within months of the cessation of the *Staatsbote*, Melchior Steiner and Carl Cist began publishing a successor, the *Philadelphisches Staatsregister*, which reported extensively on the concluding phase of the war and on the peace negotiations.[217]

[215] Durnbaugh, *Brethren in Colonial America*, pp. 419–23; Hocker, *Sower Printing House*, pp. 110–14; Knauss, 'Christopher Saur the Third.'

[216] *Henrich Millers, des Buchdruckers in Philadelphia, nöthige Vorstellung an die Deutschen in Pennsylvanien* (Philadelphia, 1778), signed July 22, 1778; 'A Robbery of a Printing Office,' *Pennsylvania Packet*, July 25, 1778.

[217] The *Philadelphisches Staatsregister* was published weekly from July 21, 1779, to sometime in 1781. From May 2, 1781, Steiner published the weekly alone, but with the editorial support of Johann Christoph Kunze and Justus H. C. Helmuth. He

The proliferation and regionalization of German weeklies after the war has already been mentioned.[218] It reflected the growth, mobility, enterprise and, beginning in the 1790s, the party politics of post-Revolutionary America. No doubt it took a pioneering spirit and great enterprise on the part of the later German journeyman printers to set up presses in the country towns of the middle and southern states and to move westward with the urban frontier, but the character of the German-language newspaper in America had clearly been established by the three pioneers, the first two Christopher Sowers and Henry Miller.

CONCLUSION

The newspapers, almanacs, pamphlets, and broadsides that the first German printers in America published for their fellow immigrants were not a piece of cultural baggage brought over from the fatherland. The great number of religious texts they also printed may have been identical with those imported from Halle and other centers of German Pietism and missionary Protestantism. The non-religious texts, however, show almost no connection with the intellectual life in Germany. No texts of German Enlightenment thinkers or men of letters were reprinted. And news about events and conditions in Germany drew only slightly more attention from the editors than European news in general. Any nostalgic reminiscence of an ethnic homeland was missing.

In one of the last numbers of the *Staatsbote*, possibly in response to complaints about the new subscription price of six dollars, Miller published an unusual defense of the quality of his newspaper. In doing so, he looked back on his principal intellectual activity, that of translator, and made it clear that he valued it.[219] Implicitly, his defense contained a justification of the basic character of the *Staatsbote*: it was essentially a translated Anglo-American newspaper. Miller knew that in providing this service, he and the Sowers and a few other German-speaking printers had been more creative and made a more unique contribution to American life than most printers of English-language weeklies whose main tools of

---

called it *Gemeinnützige Philadelphische Correspondenz*, and continued it until 1790. See Arndt and Olson, *German-American Newspapers*, p. 559. John Dunlap's attempt at starting a second German weekly failed, possibly after the first number of *Die Pennsylvanische Gazette, oder, der Allgemeine Americanische Zeitungsschreiber*, Feb. 3, 1779.

[218] See above, notes 52 to 63.

[219] *Staatsbote*, Apr. 7, 1779.

trade were scissors and paste. They had found the German language quite capable of expressing the subtleties of the great issues of British constitutional law. Indeed their verbal inventiveness, as they groped for German expressions to express the peculiarities of British political language, built political explanations into the very phraseology they used. So for the expression 'virtual representation,' the German printers used the clumsy but directly explanatory phrase 'wesentlich, obwohl nicht-förmlich im Parlament vorgestellet,' that is, 'essentially, if not formally, represented in Parliament.'

The editors conceived of their readers primarily as British subjects in America and only secondarily as an ethnic minority. Their attitude toward national identity was different from the nineteenth-century ideas with which we are familiar. The acceptance of feudal practices by which the extension of a prince's rule over foreign territories and peoples by nothing more than a marriage contract, made mobile subjects feel equally free to change their allegiance from one ruler to another. There was no reason to feel guilty about leaving one 'people' and joining another. The founders of the German Society of Philadelphia in 1764 saw no difficulty at all in styling themselves 'Seiner Königlichen Majestät von Großbritannien deutsche Unterthanen in Pennsylvania' ('His Royal Majesty of Great Britain's German Subjects in Pennsylvania').[220]

It was as inhabitants of the British colonies in America that the German immigrants shared in the development of a politically relevant public. That modern development had begun in England when, after the Glorious Revolution, the licensing and censorship laws had become the most liberal in Europe and had allowed London to become Europe's newspaper capital with several weeklies and dailies.[221] In 1704 the first weekly had been published in the colonies. In 1739 Christopher Sower joined the growing number of newspaper publishers in the colonies. After several unsuccessful attempts by others, Henry Miller, profiting from the newly aroused interest in world affairs during the Seven Years' War, started the second German newspaper in 1762. Both newspapers, together with a number of German-language broadsides and pamphlets,

[220] Minutes of the first meeting of the Society, quoted in Harry Pfund, *History of the German Society*, p. 30. For a full treatment of 18th-century ideas of citizenship see James H. Kettner, *The Development of American Citizenship, 1608–1870* (Chapel Hill, 1978).

[221] Frederick S. Siebert, *Freedom of the Press in England, 1476–1776: The Rise and Decline of Government Control* (Urbana, Ill., 1965).

faithfully reflected the movement toward independence. Miller became a Whig agitator, Sower defended colonial rights until the summer of 1775 but shied away from the radical step toward independence, and his sons became active loyalists.

The German-language press played a major role in the political culture that sustained the transformation of colonial territories and provincial societies into an independent American nation-state. It helped create an enlightened, politically relevant public opinion that gave practical meaning to the central principles of enlightened politics, popular sovereignty and the accountability of the rulers to their electors. In doing so it also played an active role in the process of nation-building. It helped the German-speaking minority to feel part of and to function in a larger national whole. And it did all of this in ways that were not much different from the ways by which the English-language press all over the colonies helped integrate their diverse audiences into a national community.

Appendix A

German-language publications, other than newspapers, with political content, 1764–1783

The source for the following list is Charles Evans's *American Bibliography*, 14 vols. (Chicago and Worcester, 1903–59) and Roger Bristol's *Supplement to Charles Evans' American Bibliography* (Charlottesville, 1970). Most of these appear in microform in the AAS–Readex Microprint Corporation series, Early American Imprints. Items in Evans are entered under the Evans numbers. Those items in Bristol that appear in the AAS–Readex set are entered under separate Microprint numbers. A few non-Evans items, held by the American Antiquarian Society in Worcester, have been added. The term 'political content,' for the purposes of this list, is taken to mean texts that address current or past problems of society as a whole, texts that are not primarily religious (in the sense of being oriented toward personal salvation and consolation) and not primarily instructional and informative, such as spelling books and handbooks of veterinary medicine. Sermons with an explicit political message and historical narratives are included. Almanacs are not included, although occasionally they contained matters of political content. The first German–American almanac was published in 1731, and from 1747 on several of them were offered by German printers each year. They are listed in Karl J. R. Arndt and May E. Olson, *German–American Newspapers and Periodicals, 1732–1955*, 2nd rev. ed. (New York, 1965).

1764

SOWER Anonymous election-day broadsheet, 2 pages, against Franklin and for the Morris–Keppele ticket. 'Höret ihr deutsche Bürger in Philadelphia, daß euch Gott auch höre!' Not in Evans or in Microprint. At AAS.

SOWER Anonymous leaflet of 4 pages reminding German voters of Franklin's insult of the 'Palatine Boors' in 1755. *Evans 9575.*

SOWER Pamphlet of 16 pages by Sower against change to royal government in Pennsylvania and in favor of the Morris–Dickinson–Keppele ticket. *Evans 9578.*

SOWER Same, with refutation by Franklin. Text lost. *Evans 9668.*

SOWER Broadside, probably by Sower himself, in defense of proprietary government and the rights of Englishmen. *Evans 9828.*

MILLER Petition to governor with frontier grievances. *Evans 9631.*

MILLER Dickinson's speech against change to royal government, with historical introduction, 50 pages. *Evans 9643.*

MILLER Galloway's speech answering Dickinson. *Evans 9673.*

MILLER Anonymous pamphlet for change to royal government. *Evans 9713.*

MILLER Broadside with song about Paxton Boys; against housing the Indians in the barracks and feeding them. *Evans 9715.*

MILLER Broadside against Franklin's reappointment as agent of the colony in London. *Evans 9803.*

MILLER Pamphlet against Franklin and change to royal government. *Evans 9865.*

ARMBRUSTER Pamphlet in favor of change to royal government. *Evans 9576.*

ARMBRUSTER Same subject matter. *Evans 9577.*

ARMBRUSTER Same subject matter. *Evans 9655.*

ARMBRUSTER Pamphlet of 8 pages by 'A Farmer' recounting the Paxton Boys affair. *Evans 9698.*

ARMBRUSTER Broadside with satirical poem on armed Quakers from Philadelphia guarding Indians. *Evans 9830.*

UNKNOWN PUBLISHER Pamphlet of 31 pages by Franklin on recent Indian massacre in Lancaster County. Translation of *Evans 9667. Evans 9666.*

1765

SOWER   Pamphlet against Franklin. *Evans 9904.*

SOWER   Broadside by Sower himself in support of sending delegates to Stamp Act Congress in New York. *Evans 10162.*

MILLER   Broadside in favor of Franklin. *Evans 9902.*

MILLER   Broadside with resolutions of Pennsylvania Assembly in answer to Sower's broadside of Sept. 28, 1765. (See *Evans 10162.*) *Evans 2611.*

1766

MILLER   Franklin's interrogation before Parliament. *Evans 10304.*

MILLER   Sermon by Mühlenberg, pastor of the German Lutheran Church of Philadelphia, in commemoration of the repeal of the Stamp Act. *Evans 10401.*

1768

MILLER   Pamphlet with song on William Tell and how the Swiss defended their liberty. *Evans 11068.*

1769

UNKNOWN PUBLISHER   New York election broadside in favor of John Cruger and De Lancey. *Evans 11389.*

UNKNOWN PUBLISHER   New York election broadside, also in favor of John Cruger and De Lancey. *Evans 11390.*

UNKNOWN PUBLISHER   New York election broadside in favor of Philip Livingston ticket. *Evans 11455.*

1772

MILLER   Broadside with resolutions of the Patriotic Society of the City and County of Philadelphia in favor of fair election practices. Membership described as 'a number of respectable merchants, artisans and freeholders.' No ethnic categories. *Evans 12525.*

1773

MILLER   Broadside by 'Publicus' in defense of the new Pennsylvania excise law. Translation of *Evans 12967. Evans 12968.*

1774

MILLER   Broadside by 'Ackermann,' addressed to the people of Pennsylvania and designated as Letter I. *Evans 13113.*

MILLER   Anonymous broadside of May 1774 calling for suspension of business on June 1 in protest against the Boston Port Bill. *Evans 13114.*

1775

MILLER   Excerpts from the journal of the Continental Congress, 76 pages. *Evans 13735.*

MILLER   Anonymous broadside of 2 pages calling upon the members of the companies of Associators of the City of Philadelphia to sign the articles proposed by the Assembly as soon as possible, Oct. 1775(?). *Evans 14508.*

MILLER   John Joachim Zubly's brief history of the struggles of the Swiss in defense of their liberties. *Evans 14139.*

MILLER   Epistle, explaining and defending the measures of the First and Second Continental Congresses, by the German Society of Philadelphia and the German Lutheran and Reformed churches of Philadelphia to the Germans in New York and the Carolinas. Aug. 1, 1775; 11 pages. *Evans 14394.*

MILLER   Speech by the Earl of Chatham in Parliament on Jan. 20, 1775, in favor of the rights of the colonists. *Evans 14407.*

MILLER   Address of the Continental Congress to the inhabitants of Ireland, May 16, 1775. *Evans 14574.*

MILLER   Excerpts of 66 pages from the journal of Pennsylvania's Provincial Congress. *Bristol B4142* (Microprint 42957).

MILLER (?)   Broadside with song against George III. *Bristol B4028* (Microprint 42861).

PUBLISHER UNKNOWN   Broadside with war song against George III. Not in Evans or in Microprint. At AAS.

1776

SOWER   Public statement against independence by the Society of Friends of Pennsylvania and New Jersey, dated Jan. 20, 1776, 8 pages. *Evans 14766.*

SOWER   Excerpts from the journal of Pennsylvania's Provincial Convention of July 15, 1776, 67 pages. Translation of *Evans 14977. Evans 14978.*

MILLER Militia regulations by Pennsylvania's Provincial Congress. *Evans 14996.*

MILLER Declaration by Continental Congress on Dec. 10, 1776, urging fresh defense efforts. *Evans 15174.*

DUNLAP Broadside with resolves of a mass meeting in Philadelphia on Nov. 8, 1776. *Bristol B4337* (Microprint 43135).

STEINER & CIST Paine, *Gesunde Vernunft* [*Common Sense*]. *Evans 14963.*

STEINER & CIST Broadside with call for more volunteers by Continental Congress, Dec. 12, 1776. *Evans 14987.*

PUBLISHER UNKNOWN Four-page leaflet calling for the election of a constitutional convention for Pennsylvania. Translation of *Evans 14642.* In reaction to May 15 resolution of Continental Congress. *Evans 14643.*

PUBLISHER UNKNOWN Broadside on resolves of Committee of Lancaster, Feb. 29, 1776. *Bristol 4239c* (not in Microprint).

1777

SOWER (?) Song rhymed by a German mercenary, A. Emmerich, celebrating the British victory at Fort Montgomery. *Evans 15251.*

SOWER Appeal by a German mercenary to German civilians in America to join the British side in the war. *Evans 15295.*

SOWER Broadside by General Howe offering land to natives who joined the king's army. Translation of *Evans 15327. Evans 15328.*

MILLER Broadside with proclamation by Pennsylvania Council of Safety asking the population to treat prisoners of war properly. Jan. 1, 1777. *Evans 15521.*

MILLER Broadside by Pennsylvania Council of Safety announcing that militia would be quartered in homes of those in Philadelphia who did not join the Association. Translation of *Evans 15522. Evans 15523.*

STEINER & CIST Address by New York's Provincial Congress to their constituents. *Evans 15471.*

STEINER & CIST Militia Act of Pennsylvania. Translation of *Evans 15503. Evans 15504.*

BAILEY Broadside with petition of inhabitants of Lancaster County to the Assembly demanding convention to change the constitution of Pennsylvania. *Evans 15379.*

BAILEY   Broadside with resolves of freeholders of Lancaster County. *Bristol 4490a* (not in Microprint).

BAILEY   Broadside by Washington ordering the thrashing of grain at certain times within 70 miles of his headquarters near Valley Forge. Dec. 20, 1777. *Evans 15635.*

LOUDON   Broadside by New York Provincial Congress of Nov. 16, 1777, encouraging German mercenaries to desert and settle in America. *Evans 15687.*

UNKNOWN PRINTER   Broadside with resolution by Continental Congress of Oct. 8, 1777, outlawing any aid to the British troops in Philadelphia, such as selling them food. *Bristol B4621* (Microprint 43392).

UNKNOWN PRINTER   Broadside by 'A Farmer,' 'Letter I,' demanding revision of Pennsylvania constitution. *Evans 13113* (wrongly dated 1774 by Evans).

1778

MILLER   Broadside written by Miller describing how Sower III stole his best press and types when Howe evacuated Philadelphia. *Evans 15911.*

STEINER & CIST   Broadside by the General Assembly of Pennsylvania announcing the Constitutional Convention of 1779. *Evans 15966.*

BAILEY   Text of the Articles of Confederation. *Evans 16106.*

RIVINGTON   British broadside announcing the Carlisle peace Commission. Translation of *Evans 15832. Evans 15834.*

1779

STEINER & CIST   Sermon by Hugh Henry Brackenridge held in German Reformed Church of Philadelphia in honor of the war dead. Translation of *Evans 16213. Evans 16214.*

1780

UNKNOWN PUBLISHER   Pamphlet of 16 pages by Sower III addressed to the Germans of Pennsylvania and the neighboring provinces to win them for the king's side. *Bristol B5187* (Microprint 43897).

1781

UNKNOWN PUBLISHER   Broadside by Pennsylvania's Executive Council urging lieutenants of the militia to present their expenses to the Council. Translation of *Bristol B5336*. *Bristol B5335* (Microprint 44020).

1782

STEINER   Sermon by Johann Christoph Kunze, pastor of the German Lutheran Church in Philadelphia, on reopening of the church after its desecration by the British. *Evans 17569*.

STEINER   Address by Pastor Johann Christoph Kunze about the German Society of Pennsylvania. *Evans 17570*.

STEINER   The Act of Incorporation of the German Society of Pennsylvania. *Evans 17676*.

STEINER   Constitution of the German Society of Pennsylvania. *Not in Evans or Bristol* (Microprint 44202).

HURTER   Letters exchanged between Emperor Joseph II and archbishop of Trier /Trèves concerning the exercise of religion. *Evans 17568*.

1783

BAILEY   Text of the Paris peace treaty. *Evans 18254*.

CIST   Pamphlet of 35 pages encouraging German mercenaries to stay and settle. *Evans 18291*.

1784

BAILEY   Text of the Constitution of Pennsylvania. *Evans 18690*.

STEINER   Broadside by 'A free German citizen of the state' addressed to the German citizens of Pennsylvania in favor of amending the state constitution. *Evans 18485*.

STEINER   Sermon by Johann Christoph Kunze on the end of the war and the peace treaty. *Evans 18548*.

STEINER   Text of the constitution of Pennsylvania and the Report of the Council of Censors, 49 pages. *Evans 18691*.

STEINER   Text of the journal of the Council of Censors, 147 pages. *Evans 18713*.

Appendix B
Henry Miller's Essay 'On the General Usefulness of Newspapers'

In the preceding paper, quotations from the German newspapers have, with a few exceptions, been translated into English, and readers of German have been deprived of listening to the Sowers' and Miller's real language. To provide at least one extended sample of the German used by these printers, the essay on newspapers that Miller published in the *Staatsbote* of May 31, 1774, is here presented in full. Since the text ends with a reminder to subscribers to pay their debt to the printer, we may assume that Miller himself was either the author or the translator.

Von der allgemeinen Nutzbarkeit der Zeitungen

Unsere Vorfahren waren gezwungen sich viele Unbequemlichkeiten gefallen zu lassen, und durften ihre Bedürfnisse nicht weit ausdehnen. Sie hatten keine Ermunterung, und begnügten sich derohalben mit solchen unmittelbaren Nothwendigkeiten, als ihnen ihre kleine Nachbarschaft verschaffte. Sie hatten keine grosse Lust zum Lesen, und die schönen Wissenschaften erhielten wenig Aufmerksamkeit. Häuslicher Fleiß beschäftigte ihre Zeit, und ließ ihnen wenig Musse für andere Ergötzlichkeiten. Nun da unsere Neue Welt die Eifersucht der Fürsten der Alten reizte um die Oberherrschaft in dieser zu streiten, so begaben die Jünglinge, die bisher ihren Vätern in Anbauung des Landes beygestanden hatten, sich freudig in die Kriegsdienste und zogen voller Muth in den Streit gegen ihre Feinde, die ihr Vaterland zu verheeren suchten. Die Eltern wurden nun begierig, den Zustand dieser jungen Krieger zu wissen; sie ergriffen voller Ungeduld die Zeitungen und lasen einen Bericht von jeder Schlacht, indem ihre Furcht sie jedesmal sorgen ließ, daß ihre Söhne geblieben wären.

Die Zeitungen waren Anfangs das Bekanntmachungs-Mittel von Politischen Neuigkeiten, entdeckten die Geheimnisse der Rathschläge der Staatsverwalter, und prophezeyten dem Publico Krieg oder Frieden. Doch ihr Plan ist nach der Zeit wesentlich verändert und verbessert, und jetzt das Mittel geworden allgemeinen Unterricht zu erhalten.

Die Menge der Leute, denen sie in die Hände gerathen, machte daß man befand, daß sie die besten und bequemsten Wege waren, unsere eigene Bedürfnisse bekannt zu machen, und zu Abhelfung fremder unsere Dienste anzubieten.

Reisen wurden gleichfalls nach und nach leichter, und Entfernung war nicht länger ein Hinderniß für ihren Umlauf.

Man darf nur einige wenige Schillinge für eine Anzeige anwenden, so kan man sogleich tausenden, in kürzerer zeit denn sonst geschehen könte, seine Bedürfnisse bekannt machen. Ist ein Pferd gestohlen, ein Haus erbrochen, eine Räuberey begangen, so wendet man sich sogleich an die Drucker der Zeitungen, und der Erfolg davon ist oftmals so glücklich, daß durch die Bekanntmachung davon die Thäter durch dieses Mittel allein ergriffen, und zu verschuldeter Strafe gebracht werden. Ein Mann, der ein lediges Haus, oder einige wenige Acker von seinem Lande zu verlehnen hat, darf jetzt weiter nichts thun als solches bekannt machen, so wird er bald einen Mietmann finden; und der Mann von einem unterfangenden Geiste, der aber in seinen nützlichen Unternehmungen durch Geldmangel abgeschreckt wird, mache nur eine gute Sicherheit bekannt, und sogleich wird ihm Geld so viel er verlangt, angeboten. Kurz, es kömmt kaum eine einzige Sache im gemeinen Leben vor, deren wir bedürftig sind, die eine Anzeige nicht leichter verschaffen könte, als einiges andere zu erdenkende Mittel. Jederman ist jetzt von diesen Vortheilen überzeugt, und daher kommen die häufigen Anzeigen in den Zeitungen vor. Sie machen einen beträchtlichen Theil ihres Inhalts aus, und sind Leuten, die in Geschäften stehen, sicherlich das Allerwichtigste.

Die Zeitungen legen uns eine Verschiedenheit von Sachen vor, nachdem sie entweder sich mit den feinern Diensten der Gelehrsamkeit beschäftigen, oder aber die Verknüpfungen unter den Menschen weiter auszudehnen suchen.

Personen von jedem Alter und Geschäfte vereinigen sich ihren Umlauf zu befördern. Die Alten und Schwachen, welche ihr kränklicher Zustand von der geschäftigen Welt ausschliesset, verlangen gleichwol zu wissen, wie die Sachen gehen, und lesen daher die Zeitungen. Der Kaufmann weiß durch Hülfe der Zeitungen die Abfahrt, Reisen und Ankunft seiner Schiffe, nebst dem Zustand der auswärtigen Angelegenheiten. Der Landmann siehet den Zustand der Erndten in der ganzen Welt, den Preis, den das Getreyde hält, und lieset die verschiedenen Verbesserungen, die in der Landwirthschaft gemacht werden. Und der Handwerker hat eine unendliche Verschiedenheit von Nachrichten, die ihn zu gleicher Zeit vergnügen und unterrichten. Allein des grossen und unvergleichlichen Haupt-Nutzens der Zeitungen wird ein Land alsdann erst inne, wenn seine Einwohner in Gefahr sind das unschätzbare Kleinod ihrer Freyheit zu verlieren: zu solcher Zeit sind diese Blätter wie in der Schweiz die Hochwachten auf den Gebirgen, sie bringen plötzlich wie ein Lauf-feuer die Einwohner eines grossen Reichs zur Aufmerksamkeit; warnen sie vor der Gefahr, ermahnen sie auf ihrer Huth zu seyn, und durch Einigkeit und Standhaftigkeit die List ihrer Feinde zu vernichten, und ihre Freyheit zu behaupten.

Hieraus erhellet die Nutzbarkeit der Zeitungen aufs deutlichste; die Drucker derselben haben nur zu beklagen, daß so viele Leute niemals sich erinnern für selbige zu bezahlen, und halten solches für keine Schuldigkeit; da doch die Gesetze sie leicht eines andern überführen könten.

The Character and Coherence
of the Loyalist Press

JANICE POTTER and ROBERT M. CALHOON

⁊⯈ ⁊⯈ ⁊⯈ ⁊⯈ ⁊⯈ ⁊⯈ ⁊⯈ ⁊⯈ ⯇⁊ ⯇⁊ ⯇⁊ ⯇⁊ ⯇⁊ ⯇⁊ ⯇⁊ ⯇⁊

1. 'SUBSERVIENT TO THE INTENTIONS OF GOVERNMENT': THE NATURE AND DILEMMA OF THE LOYALIST PRESS

THE LOYALISTS' USE OF THE PRESS—like almost everything else they did—eludes precise definition. Strictly speaking, the term *loyalist press* refers to manifestly pro-British, anti-Whig newspapers published during the crises of 1774 to 1776 and still more appropriately to newspapers published in British-held garrison towns from 1776 through 1783. These papers abounded with anonymous opinion essays which perpetuated a tradition of support of British authority and colonial subordination in the press during the entire pre-Revolutionary controversy. Both as a *journalistic enterprise* during the War for Independence and as a *polemical form* throughout the Revolutionary era, the loyalist press is a unique source of insight into the behavior, expectations, and anguish of the American loyalists.

One way to gauge the quality and thrust of pre-Revolutionary loyalist newspaper polemics is to survey the most celebrated of the series of essays appearing under the same pseudonyms. The 'Dougliad' essays in the *New-York Gazette and Weekly Mercury* in 1770—written in response to Alexander McDougal's sensational broadside 'To the Betrayed Inhabitants of . . . New York'—were a full-scale indictment of licentiousness, turmoil, and the Cromwellian antecedents of the doings of the New York Sons of Liberty.[1] Two years earlier the same paper carried numerous installments of the 'Whip for the American Whig' by Myles

---

[1] Patricia U. Bonomi, *A Factious People: Politics and Society in Colonial New York* (New York, 1971), pp. 270–71; *New-York Gazette and Weekly Mercury*, Apr. 9–June 25, 1770, hereafter cited as *New-York Mercury*.

Cooper and other high Anglicans, a series that scourged colonial society for its hostility to Anglicanism and to constituted authority.[2] Another Anglican clergyman, Henry Caner, writing anonymously as 'Chronus' in the *Massachusetts Gazette and Boston Weekly News-Letter* in 1771–72, set forth a comprehensive rationale for protecting colonial liberty by the 'wise and prudent use of the privileges and advantages we enjoy.'[3] In 1769 William Henry Drayton and William Wragg wrote a barrage of letters to the *South-Carolina Gazette* condemning the nonimportation movement—Drayton noting that its coercive machinery institutionalized popular opposition in a new and destabilizing way and Wragg denouncing coercion and intimidation as a gross violation of traditional political conscience among the South Carolina elite.[4] The famous 'First Citizen'–'Antilon' exchange in the *Maryland Gazette* in 1773 between Charles Carroll and Daniel Dulany, though ostensibly concerned with the powers of the Maryland proprietary governor, grew into a dispute over the meaning of the British constitution, the sources of imperial authority, and the historical roots of colonial liberty.[5]

Surpassing all other loyalist newspaper polemicists was Jonathan Sewall, who published five series of essays between 1763 and 1775. Writing as 'J' in the *Boston Evening-Post* in 1763, he replied to attacks on the Bernard administration by James Otis and Oxenbridge Thacher with an argument that, Carol Berkin explains, 'espoused liberty, then redefined it in its most conservative form . . . ; endorsed the vigilance of the citizen against tyranny, but reversed the direction from which that tyranny threatened society.' As 'Philanthrop' in 1766–67 he used the

---

[2] Robert M. Calhoon, *The Loyalists in Revolutionary America, 1760–1781* (New York, 1973), pp. 255–56; see also 'Poplicola,' *Rivington's New-York Gazetteer,* Nov. 18, Dec. 2 and 23, 1773 (for the various titles of this newspaper, see Timothy M. Barnes, 'Loyalist Newspapers of the American Revolution: A Bibliography,' *Proceedings of the American Antiquarian Society* 83 [1974]: 227), hereafter cited as *Rivington's Gazetteer* for the years 1773–75 and *Rivington's Gazette* thereafter.

[3] Catherine B. Mayo, ed., 'Additions to . . . Hutchinson's History of Massachusetts Bay,' *Proceedings of the American Antiquarian Society* 59 (1949): 42; 'Chronus,' *Massachusetts Gazette and Boston Weekly News-Letter,* Jan. 23, 1772, hereafter cited as *Boston Weekly News-Letter*.

[4] Robert M. Weir, ed., *The Letters of Freeman, Etc.: Essays on the Nonimportation Movement in South Carolina Collected by William Henry Drayton* (Columbia, S.C., 1977), pp. 53–57, 86–95, essays by Drayton and Wragg from the *South-Carolina Gazette* dated Oct. 26 and Nov. 16, 1769.

[5] Peter S. Onuf, ed., *Maryland and the Empire, 1773: The Antilon-First Citizen Letters* (Baltimore, 1974), pp. 3–39.

same arguments to deflect the criticism heaped on Governor Bernard during the Stamp Act crisis, and under the same pseudonym in 1770–71 he refuted Samuel Adams's attempt to retry the Boston Massacre trials in the Boston press. As 'Philalethes' in 1773 in the *Massachusetts Gazette and Boston Weekly News-Letter*, he sought to stem the torrent of abuse being heaped on Governor Hutchinson, and as 'Phileirene' in 1775, he examined in detail the sources and impetus of the Revolutionary contagion.[6]

Finally, John Adams's and Daniel Leonard's climactic duel as 'Novanglus' and 'Massachusettensis' in the *Boston Gazette and Country Journal* and *Massachusetts Gazette and Boston Post-Boy and Advertiser* in 1774–75 raised what Bernard Mason calls 'antithetical models of society,' a Tory model of 'order and imperial stability' and a Whig model in which the 'key ingredients' were 'liberty and innovation.'[7]

While these major series of anti-Whig polemics made a thorough case for dutiful submission and restraint by the colonists, scores of individual anonymous essays elaborated on the loyalist argument in the pre-Revolutionary debate and reflected the range and seriousness of the impediments to a unified colonial opposition against British policy. Some of these articles appeared originally or were reprinted in newspapers closely identified with the Whig position while most filled the columns of identifiably pro-British or 'Tory' papers: the *New-York Gazette and Weekly Mercury* and the two *Massachusetts Gazettes* already mentioned; the *Georgia Gazette*, the *South-Carolina and American General Gazette*, *Rivington's New-York Gazetteer*, the *Boston Evening-Post*, the *Boston Chronicle*, the *Boston Censor*, and the *New Hampshire Gazette*.[8]

[6] For a convenient listing of Sewall's letters to the press except for the 'Phileirene' letters and an analysis of his ideas, see Ann Gorman Condon, 'Marching to a Different Drummer: The Political Philosophy of the American Loyalists,' in Esmond Wright, ed., *Red, White, and True Blue: The Loyalists in the Revolution* (New York, 1976), pp. 1–18 and 175–77 and Carol Berkin, *Jonathan Sewall: Odyssey of an American Loyalist* (New York, 1974), pp. 31–34, 37–43, 87–89, 97–100 and 'Jonathan Sewall: One Tory's Conception of the Press,' paper read at the St. Augustine Conference on American Loyalism, St. Augustine, Fla., Feb. 8, 1975.

[7] Bernard Mason, ed., *The American Colonial Crisis: The Daniel Leonard–John Adams Letters to the Press, 1774–1775* (New York, 1972), pp. ix–xix.

[8] Stephen Botein, ' "Meer Mechanics" and an Open Press: The Business and Political Strategies of Colonial American Printers,' *Perspectives in American History* 9 (1975): 215–17; Timothy M. Barnes, 'The Loyalist Press in the American Revolution, 1765–1781,' Ph.D. diss., University of New Mexico, 1970, chaps. 1–8; Janice Christine Potter, ' "Is

Recent scholarship, especially the work of Stephen Botein, emphasizes that colonial printers sought to perform a nonpolitical service of opening their columns to all shades of opinion, a role that became increasingly untenable during the early 1770s. As late as July 1774, James Rivington declared that 'the printer of a newspaper ought to be neutral in all cases where his own press is employed' and publish all materials submitted to him, 'whether of the Whig or Tory flavour.' Rivington's perilous neutrality collapsed when a crowd of seventy-five horsemen under Isaac Sears vandalized his press on May 10, and wrecked it completely on November 23, 1775.[9] Hugh Gaine, printer of the *New-York Mercury*, was the classic example of a colonial printer driven against every professional instinct toward a partisan role in the Revolution. Throughout the pre-Revolutionary controversy he gave balanced, objective accounts of political upheaval and published anonymous essays on both sides that were decent and moderate in tone.[10]

Rivington's sympathies undoubtedly lay with the British while Gaine, like many loyalists from the middle colonies, felt equally torn between his sympathy for colonial rights and his aversion to rebellion and violence; the important point is that neither became a partisan of the British cause until the outbreak of war and royal occupation of New York City made neutrality impossible. For a short time in September and October 1776 Gaine tried to print a paper in Newark, New Jersey, in a territory controlled by the patriots while allowing Gen. William Howe's

This the Liberty We Seek?'': Loyalist Ideology in Colonial New York and Massachusetts,' Ph.D. diss., Queen's University (Ontario), 1977; Larry R. Gerlach, *Prologue to Independence: New Jersey in the Coming of the American Revolution* (New Brunswick, N.J., 1976), pp. 236–39, 335–36; S. F. Roach, 'The *Georgia Gazette* and the Stamp Act: A Reconsideration' and C. Ashley Ellefson, 'The Stamp Act in Georgia,' *Georgia Historical Quarterly* 55 (1971): 471–91 and 46 (1962): 1–19; and John E. Alden, 'John Mein: Scourge of Patriots,' *Publications of the Colonial Society of Massachusetts* 34 (1937–42): 571–99, and Sidney Kobre, *The Development of the Colonial Newspaper* (Pittsburgh, 1944), p. 148. For loyalist essays printed in newspapers closely identified with the Whig position, see for example 'Pacificus,' *Pennsylvania Chronicle*, July 25, 1768, 'A Barbadian,' ibid., Aug. 1 and 8, 1768, 'Machiavel,' ibid., Aug. 15, 22, and 29, 1768; 'Country Farmer,' ibid., Aug. 22, 1768; 'Anticentinel,' *Pennsylvania Journal*, June 16, and Sept. 29, 1768, 'Anatomist,' ibid., Sept. 8, 25, and 29, and Oct. 13, 1768.

9 Botein, ' "Meer Mechanics," and an Open Press,' pp. 217–19, and Leroy Hewlett, 'James Rivington: Tory Printer,' in David Kaser, ed., *Books in America's Past* (Charlottesville, 1966), pp. 172–76.

10 Ann Y. Zimmer, 'Hugh Gaine, Loyalist Printer,' paper read at the St. Augustine Conference on American Loyalism.

secretary, Ambrose Serle, to manage the *New-York Mercury*. Financial losses in Newark and patriot suspicion forced him to abandon this arrangement, take refuge in New York City, and make the *Mercury* into an avowedly loyalist newspaper.[11] Rivington, who had gone to England in early 1776, returned in September 1777 and resumed publication of his paper on October 4. In his second issue he candidly and accurately affirmed his willingness to make the *Gazette* 'subservient to the intentions of government—the restoration of peace, order, and happiness through the continent—by recalling the infatuated multitude to the use of their reason and understanding and by convincing them how grossly they have been imposed upon by the misrepresentations and false glosses of their leaders in sedition and rebellion.'[12]

In addition to *Rivington's Gazette* and Gaine's *New-York Mercury*, ten other loyalist newspapers appeared in towns occupied by the British between 1776 and 1783. These included the *Royal American Gazette* in New York City from 1777 to 1783; the *Newport Gazette* in Rhode Island from 1777 to 1779; the *Pennsylvania Evening Post*, *Pennsylvania Ledger*, and *Royal Pennsylvania Gazette* in Philadelphia for varying parts of the British occupation of Philadelphia from October 1777 to May 1778; the *South-Carolina and American General Gazette*, *The Royal Gazette*, and the *Royal South-Carolina Gazette* during the British occupation of Charleston in 1780–82; the *Royal Georgia Gazette* in occupied Savannah from 1779–82; and the *East Florida Gazette* in St. Augustine in 1783–84.[13] The newspapers provided a necessary semblance of normality in towns under British military and administrative control. They spurred the economy by carrying advertisements and other information vital to merchants, artisans, and consumers; trumpeted British military successes; published the numerous official announcements for British commanders and civilian administrators; and provided a forum in which loyalists could lambast their patriot enemies, prod the British government to meet the

---

[11] Ibid. and Barnes, 'Loyalist Newspapers . . . a Bibliography,' pp. 225–26.

[12] *Rivington's Gazette*, Oct. 11, 1777, quoted in William F. Steirer, 'Losers in the War of Words: The Loyalist Press in the American Revolution,' paper read at the St. Augustine Conference on American Loyalism; Botein, ' "Meer Mechanics" and an Open Press,' pp. 217–19.

[13] Steirer, 'Losers in the War of Words'; Ralph Adams Brown, 'The *Newport Gazette*: A Tory News Sheet,' *Rhode Island History* 13 (1954–55): 11–21, 97–108 and 'The *Pennsylvania Ledger*: Tory News Sheet,' *Pennsylvania History* 9 (1942): 161–75.

needs of the king's friends, and explore the ramifications of their self-pitying and often paranoid view of recent history.[14]

The intrusion of Revolutionary politics into the workings of the press and the volatile public impact of political news and opinion in the newspapers together constitute a previously little-understood dimension of the political culture of Revolutionary America. Recent work by Timothy M. Barnes, Stephen Lucas, William F. Steirer, Anne Y. Zimmer, and Carol Berkin as well as Stephen Botein and other contributors to this volume has explored the editing, coverage, management, and social role of loyalist newspapers.[15] Little systematic attention, however, has been paid to the intellectual and ideological content and character of the great mass of signed and anonymous opinion essays in the newspapers that opposed the Revolutionary movement and vindicated British authority over the colonies. This essay attempts such an appraisal.

2. 'DISAFFECTION, PETULANCE, INGRATITUDE, AND DISLOYALTY': THE THEMES OF LOYALIST POLEMICAL JOURNALISM

In the sixteenth of his 'Massachusettensis' letters, Daniel Leonard declared, with bitter sarcasm, 'some idolaters have attributed to the congress the collected wisdom of the continent.' It was an astute observation. The decision of the First Continental Congress to impose a trade boycott enforced by local committees, coupled with its resolution for a second Congress to assemble in May 1775, significantly altered the nature of the Congress. By setting these events in motion, the Congress shifted from a gathering of representatives of the colonial assemblies

[14] Timothy M. Barnes, 'Occupational Allegiance and Political Neutralism: Loyalist Printers during the Revolutionary War,' paper read at the Pacific Coast Branch of the American Historical Association, Aug. 13, 1977; John M. Coleman, 'Joseph Galloway and the British Occupation of Philadelphia,' *Pennsylvania History* 30 (1963): 289–94; George S. McCowen, *The British Occupation of Charleston, 1780–1782* (Columbia, S.C., 1972), pp. 24–42.

[15] The participants in the session on 'The Loyalist Press' at the St. Augustine Conference on American Loyalism, Feb. 6–8, 1975, generously assisted the authors of this paper. Professors Berkin, Steirer, and Zimmer gave us copies of their papers and Professor Lucas discussed his findings with us in conversations and correspondence. Prof. Timothy M. Barnes, a commentator at that conference, placed at our disposal his extensive collection of photocopies of the loyalist press and answered innumerable questions. In addition, Profs. George A. Rawlyk and Robert M. Weir provided valuable encouragement and criticism, as did the editors of this volume, Bernard Bailyn and John B. Hench.

into an active guardian of American liberty and authoritative spokesman for American interests. Those functions required Congress to interpret the meaning of fast-moving events and respond with appropriate
boldness and vigor to British actions. 'The collected wisdom of the continent' exactly expressed Congress's new status, and Leonard's grasp of
that political reality enhances the credibility and interpretive value of
the remainder of the concluding paragraph in the sixteenth 'Massachusettensis' letter. 'It is as near the truth to say,' he continued, 'that every
particle of disaffection, petulance, ingratitude, and disloyalty that for
ten years past have been scattered through the continent, were united
and consolidated in them [the Congress].'[16]

Disaffection, petulance, ingratitude, and *disloyalty* were terms that came
easily to Leonard's pen. To the casual reader of Tory diatribes against
Whig ideology and politics they are nearly synonymous words. At face
value, certainly, they are overlapping terms which collectively describe
several facets of colonial remonstrance and resistance. But when examined in the context of eighteenth-century usage, each word connotes
values and beliefs that distinguish it from the others. *Disaffection* meant
filling otherwise faithful subjects with discontent and described the understandable reaction of people to inconsistent, abusive government; it
was therefore a process by which a people's natural affections and kindliness were eroded or subverted and replaced with malignant, persistent
resentment against constituted authority. *Petulance* depicted a range of
personality traits associated with immaturity: saucy, perverse, immodest, pert, insolent behavior. The word suggested too a more deeply en-
grained trait: wantonness—an undisciplined, animal quest for sensual
gratification. In the hands of loyalist polemicists, petulance was an unwillingness, even refusal, to admit objective reality when it clashed with
men's desires for domination over others and with their craving for freedom from all restraint. *Ingratitude* was an indisposition to acknowledge
benefits received from a government, a patron, or a family. Gratitude
implied the existence of interests that knitted groups of men together
and provided a rational basis for social cooperation and political acquiescence. Identifying interests as useful, desirable, and beneficial social

---

[16] *Massachusetts Gazette, and the Boston Post-Boy and Advertiser*, Mar. 27, 1775, hereafter
cited as *Boston Post-Boy Advertiser;* for the prescience of Leonard's observation on the
First Continental Congress see David Ammerman, *In the Common Cause: American Response to the Coercive Acts of 1774* (Charlottesville, 1974), chaps. 6 and 8.

arrangements, the idea of ingratitude presupposed that men were capable of knowing whence their livelihood, security, and prosperity came and of knowing too that posing deeper questions about human nature and destiny was a dangerous, delusive, and futile activity to pursue. *Disloyalty* was the fatal, irreversible act of rebellion against legitimate authority, the inevitably violent exposure of the vicious animal appetites which, implanted in human nature, were barely restrained by the conventions and habits of civilization and the laws and authority of legally established institutions.[17]

Instead of being merely overlapping, redundant synonyms, Leonard's four terms of abuse conveyed distinct perceptions of politics, morality, and human nature. *Disaffection* was a malignant process; *petulance* a perverted reaction to the truth; *ingratitude* a denial of rational self-interest; and *disloyalty* an ugly and destructive action. Applying these broader meanings to the analysis of anti-Whig, anti-Revolutionary, and pro-British opinion essays in the press of the Revolutionary era reveals something of the coherence of loyalist ideology. These terms were not rigorous, precise ideas in the loyalists' minds—indeed their cumulative adversities prevented them from ever developing a mature, stable system of thought—but they do provide a new and significant point of access into the interior of loyalist newspaper writing.

Most Whigs found their disillusionment with Britain a painful experience and agreed that disaffection was a protracted process in which intellectual and ideological leadership played a critical role in weaning the populace from its accustomed allegiance to the British crown. In contrast to the loyalists, however, the Whigs placed disaffection in the historical context of a struggle for political and religious liberty stretching from the eighteenth century back to the Middle Ages. Recent British encroachments on colonial liberty represented to them an aberration from that long historical movement—a tragic, benumbing reminder that even prominent, august institutions and statesmen were capricious and corruptible.[18] Disaffection arose, according to the loyalist press,

[17] See 'disaffection,' 'petulance,' 'ingratitude,' and 'disloyalty' in *Dr. Johnson's Dictionary* and the *Oxford English Dictionary*.

[18] The classic analysis of disaffection from the Whig point of view was John Adams, 'Dissertation on the Canon and the Feudal Law' (1765), *The Works of John Adams* (Boston, 1851), 3: 447–64.

from the central problem of social control in a free society. 'Man is a social Animal . . . whose wants, whose natural powers of Reason, and whose capacity of improving those powers . . . demonstrate,' wrote Jonathan Sewall in the first of his 'Philanthrop' exchanges with Samuel Adams in 1771, 'that he was made for social life.' His reason, his need for companionship, and his ability to find safety in numbers dictated that man sacrifice 'part of that unlimited freedom of action . . . to which he was born . . .' to obtain and enjoy 'the more valuable blessings and benefits of *society*.' That realization of their own rationality and sociability implanted in human beings a moral obligation to 'promote the general good' and a realization that 'the public good and his own are so intimately connected and interwoven together that whatever is inconsistent with the *former* is equally incompatible with the *latter*.' For that reason, the preservation and maintenance of the public peace were a subject's 'principle' responsibility and concern.[19]

Meeting that duty confronted the good citizen with every variety of political guile, aggression, and evil. As 'dissentions and divisions' arose around him, the good citizen had to 'endeavour, within his proper sphere, to keep up in the minds of all about him an inviolable respect for the *laws*' and 'a rational submission to those in *authority*.' Expressed in these terms, obedience and acquiescence to authority required a high degree of self-consciousness and intellectuality. When individuals knew of error and abuse in government, they had a higher moral duty to restrain themselves from uttering harsh criticism lest they promote a general clamor, dishearten and discourage those entrusted with public office, and jeopardize 'that *essential subordination* upon which the well being and happiness of the whole *absolutely depends*.'[20]

Disaffection therefore sprang from a single-minded tendency to see in particular political abuses evidence 'that *all* in authority are traiterously combined in plotting the *slavery*, misery, and ruin of the society.' The subject had a moral duty to assume the '*integrity of intention*' of public officials even when they exhibited their '*human fallibility*.' After all, public officials had to meet the most exacting tests of virtue over long periods of time, operate according to legal and administrative procedures, endure without complaint a constant barrage of abuse, invective, and intimidation, and exhibit superior ability and blameless private conduct.

[19] *Boston Evening-Post*, Jan. 14, 1771.
[20] Ibid.

They therefore deserved respect and deference from thoughtful, reflective subjects. 'Arraigning, accusing, and condemning those in the most important stations,' Sewall warned, would only 'weaken the pillars of the state.'[21]

Thus in 1771 Sewall reacted bitterly to the abuse heaped on himself and on acting governor Thomas Hutchinson following the Boston Massacre. By 1775 the cruel, judgmental outlook of the people had brought government to the verge of collapse and threatened to destroy the future stability of the colonial society. 'If we look back upon the conduct of the Colonies for some years past, we may find many critical junctures where a prudent silence or a dutiful and rational remonstrance' would have exacted concessions from the British and cleared the atmosphere of rancor and crisis which harmed colonial society. Congress, Sewall complained, should therefore proceed with 'extreme caution' so that everyone in the colonies would be 'thoroughly convinced that we have truth, justice, reason, and equity for our foundation' before assaulting Parliament and the crown with hasty, ill-considered, patently erroneous grievances. Once again, he lamented, very few men had enough sophistication and toughness to perceive that tact, discretion, and patience were the foremost defenses for colonial liberty. 'Such is the unhappy frailty of the human mind that we are in general less attentive to the calls of reason and prudence than the suggestions of passion, prejudice, and vicious habits.'[22]

To counteract the infatuation that gripped the public mind, Daniel Leonard declared, involved telling people with painful bluntness that their conduct was dangerous and self-destructive. Was it unduly censorious to accuse the 'leading Whigs' of deliberately misleading their unwary contemporaries? Leonard asked; 'Whoever has been conversant with the history of man, must know that it abounds with such instances.

[21] Ibid.; see also 'A Suffolk Yeoman,' *Boston Weekly News-Letter*, Dec. 29, 1774; 'Philo Patria,' ibid., Dec. 22, 1774; 'C.,' ibid., Feb. 16, 1775; 'Mercator,' *Rivington's Gazetteer*, Aug. 11, 1774; 'Major Benjamin Floyd and a great number of others,' ibid., Apr. 6, 1775; 'An Answer to the Declaration of the General Congress,' *Pennsylvania Evening Post*, Mar. 25, 1778.

[22] *Boston Weekly News-Letter*, Apr. 6, 1775; for an exhaustive historical argument that the 1692 Charter did not fetter in any way the authority of the crown in Massachusetts, see 'A.Z.,' ibid., Mar. 2, 1775, and also the major pro-administration arguments in the controversy over the removal of the General Court from Boston by 'Verus,' 'Aequitas,' and 'Chronus,' in ibid., May 16, July 18, 1771 and Jan. 2, 1772.

The same game, and with the same success, has been played in all ages, and all countries.' The 'game' was to enflame—to politicize—the 'bulk of the people' who had neither the 'inclination or opportunity' to inform themselves about public life but who carried within themselves 'a latent spark' of outrage and animal energy 'capable of being kindled into a flame.' The manipulation of that human weakness, Leonard insisted, 'has always been the employment of the disaffected. They begin by reminding the people of the elevated rank they hold in the universe, as men; that all men by nature are equal; that kings are but the ministers of the people; that their authority is delegated to them by the people for their good, and they have a right to resume it, and place it in other hands, or keep it themselves whenever it is made use of to oppress them. . . . Thus the seeds of sedition are usually sown, and the people are led to sacrifice real liberty to licentiousness which gradually ripens into rebellion and civil war.'[23]

The shameless dishonesty and diabolical cunning of the agitator therefore combined with the emotional immaturity and suggestability of his audience to create a powerful dynamic propelling society toward anarchy. 'If you are so hurried along with the tide of general fanaticism which runs so strong at this day as to believe those *pretended* grievances, which are held up to the public view, to have any *real* foundation,' Sewall declared, 'you will perhaps think that nothing but a malignant party spirit . . . can stimulate me to thus arraign and condemn the proceedings of the Continental Congress.' There was, he insisted, a legitimate human basis for his intransigence 'when I see your fears alarmed, your tempers irritated, and passions inflamed, without any just cause, by men, the sole motives of whose conduct are envy, malice, or ambition, I think myself justifiable in attempting to expose the errors and defeat the inimical designs of such men.'[24]

Once functioning in tandem, 'the minds of the multitude' and their 'crafty deceivers' communicated through language almost perfectly suited for conspiracy and sedition. Once men's 'passions are engaged, . . . their reason is lulled into a perfectly stupid lethargy, and then mere sounds govern their judgments. The words king, parliament, ministers, governors, mandamus councillors, revenue, tea &c. carry the idea of

[23] *Boston Post-Boy Advertiser*, Dec. 26, 1774.
[24] *Boston Weekly News-Letter*, Mar. 30, 1775; see also 'A.B.C.,' *Boston Evening-Post*, Sept. 20, 1773; 'Protector Oliver,' *Rivington's Gazetteer*, Feb. 9, 1775.

slavery with them, while with as little color or reason the words congress, charter, patriots, delegates, charter councillors, independence,
coffee, &c. carry with them all the powers of necromancy [i.e., magic]
to conjure down the spirit of tyranny.'[25] 'Citizens,' it appeared, 'have
been deluded by the cry of Liberty.' Virtually mesmerized by such slogans, the mob committed numerous 'violences' in the name of liberty
and engaged in ritualistic and bizarre behavior—they marched around
a field to a liberty pole, where some of their members harangued the
rest, and then they elected committees to undertake the most trivial
tasks.[26] 'Are there not many among them whose case we may lament,'
wondered one supposedly bewildered observer, 'who at some seasons
appeared frantic, superstitious and in some degree idolators by their
veneration for a tree and the number 92 . . . [and] their sacrifice on the
annual solemnity or feast of dedication of the juice of lemons, wine &c.
which, with the temper and behaviour of the votaries, appear to have
some resemblance of the ancient Bacchanalia?'[27]

Disaffection, then, was like a poison infused into the populace to
erode their reason, benevolence, and loyalty, and to evoke, instead,
their passions, malignity, and licentiousness. Such baser instincts, which
many loyalists believed lurked beneath the surface of mankind's rationality and kindliness, should be curbed by individual self-restraint and
by the authority of the institutions of church and state. When, however,
these barriers were broken down by unscrupulous intriguers who aroused
the public by appeals to its passions, the less noble and more irrational
side of human nature was exposed. The loyalist assumption that a small
cabal of designing, crafty, and self-interested men had played upon
weaknesses in human nature to bring out men's baser instincts and in
this way to infuse disaffection into the populace was basic to their interpretation of the Revolution. Americans were rebelling, according to
many loyalists, not because of concrete and well-founded grievances but
because of the concerted designs of a well-organized and disaffected
minority to subvert the authority of legally established institutions and
undermine America's allegiance to the mother country.

For the loyalists petulance was an attribute of human depravity—con-

[25] 'Plain Heart,' *Boston Weekly News-Letter*, Feb. 16, 1775.
[26] 'Anti-Licentiousness,' *Rivington's Gazetteer*, Apr. 20, 1775.
[27] 'Z.T.,' *Boston Evening-Post*, May 15, 1769.

clusive evidence that most people were unfit for political responsibility; only subordination of subjects to their rulers and the maintenance of social hierarchy protected society from the perverse childishness of the disobedient and restive. Whig ideology, on the other hand, rested on a far more comprehensive inquiry into human nature. Only a people imbued with a sense of a social covenant and determined to regulate the exercise of power through constitutional means, Whig ideology contended, could guard against the greed and aggression that were intrinsic to human nature.[28]

The loyalists' judgmental rhetoric betrayed their exasperation with the public's tolerance of disorder and disrespect for authority. 'Wake up my friends,' an anonymous loyalist exhorted his readers, 'act like men, like free men, like reasonable creatures. . . . See and judge and act for yourselves.' 'Truth,' he proclaimed, 'delights in free enquiry'; therefore, he was appealing to the colonists to read and consider both the patriot and loyalist points of view.[29] Daniel Leonard also pleaded with his readers to 'divest' themselves of 'prejudice' and to 'hear and weigh everything that is fairly adduced on either side of the question with equal attention and care.'[30] Similar attempts to persuade the public to reflect dispassionately on both interpretations of the Anglo-American crisis were made by other loyalists. The Boston *Censor*, for instance, asserted that 'truths' were arrived at by 'compar[ing] discordant opinions,'[31] and an unknown New York loyalist proclaimed, 'The ears of a genuine son of liberty are ever open to all doctrines; it is his glory to hear them, examine them, to adopt them if they are true, to confute them if they are false. . . .'[32] Yet loyalists themselves seemed to sense the futility of their endeavors to convince the public and their opponents of the need for an open and dispassionate discussion of Anglo-American issues.

The touchstone of patriot resistance, various loyalist writers declared, was its petulant refusal to listen to or tolerate criticism. A Massachusetts loyalist denounced the Worcester Resolves for advocating that loyal Americans refrain from subscribing to loyalist newspapers like the *Mas-*

---

[28] Bernard Bailyn, *The Ideological Origins of the American Revolution* (Cambridge, Mass., 1967), pp. 55–60.

[29] 'Plain Heart,' *Boston Weekly News-Letter*, Mar. 2, Feb. 16, 1775.

[30] *Boston Post-Boy Advertiser*, Dec. 12, 1774, Feb. 20, 1775.

[31] [Boston] *Censor*, Nov. 30, 1771.

[32] 'T.W.,' *Rivington's Gazetteer*, Dec. 15, 1774; see also 'Conciliator,' *Boston Post-Boy Advertiser*, Feb. 6–13, 1775; 'A Farmer,' *Rivington's Gazetteer*, Dec. 2, 1773.

sachusetts Gazette and likened the patriots to the Catholics who supposedly kept their parishioners in 'total heathenish ignorance' so that they could be more easily controlled.[33]

Jonathan Sewall denounced the patriots as a 'set of *enthusiastical* persons, who seem to think they have a right to tyrannize over their fellow creatures, and to threaten, insult and abuse everybody that cannot think and speak with them upon the state of our public affairs.'[34] The perverse unwillingness of the patriots to tolerate other points of view was also condemned by Myles Cooper, who asked rhetorically, 'Can they be friends to liberty, who will not allow any to think or speak differently from themselves, without danger? Will they compel the society to act according to their arbitrary decisions, and yet tell us we are free?'[35] Such intolerance and abusiveness, Daniel Leonard declared, was the product of 'an illiberal, bigoted, arbitrary, malevolent disposition.'[36] 'Whoever contradicts a prevailing humour,' explained the author of a prolonged reply to Dickinson's *Farmer's Letters*, 'draws upon him the clamor of the multitude. The voice of a modest and impartial enquirer is often drowned in the popular cry. Wild enthusiastical rant, disconnected and unintelligible declamation which only serve to heat the world without instructing it, pass upon the world for truth and solid reasoning.'[37]

The patriots' use of intimidation and coercion to silence those whose views were incompatible with their own, the loyalists alleged, opened the door to various excesses and naive ideas about the possibility of imposing virtue on a people. A taste of coercive power over their fellow men so intoxicated the people that they lost the sense of purpose and discrimination that had dignified the parliamentary leaders in their opposition during the early stages of the English civil war:

> Treating all men as mortal foes,
> Who dare their high behests oppose.
> Stark raving mad with party rage,

[33] 'Plain Heart,' *Boston Weekly News-Letter*, Mar. 2, 1775; 'A Card,' *Rivington's Gazetteer*, Mar. 9, 1775, called the Revolutionaries 'Protestant Jesuits'; see also 'Yeoman,' *Boston Weekly News-Letter*, Dec. 10, 1772.
[34] 'Phileirene,' ibid., Feb. 9, 1775.
[35] 'Poplicola,' *Rivington's Gazetteer*, Dec. 2, 1773.
[36] *Boston Post-Boy Advertiser*, Feb. 20, 1775.
[37] 'Letters . . . which contain a compleat Answer to the Farmer's,' *Boston Evening-Post*, Feb. 6, 1769.

With coward arms, those foes engage.
. . . Dares the poor man impartial be,
He's doomed to want and infamy . . .
Sees all he loves a sacrifice,
If he dares publish, ought—but lies.
. . . Alas, vain men, how blind, how weak;
Is this the liberty we seek?
Alas, by nobler motives led
A Hampden fell, a Sydney bled.[38]

As the loyalists tried to analyze the perverse, petulant, abusive tide of American behavior, they perceived a new kind of Revolutionary justice operating according to its own rules and imposing its own exalted standards of public virtue. The patriots did not appreciate the impossibility of imposing a new morality on their fellow men because they were blinded to the monstrous evil of intimidation and coercion. 'You vainly imagined to force . . . belief [in] the treasonable articles of your absurd creed,' Sewall complained, 'by extorted *confessions, acknowledgements, recantations,* and *submissions.*' How could the patriots be so gullible, Sewall demanded to know, as to place any credence in extorted, coerced conversions to their cause. Only 'inebriated and intoxicated devotees of rapine and licentiousness' could be so deluded and irrational 'as to suppose that any promises, declarations, and engagements thus extorted can be binding upon those unhappy victims to popular frenzy.'[39] 'Union,' another loyalist argued, 'can then only be right when the principles upon which it is founded are so.' These principles involved 'bring[ing] us over by argument and conviction not terror.' 'It is from such a temper alone that a permanent union can be formed.'[40]

In addition to being associated with an obstinate and aggressive intolerance of dissenting views, petulance was related to the apparent churlishness and undisciplined character of the colonists. One of the most thoughtful considerations of the later manifestation of petulant behavior was the high-Anglican series 'A Whip for the American Whig.' Only a powerful, conservative church that was closely allied with the government, the 'Whip' argued, could inculcate enough respect for authority and decorum in public affairs to prevent liberty from degen-

[38] *Rivington's Gazetteer,* Dec. 8, 1774.
[39] *Boston Weekly News-Letter,* Jan. 12, 1775.
[40] 'Agrippa,' *Rivington's Gazetteer,* Mar. 30, 1775.

erating into licentiousness and to restrain the passionate enthusiasts from trampling on the rights of the reasonable, dutiful subjects. 'Religion is so confessedly advantageous to society that every reasonable man must endeavor to advance it,' Myles Cooper posited, if only from the selfish motive of 'increasing the happiness of the community of which he is a member.' Reason and self-interest might incline some people to practice 'honesty and obedience of government,' but, for most men, the 'sallies of ambition' and 'the unresisted desire of unlimited freedom' could only be inhibited by the prospect of 'future rewards' for 'virtue' and 'punishment of vice.' By training people in self-discipline and reinforcing continually men's moral duty to respect and obey legitimate authority, religious teaching established 'that *order* and *harmony* so requisite to the just motion in the springs of every political system.'[41]

Deeply imbued with enlightenment ideas about equilibrium among theoretical political orders, the 'Whip' series saw the Church of England and the British crown subtly using each other—the church receiving protection and sponsorship, the crown enjoying a gentle, noncoercive way of influencing its subjects. 'This prerogative [by which the king was head of the church] tends . . . to create a reverence and veneration for the prince as head of two bodies united, as defender of . . . religious as well as civil privileges: a reverence extremely well adapted to engage his subjects to a ready and cheerful obedience.'[42]

The incessant campaign of vilification against the Anglican church—characterized by its 'abusive' criticisms, 'Slander,' 'Invective,' and 'Billingsgate'[43]—and the misrepresentation of its role as a handmaiden of authority, the 'Whip' authors argued, undermined public respect for both religion and government. By persistently and abusively attacking the established Church of England, 'The American Whig' was in fact 'endeavouring to prejudice the cause of Christianity and to bring its ministers into disgrace.'[44] Besides leveling a blow at Protestantism in casting 'the most odius reflections on the Reformation,'[45] Livingston and Smith, by attacking the established church which was 'so interwoven' with the constitution of the British state 'that the one must be

[41] 'A Whip for the American Whig,' No. 22, *New-York Mercury*, Sept. 5, 1768.
[42] Ibid., No. 32, Nov. 14, 1768.
[43] Ibid., No. 2, Apr. 11, 1768.
[44] Ibid., No. 19, Aug. 15, 1768.
[45] Ibid., No. 14, July 4, 1768.

bent and torn to pieces with the other,' were attempting to 'inflame the passions of the populace and so root their prejudice that they become, in a great measure, invincible.'[46]

Petulance was therefore a mixture of impatient irrationality and limited but dangerous cunning. The Tryon County magistrates and grand jurors, on March 16, 1775, denounced 'the artifices used by violent and designing men to practise on the easy credulity of the good people.'[47] 'These inconsiderate people,' complained Bellisarius, 'have made themselves idols, viz. Liberty Trees, Newspapers, and Congresses, which by blindly worshipping, have so engrossed their minds, that they neglect their honest professions and spend all of their time' in 'taverns where they talk politicks, get drunk, damn King, Ministers, and Taxes and vow they will follow any measures proposed to them by these demagogues, however repugnant to religion, reason, and common sense.'[48] To some loyalists, the impulse behind petulant opposition to all restraint was narrow self-interest: 'smuggling merchants' who, 'finding themselves too closely watched,' conspired to subvert all British authority in America. Resistance was clearly directed by 'unprincipled, factious, designing men whose interest it has been to keep alive the coals of sedition.'[49] 'Every measure of the cabal' against enforcement of the Tea Act 'is an undoubted proof that not your liberties but their private interest is the object,' declared 'Popicola' in the *Norwich Packet*: 'They have too richly experienced the fruits from a contraband trade . . . to relinquish them to others without a struggle. To Liberty they can pretend no friendship. Every Step they have hitherto taken has been introductive of the most fatal tyranny, a tyranny of so high a nature as not to permit a fellow citizen even to think differently from them without danger.'[50] 'O poor *degenerate* children!,' lamented two New York loyalists. 'Such destroyers of liberty itself are a disgrace to their mother, if she is the goddess of liberty. For doth not liberty herself allow every man to enjoy his own sentiments?'[51]

[46] Ibid., No. 21, Aug. 29, 1768.

[47] *Rivington's Gazetteer*, Apr. 6, 1775.

[48] Ibid., Mar. 9, 1775.

[49] 'Phileirene,' Mar. 2, 1775, and Jan. 12, 1775, *Boston Weekly News-Letter*, see also [Samuel Seabury], 'The Congress Canvassed,' *Salem Gazette*, Jan. 13, 1775.

[50] *Norwich Packet*, Nov. 25 – Dec. 2, 1773.

[51] John Grou and John Peters in *Rivington's Gazetteer*, Sept. 2, 1774; see also 'An Answer to the Declaration,' *Pennsylvania Evening Post*, Feb. 24, 1778.

Conniving, avaricious politicians fed upon each other's weaknesses. 'A New York Freeholder' commended the Athenian statute drafted by Solon that imposed banishment or forfeiture of property on any citizen who stood aloof from a controversy that divided society into two fiercely antagonistic factions. 'Designing, passionate, or selfish persons,' this writer explained, 'are generally the promoters of faction in every state whereas men of real merit and judgment are naturally averse to tumults and fly from the boisterous haunts of discord.' 'Temperate, discreet colonists,' 'America's Real Friend' lamented, 'have been too indolent; whilst restless spirits [have] . . . led the inconsiderate into the deep gulphs of sedition, where they lost virtue, loyalty, and good manners.'[52]

Petulance was most dangerous because it perverted natural communication between parent state and subordinate colonists. 'Far from exciting our gratitude or satisfying our uneasiness and discontent,' Isaac Wilkins declared in the New York Assembly, the repeal of the Stamp Act 'has only emboldened us to make further encroachments upon [British] authority. We foolishly attribute this gentle conduct towards us to fear and to a consciousness of her inability to compel us to submission.' Colonial antagonism and hostility to Britain, Wilkins complained, displaced normal relations with the colonists' 'kind and indulgent mother . . . whose arms are open to receive all such of her children as will return to their duty.' Only 'detestable parricides' would stab a mother's 'bosom' simply to gratify the desire of 'Ungrateful brethren' in Boston. The only way to secure redress of grievances from a firm and loving parent was to argue the undue exercise of power, not the illegitimacy of superior authority.[53] To the Anglican rector Henry Caner, the American opposition to British measures was marked by a childlike peevishness. Some American liberties had been 'infringed,' he admitted, but 'will it therefore follow that like froward children we should peevishly throw away the rest, because some things have been taken away?' Instead, he advised that the colonists adopt attitudes of 'peace and submission, union and harmony' to prevent all blessings from being taken away.[54] Another observer castigated the unruly and licentious methods adopted by the patriots in the dispute with Britain when he asserted, 'Sirs, is

[52] 'A New York Freeholder,' *New-York Mercury*, Oct. 10, 1774; 'America's Real Friend,' *Rivington's Gazetteer*, Feb. 16, 1775.
[53] Ibid., Apr. 6, 1775.
[54] 'Chronus,' *Boston Post-Boy Advertiser*, Dec. 2, 1771.

mobs, bullying, riots, treasons, rebellions &c. the only effectual method for you to prosecute, to obtain his Majesty's and parliament's favour?'[55] Insolence and wantoness described the Continental Congress's approach to the Anglo-American dispute, according to an unknown loyalist who contended that instead of pursuing 'wise and prudent' courses of action, the Congress adopted 'rude, insolent and absurd resolves' and 'wantonly' altered the 'constitution.'[56] The colonists made fools of themselves when they 'gravely assert that [the British] people long famed for wisdom and love of liberty' would spend 'a thousand years in compounding and rearing up a constitution out of the materials of the different simple forms of government' and in the end 'select nothing but the tyrannical forms of each.' Too much of the history of England had gone into the making of the constitution that the colonists now found oppressive and too much blood had been spilled in defending it against domestic and foreign tyrants for colonial diatribes to weaken British resolve to maintain parliamentary supremacy. 'Arguing from the abuse' of parliamentary and royal power 'rather than from the use' of those 'things,' the colonists would only forfeit any right to be taken seriously as commentators on British constitutionalism.[57]

To some loyalist writers, the Bostonians, who appeared to be spearheading the American opposition to Britain, epitomized the petulance characteristic of the patriots. Several loyalists criticized their intolerance and desires for domination over others. Peter Oliver in his 'Address' to the Massachusetts militia depicted other Americans' attitudes toward Massachusetts as follows: '*the Massachusetts have a different interest from the rest of the Continent; they are a set of brave, hardy dogs; and are always encroaching upon their neighbours.*'[58] The Anglican authors of 'A Whip for the American Whig' reminded their readers that it was the people of Massachusetts who hanged the 'poor, harmless, inoffensive Quakers,' while another defender of the Anglican church recounted the history of seven-

[55] 'John Herbert,' *Boston Evening-Post*, Mar. 13, 1769.

[56] 'A Freeholder of Essex and a Real Lover of Liberty,' *Rivington's Gazetteer*, Jan. 5, 1775.

[57] 'Cato,' 'To the People of Pennsylvania, VII,' *Pennsylvania Gazette*, Apr. 10, 1776; see also 'An Answer to the Declaration,' *Pennsylvania Evening Post*, Feb. 17, 1778.

[58] [Peter Oliver], 'An Address to the Soldiers of Massachusetts Bay who are now in Arms against the Laws of their Country,' *Boston Weekly News-Letter*, Jan. 11, 1776.

teenth-century Puritan bigotry.[59] The New England clergy, in the opinion of 'Bellisarius,' were 'the instigators and abettors of every persecution and conspiracy.'[60] A Quaker in Massachusetts itself shared the same view of the intolerance of his fellow colonists: 'we tell thee friends we esteem George [III] a good sort of a Man . . . he is willing every Man should worship God according to his Conscience . . . which the town of Boston is not.'[61] The 'insidious' actions of the First Continental Congress, which were comparable to those of the 'Spanish Inquisition,' were, in the eyes of one loyalist, 'borrowed from the seditious Bostonians.'[62] The wantonness and self-righteousness associated with the Massachusetts capital was suggested by a group of New York freeholders who spoke of the 'rebellious Saints at Boston.'[63] A Massachusetts loyalist satirized the insolent and immodest behavior of the Bostonians by contriving a conversation in which a 'high Patriotic Bostonian' was made to say 'do not we in Boston live at the fountainhead of political knowledge and are we not to be believed?' In light of such patriot self-perceptions, the author concluded that it was dangerous to speak unless one were unalterably opposed to Britain and that the liberty of the press was for patriots only.[64] In describing the endeavors of the 'cunning' and 'zealous' patriots in the late 1760s to arouse the passions of the multitude, 'Z.T.' of Massachusetts paused 'to consider the part acted by the town of Boston.' 'Their spirited resolves and instructions, polemical writings and . . . practices, and their undue influence and example must have had some effect,' he reasoned. 'Did not the inhabitants of that town on all occasions keep up such a perpetual din to people from the country about politics, that they were even confounded with the clamour of it?,' he began. 'They so abounded with politicians, or the echoes of them,' he continued, 'that in all companies, the poor countryman must hear them display their oratory or vociferations, whether they would or not.' Besides being assertive and rabble rousing, the Bostonians were cunning and intolerant: 'if any one did offer to oppose them in their extravagant

[59] *New-York Mercury*, Apr. 25, 1768; see also 'Anatomist III,' *New-York Journal*, Oct. 13, 1768, and 'A Dissenter,' *Boston Evening-Post*, January 11, 1773.

[60] 'Bellisarius,' *Rivington's Gazetteer*, Mar. 9, 1775.

[61] 'A Letter from a Quaker,' *Boston Evening-Post*, Jan. 25, 1773.

[62] 'America's Real Friend,' *Rivington's Gazetteer*, Feb. 16, 1775.

[63] 'Major Benjamin Floyd and a great number of others,' ibid., Apr. 6, 1775.

[64] 'Dialogue Between a high Patriotic Bostonian and a plain honest countryman,' *Boston Weekly News-Letter*, Jan. 14, 1773.

flights and invectives . . . he might depend upon being ill treated; and called a d – g sl – ve, t – ry, or f – – l; and it was also very difficult for a countryman to find where he might set in quiet to drink something . . . for there are those who are more ready to stir up sedition or slander than to stir a bowl of punch; by which practices the weaker sort are misled, and the less credulous abused.'[65]

Petulance, associated with insolent, pert, and undisciplined behavior, a childish unwillingness to consider seriously the reasoned arguments of critics, and an aggressive intolerance of dissenting views, was regarded as being a fatal weakness of the patriots. It led them, according to loyalists, to ignore the best long-term interests of the colonies—a reconciliation with the mother country—which required mature, prudent, discrete, and dutiful representations of colonial grievances to a supposedly just mother country, and to persevere in the belligerent, irresponsible, and shortsighted courses of action that were aggravating the dispute with Britain.[66] And to many loyalists, it was this kind of insolent, provocative, and uncompromising behavior on the part of the patriots that was largely responsible for the crisis in Anglo-American relations. After discussing at length the high-handed, unrestrained and intolerant patriot methods, 'Z.T.' stated 'that it may be justly concluded that such proceedings were greatly instrumental to our present distresses.'[67] Henry Caner also believed that if 'our affairs . . . are not so eligible now it is manifestly owing to the improper conduct of our officious patriots. . . .'[68] The Boston Port Bill, in the opinion of a 'New York Freeholder,' was the result of American 'provocation.'[69] Daniel Leonard was distressed at the measures adopted by the Continental Congress, which he felt would 'irritate and enrage the inhabitants of the two countries, against each other, beyond a possibility of reconciliation'; however, the tone of the resolves could be explained to some extent by the fact that 'some of the most influential of the members were the very persons that had been the *wilful* cause of the evils they were expected to remedy.'[70] And a group of loyalists in White Plains, New York, declared, 'our disapprobation of

[65] 'Z.T.,' *Boston Evening-Post*, May 15, 1769.
[66] 'Juba,' *Rivington's Gazetteer*, Sept. 2, 1774.
[67] 'Z.T.,' *Boston Evening-Post*, May 15, 1769.
[68] 'Chronus,' *Boston Post-Boy Advertiser*, Jan. 6, 1772.
[69] 'A New York Freeholder,' *New-York Mercury*, Sept. 26, 1774.
[70] *Boston Post-Boy Advertiser*, Mar. 27, 1775.

many hot and furious proceedings against the measures taken by the mother country, as, in our opinion, they will rather tend to ruin this once happy continent, than remove grievances.'[71]

Moreover, the patriots' attempts to intimidate or coerce those who held opposing views convinced many loyalists that, while mouthing shibboleths about liberty, the patriots were in fact infringing the most basic civil freedoms of Americans. This conviction led several loyalist writers to conclude that the most substantive threat to their freedom emanated not from Britain but from the patriot congresses, committees, and mobs in their midst. As early as November 1773, Myles Cooper advised his readers that 'while we are watchful against external attacks upon our freedom, let us be on our guard, lest we become enslaved by . . . tyrants within.'[72] 'Take heed,' another loyalist warned, 'that while the words tyranny and oppression are bandied about, and fixed on Britain, you are not unawares enthralled at home.'[73] After denouncing the tyrannical implications of the First Continental Congress's Association, one loyalist declared, 'I shall not dare to think or act, but I shall be in danger of being held up as an enemy to my country. . . . Am I to be a slave? I will then be a slave to a King and a Parliament.'[74]

The charge of ingratitude touched a sensitive nerve in Whig consciousness. The Revolutionary generation had become increasingly enmeshed in its dependence on British consumer goods, capital, and credit. The price of this economic anglicization, Marc Egnal and Joseph A. Ernst argue persuasively, was periodic liquidity crises and the erosion of colonial mercantile independence in the marketplace.[75] Against this background of provincialism and uncertainty, many colonists groped toward a reassessment of the benefits they enjoyed as subjects of the empire. Loyalist writers to the press, in contrast, boldly seized the issue of colo-

[71] 'Subscribers, Freeholders, and Inhabitants of White Plains in the County of Westchester,' *Rivington's Gazetteer*, Jan. 12, 1775; see also 'A Freeholder of Essex and a Real Lover of Liberty,' ibid., Jan. 5, 1775.

[72] 'Poplicola,' ibid., Nov. 18, 1773.

[73] 'Philo-Libertas,' ibid., Oct. 18, 1774.

[74] 'A Freeholder of Essex and a Real Lover of Liberty,' ibid., Jan. 5, 1775; see also 'Declaration of the Grand Jury and Magistrates of Tryon County,' ibid., Apr. 6, 1775; 'Anti-Licentiousness,' ibid., Apr. 20, 1775; 'Phileirene,' *Boston Weekly News-Letter*, Jan. 12, 1775; 'X.,' ibid., June 16, 1774.

[75] Marc Egnal and Joseph A. Ernst, 'An Economic Interpretation of the American Revolution,' *William and Mary Quarterly*, 3d ser. 29 (1972): 3–32.

nial self-interest in imperialism and made it their own. Ingratitude for the benefits of the empire weakened the fabric of colonial subordination, the loyalist press argued, because men ignored their own best interests, misunderstood the reciprocal benefits that colonists and the British nation received from the imperial connection, and lacked the patience and sophistication to engineer a reconciliation of the imperial controversy which would preserve American liberty without destroying the empire. Concerned with economic interests, with the preservation of stability and harmony in society, and a pragmatic approach in dealings with imperial authority, the denunciation of patriot ingratitude was grounded in reason and experience.

'It is impossible to review the advantages we derive from our connection with Great Britain,' 'A Philadelphian' declared, 'without wishing it to be perpetual. We are formed by her laws and religion: we are clothed by her manufacturers and protected by her fleets and armies. Her kings are the umpires of our disputes, and the center of our union. In a word, the Island of Britain is the fortress in which we are sheltered from the machinations of all the powers of Europe.' Here was the classic loyalist view of the nature of the empire which portrayed Britain as a dynamic culture from which law, religion, military security, and political authority flowed irresistibly to weaker, far-flung colonial societies. The colonists, this writer maintained, were instinctively anxious and insecure about their own ability to survive in a world of powerful assertive European nations. It was therefore axiomatic that a 'review' of imperial benefits would strengthen people's identification with the empire: 'no wonder . . . we look forward with horror to those conclusions which must attend ([for] ages hence) our separation from that country.'[76]

The stabilizing effect of the British tie was emphasized by Isaac Wilkins, who argued, 'Shall we not derive strength, protection and stability from that oak around which we have so long twined ourselves and under the shadow of whose branches, we have so long flourished in security'; it is 'our interest' and 'our duty' to 'cultivate the closest and most intimate union with her [Britain].'[77] Other loyalists stressed the security and freedom guaranteed to the colonists by the British constitution. To

[76] *Pennsylvania Gazette*, May 18, 1774.

[77] Isaac Wilkins, 'Speech to the New York General Assembly,' *Rivington's Gazetteer*, Apr. 6, 1775; see also [Joseph Galloway], 'A West County Farmer,' *Pennsylvania Gazette*, June 16, 1768.

Henry Caner, the English constitution was 'most perfect,' most 'favourable to Liberty,' and a constitution under which 'the subject enjoys more liberty, is more secure in his property, and in the enjoyment of every valuable blessing and Privilege than the subject of any other nation under Heaven.' Similarly, a group of loyalist Associators joined together 'to declare our firm and indissoluble attachment to our most gracious Sovereign George the third . . . and with grateful hearts to acknowledge that we are indebted to his paternal care for the preservation of our lives and fortunes.'[78] In the opinion of another loyalist, the unity, harmony, and vitality of the various colonies depended on the maintenance of the British tie. 'The superintendence and mediation of Great Britain seems to be necessary to balance . . . the different interests of the several plantations and colonies, and to direct, command and govern the operations and powers of *each* for the benefit and defence of *All.*' Furthermore, he contended, 'protected by her navy and armies, we shall rise with fresh vigour and strength, and see her free and well balanced constitution gradually communicated to us. In a state of separation, on the contrary, ages may pass, and rivers of blood be shed before any regular form of government could be adopted and fixed on a firm basis.'[79] An important factor in colonial economic growth and prosperity, declared 'Rusticus,' was Britain's 'readiness to increase our industry and protect us from foreign injuries. . . . Surely some returns of gratitude, such as become a free and liberal people are justly due for favours received.'[80]

Though mutual interest and obligation knit the empire together, the relationship of the colonies to their parent state depended upon British restraint in the use of imperial authority and colonial passivity in responding to British measures. 'Eugenio' felt unable to conceive of the empire in terms other than those of 'a parent and her children. . . . I look upon it as the duty of Great Britain,' he declared, 'to give her colo-

[78] 'Chronus,' *Boston Post-Boy Advertiser*, Dec. 2, 1771; 'Form of an Association in Cortlandt's Manor,' *Rivington's Gazetteer*, Feb. 16, 1775; see also 'Philanthrop,' *Boston Evening-Post*, Jan. 14, 1771; 'A New York Freeholder,' *New-York Mercury*, Sept. 12, 1774.

[79] 'Extract of a Letter from London,' *Rivington's Gazetteer*, Feb. 16, 1775.

[80] 'Rusticus,' *Pennsylvania Packet*, Jan. 2, 1775; see also 'Rusticus,' *New-York Mercury*, Jan. 16, 1775; 'An Account between Great Britain and her Colonies,' ibid., June 6, 1774; 'Phileirene,' *Boston Weekly News-Letter*, Jan. 26, 1775; 'Mr. Cruger's Speech in Answer to Lord North,' *Rivington's Gazetteer*, July 13, 1775.

nies that countenance and protection to which as children they are certainly entitled, . . . not only defense of person and property against our common enemies abroad, but [also] the preservation of our essential rights and liberties.' He counted on 'mutual forebearance' to compensate for 'any little appearances of severity on one side or petulancy on the other.' The need for such familial goodwill was imperative: 'I can easily foresee that unnumbered calamities must burst upon these American colonies unless present difficulties between them and the parent land be speedily adjusted.' If the British abridged colonial rights, then colonial self-interest required an added measure of toleration and acquiescence; conversely, the British needed to allow their headstrong children a healthy latitude in coping with the requirements of imperial policy.[81]

The colonists' ingratitude—their unwillingness to recognize the past, present, and future benefits derived from the imperial tie—led them, according to loyalists, to countenance a rebellion that was totally unnatural. The adjective *unnatural*, used frequently by loyalists to describe the Revolution, reflected their belief that the colonies and Britain were naturally tied to each other by the bonds of culture, history, and mutual interest. Severing such a beneficial and deeply rooted link was contrary to the dictates of both reason and colonial self-interest. Because of the 'infatuated blindness'[82] of the colonists to their 'true interest' and their ingratitude for past British aid and benevolence to the colonies, the patriots could assert what appeared to loyalists to be totally inconsistent with reason and history: that Britain was no longer the mother who 'nourished, protected and established us,' but had become a tyrant.[83] That such a perception of Britain was totally irreconcilable with common sense and history was asserted forcefully by Daniel Leonard: 'Are we to take up arms and make war against our parent, lest that parent, contrary to the experience of a century and a half, contrary to her own genius, inclination, affection and interest, should treat us or our posterity as bastards, and not as sons, and instead of protecting, should enslave us?'[84]

[81] *Pennsylvania Ledger*, Jan. 28, 1775; see also 'Massachusettensis,' *Boston Post-Boy Advertiser*, Jan. 2, 1775; 'Phileirene,' *Boston Weekly News-Letter*, Jan. 26, 1775; 'Isaac Wilkins' Speech,' *Rivington's Gazetteer*, Apr. 6, 1775; 'Form of an Association in Cortlandt's Manor,' ibid., Feb. 16, 1775.

[82] 'Phileirene,' *Boston Weekly News-Letter*, Jan. 26, 1775.

[83] 'Isaac Wilkins' Speech,' *Rivington's Gazetteer*, Apr. 6, 1775.

[84] 'Massachusettensis,' *Boston Post-Boy Advertiser*, Mar. 20, 1775.

The debate in Philadelphia in the spring of 1776 over the alternatives of independence and reconciliation matched the infectious radicalism of Thomas Paine's *Common Sense* against Provost William Smith's deft, adroit advocacy of delay, caution, and patience as bulwarks of colonial liberty. 'I am bold to declare and hope yet to make it evident to every honest man,' Smith asserted, 'that the true interest of America lies in reconciliation with Great Britain upon constitutional principles, and . . . upon no other terms.' Smith's bold pronouncement was at once aggressive and flexible. Inclusion in the empire was not merely a negative restraint, he explained, it was also a source of insight, capability, and strategy for the colonists. 'We [have] considered our connection with Great Britain as our chief happiness' because under it 'we flourished, grew rich and populous. . . . Let us then act the part of skillful physicians and wisely adapt the remedy to the evil.'[85]

Smith realized that there was a broad coalition of moderates in Pennsylvania who feared the social disruption that would accompany independence and civil war. The Pennsylvania social order—with its numerous ethnic and religious factions and its divided political elite—was more than any other colony susceptible to this argument. 'The world has already seen numberless instances of fine-spun political theories which, like the quackeries of mountebank doctors, are to cure all the political evils to which human nature is liable,' Smith observed. Sweeping programs of political purification, he went on, invariably ran afoul of a 'thousand little passions and interests' which protected people from the arbitrary whims of ambitious rulers and agitators. Independence won through armed rebellion, he warned, would produce 'every convulsion attendant upon revolutions and innovations in government untimely attempted or finally defeated: the loss of trade for want of protection, the consequent decay of husbandry, bloodshed and desolation, . . . an exchange of the easy and flourishing condition of farmers and merchants for a life at best of hardy poverty as soldiers or hunters.' Smith saw the society and economy of the middle colonies as rich, expansive, and rewarding while the political system governing the province was brittle, inexperienced, and vulnerable. While 'agriculture and commerce have hitherto been the happy employments by which these middle colonies have risen in wealth and importance,' all of these at-

[85] 'Cato,' 'Letter to the People of Pa., II,' *Pennsylvania Gazette*, Mar. 13, 1776.

tainments could be lost if the British ceased protecting the colonies from the grasping designs of other European powers. Even a successful revolt against the mother country would leave the Americans discredited in the eyes of mankind as a 'faithless people,' and an abortive rebellion would disrupt the fragile infrastructure of trade, credit, and the honoring of civil obligations. 'To see America reduced to such a situation may be the choice of adventurers who have nothing to lose or of men exalted by the present confusions into lucrative offices which they can hold no longer than the continuation of the public calamities,' Smith declared. It was not only the bloodshed and dislocation of a civil war that alarmed him, but the emergence into leadership positions of new men hungry for recognition and impatient with the pace of advancement under imperial rule. Surely the 'great and valuable people in *America*, who by honest industry have acquired a competency and have experienced a happy life,' would do everything in their power to avoid an abrupt shift in leadership and power.[86]

The trouble with this conservative calculation, Smith acknowledged, was that 'the people generally judge aright [only] when the whole truth is plainly laid before them, but through inattention in some and fondness for novelty in others' only 'one side' in the imperial controversy was receiving wide circulation and appreciation. Politicians abused the privilege of addressing a public audience when, like the advocates of independence, they exaggerate or conceal facts, . . . state but one side of a question, . . . warp the judgment [of their audience] by partial representation, . . . give railing for reason, invectives for arguments, and . . . urge the people into hasty resolutions by addressing [men's] passions rather than [their] sober reason.'[87] Reconciliation, therefore, required a calm, dispassionate citizenry capable of hearing all of the arguments on both sides of the imperial dispute and secure enough to resist being stampeded into precipitous action. Smith conceded that independence could be legitimately declared if the whole community became 'convinced by better arguments than declamations and abuse of things venerable and ancient that future connection with *Great Britain* is neither possible nor safe.'[88] For all practical purposes, he argued, the colonists had already declared de facto independence by preparing to resist Brit-

86 'Rationalis,' ibid., Feb. 28, 1776.
87 'Cato,' 'To the People . . . VIII,' ibid., Apr. 24, 1776.
88 'Cato,' 'To the People . . . III,' ibid., Mar. 20, 1776.

ish coercion and by asserting broad claims of colonial liberty. 'It is our duty to continue this resistance till Great Britain is convinced (as she must soon be) of her fatal policy and open her arms to reconciliation.' Resolute but not offensive, united and eschewing factional agitation, the colonists, Smith argued, could secure redress without resorting to violence or rebellion. 'Upon such a footing we may again be happy. Our husbandmen, our mechanicks, our artificers will flourish. Our language, our laws, our manners being the same as those of the nation with which we are again to be connected.' It was an appealing formula. Political calm would restore a flourishing economy; an easing of imperial tensions would enable British culture to continue to serve as a stabilizing force in the diverse society of the middle colonies. Having shown firmness and patience in dealing with British encroachments, the imperial 'connection will become more natural and we shall more easily guard against foreign innovations.' '*Pennsylvania*,' Smith concluded, making his point unmistakably clear, 'has much to lose in this contest and much to hope from a proper settlement of it.'[89]

Loyalist writers stressed that colonial ingratitude was a self-inflicted wound that deprived the Americans of the leadership of some of their most courageous and unselfish fellow citizens. 'Does not that man deserve to be heard with candour,' asked 'A Philadelphian,' 'who desires not to counteract the general sentiments of his countrymen but thinks it a duty incumbent upon him to endeavor to guard against an evil which may have a tendency to destroy the hope of every virtuous patriot—a hope of our united efforts may be a means to a redress of grievances [and] that the lasting and happy union may be restored between the Mother Country and her Colonies?' By identifying liberty and happiness with the maintenance of political calm and unity, the loyalists were able to depict ingratitude as a cast of mind into which people slipped when they tired of the burden of supporting a common public consensus—a middle position enjoying the widest possible support. The emotional gratification of fracturing that consensus by abusing individuals

---

[89] 'Cato,' 'To the People . . . IV,' ibid., Mar. 27, 1776; on Smith's use of the press, see Don R. Byrnes, 'The Pre–Revolutionary Career of Provost William Smith, 1751–1778,' Ph.D. diss., Tulane University, 1969; on Smith's emphasis on social pluralism and instability in Pennsylvania, see Stephen Lucas, 'Between Protest and Revolution: The Ideology of Reconciliation and the Popular Debate over Independence,' paper read at the St. Augustine Conference on American Loyalism, and *Portents of Rebellion: Rhetoric and Revolution in Philadelphia, 1765–76* (Philadelphia, 1976), chap. 7.

was, lamentably, very strong.[90] 'Such is the violence of our disputing parties,' wrote 'A Moderate Man,' that whoever differs from either is immediately stigmatized as a *whig* or a *tory*, . . . terms of disgrace according as they are applied by these parties to each other. Many of those who suffer such vituperation 'are really pursuing that which appears to them for the interest of the community.' What was remarkable about this persecution of the innocent moderates, 'A Moderate Man' explained, was a new self-consciousness and sense of political purpose which the experience instilled into the personalities of apolitical novices: 'to moderate these party heats, to draw that zeal into a channel where it would really be serviceable, is the duty of every member of the community,' he concluded; only when 'mutual forebearance, amity, and love' replace 'hard words' can 'any society' become 'quiet and happy.'[91]

To execute this kind of political therapy, urged 'A Farmer' in the *Pennsylvania Packet*, 'let us equally shun the benumbing stillness of *overweening sloth* and the feverish activity of ill-formed zeal which busies itself in maintaining little, mean, and narrow opinions.'[92] The most self-conscious newspaper advocacy of a fresh mental outlook in the pursuit of reconciliation appeared in a series of essays by Richard Wells in the *Packet* in the summer of 1774. 'The more I consider the importance of the present controversy,' he declared, 'the more I am convinced of the need of wisdom in our councils. . . . Reason must command our forces. . . . The sparkling ideas of a warm imagination are too apt to soar into the regions of danger and, without providing a proper retreat, involve the bold adventurer in unthought of perplexities.' Resisting parliamentary violations of the colonists' constitutional rights, Wells insisted, required rigorous self-control and disciplined use of imagination. '*I contend with a zeal which convinces me that I am right* that we must not pass by the present temper of the times' for a time of crisis was precisely the moment when a high sense of responsibility could offset men's rashness and mindless aggression. 'Our passions cannot always remain upon the stretch; [soon] we shall gently relax from the severity of strict right and heedlessly and gradually slide down the hill of [mere negative] opposition

[90] *Pennsylvania Gazette*, Sept. 7, 1774.
[91] *Boston Weekly News-Letter*, Feb. 2, 1775.
[92] *Pennsylvania Packet*, Feb. 27, 1775.

[allowing] our rulers [to] become tyrants and from a country of happy freemen, we shall degenerate into a land of abject slaves.'[93]

Pleading for a cautious, deliberate response to British encroachments, Wells advocated a circuitous strategy in which the Americans would ask the king to instruct his governors to recommend to the assemblies the gathering of a continental congress to draft *'an American Bill of Rights.'* Colonial negotiators could then carry this document to London and bargain for British approval of a 'legal and firm contract.' Such a process would recognize that the empire was an amalgam of many activities, motives, and purposes: ' 'tis offensive [and] defensive, connected [and] independent, a mixture of rivalry and friendship, a greater [entity] subordinate to the lesser, and yet all bound together by one interest and affection.' By conceiving of the empire as a source of vast material benefits to the colonists, the advocates of reconciliation pointed within the social order itself for insights and wisdom to guide their fellow citizens in confrontation with British power.[94]

Confronted with an apparently brutish and immoral British regime, the Whigs looked deeply into their collective selves as the final crises of 1774–76 crashed around them. Externally, they assumed a posture of defiant disobedience. As they prepared for defensive, hopefully peaceful, resistance to the Coercive Acts, they discovered their ability to decentralize resistance through local committees of inspection and correspondence and also how to entrust direction of the common cause to a continental congress. Surprised and emboldened by these discoveries, the leaders of resistance scarcely realized how much they had accelerated the pace of events leading toward independence and war.[95] A few years earlier, a unified movement for national independence would have been inconceivable; to the loyalists watching, the spectacle was incomprehensible and outrageous.

Overt, deliberate, violent disobedience to constituted authority, the

[93] Ibid., June 22, 1774; see also 'Anti-Tormentor,' ibid., Nov. 21, 1774.

[94] Ibid., July 20, 1774; see also 'Amor Patriae,' *Boston Weekly News-Letter*, Jan. 19, 1769; 'A Plan of Reconciliation,' *Rivington's Gazetteer*, Nov. 2, 1775; 'Isaac Wilkins' Speech,' ibid., Apr. 6, 1775.

[95] Pauline Maier, *From Resistance to Revolution: Colonial Radicals and the Development of American Opposition to Britain, 1765–1776* (New York, 1972), chap. 9 treats the interior of these tactics and perceptions while Ammerman, *In the Common Cause*, examines their external thrust and impact.

loyalist polemicists declared, was rebellion—the ultimate outrage against God and society. 'Rebellion is the most atrocious offence that can be perpetrated by man,' exhorted Daniel Leonard; 'it dissolves the social band, annihilates the security resulting from law and government; introduces fraud, violence, rapine, murder, sacrilege and the long trail of evils, that riot uncontrouled in a state of nature.'[96] In one of the most cogent and informative loyalist newspaper polemics, 'Plain English' in February 1775 depicted the threshold of rebellion in a listing of twenty-nine specific acts of aggression against 'people, who from a sense of their duty to the King and a reverence for his laws, have behaved quietly and peaceably.' 'Barbarous cruelties, insults, and indignities, . . . disgraceful even for savages to have committed,' composed his profile of 'lawless mobs and riots.' 'Plain English' perceived clearly that the abuse and intimidation of known allies of the crown and of all officials who refused to renounce the legitimacy of the Coercive Acts radically changed the framework of politics in Massachusetts. The assertion of the will of the people and the physical power that large numbers of people could exert created a new atmosphere of fear and terror in the province. 'Last August a mob in Berkshire forced the justices of the court of common pleas from their seats and shut up the court house,' the enumeration began; 'they also drove David Ingersoll, Esq. from his house and damaged the same. . . . Col. [Thomas] Gilbert of Freetown, a firm friend to government, in August last, being at Dartmouth, was attacked at midnight by a mob of about an hundred but by his bravery [and] with the assistance of the family where he lodged, they were beat off.' 'Mr. [Jonathan] Sewall, his Majesty's attorney general for this province was obliged to repair to Boston for refuge; his elegant house at Cambridge was attacked by a mob, his windows broke, but they were beat off by the gallant behaviour and bravery of some of the young gentlemen of his family.'

Rebellion, 'Plain English' sensed, was more than the seizure of power through physical coercion and violence. Random, spontaneous acts of aggression created an aura of their own—unintended and unanticipated by the perpetrators of such conduct—which corroded the structure of civility and acquiescence to authority that were essential to civil gov-

---

[96] *Boston Post-Boy Advertiser*, Feb. 6, 1775; see also 'Chaubullagungamuggensis,' *Rivington's Gazetteer*, Sept. 22, 1774 ('I cannot but consider the present opposition to Parliament as resistance of lawful authority and the beginning of a rebellion') and 'Tranquillus,' *Pennsylvania Gazette*, Sept. 7, 1774.

ernment. Daniel Leonard was not only forced to evacuate his fine house in Taunton, but also compelled to watch as the mob fired bullets into the empty structure as a ghoulish gesture of their determination to destroy every vestige of support for the crown. Vandals cut hair from the mane and tail of Timothy Ruggles's fine horse. At Worcester a crowd of 5,000 required thirty judges, sheriffs, and lawyers to walk bareheaded between two columns of armed men and then signify their compliance with the closing of the courts in defiance of the Coercive Acts. It was the mobs' insistence on symbolic victories that revealed to 'Plain English' their design of destroying the symbols of authority and self-respect held by men of accomplishment and social standing in the community. 'Daniel Dunbar of Halifax, an ensign of militia there,' this account explained, 'had his [regimental] colours demanded by the mob, some of the selectmen being the chief actors; he refused; they broke into his house, took him out, forced him upon a rail and was held on it by his hands and legs and tossed up with violence.' When Dunbar 'resisted' being put 'on the rail, they seized him by his private parts to drag him on it, then beat him and after keeping him two or three hours in such abuses, he was forced to give his colours up to save his life.'[97]

In the extreme form of rebellion, political disobedience was a mania compounded from the guilt and desperation of evil leaders. 'Your officers, my countrymen!,' Peter Oliver appealed to Massachusetts militiamen in January 1776, 'have taken great pains to sooth and flatter you, that you may not quit your posts and forsake *them* until they have accomplished their ambitious and desperate schemes. Your leaders know that they have plunged themselves into the bowels of the most wanton and unnatural rebellion that ever existed; they think that by engaging large numbers to partake in their guilt that they shall appear formidable, and that by so numerous an appearance the hand of justice will not dare to arrest them.' That desperate gamble, that willingness to plunge society into chaos without any consideration of the consequences, generated powerful destructive energies. In what would be a preview of his full-scale history of the Revolution, Oliver narrated the 'origin and progress of the publick disorders which . . . terminated in a most unnatural and ungrateful rebellion.' By systematically engaging in smuggling, a group of merchants had accustomed themselves to 'defrauding

[97] *Boston Weekly News-Letter*, Feb. 23, 1775; *Rivington's Gazetteer*, Mar. 9, 1775.

King,' 'injuring and publickly ruining' their fellow subjects, and 'by degrees' abandoning every pretense to virtue and responsibility. In the pursuit of illegal gain, the smugglers enlisted as an ally James Otis, Jr., who through oratory and radicalism 'swore he would set the province in a flame if he died in the attempt.' But the flame that Otis ignited and fanned, because it originated in compulsive ambition and vindictiveness, was the 'sort of flame that consumes not only a man's property but also [this] understanding.' To offset the 'popular commotions' aroused by an attack on the authority of Parliament, Otis felt 'it was necessary to enlist a *black regiment*' of clergymen to cast an aura of religiosity on these turbulent and vicious actions. What had started as an opposition to the acts of trade became a torrent of perverted moral outrage: 'the press roared out its libels; the sacred desk . . . sounded the trumpet of sedition and rebellion. . . . Libertinism, riot, and robbery soon became the effects of this sort of public spirit; houses were plundered and demolished; persons were beat, abused, tarred and feathered; courts of justice were insulted; the pillars of justice were destroyed; and no way to escape the torrent of savage barbarity but by paying obeisance to the sovereign mandates of a mob.' In this macabre setting, the drama could lead only to death and desolation. 'Garretts were crowded with patriots; mechanicks and lawyers, porters and clergymen huddled promiscuously into them; their decisions were oracular, and from thence poured out their midnight reveries: . . . to form an independent empire' in which 'all the friends of licentiousness were to be reimbursed out of the estates of the friends to government.'[98]

Rebelliousness, the loyalists concluded, was therefore an irreversible contagion sustained by the desperation of its fomenters and the fear and ignorance of its growing circle of adherents. Once they employed violence and deceit, the patriots could not hope to control and regulate the behavior of their own supporters; the most ambitious and most cowardly among them would always succumb to the temptation to commit fresh outrages. The career of Nathanael Greene, 'A British American' in Charleston wrote in May 1781, illustrated perfectly the way in which 'political phrenzy' elevated the most 'infamous' men to positions of profit and power. Greene's avarice had been whetted by speculation in Rhode Island paper currency; his ambition ignited when he inveigled

[98] *Boston Weekly News-Letter*, Jan. 11, 1776.

his way into Washington's favor early in the war. His early attachment to the dignified and upright Washington was further evidence of his unscrupulous behavior. Washington, at the outset of the war, was known to have doubts about the wisdom of independence. Greene must have known that Washington's heart was not wholly committed to the patriot cause and must have planned to consign 'Washington to oblivion' and take his place. 'Did you indeed expect Washington would resign?,' 'British American' demanded. 'Is it possible ambition had so totally obliterated humanity that'—unlike Washington—'you could look forward to the redoubled calamities of war and ruin of your country without emotion? Recent experience answers you could. . . . The deliberate murders committed in cold blood, under your influence and direction in the Carolinas in the space of two months, exceed the number ever committed in any one war recorded in the history of Europe. . . . Entrusted with a separate command, . . . your vanity has been partly gratified, . . . and the peaceable inhabitants of America now feel, what they might have long expected, from such a commander as you are.'[99]

Disobedience and rebellion, the loyalist press maintained, dissolved the delicate network of social relationships that held human aggression under control and enabled people to live in peace and security. By drawing large numbers of people into lawless behavior and by creating large geographical areas where no law or constituted authority functioned, warfare accelerated and magnified this process of social disintegration and moral abandon. Among the most vivid documents illustrating these conditions and expressing this point of view was the narrative of Levi Smith, a South Carolina loyalist militia officer, which told of his capture and imprisonment by the patriots in the South Carolina back country during May and June 1781. Disobedience and rebellion generated rampant falsehood, Smith complained; 'our enemies have been indefatigable in propagating and screaming accounts of every circumstance by which they feel themselves aggrieved or improperly treated by our government' while 'a uniform silence prevails on our side under the hardest usage, . . . although we have had by far the greatest reason to complain.' Loyalist prisoners of the patriots, Smith testified, had received 'the most cruel treatment' from their captors, and these

[99] [South Carolina] *Royal Gazette*, May 30–June 2, 1781; see also 'Drusus,' *South-Carolina and American General Gazette*, Aug. 2, 9, 1780 and in [S.C.] *Royal Gazette*, May 2–5, 1781.

'shocking' atrocities should be made known to the whole world. Skeptical readers of his narrative, Smith suggested, could consult numerous loyalist refugees and British soldiers—several identified by name—who had been eyewitnesses to the outrages he had seen.

Smith's story was a grisly one. Upon capture he had been stripped to his undershirt and forced to run for a mile ahead of his mounted captors. When he collapsed, the patriot soldiers beat him with the flat edges of their swords. Once confined in Francis Marion's camp, he arranged to be exchanged for Samuel Cooper, a patriot held by Lord Rawdon. Cooper's brother, William, one of Smith's captors, initiated the exchange. For the next few days he was treated leniently, even allowed to go fishing with a single guard and visit his wife and children while awaiting the prisoner exchange to be completed. Then on the afternoon of May 14, the patriots captured a British outpost and confined their new loyalist and British prisoners, along with Smith, in a mill house. The American commander, Col. Francis Lee, then ordered the hanging of a young loyalist militia officer named Fulker who was accused of turning a sick woman from her house and thereby causing her death. Next the Americans condemned two loyalist militiamen to death. For carrying intelligence to the British army, Priv. John Jackson 'was hurried off, stripped, and tied up [by the neck] about dark, and left hanging all night . . . while Fulker's body, which had been cut down to make room for him, lay naked under the gallows.' The following day a militiaman named Hugh Maskelly, charged with various forms of collaboration with the British, was led off to the gallows with 'only an old dirty shirt tied round him,' executed 'without the slightest trial or hearing.' To his horror, Smith discovered that he was next on Francis Lee's execution list. Demanding to know the charges against him, Smith was charged with having had a part in the burning of the tavern of a Mrs. McCord, whom Smith knew as 'a person of notorious disaffection to the British cause.' Protesting he had known nothing of the burning until two hours after it occurred, Smith convinced several Continental officers standing nearby that he deserved a trial. Nevertheless, 'I was now made ready for execution. The old dirty hunting shirt was taken from Maskelly's body and wrapped around mine.' Fearing that Rawdon would retaliate by executing his brother, Samuel, William Cooper got a message to General Marion who arrived at the improvised gallows in time to save Smith's life.

Greene then ordered Smith put in irons. While waiting further disposition of their cases, the loyalist captives in Greene's camp underwent a further ordeal. John McCord, the son of the woman whose tavern had been burned by the patriots, arrived in the camp with a group of loyalist prisoners in chains. These prisoners brought harrowing rumors. A few days earlier, their reports contended, McCord had taken fourteen loyalist militiamen prisoner and handcuffed them in seven pairs. Marching these prisoners to Greene's headquarters and fearful of being overtaken by pursuing patriots, McCord had ordered two of his subordinates to shoot the prisoners in cold blood. 'All . . . died except one Joseph Cooper. . . . The person who was handcuffed with him was named Conrad Millar and was shot first. The murderer . . . loaded his piece again' and 'with great deliberation took sight at Cooper, who moved his head on one side when he perceived him drawing the trigger. . . . The bullet passed through the right side of his neck and he fell; upon which one of the guard run his sword through his neck to make sure of dispatching him and observed he had never seen a son of a bitch bleed so much in his life.' Miraculously, Cooper did not die from these wounds. He dragged his dead companion and himself under a shade tree. The next day, the 'stench' of Millar's body attracted the attention of two women in the neighborhood. They returned with a knife, cut off Millar's arm below the elbow, and moved Cooper to a house where his handcuff could be broken off and his wounds treated. (Some of these details Smith learned later when both he and Cooper were safely in Charleston.) News of this atrocity filled Greene's camp and so terrorized many loyalists that, fearful of the same fate, they enlisted in the rebel cause to escape captivity. Smith, however, refused to renounce his British allegiance. By this time Greene was in possession of captured documents showing that, prior to his capture, Smith had provided the British with military intelligence. 'He asked me if I did not deserve death, as I was American born. I told him that the province had been conquered and that I had, of course, become a British subject.' Apparently taking account of Smith's previous mistreatment, Greene paroled him to a nearby plantation to regain his health, and Smith—with some moral qualms—took the chance to escape and, still clad in Hugh Maskelly's bloody shirt, found safety with Lord Rawdon's force which was marching to relieve Fort Ninety Six.[100]

[100] [S.C.] *Royal Gazette*, Apr. 13–17, 1782.

Rebellion, in these gruesome terms, was the natural, predictable outgrowth of all of the political opportunism, social degeneracy, and perverted communalism that had precipitated the upheaval. It fused all of these symptoms into a single fatal malady. The process of disaffection climaxed in a state of rebellion where the whole network of social relations and the traditional authority of institutions of church and state, which restrained passions and inculcated morality, were undermined to unleash the thinly veiled depravity of mankind. Released from the restraints of law and morality and aroused by a cabal of cunning and aggressive intriguers, the passions of the populace knew no bounds. Atrocities took place, often without the knowledge of the Revolutionary leaders themselves, which were unimaginable in a civilized community. For Daniel Leonard this descent into barbarity was what rebellion meant: 'a state of war, of all against all . . . [where] might overcomes right; [and] innocence itself has no security.'[101] America had been led down the fatal road to rebellion, in the opinion of the loyalist press, by a minority of crafty and aggressive patriots who displayed an incomprehensible ignorance of the best long-term interests of the colonies and an obstinate refusal to take account of the reasoned appeals of critics. They had plunged the colonies into an irrational, unjustifiable, and self-destructive war against a mother country whose benevolence, protection, and aid to the colonies, and whose commitment to constitutional liberty, should have evoked Americans' gratitude rather than their disloyalty. Calm, dispassionate colonists who tried desperately to warn their fellow Americans of the dangerous route that they were embarking upon were, loyalist writers contended, intimidated, coerced, and silenced by patriots who would brook no opposition. As was often the case, Daniel Leonard summarized succinctly the loyalist view of the Revolution when he proclaimed, 'the annals of the world have not yet been deformed with a single instance of so unnatural, so causeless, so wanton, so wicked a rebellion.'[102]

[101] *Boston Post-Boy Advertiser*, Feb. 6, 1775.
[102] Ibid., Mar. 20, 1775.

3. 'TO MAKE BLIND EYES BLINDER AND THE DECEIVED PEOPLE [TO] IMAGINE VAIN THINGS': THE ULTIMATE MORAL INDICTMENT OF THE REVOLUTION

The corpus of loyalist essays in the press of the Revolutionary era depicts the psychic turmoil wrought by a radical change in the political culture. As old patterns of acquiescence collapsed, as new standards of political morality came to dominate public affairs, and as the pace and tempo of events accelerated, the loyalists' sense of identity, probity, and composure came under severe stress. Internalizing a political culture that was rapidly disappearing and assigning themselves a new role as agents of virtue and reason in a world gone mad, the writers of the loyalist press illustrate the intimate connection between the human spirit and the larger culture of values, expectations, and behavioral norms within which people live. Convinced that the dominant culture of their society no longer motivated people to adopt proper conduct, they sought to 'revitalize' it—to make it satisfying and coherent once again. They tried to understand the plight of a strife-ridden and war-torn political order by rethinking and recasting their own deepest yearnings and aspirations in a manner that would harmonize once again their inner and outer worlds.[103]

Simply recognizing the disparity between their own perception of the truth and the motivations and impulses of the patriots liberated the loyalist writers from uncertainty and apprehension. An open letter to 'Peyton Randolph' by 'Grotius' in January 1775 gained momentum and accusatory power as it identified the tension: 'how then, Sir, could you thus attempt to make blind eyes blinder, to make the mad Americans rage, and the deceived people imagine vain things. How could you thus set yourselves and take counsel against the Lord's anointed—stimulating the inhabitants of this continent to wage war with their parents and rebel against their lawful sovereign after declaring yourselves his most *loyal subjects* and avowing an *affection and regard for your fellow-sub-*

---

[103] See Anthony F. C. Wallace, 'Revitalization Movements,' *American Anthropologist* 58 (1956): 264–81; Clifford Geertz, 'Thick Description: Toward an Interpretive Theory of Culture,' in *The Interpretation of Cultures: Selected Essays* (New York, 1973), chap. 1; Peter Berger and Stanley Pullberg, 'Reification and the Sociological Critique of Consciousness,' *History and Theory* 4 (1965): 196–211; and George Grant, *Lament for a Nation: The Defeat of Canadian Nationalism* (Toronto, 1965).

266

jects?' 'Grotius's' dialectic between morality and disobedience was so taut and highly charged that his argument fairly leaped from assumption to prescription: 'surely you could not suppose' that the Continental Association was 'a healing measure, tending to an accommodation of our unhappy differences. You must know your preamble was calculated to blind the reason and enflame the passions of Americans, and your association an open act of hostility which could not fail to sharpen the resentments of an affronted, powerful nation, jealous of their rights and tender of their honour.'

It was this insensitivity to the known and natural predispositions of British national sentiment that represented for 'Grotius' the clearest evidence that the patriots were ignoring the most obvious moral and political realities: 'Englishmen, Sir, can never submit to [the] despotism' of illegal committeemen; 'an Englishman cannot tamely look on and see bread snatched by ruffians from his children's mouths—it is too much for human nature to bear—it will drive men to desperation, and must surely be productive of confusion and bloodshed.' By the grossness and barbarity of their behavior, 'Grotius' explained, the patriots would goad humane British rulers to unleash the severe retribution at the hand of a long-suffering, almost infinitely patient, parent finally driven to impose discipline. 'It is strange indeed,' he concluded incredulously 'that wise men should hit upon treason and rebellion as a means of *pacifying* an *offended sovereign*; upon *violence* and *robbery* as the preservatives of *civil liberty*.' Reason and elementary political judgment indicated that just the opposite was true; 'how much more certainly would the tendency of a gentle, peaceable, orderly conduct have been to obtain these desirable ends!'[104]

By adopting a system of moral absolutism, the loyalist press maintained, the patriots dehumanized the British—forgetting the human feelings that ingratitude and rebellion aroused in the minds and hearts of British rulers. When the New York Constitutional Convention, in early 1777, castigated Britain for its coercion and abuse of colonial Americans who had a long record of loyalty and service to the empire, 'Integer,' in Gaine's *New-York Mercury*, seized the polemical initiative. Incredulously, he quoted the convention's characterization of 'the in-

---

[104] *Boston Post-Boy Advertiser*, Jan. 30, 1775; for a similar diagnosis of British sensibilities see 'Scotus Americanus,' *South-Carolina Royal Gazette*, June 8, 1780 and 'Planter,' ibid., Dec. 19, 1780.

habitants of Britain' as a 'nation and people bound to us by the strongest ties; a people by whose side we have fought and bled; whose power we have contributed to raise, who owe much of their wealth to our industry, and whose grandeur has been augmented by our exertions.' 'Gentle reader,' retorted 'Integer,' 'here is a great deal of matter in a few words. . . . "Bound to us by the strongest ties"; I suppose the Convention meant by saying this to give us a proof of their great strength in having burst those ties asunder. . . . "Whose power we have contributed to raise"; that is, Great Britain had no power till after she had drained herself of people in order to strengthen us, that we might strengthen her.' By making their own ego the center of their political culture, 'Integer' explained, the New York patriots had 'totally inverted . . . the order of things' in claiming that the British had reduced them to being *miserable slaves.*' 'All of us know,' 'Integer' scornfully declared, 'what wretches, what Israelites in bondage, we have hitherto been till our good representatives . . . undertook our deliverance. Nobody could possess his farm or dispose of his merchandise; nobody lived in peace or security. Nobody could even say that he had life or property before we were under the direction of our Congresses, Conventions, and watchful committees.'[105]

Imbibing unnatural and untried doctrines about their obligations as subjects, the loyalists contended, the patriots became victims of their own desperation. 'It was the universal and professed maxim' at the outbreak of hostilities with Britain, wrote the Reverend J. J. Zubly under the pseudonym 'Helvetius' in the *Royal Georgia Gazette* in 1780, that '*if we succeed we will be called a revolution and deemed a rebellion if we miscarry.*' This 'neck or nothing' frame of mind anesthetized the patriots from the pain of anticipating the 'ruin and destruction . . . coming on apace.' 'Helvetius' had even heard South Carolina patriots say, 'we must not look to the consequences,' as though the very possibility of defeat and punishment, seriously considered, would be enough to unnerve the radicals. 'Upon no other principle than the prospect of success, and that success would abolish the criminality of the means,' he concluded, 'would men that have any regard for their lives engage in any desperate action.' The rebellion not only ignored the truth and gloried in violence, injustice, and irresponsibility, it necessarily converted truth into

[105] *New-York Mercury*, Mar. 3, 1777.

268

falsehood and good into evil: 'upon this plan . . . men must place per-
jury in the room of a lawful oath, to murder must be no crime; rapine
and violence hold the place of equity and justice, nor can any design be
too dark or any action too villainous for men that expect to succeed in
wickedness.' By this circular morality, the Revolution became a self-
justifying endeavor in which 'success will sanctify . . . all the measures
made use of to obtain it.'[106]

Bound together by their desperate flight from reality, by an abandonment of traditional moral norms, and by the perversion of the truth, the
Revolutionaries had plunged their society into a moral and social mo-
rass. 'Before the interruption of regal government [in South Carolina],
plenty, affluence, and increasing prosperity seemed to combine to render the people happy, while poverty, wretchedness, and ruin characterize the era of democratick oppression,' wrote 'Drusus' in the *South-
Carolina and American General Gazette* early in British reoccupation of the
province. Yet pacification and submission to British authority was not
yet complete. 'Can any man be so absurd as to imagine that the inhabitants of this country were subjects to Congress?' If Congress could not
provide protection and military security for the people living under
British occupation, how could it claim allegiance?, 'Drusus' demanded.
In theoretical terms, no confederation even existed until the Articles of
Confederation were ratified. In practical terms, the disintegration of the
insurrectionary administration in South Carolina was ample evidence
of Congress's artificiality and illegitimacy. 'If . . . this MIGHTY STATE
[i.e., South Carolina from 1775 to 1780] in possession of *legislative authority*' and an '*executive*' inflicting 'vengeance and confiscation against
the refractory and, exercizing arbitrary and despotick power in violation of every principle of the constitution, could not prevent its DISSO-
LUTION, can it be reasonably supposed . . . that Congress, aided by a
few republican enthusiasts in this province will be able to reestablish its
independency and participation in the union?'[107]

In their quest for a coherent understanding of the Revolution—for a

[106] *Royal Georgia Gazette*, July 27, 1780; 'Helvetius' was the Reverend J. J. Zubly, a
Presbyterian clergyman who frequently referred to his Swiss origins and whose diary
(Georgia Historical Society, Savannah) bore an acrostic which spelled 'Helvetius.'
Zubly was a classic case of a 'Whig-loyalist' who vigorously defended colonial liberty
before 1775 and reluctantly became a loyalist in 1776; see Calhoon, *Loyalists in Revolutionary America*, pp. 180–82 and Bailyn, *Ideological Origins*, pp. 169, 181–82, and 217.
[107] *South-Carolina and American General Gazette*, Aug. 2, 1780.

reasonable way of dealing with capricious, illogical events—the writers of the loyalist press commented astutely on revolutionary behavior. They noted, as we have seen, the symbiotic union of moderation and radicalism in Whig rhetoric: a defense of the existing social order that magnified to fantastic dimensions the evil potential of British policy and heightened the moral drama of colonial opposition. The resulting tension within American society was excruciating, and the loyalists noted the release of guilt and desperation into every political transaction. Aware that this emotional energy needed to be channeled and conserved, some patriot leaders advocated Spartan discipline, and others struggled to construct and operate constitutional government. Unable to appreciate those corrective, self-denying measures by the Revolutionaries, some of the most thoughtful and knowledgeable loyalist polemicists believed that they alone lived in a world of discipline and constraint. 'There are bounds to all human power,' 'Helvetius' declared in the *Royal Georgia Gazette*; 'the doctrine of non-resistance has long and deservedly been exploded, but its opposite, like some powerful and dangerous medicine, ought to be handled with the utmost caution, lest it become a dangerous weapon in the hands of a madman.' The history of modern Europe, explained Zubly—who chose the name 'Helvetius' because he was a Swiss emigrant—showed that civility and maturity were the mark of people who did not resist every injustice or jealously guard every scrap of power. 'The Swiss never revolted,' and ever since the height of the Roman Empire they 'pleaded, petitioned, and appealed' against imperial encroachments but 'suffered' with grim dignity rather than 'taking up arms or revolting.' The Spanish Netherlands, 'Helvetius' continued, did revolt against Phillip II, goaded to violence by the Duke of Alva's barbarous suppression of the Dutch Protestants; in marked contrast with the American Revolutionaries who casually printed millions of dollars of worthless currency and boasted of their national greatness, the Dutch were tenacious, humble, and soft-spoken. Even courage and genuine patriotism, 'Helvetius' concluded with a final example, did not guarantee success to a people fighting for their freedom. The Corsicans had fought bravely for more than forty years against their Genoese overlords only to have 'the French, like true politicians, after weakening both parties at last make a conquest of it for themselves'—inflicting cruel atrocities on the Corsican patriots. The lesson of history was clear: 'intestine commotions and civil wars are productive of such infinite mischiefs that humanity shudders at their approach, and very great evils and just complaints grow foul and unworthy of the resentment they might otherwise deliver, where the evils produced by an intestine war for redress are thrown into the opposite scale of the balance.'[108]

'Helvetius' skillfully arranged a series of quotations from Emmerich de Vattel's treatise on international law. This humane and rational commentary on the limitations of military power as an agent of change placed extremely narrow limits on the meaning of a just war. Vattel observed that while legitimate national interests were at stake in many wars, the passions and aggressiveness of particular rulers were more intimate causes of conflict. He underscored—in the passages 'Helvetius' quoted—the futility of war as a means of achieving social change; war itself settled nothing, it only compelled a defeated national to submit to negotiation. If peace settlements depended on 'exact and punctual' compliance by all parties, no war would ever end short of the utter desolation and annihilation of the losing side. Because warfare itself spawned so much incidental injustice, a war was never an instrument of justice. The civilized way to end a war, Vattel insisted, was for both sides to strike an imperfect bargain and 'extinguish differences by the most equitable' feasible arrangements. On the basis of these terms, the concessions proposed by the Carlisle Commission in 1778 conceded virtually every American claim short of independence. 'Is it a just and lawful plea against generous offers of peace,' he demanded, 'that they cannot be accepted because those to whom they were made' are allied to France? Is fear of insulting an opportunistic ally a valid reason to perpetuate a dreadful war?

Ultimately, the unity of the moral order—which the Revolution had so savagely torn—depended not on history or philosophy but on God's final judgment. Looking forward to that vindication, 'Helvetius' defined the Revolution in much of its complexity: 'The penalty due to obstinate rebellion in this life is a trifle not to be mentioned with what you must expect when all of the ghosts of the slain, every drop of innocent blood you spilt, every act of violence you concurred in or committed, all the confederates of your crime whom you have forced or seduced, every injured widow's groan and every orphan's tear whom

---

[108] *Royal Georgia Gazette*, Aug. 3, 1780; see also 'An Address to the People of this Country by an American Loyalist,' *South-Carolina Royal Gazette*, Dec. 25, 1780.

you have ruined, the spoils of the honest and innocent whom you have robbed, every friendly warning which you rejected, will at once arise in judgment against you and render you as compleatly miserable as you have rendered yourselves distinguishedly wicked.'[109] No single sentence in all of the loyalist press dealt so comprehensively with the nature and impact of the Revolution. In a single spacious and ominous image, Zubly juxtaposed the innocence, agony, spiritual and physical isolation, virtue, and brutalization of the loyalists with the destructive force and inner nature of revolution: the self-justifying use of violence, the way coercion expanded outward until it overwhelmed even the weak and helpless, and the patriots' determination to pay any price—moral or material—to insure the permanence of their new regime.

The loyalist press did not enunciate a fully developed alternative ideology or a coherent political code, nor did it refute very cleverly the novel and untested features of patriot constitutionalism and mission. But it did articulate a profound sense of moral estrangement from the values that the Revolutionaries claimed for themselves and that permeated their republicanism. Loyalist pamphleteers, Leslie F. S. Upton argues, failed to confront the colonists with 'the conventional wisdom' of Georgian political orthodoxy.[110] Writers to the loyalist press operated at the more elemental level of moral self-vindication. They internalized their perceptions of upheaval and vented the anguish they felt as innocent victims of a cruel and unnatural rebellion.

[109] *Royal Georgia Gazette*, Sept. 28, 1780; see also ibid., July 27, Aug. 31, Sept. 7, and Oct. 12, 1780; to appreciate Zubly's skillful use of Vattel, cf. James Turner Johnson, *Ideology, Reason, and the Limitation of War: Religious and Secular Concepts, 1200-1740* (Princeton, 1975), pp. 240-53.

[110] Leslie F. S. Upton, 'The Dilemma of the Loyalist Pamphleteers,' *Studies in Burke and His Time* 18 (1977): 71-84.

British Correspondence in the Colonial Press, 1763–1775: A Study in Anglo-American Misunderstanding before the American Revolution

PAUL LANGFORD

FEW FEATURES of the colonial press in the years between the Peace of Paris of 1763 and the Declaration of Independence, the decisive years for the developing rupture between Britain and America, are more striking in retrospect than its preoccupation with events in the mother country. The news from England figured in the pages of American newspapers to a varying but almost always impressive extent. Throughout the thirteen colonies, in the typical weekly or semiweekly edition, the heading 'London,' with its attendant columns of news and articles, had a way of driving more local information either to an inferior position or indeed off the page altogether. Even news from close at hand, hailing from colonial centers other than that in which a particular paper was published, frequently masked yet more transatlantic material. Headings like 'Philadelphia,' 'New York,' and 'Williamsburg' in the Boston journals, for example, often indicated merely that the London news reproduced below them had been obtained at second hand from other colonial papers, rather than by more direct means. Only when events of particular importance took place in North America itself were such items reduced to relative and temporary insignificance, and the twentieth-century reader of these newspapers might be forgiven for concluding that colonists found the reports from the imperial metropolis of far more consuming interest than

273

those from his own or neighboring colonies.[1] It is a fact, and a rather remarkable one, that in this respect colonial papers were almost indistinguishable from the journals of the provincial press in Britain itself, though the former were produced for a society far more autonomous, far more remote, far more self-reliant, than that of the colonies.

In accordance with that pursuit of plagiarism which was the fundamental basis of all eighteenth-century journalism everywhere, much of the material published in an attempt to satisfy the colonial hunger for transatlantic information was derived in the first instance from newspapers and magazines produced in London. There were exceptions: captains who plied to and from Liverpool, Bristol, or Glasgow brought copies of the local publications, and even ships docking from London sometimes carried copies of such papers as the *Sherborne Mercury* and the *Bath Chronicle*, or other West-country journals, which could be obtained at Falmouth or Penzance.[2] But since all such publications depended themselves on the metropolitan press for the great bulk of their material, these exceptions were of little practical importance. In any case it is plain that American editors relied primarily on the London newspapers proper, occasionally with bizarre results. In an extreme case the *New-York Journal* published in its issue of January 1, 1767, a letter written by a merchant which was taken from the *Public Ledger* of London but which the *Ledger* had actually reprinted from the *Maryland Gazette*. A few printers like Edes and Gill of the *Boston Gazette* and John Mein of the *Boston Chronicle* would acknowledge their sources on occasion, but most who cheerfully appropriated whatever they could lay hands on by way of British journals did not bother. In either event the reliance on the newspapers of the capital was almost total.

The results of this dependence are of course important, particularly for what they reveal about the kind of information accessible to the colonial newspaper audience and the kind of selection process employed by editors and printers. A full-scale study of these problems has yet to be attempted, doubtless because of the difficulties involved in coordinating and comparing journals on either side of the Atlantic, and

[1] See Richard L. Merritt, *Symbols of American Community, 1735–1775* (New Haven, 1966) for a highly tendentious and arguably quite fallacious view that the press was increasingly expressing a preoccupation with specifically American concerns in the 1760s and 1770s.

[2] See, for example, *Boston Gazette*, Aug. 22, 1768; *New-Hampshire Gazette*, July 15, 1774.

though much has been done to elucidate the role in the American Revolution of the colonial press,[3] its use of specifically British material is still a subject of some obscurity.

The information so eagerly sought from the metropolis by the colonial printers was limited in several respects. In the first place, the materials acquired from England were necessarily affected by the restrictions which generally hampered the metropolitan press. Scurrilous and violent, irresponsible and scandalous though the eighteenth-century press appears by modern standards, it was in practice extremely limited as a source of political comment or information. London newspapers were hemmed in by a common law which made ministerial prosecution of adverse or so-called 'seditious' comment extremely easy and by a parliamentary law that made description or discussion of political matters peculiarly difficult.

It is true, as is well known, that the picture was changing quite dramatically in precisely the period of the American Revolution. After the effective proscription of general warrants for arrest of persons and seizure of papers which followed the celebrated Wilkes affair of 1763–64, government restraints on freedom of the press were much less powerful, and after the notorious Printers' Case of 1771, the Commons effectively gave up attempts to prevent reporting of its debates for all practical purposes.[4] But the consequences of this liberalization did not entirely eliminate all forms of deterrent censorship on the one hand, or the flow of government-inspired propaganda on the other. And the advances that were made came too late to affect the Anglo-American quarrel. Only in 1774, for example, did reporting of parliamentary debates really become extensive and widespread, so that the crises that followed the Stamp Act of 1765 and the Townshend Duties of 1767, if not the Coercive Acts of 1774, had to be followed in London and consequently in the colonies with nothing but the barest outlines of Parliament's activities. And at no point in this period did journalists

---

[3] The standard authority, despite its somewhat controversial conclusions, remains Philip Davidson, *Propaganda and the American Revolution, 1763–1783* (Chapel Hill, 1941). Also valuable is A. M. Schlesinger, *Prelude to Independence: The Newspaper War on Britain, 1764–1776* (New York, 1958).

[4] See P. D. G. Thomas, 'The Beginning of Parliamentary Reporting in Newspapers, 1768–1774,' *English Historical Review* 74 (1959): 623–36, and 'John Wilkes and the Freedom of the Press (1771),' *Bulletin of the Institute for Historical Research* 33 (1960): 86–98.

feel free to describe in detail the personal views and activities of politicians. Given the obsession of the London world with the politics of the 1760s, it is indeed remarkable how restrained much of the newspaper treatment was. Wild and extravagant stories about Bute and the king's mother were one thing; well-informed and plausible reporting of the political scene was generally a quite different matter.

Only in its discussion of the constitutional and economic arguments involved in the American drive for self-rule was the press utterly uninhibited and informative. Throughout the 1760s journals like the *London Chronicle*, the *Public Advertiser*, and the various *Evening Post*s, to name only the most enduring and well-known, published controversial argument and debate with great gusto. Inevitably much of it concerned America, and though the great majority of articles, almost all of them in the form of letters to the publisher, were unsigned, they were of considerable interest to the colonial audience which read them at second hand. Even these, however, were of limited value, given their primary attention to matters of abstract argument and principle rather than to practical politics. They added bulk to the readable matter already provided by pamphlets published on both sides of the Atlantic and by the journalistic debates that went on unceasingly in the colonies themselves, but they told Americans little about the attitudes of the British public or the specific views of any but the leading pro-American politicians. Finally, the materials published about America in London necessarily took account, silently, of the assumptions and attitudes of English readers. For the historian, incapable of the contemporary's close acquaintance with the views of the period, this natural failure to explain what was considered obvious at the time almost inevitably creates distortions; but it did the same for the colonial reader at the time. Americans had no means of knowing what had been assumed by editors in London, and had to take at face value news and comments that had been published with special resonances in mind.

Fortunately, the extracts and abstracts of material acquired through the London newspapers were not the only items concerning England to appear in the colonial press. There also appeared direct reports from Britain in the form of journalistic letters, printed without the identity of the author. 'Letter from a gentleman in London to his friend in New York,' 'Letter from a merchant of Bristol to a gentleman in Boston,' 'Letter from a house of eminence to a merchant in Philadelphia'—

such were the variations on the main theme, though many were simply printed as 'Letters from London,' or 'London letters.' Few issues of any colonial journal in the 1760s and early 1770s passed without examples of this genre, and some issues, printed just after several ships reached port simultaneously or at moments of great controversy and interest, were packed with them. As with the more conventional items taken from the British newspapers, the letters were reprinted extensively, not merely by the less important publications in the smaller colonies, which always drew on the more important journals of Boston, Philadelphia, and New York, but by the major newspapers in the key centers themselves. A typical example is the London letter of May 11, 1767, which was printed first in the *Boston Gazette* on July 6, then, on July 9, in the *New-York Journal* and Parker's *New-York Gazette*, and finally in the *Pennsylvania Gazette* on July 16. The Philadelphia press in particular first published many items that were quickly reprinted in New York and Boston. But some letters traveled much greater distances and at a much slower rate. Thus a London letter dated May 12, 1774, was printed initially in the *Boston Evening-Post* on July 11, immediately found its way into the nearby *New-Hampshire Gazette* on July 15, and eventually appeared in the *South-Carolina Gazette* on October 3. Similarly in 1765 the *Newport Mercury* relied heavily on the South Carolina press, no doubt by virtue of the coastal trade between New England and Charleston.[5] For obvious reasons such long-distance journalistic migration was less common than the constant interchange of reports between New York, Philadelphia, and Boston, but in either case the size of readership achieved by many of the letters allegedly originating in England was most impressive.

As will be seen, the value of these letters can easily be exaggerated. Even so they were and are more important than the routine information taken from the London newspapers, for they shared almost none of the defects of the latter. Since they were printed only in the thirteen colonies, they could be less inhibited than they would have been if printed in England. In the colonies there were of course attempts in the eighteenth century to censor or at least restrict the activities of newspapers, with some spectacular results, such as the Zenger case. Even so, the colonial journals were far less restricted than their trans-

[5] See, for example, the issues of May 6, May 20, Nov. 11, 1765, which printed long letters from London (clearly Charles Garth's) by way of the *South-Carolina Gazette*.

atlantic counterparts, especially when it came to the reporting of distant events. The observations on personalities and politics that were normally eschewed in the London press were entirely beyond the control of government in America, and the 'London letters' consequently form a freer and more explicit commentary on events in London than the reporting in the English press. And, no less important, letters written with a colonial readership in mind, whether or not intended for publication by the writer, had a quite different focus and a quite different perspective from publications in the English newspapers. Their obsession with anything that might have an impact on America, and their basic object of supplying information that would be of interest to Americans, were in a sense as misleading and distorting, arguably more so, than the items published in London newspapers. But they filled precisely that vacuum that made it so difficult for colonists to learn the basic attitudes and activities of Englishmen concerning the colonies, and formed a critical element in the colonial impression of the scene in Britain. A few of these letters reveal more about the colonial picture of British policy and British attitudes than a host of polemical articles debating nice points of constitutional doctrine and dispute.

The utility of this form of journalism was amply appreciated in the colonies themselves. Until the war largely destroyed direct and publicly avowable correspondence with London, newspaper editors were delighted to print 'letters' from Britain, whether they were original items or were pillaged from other American journals, not least because the London newspapers themselves were so deficient in news of importance to America. Thus the *Boston Chronicle* observed in August 1768 that the 'public prints' from England were 'wholly taken up with their own concerns,' and admitted that 'We can collect no intelligence from [them] respecting American affairs, but by letter.'[6] Even with competing information available, the letters were especially prized. John Mein, the publisher of the *Chronicle*, clearly regarded them as a particularly strong selling point when he announced the establishment of his newspaper in November 1767.[7] Apart from the regular London newspapers, he declared in his preliminary advertisement, he had made arrangements for a private correspondence with the capital and had been promised a wealth of anecdotes 'which the papers at home are some-

[6] Aug. 1, 1768.
[7] Nov. 19, 1767.

times cautioned against inserting.' Whatever the justice of Mein's claims of superiority in this respect, they were entirely typical of printers' and publishers' anxiety to command a continuing and reliable supply of information from the horse's mouth, unfettered either by the Englishman's laws of libel or his disinterest in America's affairs. In any event the result is a veritable mine of information about the impressions that Americans gained of the mother country's doings and attitudes, impressions of considerable importance in explaining the colonial reaction to imperial policies.

There is no simple or entirely straightforward way of describing the character of this shaping force. Quantification is difficult except in the crudest possible terms.[8] On the other hand it is possible to state some reasonably clear conclusions about the general drift of the information conveyed in the published letters. Indeed, given the potential diversity of descriptive and interpretative comment that might be expected from hundreds of letters published in this period, the extent to which they agree, the way in which they tended to form a composite and consistent picture for their readers, is little short of remarkable.

A striking feature of this picture, for example, was the great emphasis laid on the allegedly good intentions of the great majority of British people toward America. The sentiments of the public at large, as opposed to those who were directly responsible for the conduct of imperial policy, were naturally a matter of the greatest possible interest to Americans; what is astonishing is that the correspondents who were quoted in the newspapers were so optimistic about them. Few letters failed to make some reference to 'our friends,' 'those in our interest,' 'the friends of America,' or some similar grouping. Moreover, the constant refrain, from the time of the first great crisis in Anglo-American relations over the Stamp Act in 1765–66 to the moment when full-scale war became unavoidable in 1775, was the large size of the block of friends and their constantly increasing number, at any rate outside government itself.

There were moments when such reports were not entirely implausible, notably in the winter of 1765–66. Then the *Boston Gazette* assured its readers that 'the City and Country are all in your Favour,' and

---

[8] See, for example, the useful article by Benjamin W. Labaree, 'The Idea of American Independence: The British View, 1774–1776,' *Proceedings of the Massachusetts Historical Society* 82 (1970): 3–20.

that 'the Friends to America are very powerful and disposed to assist us to the utmost of their Ability,' while Holt's *New-York Gazette* made similar claims for 'the Nation in general.'[9] Such observations are amply supported by other evidence, and perfectly justified by the activities of mercantile pressure groups and the profound economic depression, both of which were operating to create a strong and successful demand for the repeal of the Stamp Act in England.[10] But at other times in these years, the constant assurances crossing the Atlantic as to the popularity of the American cause in Britain were highly misleading. In the spring of 1767, for example, in the wake of repeated reports in London of renewed and mounting opposition to imperial authority in New York and Boston, the tide was clearly running strongly against America in almost all circles. The parliamentary session of 1767, which produced the hated Townshend Duties, the establishment of independent salaries for colonial officers and judges, the institution of the new American Board of Customs Commissioners, the act that threatened to suspend the New York legislature unless the imperial mutiny act were enforced in that province—all this testified to a deep and growing resentment of colonial insubordination. As one politician later observed, long after Charles Townshend himself had died, 'it was not the opinion solely of one man, but of many, that some plan of taxation ought to be adopted, and that opinion had so pervaded the nation at large, that it was absolutely necessary to do something. . . . A chancellor of the exchequer, who at that time had not attempted something of the kind, would have been looked upon as blameable.'[11]

Yet little of the strong tone of hostility that characterized British thinking about the colonies at this time was communicated to American newspaper readers. On the contrary, journals like the *Pennsylvania Gazette* cheerfully assured their audience that 'all our Grievances will be redressed.'[12] The same optimism was expressed two years later, at another low point in Anglo-American relations when the riotous opposition of Boston to its new customs administration, the impudence

[9] Feb. 17, 1766; May 19, 1766; Jan. 30, 1766.

[10] See Paul Langford, *The First Rockingham Administration, 1765–1766* (Oxford, 1973), chaps. 4, 5, and P. D. G. Thomas, *British Politics and the Stamp Act Crisis* (Oxford, 1975), chaps. 9–12.

[11] John Wright, ed., *Sir Henry Cavendish's Debates of the House of Commons during the Thirteenth Parliament of Great Britain*, 2 vols. (London, 1841–43), 1: 213.

[12] May 7, 1767.

of the Massachusetts Assembly in marshaling colonial resistance to the Townshend Duties, the summoning of a convention in Boston, and the initiation of nonimportation agreements in several provinces all conspired to enrage opinion in Britain against New England in particular and America in general. Yet the reports in the colonial press were uniformly encouraging. Bostonians themselves were assured that 'The Friends of America increase upon the Measures that have been pursued,' and in Philadelphia it was similarly asserted that 'New partisans arise every day, to espouse our cause.'[13] Still more emphatic was the assurance printed in Rind's *Virginia Gazette*: 'As to the political conduct of your country, you have the approbation of every Englishman.'[14]

Equally striking and in the last analysis arguably more important was the thoroughly misleading reporting of attitudes between 1773 and 1775, the decisive period for the final breakdown in relations between mother country and colonies, the period that saw the Boston Tea Party, the Coercive and Quebec Acts, the creation of a revolutionary organization at central and local levels in the colonies, the first bloodshed at Lexington and Concord, and finally the drift to war and irrevocable rupture. Yet throughout this darkening period, colonists were forever being told that British public opinion was fundamentally on their side. Thus at the time of the Boston Port Bill, when even those in England who genuinely regarded themselves as supporters of colonial liberty found it impossible in the prevailing climate of opinion to defend the actions of Boston, readers of the *Boston Evening-Post* were informed by separate correspondents that 'the people in general applaud our conduct as well as the members of the greatest honor and abilities in both houses,' and 'the People here in general are in favor of the Bostonians, and say they have been greatly imposed upon.'[15] A more complete misrepresentation of the true state of opinion in and out of Parliament in Britain could hardly have been invented. Nor did the tone alter thereafter. Throughout 1775 the same impression was continually fostered, the same fundamentally incorrect interpretation offered. Only in 1776, and in the case of some newspapers only when the supply of letters itself dried up, did this stream of misrepresentation cease. The very last London letter available to the *Connecticut Courant* in June 1776 asserted, in

[13] *Boston Weekly News-Letter*, Jan. 5, 1769; *Pennsylvania Gazette*, Feb. 9, 1769.
[14] Sept. 21, 1769.
[15] May 9, 1774; July 18, 1774.

now modified but still basically optimistic terms, 'I think your friends increase rather than diminish'—this at a time when war fever in England was rampant and when all hope of an accommodation, let alone reconciliation, had been abandoned even by the advocates of a liberal and conciliatory policy.[16]

This constant belief in the fundamental benevolence of the British was only one element in a larger composition with many corresponding elements. Closely connected, for instance, was the notion that America's misfortunes were to be laid at the door of a small and sinister group of ill-intentioned ministers, a veritable cabal of the crown's evil advisers. A handful of these malevolent enemies both of America and the empire's true interest were blamed for every grievance in the colonies. Bute, Grenville, the Bedfords, and North, these and their lackeys alone were responsible for tyrannical and oppressive measures. The Stamp Act, for example, which, at the time it was passed, was utterly uncontroversial and almost totally unopposed in England, was treated as entirely the work of Grenville and his colleagues, completely unaided either by the crown or the people. 'It is not your Mother Country; it is not your king oppresses you; but it was a bad Ministry, who carried Things so far, as to bring universal Odium on themselves.'[17] The destruction of Grenville's ministerial career at the hands of the king in July 1765 made it difficult to blame him for subsequent measures, though his name long thereafter remained a byword for vicious and irresponsible imperial government. But the rather misleadingly named group, the Bedfords, were in office for much of the 1760s and 1770s, and they could be conveniently blamed for Britain's misdeeds. Hillsborough in 1768 and 1769 as secretary for the colonies, and North, as prime minister from 1770, were obvious targets, and the administrations of which they were part were invariably pictured as plotting to deprive more representative Englishmen of their influence.

Faith in Parliament was very slow to die. In 1766, for example, it was assumed that the passage of the Stamp Act, insofar as it was not simply the work of Grenville, was a temporary and uncharacteristic aberration on the part of a particular Parliament. 'We flatter ourselves a new Parliament will have the interest of our Colonies so much at Heart, as not to take up the Business again,' the readers of the *Boston*

[16] July 16, 1776.
[17] *Pennsylvania Gazette*, Jan. 16, 1766.

Gazette learned.[18] Even the Townshend Duties of 1767 could be seen as the product of the same generation of legislators, and it was easy to assume that when Parliament was dissolved in 1768 the electors of Great Britain would cleanse it of all its impurities. Thus Virginians were informed during the first session of the new Parliament that the running battle that Hillsborough and his colleagues seemed to be conducting with the Boston populace and the legislature of Massachusetts Bay would be decided by firm and favorable intervention on America's behalf by the House of Commons. 'The affair of Boston, being totally ministerial, when it comes to be fully debated, and all the papers are before the House, it is very possible the Ministry may be overset.'[19]

When Parliament failed to oblige its American friends by overturning either the ministry or its colonial policies, American hopes returned to the people once again. 'I am sorry to say,' one letter in the Philadelphia press reported in April 1769, 'the Temper of Parliament does not at present appear favourable to your Cause, but without Doors you gain Ground daily.'[20] And always the one absolutely inadmissible fact, something that could never be conceded, was that the public at large sympathized either with a tyrannical ministry or a corrupted Parliament. Britain's imperial policies were always pictured as the systematic conspiracy of a handful of ministers against the interest and desires of the community at large. As Gaine's *New-York Gazette* (itself by no means a radical journal) reported on the very brink of war between the two countries, 'The greatest Part of the Nation wish well to America, and detest the present Politicks; so that it is a War of Administration only.'[21]

The colonial press made efforts to explain this ministerial conspiracy. The ministers, it was claimed, were actually the Tories and Jacobites of George II's reign—hence their desire to tyrannize in England and America alike, and hence their utterly corrupt and unrepresentative character.[22] A simpler explanation was that greed and profiteering underlay the political actions of the government. This note was sounded early in the history of Anglo-American discord. One characteristic

---

[18] Feb. 27, 1766.
[19] Rind's *Virginia Gazette*, Feb. 23, 1769.
[20] *Pennsylvania Gazette*, Apr. 6, 1769.
[21] Sept. 11, 1775.
[22] *Boston Gazette*, Apr. 21, 1766; *Pennsylvania Gazette*, Aug. 10, 1769.

letter in August 1765 explained, 'I must . . . take leave positively to declare, that *all measures prejudicial to the interest of America, ever yet taken, have been not only proposed, but even very warmly recommended by mean mercenary hirelings or parasites among yourselves, who for a little filthy lucre would at any time betray every right, liberty and privilege of their fellow subjects. Most men of sense in England are now convinced that they have been most miserably deceived and deluded by the accounts received from placemen in the colonies, and the seekers of such places, who are and have been from hence.*'[23] Thomas Hutchinson of Massachusetts and his circle were rarely free of such charges in subsequent years, but there were other lines of attack too. One reporter alleged that Bourbon gold—'the Power of French Money'—lay behind the intrigues of the ministers, a charge that not even the opposition in England thought of fabricating.[24] And in a significant comment about the apparent failure of the London newspapers to endorse the impressions constantly reported by the letters printed in the colonial press, one letter in the *Boston Gazette* explained, 'you must know that the public papers are all so severely watched, and such powerful imprimaturs placed over them, that they will not print anything which tends to open men's eyes lest the honest part of the nation should seek revenge against their oppressors and destroyers.'[25] Nothing, it seemed, could be permitted to give the impression that the people of Great Britain as a whole actually supported the policies that were so hateful to their transatlantic compatriots. The ultimate point in this logic was reached in 1775–76 when the newspapers predicted that full-scale rebellion and civil war in England itself were imminent. The *Maryland Gazette* printed a report that North's ministry would be toppled by main force, while Gaine's *New-York Gazette* reported that Britain was on the brink of civil war in the summer of 1775.[26] The *Pennsylvania Gazette* provided circumstantial details, claiming that in London, there were '*ten* for America to *one* against it,' and prophesying a rising by 16,000 laborers and tradesmen, notably in Spitalfields.[27] In this journalistic climate it came as no surprise to colonists to read in the *Essex*

---

[23] *Boston Gazette*, Aug. 5, 1765.
[24] *Pennsylvania Gazette*, Apr. 13, 1769.
[25] May 1, 1769.
[26] Mar. 23, 1775; July 31, 1775.
[27] Dec. 13, 1775.

Journal that Lord North had actually felt compelled to flee to France, leaving behind him a country torn by civil strife.[28]

Naturally if those who were responsible for the measures that alienated America were dangerous impostors and conspirators, those who at any time expressed sympathy for the plight of the colonists were seen as heroes. The outstanding example is the elder Pitt, who had already earned himself a place in colonial affections by his record as a war minister, and whose canonization in American eyes was completed by his celebrated speech of January 14, 1766. That speech, which included a bitter attack on the Stamp Act and involved Pitt in a thoroughgoing defense of the colonial interpretation of the imperial constitution, led to his veneration and even idolatry in America. Pitt's own role in the repeal of the Stamp Act was in reality quite limited; he was not in office at the time, and his own views, extending as they did to a conviction that parliamentary taxation in the colonies was illegal, were totally out of tune even with those of the great majority of the ministers, M.P.'s, and merchants who secured repeal. They deliberately coupled repeal with the passage of the Declaratory Act, asserting the right of king and Parliament to impose laws on the colonies binding 'in all cases whatsoever.' But for much of America, Pitt was the true author of repeal and richly deserved the credit for it. His speech against the Stamp Act, unlike almost all other parliamentary performances in this period, was printed and reprinted not merely in London but in North America; his praises were sung both in the colonial press and at public gatherings; and a great demand arose for statues and portraits of the Great Commoner.[29] Thus from New York a friend of the Rockingham ministry, which was actually responsible for the repeal of the Stamp Act, reported, 'It appears as if that Province had decreed a Statue of Brass in Honour of His Majesty's grace and favour to the colonies on this occasion—and another to Mr. Pitt as the Great Instrument in effecting the repeal—It is strange if not incredible that America acknowledges so little to the present Ministry on this occasion.'[30] Some British contemporaries were also mystified and

[28] *Essex Journal*, Aug. 11, 1775; see also Pauline Maier, *From Resistance to Revolution: Colonial Radicals and the Development of American Opposition to Britain, 1765-1776* (London, 1973), p. 251.

[29] For the impact of Chatham's speech on the colonies, see, for example, *Letters of a Loyalist Lady* (Cambridge, Mass., 1927), p. 13.

[30] Sheffield City Library, WWM.R 55-4.

indeed irritated by this worship of Pitt. John Fothergill, for example, wrote to Pemberton in Pennsylvania,

> I think the Americans have gone unwarrantable and ungrateful lengths in ascribing all their advantages to the late great Commoner. You are less obliged to him than you suspect, but you are Americans, warm, passionate and an Englishman in excess. You are solely obliged to the steadiness of the late administration under Providence and to the few individuals here whom I have formerly mentioned. Lord Chatham coincided in the Stamp Act, I mean in *repealing* it, and by this, gave great weight to the ministry. But he opposed divers of the regulations so beneficial to you, the free ports especially. . . . I mention these circumstances chiefly to show how much many of the colonies are misled. They overlook those who have actually served them and most essentially; they are erecting statues to a man who however he may deserve it on other occasions, in this has much less merit than you imagine.[31]

But there was no altering the colonial view. The simple equation arrived at on the basis of Pitt's famous speech and the apparently simultaneous repeal of the stamp tax was sufficient to establish in colonial minds the clear and overwhelming impression that Pitt was their great champion and savior. And given the tone of the reporting from London this was scarcely surprising. An account printed in the *Boston Gazette* in April 1766 pictured Pitt as 'outdoing his usual Outdoings in the Cause of Liberty and his Country' and observed that he 'spoke with more Eloquence than ever did Cicero.'[32] Similar was the letter from a Londoner to an inhabitant of New Jersey published in Holt's *New-York Gazette* on May 1. 'Our glorious HERO, our former deliverer, stood forth; and almost alone, supported our feeble unfashionable dying Cause. He struck at the Root; he openly denied the right of Parliament to impose internal taxations on the Colonies. With the eloquence of a *Demosthenes*, —with the cool reasoning of a *Hampden*,—with the warmth of an American enthusiast, did this *Great Man* plead our desperate cause, and that of liberty, in defiance of R – – – l favour, popularity, friends, relations, dangers and disease. For Hours could I expatiate, in heaping encomiums upon the Saviour of our Country; but you will hear them from

[31] Sept. 30, 1766, in B. C. Corner and C. C. Booth, eds., *Chain of Friendship: Selected Letters of Dr. John Fothergill of London, 1735–1780* (Cambridge, Mass., 1971).
[32] Apr. 21, 1766.

all quarters.' Such reporting was scarcely calculated to put the activities of Pitt in perspective.

The result was that much was to be forgiven or rather misunderstood in Pitt's subsequent record on matters affecting the Americans. Naturally when he returned to power himself in July 1766 and formed a new administration the euphoria in the colonies was intense. The disillusion and unpopularity that in London followed the announcement that Pitt was taking an earldom and a pension and leaving the House of Commons, the scene of his great triumphs, were less in evidence in America, where the press instead looked forward to a great era of prosperity and harmony for the empire, under the leadership and guidance of America's own special guardian. As the *Pennsylvania Gazette* pointed out, 'you have now got into the Hands of a Ministry, who in Fact, did you the essential Service of getting the Stamp Act repealed.'[33] In the event, the record of the Chatham administration in this area was sadly at variance with colonial expectations. Yet those who were so quick to condemn Grenville and his friends for the Stamp Act were less ready to blame Chatham and his friends for the Townshend Duties. The result was the adumbration of contradictory notions. Where Grenville and later Hillsborough and North were charged with forcing through Parliament policies that were allegedly secured by corruption and were totally unacceptable to the nation, the measures of the Chatham administration were explained on the grounds that opinion in Parliament and elsewhere would not allow a more liberal policy. Thus the repressive Suspending Act, which invalidated New York laws until provision was made for supplying Gage's troops, was explained to readers of the *Pennsylvania Gazette* in the following terms:

> The ministry have, in fact, been greatly embarrassed with this affair, being pressed upon it by the opposition early in the session, which drew from them an inconsiderate promise, that they should take some measures or other, which they hastily admitted were necessary, in order to support the sovereignty of the country; for there is reason to think, that had they been left to themselves, they would gladly have let the matter sleep, and given the colonies some time to recollect themselves, and to have come voluntarily into what is here called their duty. But the opposition will not suffer this.[34]

[33] Nov. 13, 1766.

[34] Aug. 27, 1767. See, on this affair, N. Varga, 'The New York Restraining Act: Its Passage and Some Effects,' *New York History*, 37 (1956): 233–58.

The truth was that the leading Chathamites were deeply angered by the apparently rebellious tactics of the New York Assembly and had every intention of taking strong action to assert the authority of government. Shelburne himself strongly supported firm measures and described the Assembly's tactics as 'infatuated conduct' which 'precludes I am afraid all consideration of the merits or principles of it.'[35] Such a statement would have surprised the Americans who continued to believe that Shelburne was a true friend, one who supported them when in opposition and when in office between 1766 and 1768 was only prevented from protecting their interests by the power of others. The description in the *Boston Chronicle* in March 1769 was typical; he had 'always been a friend to the colonies, though sometimes, when in place, he had been obliged to swim with the tide.'[36]

The sympathy and generosity with which colonial journals treated the Chatham Whigs were similarly, though in slightly lesser measure, extended to their distant cousins, the Rockingham Whigs. The fact that Rockingham and his colleagues had been in power at the time of the repeal of the Stamp Act, and the fact that thereafter they were continuously in opposition to the crown, providing a natural focus of organized opposition, automatically made them of interest and importance in the minds of colonial opponents of the same government. To a great extent, however, the colonists quite misunderstood the position of the Rockingham party. At least Chatham supported the American notion that the power of taxation was located only in the provincial Assemblies; but Rockingham, Burke, Dowdeswell, and their friends were irrevocably committed to the contrary notion, that the sovereign power of Parliament was unlimited and inescapable. They had admittedly taken the initiative in repealing the Stamp Act itself in 1766. But their reasons for doing so were more the result of the arguments and pressures of the mercantile and manufacturing lobby in England than of a conviction that the colonies had justice on their side.[37] Moreover, it was Rockingham who had ensured that the repeal of the stamp tax would be accompanied and, as it were, offset by the Declaratory Act. That statute, which was introduced not merely because it was

[35] Lord E. Fitzmaurice, *Life of William, Earl of Shelburne*, 3 vols. (London, 1876), 2: 44.
[36] Mar. 27, 1769.
[37] Langford, *First Rockingham Administration*, chap. 4.

necessary to bring the House of Commons around to support a policy of repeal but because the Rockinghams were entirely convinced of its validity, destroyed any doubts in Britain about the right of Parliament to tax the colonies, and in a sense it was a logical preliminary to the measures of taxation later administrations produced.

Nor was the subsequent record of the Rockinghams in opposition altogether encouraging from the American point of view.[38] They did little to oppose the substantive measures that so aggrieved America in the late 1760s and early 1770s, seemed anxious to obstruct ministers rather than their measures, and generally showed little desire to support the violent and extreme demands of Americans in these years, though they liked to project themselves as fundamentally well-disposed toward the colonies. Americans who made contact with them, like William Samuel Johnson, the Connecticut agent who arrived in England just after the repeal of the Stamp Act, were disappointed by their attitude, and tended to conclude that 'Opposition [would not] take up our cause with spirit, at least, if they do, I fear it will be only so far as may serve the purposes of pure opposition, not upon the great principles upon which we stand, and if so, what they will do, will lose much of its weight.'[39] The attitudes of the Rockinghams in this area are a complex matter and it would be absurd to delineate them as enemies of America, even in the limited sense that Grenville and Townshend were. But on their record, there is little to substantiate the idea that in fact they were friends of America in the sense the colonists intended.

Yet repeatedly in the late 1760s, when the Rockinghams were exceedingly silent and ambiguous on the subject of America's rights, the colonists were assured of their good intentions and potential influence. In 1769, for example, they were frequently encouraged to believe that the Grafton administration would soon be displaced and a new Rockingham ministry would emerge to restore liberality and harmony to the empire, and in particular would repeal the obnoxious Townshend Duties in their entirety. In New York it was announced that the 'Rockingham Party would soon come into the Ministry who would repeal

---

[38] See Paul Langford, 'The Rockingham Whigs and America, 1767–1773' in A. Whiteman, J. S. Bromley, and P. G. M. Dickson, eds., *Statesmen, Scholars and Merchants: Essays in Eighteenth-Century History presented to Dame Lucy Sutherland* (Oxford, 1973).

[39] *Collections of the Massachusetts Historical Society*, 5th ser. 9: 406.

the Acts we complain on,'[40] while in Philadelphia it was firmly declared that the ministry was about to disintegrate. 'The Bedford Part of it will give Way, when the Rockingham Friends will supply their Places, which would be a happy Circumstance both for Great-Britain and her Colonies.'[41] And in Boston one reporter waxed eloquent and euphoric about the inestimable benefits to be derived from a ministry led by the Marquess of Rockingham himself. 'The whole minds of the troubled continent would unite; he would be a common center to a system of blessings to the present, as well as to ages yet to come.'[42] Such rhetoric was altogether misleading. In the first place, the actual prospects of the Rockinghams' getting into power at any time in these years were exceedingly remote; in the second, even if they had succeeded in doing so, it was by no means clear that their policies would have differed substantially from those of the harassed Hillsborough or Grafton and North. But colonists were in no position to form a clear or accurate impression, informed as they were by highly colored communications from England.

Equally misleading was the stress placed on the attachment to the American cause of the radical politicians of the 1760s and 1770s, the Wilkesites and their allies. No doubt rightly, much importance has been attributed by historians to the connections between radicalism in America and radicalism in Britain,[43] and it is naturally reflected in the colonial newspapers and their reporting of events in England. The journals were full of information concerning the Middlesex election and its dramatic repercussions in 1769 and 1770, and indeed it is impossible to resist the impression that American readers were every bit as interested in this aspect of British politics as were their transatlantic fellow subjects. However, it is no less difficult to resist the impression that the real connection between the grievances of America and those of England was greatly exaggerated, and in particular that the true concern of Wilkes and his friends with events in America was vastly overrated. From the beginning Americans were assured that the Wilkesites were effective and influential friends of the colonial cause. Wilkes himself was described as 'an Enthusiast, for AMERICAN Liberty,' and his

[40] *New-York Journal*, Mar. 30, 1769.
[41] *Pennsylvania Gazette*, June 8, 1769.
[42] *Boston Chronicle*, May 1, 1765.
[43] In general see Maier, *From Resistance to Revolution*.

friends, or rather 'All Mr. Wilkes's friends,' as 'friends to America; some of them talk of seeking a shelter from arbitrary power in those peaceful deserts. Mrs. Macaulay the celebrated female historian, talks of ending her days on the banks of the Ohio.'[44] More important, the wider movements associated with this sudden outcrop of radical discontent were assumed to be closely interested in the affairs of America. London, as the obvious focus of Wilkesite activities, was naturally given a particularly significant prominence. Thus New Yorkers were informed in 1769 that 'the majority of citizens of London espouse the cause of America very warmly,' and a year later Philadelphians were told that 'the City of London, which is in full Opposition to the Measures of Administration, unites the Cause of America with their own.'[45] And when the petitioning movement, which grew out of Wilkes's misfortunes, spread to the provinces, the same picture was conveyed. 'A Spirit of Discontent,' it was reported, 'rather increases than subsides, throughout the Kingdom; and one Article of Complaint pretty universally adopted, is AMERICAN GRIEVANCES.'[46]

Yet such claims were distortions of the truth. The evidence for the sympathy of out-of-doors movements with American grievances is strictly limited. None of the provincial county petitions in 1769–70 was at all concerned with colonial grievances; all of them were exclusively devoted to the constitutional rights of English electors, or in some cases to local demands.[47] Only a handful of urban petitions and instructions bothered to list America among their concerns, and then as a matter of little interest and low priority. Canterbury, for example, drew up eleven resolutions of which nine related to the Middlesex election, one to a recession in the Kentish leather trade, and only one to America. Even that was confined to a mild statement in favor of healing existing divisions between mother country and colonies 'by every lenient and constitutional Method.'[48] In the metropolis itself there seemed little desire to adopt the ground taken up by radicals in America. Much

[44] *Pennsylvania Chronicle*, Apr. 3, 1769; *New-York Journal*, Apr. 27, 1769.

[45] Both Parker's and Gaine's *New-York Gazette*, Oct. 30, 1769; *Pennsylvania Chronicle*, Sept. 4, 1770.

[46] *Massachusetts Gazette*, Nov. 30, 1769.

[47] For a detailed study of these petitions, though in a domestic context, see George Rudé, *Wilkes and Liberty* (Oxford, 1962), chap. vii.

[48] The resolutions, widely recorded in the British press, were also printed, for example, in the *New-York Journal*, May 4, 1769.

was made in the colonies, for example, of the great petitions from the Middlesex electors and London Livery in 1769, for both apparently joined America's grievances with those of the capital. Yet the reality was not impressive. The Middlesex petition consisted of thirty-four clauses, thirty-three of which were concerned exclusively with the domestic implications of the Wilkes affair. Only the last mentioned America, and that rather enigmatically. 'The same Discretion has been extended by the same evil Counsellors to your Majesty's Dominions in America, and has produced to our suffering fellow Subjects in that Part of the World, Grievances and Apprehensions similar to those of which we complain at home.'[49] Similarly cryptic and obscure reference was made to America in the London petition, and indeed the same unreadiness to adopt the clear arguments and complete hostility of the colonies was to be evinced in the metropolitan petitions that six years later preceded the outbreak of war. Nor is it clear that there was much that was authentic in such demonstrations of halfhearted solidarity with the colonies. Arthur Lee claimed the credit for inserting the final clause in the Middlesex petition—'The subject was novel, supported only by myself, almost a stranger, and appeared to many of the leading men to be foreign to their purpose'[50]—as well as for other cases of British concern with American liberties; and his brother William was to make similar claims for himself in 1775.[51] As a result of such activities in London and the subsequent reporting of the results in America, the actual concern, even of radicals, in England with colonial grievances was apt to be considerably exaggerated.

This is not to say that the Wilkesites themselves were not interested in the possibilities of political advantage offered by the Anglo-American confrontation. They went out of their way to flatter the Americans who had dealings with them, and Wilkes had particular cause to welcome the cooperation of colonial radicals who, in the case of South Carolina, for example, granted a substantial sum of money for his relief. But neither Wilkes nor many of his friends had an enduring or deep concern with colonial grievances, and while it is quite true that pro-Americanism as a phenomenon was far more marked in the

[49] Printed in the colonial press, for example, in the *New-York Journal*, Aug. 10, 1769.
[50] Richard H. Lee, *Life of Arthur Lee, Ll.D.* (Boston, 1829), pp. 245–46.
[51] *Letters of William Lee*, ed. Worthington C. Ford, 3 vols. (New York, 1891), 1: 152–53.

metropolis, especially among the religious dissenters, than it was elsewhere, the basic fact was that few Englishmen sympathized with the American's right to tax himself. The House of Commons's action in apparently depriving the Middlesex electors of their constitutional rights provoked a widespread and authentic voice of protest; its action in taxing the colonies was fundamentally uncontroversial in Britain, especially in the country at large. The impression created in America that English political society was seething with radicalism and rebellion in general, and eager to take up the cudgels on America's behalf in particular, was quite at variance with the facts.

Even when the American press admitted that the friends of the colonies might be temporarily powerless or the people of England temporarily blind to their true interest, it continued to encourage the notion that rescue lay just around the corner. It is particularly significant, for example, that the letters published in the colonies strongly supported the view that British society and the British economy were deeply vulnerable to the pressures that America could bring to bear in the cause of political change. It may be that the colonial pressure groups needed little encouragement to resort to the economic embargoes that were their principal weapon before the bloodshed of 1775 and the resulting war. However, they certainly had no need to fear contradiction from England. Even the nonimportation movement of 1765–66 was openly encouraged in the letters from London, and the later ones were similarly urged on from England.[52] The notion that the industrial economy of England and Scotland, already so vital to the country's prosperity and social stability, was an easy prey to the withdrawal of the colonial market in North America, was of course much strengthened by the repeal of the Stamp Act, which contrived to give the impression, albeit mistakenly, that political concessions could invariably be obtained by the use of economic weapons. However, in the following years London correspondents did much to reinforce this impression. As early as the summer of 1767, almost before the Townshend Duties had been established, one letter printed in the *Boston Gazette* stressed the potential benefits of nonimportation. 'Should your demand cease for a Year or two, the utmost you can desire would be effected for you here without any unconstitutional Opposition on your Parts.'[53] A year later, just

[52] *Massachusetts Gazette*, Jan. 9, 1766.
[53] Sept. 28, 1767.

before the nonimportation agreements were actually adopted, the encouragement was stronger still. 'Distress among the manufacturers and merchants would be the certain consequences of such a conduct, people in general would have their eyes opened, they would soon feel the fatal effects of the late acts of parliament, a feeling must bring conviction, and daily create new friends with the increase.'[54] And in 1769 when the embargoes were actually operating, much friendly advice was offered, with the strongest warnings against surrender or discontinuance of the campaign.[55] A similar chorus was raised in 1774 before and during the final and most effective of the nonintercourse campaigns. One assertion in the *Boston Gazette* in December 1774 may stand for all. 'If the colonies are firm for one year, and neither import or export, it would establish American freedom for this country cannot support itself without the colonies.'[56] Nor was plausible circumstantial detail wanting in this torrent of encouragement and information. In Virginia it was observed that nonimportation 'in less than twelve Months will bring the People of this Country to Reason, and force them, contrary to their Inclinations, to do the Americans Justice; for they have no Trade, but what is against them, save to Ireland and America.' And a supporting letter added, 'I was at Nottingham, Leicester, and Birmingham, not long ago, and great indeed were the Complaints of the Stagnation in Trade; the Manufacturers were absolutely in the greatest Want.'[57] Both the details and generalities in this case were misleading, if not deliberate falsehoods. As it happened, Britain suffered relatively little by the economic warfare launched from the colonies, and was not at all distracted by it from her determination to discipline them. Even earlier, the effectiveness of the American nonimportation campaigns had been strictly limited. The boycott of 1768–70 did not procure the total repeal of the Townshend Duties, and even the Stamp Act was repealed for far more complex reasons than the embargo organized in the colonies.[58] But it is difficult to find a word in the information transmitted across the Atlantic that would have tended to warn America that their economic sanctions would be anything less

[54] *Pennsylvania Gazette*, Aug. 11, 1768.
[55] *Boston Gazette*, June 19, 1769, Sept. 8, 1769; *New-York Journal*, May 22, 1769.
[56] Dec. 5, 1774.
[57] *Virginia Gazette* (Purdie and Dixon), Oct. 6, 1774.
[58] See Langford, *First Rockingham Administration*, chap. 4.

than devastating. Everything the colonists learned of the situation in Britain seemed calculated to reassure them on this score.

The effect of the stream of misleading information contained in the letters from England printed in the colonial press cannot be precisely calculated. Certain things, however, are clear. The tone and tendency of these letters closely corresponded with the tone and tendency of the American picture of Britain and its policies generally. Indeed, every feature of the picture created by reporting from England confirmed the prejudices of colonial opponents of Britain. The nature of the Revolutionary mentality is now well known for its brooding suspicion of Britain's contemporary governmental system, its excessive faith in the freedom-loving character of true and old England, its conviction, in short, that the policies that were so unpopular in America were part of a vicious conspiracy on the part of the crown's ministers who were imposing on England as much as on America, and that America was the battleground for a great conflict between these forces of political evil and traditional ideas of liberty.[59] The structure of this mentality, its historical antecedents and strangely conservative concept of political liberty, is now a matter of record; moreover the picture that resulted was both powerful and plausible, powerful in that it did much to fuel the enthusiasm and fervor of the Revolutionary movement, plausible in that so much that was happening in the British Empire seemed tailor-made to fit it. But passably accurate reporting from London of the actual attitudes of the politicians, parliamentarians, and above all the public would have created severe difficulties for those who subscribed to such views.

Admittedly there were occasional letters that purported to describe the extent of anti-Americanism in England. Most of these appeared in 1767 at the time of the Townshend Duties, and even then they were so few that their status is that of the exception that proves the rule. Nonetheless their impact is intriguing as a pointer to the likely effects if they had occurred in far greater number. For example, one letter in the *Boston Gazette* for March 2, 1767, was headed London, December 13, 1766, and gave an account of politics in the capital that accorded ill with the usual descriptions. Its writer observed that 'there is a spirit rising in Parliament very different from that which prevailed during

---

[59] The outstanding account is Bernard Bailyn, *The Ideological Origins of the American Revolution* (Cambridge, Mass., 1967), esp. chaps. 3, 4.

the last Session,' pointed out that the ministers seemed intent on a new and tough line in colonial affairs, and above all declared that Pitt himself had 'quite changed his colours.' The local reaction to this, one of the few accurate reports of the situation in London at any time in this period, was significant. The printers of the *Boston Gazette* assured readers that this depressing observation need not be taken seriously, for it was a 'very dirty anonimous extract' and a 'wicked libel,' smacking of the 'Temper of the remaining Dregs of a Party, who not a Twelve month ago, were exerting every Nerve to enslave this Continent, but fail'd in their Attempt.' Equally significant was the reaction of one reader who regarded such stuff as amounting to an argument for censorship or at least editing. 'I cannot but think it injurious, and of bad Tendency,' he wrote, 'to insert any Thing of the like Import, without giving the Name of the Writer, or adding some Reflection or Notification, to antidote his Poison. I am convinced, if the Names of these Writers were to be publish'd, we should find them of the Party who have all along used their utmost Endeavours to enforce the Stamp-Act.'[60] Unpalatable truths produced similar reactions elsewhere. When the *New-York Journal* printed a 'genuine letter, wrote by a gentleman, who never was in America,' which commented adversely on the insubordination of the New York Assembly in the matter of the province's refusal to obey the Mutiny Act, it hastened to reassure its readers that the gentleman concerned was 'a Grenvillian doubtless.'[61]

Such bitter reactions to reporting that failed to conform to what Americans liked to think of their fellow citizens in England are indeed significant; but the examples are too few to do more than confirm the overall impression. Only in 1775–76, too late to make any difference in practical terms, did the idea gain currency that it was after all the great bulk of the British nation that was bent on tyranny, as the colonists saw it, and not merely a little knot of conspirators in Whitehall. Much attention has traditionally been paid to the significance of the sudden hostility to the king himself at this time, epitomized in Paine's *Common Sense* and reflecting a readiness to question fundamentals in a new and revolutionary way.[62] But whether an accurate picture of Brit-

[60] Sept. 28, 1767.
[61] June 18, 1767.
[62] See Maier, *From Resistance to Revolution*, p. 261; see the same work for other and similar examples of the disillusionment.

ish attitudes toward America would have made a difference then or even five years earlier is a matter of speculation. If nothing else, however, it would have forced the colonists to cope with some awkward and disturbing facts. As it was, there was no need for agonizing over such matters as the basic alienation from America of British public opinion. For almost everything reported from London corresponded perfectly with the assumptions and attitudes that already existed or that were growing apace, and the truth was allowed to slumber beneath the theory of conspiracy which throve in the 1760s and 1770s. The comment in one London letter published in New York and reprinted in Virginia in June 1773 neatly epitomizes the connection between radical theorizing in America and the reassuring information conveyed from Britain. 'A Plan of Despotism and arbitrary Power has incessantly been pursued, during the present Reign. Through all the ministerial Changes and Manoeuvres, that has still been the grand Object in View, and may explain all those intricate Movements of Government, which otherwise appear mysterious and unaccountable, especially with Regard to the Colonies.'[63]

Additional evidence of the results of defective and misleading reporting is amply provided by the comments of contemporaries in a position to observe the effects of transatlantic journalism. Particularly striking is the testimony of those Americans of varying political complexion who actually went to Britain and found themselves compelled to revise the picture of British attitudes that they carried with them. The many colonists who already knew England or had been there before the troubles began with the Stamp Act are of course unhelpful in this respect; but those who first crossed the Atlantic in the late 1760s or early 1770s and whose preconceptions of Britain had largely been received from what was reported in the newspapers provide a useful test of the prevalent misapprehensions. Thus Samuel Barrett, a New England merchant, visited London in 1766–67 and was so struck by the realities he found there that he felt bound to communicate his surprise to Thomas Cushing, the speaker of the Massachusetts Assembly. The essential fact, he insisted, was that British opinion was infinitely more anti-American than was popularly supposed in the colonies, and moreover 'this Spirit of Acrimony [was] unhappily, too generally and

[63] *Virginia Gazette* (Purdie and Dixon), June 9, 1773.

with too much Facility admitted, and apparently gaining strength every Day.' The customary colonial explanation of events in England he strongly discounted, and particularly the notion popular in America 'that some internal Foes, some Persons disaffected to our Interest among ourselves, have wrote home to our Disadvantage.' The truth was that there were quite sufficient of 'our Enemies resident in England' to account for America's tribulations, and Barrett himself, scarcely very radical by colonial standards, was appalled to find that in England 'I advance Positions so very unpopular.'[64]

Similar testimony is supplied by William Samuel Johnson, the special agent for Connecticut, who was perhaps more representative of the radical New England mentality, and was in London in the late 1760s. Throughout this period, his letters to friends at home were at odds with the kind of impression normally given in the newspapers. Unlike the latter, he found few friends of America in England, considered that ministers were all too representative of parliamentary and public opinion, and expected little of weapons like the nonimportation campaign. Typical was his observation in January 1769 on the hopelessness of working up an effective opposition to the Townshend Duties. 'It is surprising,' he remarked, 'how few friends we have there, who are so upon real principles, I fear I could not name above five or six; but those who will be so upon the ground of opposition may be pretty numerous, though I fear all too few to stem the present tide, which sets strongly against the Colonies.'[65] Thomas Hutchinson perhaps put his finger on the problem when he pointed out the incompatible nature of opposition in England and opposition in America. 'The Opposition in this kingdom is not to the Constitution nor to any particular law but to the Persons in Administration. Opposition in the Colonies is to the Constitution itself and the Authority of the Kingdom over them.'[66]

Hutchinson of course had sentiments of his own utterly dissimilar to Johnson's, as did the other loyalists who flocked to London in the 1770s. Nonetheless their commentaries on British politics are equally revealing. Samuel Curwen, for instance, made some interesting discoveries

[64] July 20, 1767, Salisbury MSS, American Antiquarian Society.

[65] *Collections of the Massachusetts Historical Society*, 5th ser. 9: 309.

[66] Quoted in Mary Beth Norton, *The British-Americans: The Loyalist Exiles in England, 1774–1789* (London, 1974), p. 47.

when he arrived in London from Philadelphia in 1775, discoveries that he recorded in his journal and in his letters to his wife, who had remained in Pennsylvania. 'The capital mistake of our people,' he wrote, 'in believing the reports of mobbs, riots and insurrections in this country has not a little contributed to that delusion so universal in America, which designing men have raised. There is not the least grounds for it; people of all ranks are too much employed by their business and pleasures to suffer an interruption in either for the sake of America; her claims almost every one even of her warmest friends disallow.'[67] And again in September 1775, when the colonial newspapers were busy assuring their readers that Britain would shortly give way, he wrote, 'I wish I could make it to be believed, for it is a very important and alarming truth; no relief can be expected from Great Britain, the king and his servants are inflexible, nor do the people incline to suffer themselves to be diverted from their business and pleasure to risk their head and estates to support claims, all here almost to a man (whatever is suggested to the contrary) consider as an indignity and wrong to this Country, an independence on the British legislature, which they are to believe is now the only point in dispute.'[68]

This kind of discovery was not uncommon among loyalists. Ironically they, of all people, were taken aback by the extent of anti-Americanism that they found in England. Paradoxically many of them suffered during their English sojourn thanks to the disposition of the British to abuse and vilify any American they happened to find in their midst. Most loyalists expected to find a degree of resentment against the colonial rebels in the mother country; but the revulsion against all things colonial among all but the most sophisticated was surprising and, to men like Samuel Curwen, distasteful. Their distress was extreme; as Dr. Peter Oliver, the son of the chief justice, observed just after the war, 'We are obliged to put up with every insult from this ungrateful people the English, without any redress.'[69] Such was the unpleasantness of the loyalists' experience that some of them, like Curwen himself, came deeply to question and even regret their own action in deserting their compatriots.

[67] *The Journal of Samuel Curwen, Loyalist*, ed. Andrew Oliver, 2 vols. (Cambridge, Mass., 1972), 1: 62.

[68] Ibid., 1: 71.

[69] Quoted in Norton, *British-Americans*, p. 60.

If it is plain enough that colonial audiences were badly misinformed about their fellow subjects' feelings in Britain, it is less easy to attribute causation or culpability. It would be natural, for example, to assume on the basis of the generally remarkable degree of agreement among the various correspondents from Britain that conscious propaganda and perhaps imposture were involved. Yet there is little evidence of American opponents of government masquerading as reporters of British news in America. This is not to say that colonial radicals were not masters of the arts of propaganda. Sam Adams memorably observed that 'We cannot make Events; Our Business is merely to improve them,'[70] and there is ample evidence that he and like-minded Americans were adept at the manipulation, indeed the fabrication, of information and comment. In particular one remark of William Livingston, the New York controversialist, though not related to news from Britain, leaves no doubts on this score. 'I have sent Collins [of the *New-Jersey Gazette*],' he wrote in 1778, 'a number of letters, as if by different hands, not even excluding the tribe of petticoats, all calculated to caution America against the insidious arts of enemies. This method of rendering a measure unpopular, I have frequently experienced in my political days to be of surprising efficacy, as the common people collect from it that everybody is against it.'[71] However, it was one thing for an American resident in the colonies to compose plausible if fraudulent documents claiming to represent colonial opinion; it was another to attempt to represent opinion in Britain. For that, an unusual degree of knowledge and insight was required. There are a few documented cases of such fraud, but these were so implausible as to be ludicrous. Typical was a spoof letter claiming to come from London in early 1774 and bitterly attacking Hutchinson. The printer who published it, Isaiah Thomas, was far from being a friend of the establishment in Boston, and his paper, the *Massachusetts Spy*, was characterized by an aggressive radicalism. Nonetheless he took care to disassociate himself from the letter by announcing that it was 'inserted by desire,' and it is difficult to believe that a letter addressed from Bagpipe Alley, Scotland Yard, was meant to be taken entirely seriously.[72] Similarly, the *Massachusetts Gazette* was accused by its rival the

[70] Quoted in Maier, *From Resistance to Revolution*, p. 225.
[71] Davidson, *Propaganda*, p. 12.
[72] Mar. 17, 1774.

300

Boston Gazette (not one of the most impartial of journals) of 'making Extracts from Letters never received,'[73] and also in Boston John Mein (on the other side of the political fence) was involved in at least one case of imposture. With much circumspection Mein's *Boston Chronicle* printed what it described as an extraordinary letter, purporting to come from London, though it had been 'thrown into the yard before the house, and was picked up by a neighbour who delivered it to one of our servants.' The orthography of the letter was more than a little defective, and its gist, that Bernard was to be given a pension from a new tax on the colonies and that Hutchinson was to become governor with a salary derived from a new duty on American woolens, was wild even by New England standards. As Mein concluded in print, it 'appears to have been sent us with a design to impose on the public.'[74]

Such examples suggest that not more than a handful of the misleading letters from Britain, and those readily recognizable at the time and since, were deliberately perpetrated frauds. An alternative and superficially more plausible explanation of the flow of misrepresentation is that the printers and publishers, together with those politically interested parties who concerned themselves in such matters, exercised on letters from England the same editorial arts that they practiced on English newspapers, selecting only what suited their purposes and deliberately distorting the resultant picture of events and opinions across the Atlantic. That they were indeed highly selective in what they printed from newspapers and pamphlets published in England is undoubtedly true. British visitors to America were always struck by the way in which the most violent and abusive of the publications sent from England were reprinted locally. Typical was the complaint of Henry Hulton that radicals in Boston were sustained 'in their resistance by the accounts and publications received from home.'[75] In this case it was the *Boston Gazette* that offended by printing part of the London radical paper *The Whisperer*, but its action was entirely representative of the press at large. It would not be surprising, therefore, if such a strategy were extended to manuscript materials received in America and subsequently published. In fact, however, there is no

---

[73] *Massachusetts Gazette*, Mar. 13, 1766.

[74] Jan. 30, Feb. 2, 1769.

[75] W. Brown, ed., 'An Englishman Views the American Revolution: The Letters of Henry Hulton, 1769-1776,' *Huntington Library Quarterly* 36 (1972).

reason to believe that this was actually the case. As has been seen, the colonial newspapers were not averse to printing an occasional letter opposing the American cause; on the contrary such materials gave them and their correspondents an opportunity to expand at considerable length on the iniquities of their enemies. Two of the most radical and politically minded of the journals of the mid-1760s, the *Boston Gazette* of Edes and Gill and the *New-York Gazette* (later *Journal*) of John Holt, published letters of this kind on the rare occasions when they were available. Moreover, even the most party-motivated of publishers had an eye to news and novelty, and it is doubtful whether they thought seriously of distinguishing among the correspondence from England on any other basis than its interest to the readers.

In truth there need be little mystery about the selection process by which letters got into the papers. The natural sources and most convenient channels of communication shaped the flow of news and comment. Men of standing in the local community who were accustomed to receiving correspondence from friends and connections in Britain were not reluctant to pass on interesting or important news to the publishers, and the latter themselves often received such correspondence. Franklin's letters to friends in America are in some cases known to have been printed, whether through friends like Joseph Galloway, relatives like William Franklin, or business partners like David Hall. Hall similarly printed the letters of his friend William Strahan, who supplied a considerable quantity of comment and news through the middle and late 1760s.[76] Not surprisingly, then, the *Pennsylvania Gazette* was much used by other colonial newspapers as a source of well-informed London reports.

In many cases the natural channels were semiofficial. Most of the agents can have been little surprised to find their reports to their employers in the colonies published in the newspapers. The letters of Dennis De Berdt, the Massachusetts agent, were on occasion printed without any attempt to hide their authorship or addressees, though more frequently they were simply printed without acknowledgment. The letters, for example, of Joseph Sherwood, the Rhode Island agent, and of Charles Garth, the South Carolina and Maryland agent, can

[76] Franklin's letters are well known and sprinkled among the *Papers of Benjamin Franklin*, ed. Leonard W. Labaree (New Haven, 1964–   ); for examples of Strahan's, see *Pennsylvania Gazette*, May 12, 1768, Jan. 26, 1769.

be readily detected in the newspapers of the provinces concerned, and subsequently further afield.[77]

The great bulk of the letters were doubtless penned by figures of less official consequence, many of them with a 'delicacy' about 'the Risque of Publication' natural enough in view of the colonists' notorious lack of discretion in such matters.[78] But the process by which their letters were published involved nothing peculiarly sinister. The appeal and interest of authentic information from England were obvious and commercially valuable for printers who were frequently struggling for their financial existence. If American audiences got quite the wrong impression of the situation in Britain, the blame lies squarely with those who wrote to the colonies from Britain, not with those who printed their productions in America.

Though the individual identities of most correspondents cannot be ascertained, some helpful, if imprecise, generalizations can be made. For one thing, it is obvious that many of the letters, especially before the final crisis of 1774–76, came from British or Anglo-American merchants. Normal business communications between the trading communities in the colonies and the mother country must have accounted for much the greatest portion of mail crossing the Atlantic, and it was natural enough that in times of political controversy such communications should make passing or even more extended reference to matters of political interest. Few of the published letters seem to have originated in Glasgow, doubtless because the west-of-Scotland trade was predominantly with the tobacco provinces, and on a basis that employed extensive commercial management on the spot, perhaps because the business community in Scotland was bound to be more isolated and less well informed about politics than its counterparts in the more southerly centers of trade. The overwhelming majority of printed letters came from London, and to a lesser extent Bristol, with a smattering from Liverpool and other ports. Significantly, some of the

---

[77] See, for example, *Boston Gazette*, Apr. 27, 1767 (for De Berdt), *Newport Mercury*, Sept. 30, 1765 (for Sherwood) and *South-Carolina Gazette*, Apr. 20, 1769 (for Garth). The original correspondence is printed in 'The Letters of Denys De Berdt, 1757–1770,' ed. A. Matthews, *Publications of the Colonial Society of Massachusetts* 13 (1912): 293–461; *The Correspondence of the Colonial Governors of Rhode Island, 1723–1775*, ed. G. S. Kimball (Boston, 1902–3); 'The Correspondence of Charles Garth,' *South Carolina Historical and Genealogical Magazine* 26 (1925) et seq.

[78] J. Barrett to T. Cushing, July 20, 1767, Salisbury MSS, AAS.

great inland cities of England (Norwich, for example) were scarcely involved at all, precisely because their economic link with the American colonies was a tenuous one. In general, too, manufacturers, because they conducted little direct business with their ultimate customers but rather operated through the mercantile houses, seem to have been little involved. In any event, it is generally clear from the drift and phrasing of many of the letters, and from the failure of the printers concerned to omit the more mundane portions of some of them, that merchants accounted for a substantial number of published communications. And their motives in transmitting an impression of attitudes in Britain scarcely led them to convey an accurate picture.

In general, merchants who depended on the colonial trade for their livelihood had a natural tendency to convey a picture of affairs in Britain that was likely to fit rather than contradict American expectations and prejudices. Some British merchants were actually Americans by birth and radicals by conviction. Barlow Trecothick was something of a moderate, but Henry Cruger of Bristol, whose letters to his friends and family in New York were published freely there, made no attempt to hide his prejudices.[79] But even for more typical businessmen in Britain, it was only human to write what would go down well in the colonies rather than what was strictly the case, to blame for the grievances of their customers an allegedly unrepresentative government rather than the community at large, to stress the bright prospects for Anglo-American relations rather than gloomy possibilities, and to give America's concerns in general an importance in British life that they did not have for most of the public. The natural and not deliberately deceitful misrepresentations of the merchants were largely matters of tone and color, of emphasis and implication, rather than of crude falsehood or fabrication. A curious example can be seen in one of the few surviving letterbooks of British merchants in this period, that of Charles Goore, a prominent Liverpool merchant with a strong interest and extensive property in Virginia. Side by side in Goore's letterbook under January 1775, for instance, are letters both to colonial customers and British friends. To one of the former he was judicious, considerate, and cautious. 'Whatever parliament will do towards a reconciliation cannot yet be known nor do I think they will comply in

[79] See, for example, Holt's *New-York Gazette*, Apr. 24, 1766.

granting all that is demanded. Certain it is they have acted indiscreetly in laying internal Taxes on the Americans. On the other hand the Colonies assume an authority in several of their demands they have no right to but you'll find by the London Papers all and every act is to be repeald before the Colonists will submit. As parliament is not sitting its to be hoped some measures will be taken towards a reconciliation.' But to his friend, the M.P. for Liverpool, Sir William Meredith, Goore's tone was quite different. 'The Coffee houses are now crowded waiting to hear the resolves of Parliament relative to American affairs—I have upwards of £5,000 amongst the Virginians. Yet I hope the British Government will not submit to their arbitrary demands, submit now and always submit for it's evident they are resolv'd to be independent —Surely if practicable its time to stop the people of G Britain and Ireland flocking thither to transport the Convicts to the East Indies.'[80] Thus was the concerned and balanced friend of America transformed into a thoroughgoing champion of Britain's authority.

Partly this was a question of crude economic interest. Up to a point the views and attitudes of British merchants were of necessity far less anti-American than those of most of their compatriots. Few of them had the least desire to load the colonists with onerous taxes and duties, or bureaucratic restraints and burdens. Their prosperity was to a great extent dependent on the prosperity of America, and indeed in the lobbying in favor of the repeal of the Stamp Act in 1766 they convincingly displayed their desire to support relief for the colonists from grievances that were in appearance at least as crippling a burden on trade as on American liberty. But as it became clearer in the late 1760s that the colonists were opposed to the entire system of parliamentary sovereignty on which the order and coherence of the empire and its commerce were built, the merchants and manufacturers became alienated from their connections and customers in America. Once merchants became convinced that America was prepared to strike at the Navigation Acts and Britain's effective monopoly and control of plantation economies, they slowly moved from being eager champions of American demands, to bitter if reluctant opponents of them. This change of direction was already under way in the late 1760s, reflected

[80] To J. McWhirter, Jan. 3, 1775; to Meredith, Jan. 25, 1775, Charles Goore Letter-Book, 1774–83, William L. Clements Library, University of Michigan, Ann Arbor.

for example in the relative feebleness of the mercantile campaign for the repeal of the Townshend Duties; by 1775 it was largely complete, and epitomized by the attitudes of Charles Goore.

The colonists, however, remained unaware of this crucial shift of opinion among British businessmen, and the latter did not attempt to make it explicit or obvious in their correspondence. Again, what guided them was undoubtedly a desire to avoid the political controversy and economic loss likely to be consequent upon such frankness. Insufficient ardor in the cause of their clients could be a serious penalty for ambitious businessmen, and more than one of them learned a painful lesson in this respect. The brilliantly successful campaign for the repeal of the Stamp Act had been in part stimulated by the complaints in the colonies about the backwardness of British merchants in obtaining relief for America. In October 1765, for instance, John Hancock had bluntly informed his London suppliers, 'You may bid Adieu to Remittances for the past Goods, and Trade in future. . . . We are a people worth a saveing and our trade so much to your advantage worth keeping that it merits the notice of those on your side who have the Conduct of it but to find nothing urg'd by the merchants on your side in our favour Really is extraordinary.'[81] Moreover in the late 1760s there were some striking illustrations of the interest in America in the activities of British merchants, illustrations the force of which was not lost among the latter. John Norton, for example, one of the best-known London merchants trading to Virginia, suffered severely at the hands of the colonial journalists, for no fault of his own. The occasion was an address to the king, which he along with many other well-known businessmen in the capital signed in March 1769 to pledge their loyalty and support for the forces of law and order. The address had little that was political about it; on the contrary, it was a natural reaction of propertied men to the alarming violence and mobbing to which the metropolis was subject during the commotions associated with the Middlesex elections. Moreover it was not connected with any direct interest of the American colonists. However, the fact that it clearly reflected on the excesses of Wilkes's friends and connections made it peculiarly interesting to American opinion, and the press in the colonies gave the address a highly imaginative treatment:

[81] Abram E. Brown, *John Hancock His Book* (Boston, 1898), pp. 86–87.

There has been an address to the king, fabricated by the Ministry, approving of and thanking his Majesty for every Step taken by administration since his accession, and throwing an imputation of rebellion and disaffection on the association of the bill of rights, by which they in fact applaud Ministerial conduct against America, the murder of Allen, the massacre at Brentford, the not producing those condemned by a fair trial for the massacre, general warrants, rendering the habeas corpus of no effect, taking away the trial by juries, alteration of records, etc. etc.[82]

Since this obviously biased account added the names of a number of American merchants involved, including Norton, and asked, 'Queare, Are the addressors proper men to be entrusted with American business?,' it was followed by a storm that alarmed Norton and his friends not a little. Though Norton's Virginian connections eventually accepted his explanations and apologies, they did so somewhat grudgingly.[83]

Norton himself was deeply alarmed by this affair since he was well aware of the economic effects of political passions in Virginia. That he emerged with his business ultimately unaffected was largely due to the stream of letters that he and his friends published in the colonial press to counteract the bad effects of the report of the address and the stormy correspondence that arose from it. Typical was that published in Rind's *Virginia Gazette* on June 29, 1769, which explained that Norton 'hath taken every Opportunity of shewing his Regard for the Virginians, so that it is hoped the Public will receive no unfavourable Impression to the Extract from a certain letter lately published, which was evidently calculated to torture a late Address to his Majesty against Riots, etc. in England to the prejudice of this particular Gentleman and a few other American Merchants.'

[82] *Pennsylvania Gazette*, July 6, 1769.

[83] William Nelson, for instance, remarked, 'allow me the Freedom of a Friend, and I will just tell you, that I like not this Cordiality and a good understanding between the Great Men and the Merchants, as I think it has been attended with no good Consequences to the Colonies. On a former Occasion, when the Merchants stood upon their own good sense and Importance, they procured a Repeal of the Stamp-Act, but of late, the M-y seem to have cajoled them and laid them asleep; so that the Repeal We are to expect next Session must flow from the Justice and Equity of our Demand and leaves us no ground to express our Gratitude as before to that respectable Body of Men.' F. N. Mason, ed., *John Norton and Sons, Merchants of London and Virginia* (Richmond, 1937), p. 104. See also J. Norton to R. C. Nicholas, Nov. 10, 1769, Wilson Cary Nicholas MSS, Library of Congress.

Other merchants were indeed similarly treated in this affair and found the episode similarly instructive. Particularly striking was the letter that John Buchanan of London wrote to James, Dick, and Stewart of Maryland, published in the provincial *Gazette* on May 28, 1769:

> I have read over the Address again, and I don't find anyThing in it that relates to *America*; I dare say there is not one Man who signed it, but what is a Well-wisher to the Colonies; as for my Part, I have all the Reason in the World to be so, and I have always declared myself against taxing them, as a Thing unjust, upon the Principle of their not being represented. I have the greatest Regard for my Friends in *Maryland*, and considering how I am situated with them, I should be a Fool and a Madman to do anyThing that would hurt them. I have just been taking a Balance of my Books, and Effects and Debts due to me in Maryland, including the Iron-Works, amount to no less than — £: To think any Man so situated would designedly do any Thing to hurt the People of that Colony is absurd. I had my Share of Trouble a getting the Stamp-Act repealed, and I am still ready to do everyThing in my Power to relieve North-America from their present Distresses.[84]

Doubtless this was a storm in a teacup. Yet it is a clear pointer to the potential tension that existed between relatively conservative and increasingly worried businessmen in Britain and the growing revolutionary mentality in America, a tension that greatly strengthened the caution of the former in the comment and news they passed on to their connections. John Huske was one merchant who discovered that it was necessary to rehabilitate himself with his old New England acquaintances after a campaign of vilification against him at the time of the Stamp Act, and the firm of Mauduit and Crowley was similarly compelled to denounce an attempt in the American press to discourage colonial purchases from it.[85] William Molleson, the most prominent of all London's Maryland merchants, was particularly unfortunate. Heavily involved in the affair of the address of 1769, he was again under bitter attack six years later for his alleged support of North's repressive measures. According to a savage piece from London in the *Boston Evening-Post*, he was 'very busy in traducing those Americans

---

[84] July 27, 1775.

[85] *New-York Mercury*, Sept. 22, 29, 1766; *Boston Gazette*, Oct. 6, 1766; Parker's *New-York Gazette*, Sept. 11, 1769.

here, that have honestly borne their Testimony against the iniquitous Bills by their Petitions.'[86] Molleson, too, even at this late stage in the Anglo-American confrontation, was compelled to take defensive measures, including a letter of support from his friend Richard Glover which was published in the *Maryland Gazette*, describing him as 'the most eminent trader to your province who hath been more than once unwarrantably traduced in the American prints.'[87] Under pressures such as these, it need not be surprising that the businessmen who supplied so much of America's information from England hesitated to tell the truth about opinions and events there.

Even so, the tone of mercantile reporting can account only for a portion of the distortions and misrepresentations, and that the milder and less blatant portion. Far more important was the great body of information that by its tone can only have been penned by writers who were not merely strong partisans of the colonial cause and highly critical of politics in England but were also set upon provoking colonial resentments, fomenting colonial discontent, and generally keeping the level of Anglo-American friction high.

Who were these 'false friends,' as they were called in Gaine's *New-York Gazette*, who 'conveyed from hence, wrong accounts'?[88] Not, of course, a tightly knit group of sinister conspirators intent on misinforming all America. They were, however, a large and effective body of propagandists. It was a fluid, shifting group, even fractious and divided at times, and above all quite informal; but in retrospect it can be seen as a powerful force in the preliminaries to the American Revolution. Its very informality makes it difficult to describe and analyze, but of its consequence there can be no doubt. At its widest it consisted of a large community of 'gentlemen interested in the colonies,' as they tended to call themselves. For practical purposes this group was broken up into subgroups only some of which were important as far as propaganda was concerned. Most active were the American radicals who happened to be in England or deliberately went to England to influence opinion, and the congenial connections they found there. Some of them, like Johnson, the Connecticut agent, and like Josiah Quincy, a more or less casual visitor, remained only for a while; others like the

[86] *Boston Evening-Post*, July 11, 1775.
[87] July 27, 1775.
[88] Oct. 16, 1775.

Lee brothers and Stephen Sayre, who were active agitators, stayed longer and became almost fifth columnists, doing all they could to work up America as an issue in British politics. And linked to this group were the radical dissenting community (the connection between religious dissent and Wilkesite radicalism was also extremely strong in London) to which visiting Americans naturally gravitated and which indeed traditionally had close links with their coreligionists in America, especially those in New England. Many of the dissenters, particularly the more radical ones, had indeed a regular correspondence of the kind that was most likely to end up in colonial newspapers. The best-known of all of them, Thomas Hollis, was far more than a casual or unconscious manipulator of the printed word. His systematic use of his wealth and connections to send across the Atlantic a stream of quite deliberately slanted and distorted propaganda is well documented, and no doubt it played its part in the process which so misled Americans about the mother country.[89] More important still were the often wild, but also wily Lees. Arthur was in London studying law, like many southerners in the eighteenth century, and William was there in business; most of their activities were overtly political, William's culminating in the shrievalty of London in 1773 and an aldermanship in 1775. William in particular, with his friend Stephen Sayre, similarly involved in metropolitan politics, played a prominent part in enlisting the city in the campaign for concessions to America in 1774 and 1775, and Sayre was more dangerously implicated in talk of treasonable conspiracy in 1775, though in the event there turned out to be little concrete evidence against him.[90] Arthur's role was less official and public, though by his own account he did much to insert American grievances in the various radical demonstrations of the period, observing that his aim was to mix 'popular subjects here with that of America . . . and by that means to gain a more easy ear to the discussion of American grievances.'[91] His semijournalistic activities were extensive and influential. Quite apart from his polemical publications, he practically had his own network of Anglo-American correspondence for propaganda purposes.[92]

[89] See Caroline Robbins, 'The Strenuous Whig, Thomas Hollis of Lincoln's Inn,' *William and Mary Quarterly*, 3rd ser. 7 (1950): 406–53.
[90] Maier, *From Resistance to Revolution*, pp. 259–60.
[91] R. H. Lee, *Life of Arthur Lee*, p. 193.
[92] Maier, *From Resistance to Revolution*, p. 222.

Not all Americans either in the colonies or in London had time for the Lees, and Franklin's sensible contempt for the antics of Arthur, with the consequent tension between them, damaged what could have been a very powerful partnership. But they nonetheless formed the active nucleus of a community that could be highly effective on particular occasions. The American interest in London emerged en bloc only on such occasions as the petitions against the Coercive Acts in 1774, petitions that reflected the refusal even of British merchants to offer substantial assistance. But the names on those petitions are intriguing as an indication of the remarkably talented bloc of colonists in London at this time, names like the Lees and Sayre, Hugh Williamson, the celebrated Pennsylvanian, Edward Bancroft of New England, and that extraordinary group of South Carolinians in the metropolis, Ralph Izard, Henry Laurens, Thomas Pinckney, and William Hasel Gibbs, to name only the best-known.

Just how much of the correspondence that crossed the Atlantic and found its way into the newspapers came from this community will never be known, though in the case of the Lees there is ample documentation of the care with which they distributed material to the American newspapers. What matters, however, is that the kind of material they were in a position to transmit, even if they lacked the virulence or intrigue of Arthur Lee, was bound to be misleading and unrepresentative. Many of them were Americans, and well-educated and articulate ones at that, and few of them genuinely had the entree to the society of property and privilege in London, eagerly though they reported back their occasional meetings with ministers and magnates.[93] Most of them gravitated naturally to the dissenters, American businessmen, and radicals who congregated in the capital, who were unrepresentative of Britain in general, and who tended to be highly politicized. In such company, few visitors were likely to hear facts that were unpalatable, and few made a real attempt to gather them. Few, too, traveled around the country with more than superficial interest. Instead of being immersed in the natural conservatism and natural lack of concern with America that they would have found in country

---

[93] Witness the bombastic claim of one writer in the *New-Hampshire Gazette* on Feb. 4, 1774: 'You may depend upon the Truth of what I shall write you on public Affairs, as I have the most certain Information and Knowledge of all the secret and principal springs of Motion in the Government.'

towns and country parishes, and even in many more important centers, they were plunged into the hothouse world of radical London society, a world that generated considerable political controversy in the years after the Seven Years' War, but that at no time made a really effective impact on British politics. Yet this was the world, the opinions of which were normally reported back to the colonies and there accepted as fairly typical. Reports of such balanced, intelligent, and skilled observers as Franklin were colored enough; it is not surprising that less moderate and less clearheaded writers should have retailed some strange information.

And so a myth was made, a myth that can still be traced in the public pamphlets as well as in the private correspondence with which they enlightened America. For the evidence of the public writings of these propagandists tallies closely and convincingly with the evidence of their correspondence. The central element in the picture conveyed—the notion that Britons were at heart friends of America—ran through such publications even when those concerned were involved in attempting to influence British rather than colonial opinion. Thus Arthur Lee's *Appeal to the Justice and Interests of the People of Great Britain* saw the author, posing as a British member of Parliament, declaring, 'The people are interested; it is to them I speak; there is no feeling for their interests either in the cabinet or parliament'; and asking, 'Is it that a system of slavery has ascended the back stairs, the first line of which is to subjugate America?'[94] Similarly Sayre's *Englishmen Deceived* was intent on demonstrating one of the central points made across the Atlantic: 'all the real friends of freedom are, or will in a short time, be on your side: the interest of the merchant first, then the manufacturer, and finally the landholder, as they feel the distress, will in the same proportion bring on conviction.'[95] Some years later Hugh Williamson's *Plea of the Colonists* was still declaring that the claims made by ministers were incorrect; the people of Great Britain were not mindless supporters of the oppression of the colonies. On the contrary and in particular, 'the Americans in general view this subject in a different light. They believe that there is a very respectable and very numerous body of men in this kingdom, who are generally distinguished by the name

[94] (London, 1774), p. 23.
[95] (London, 1768), p. 52.

312

of Whigs, who are friends to civil liberty and perfectly averse to the idea of taxing their brethren in North America.'[96]

If this is what Americans believed, Williamson and others writing from England had largely taught it to them. Historians have traditionally and rightly remarked on the astonishing ignorance in Britain of conditions in America for which legislation was written; in its way the ignorance, or rather misunderstanding, that characterized the Americans' picture of the situation in Britain was no less important a factor in the making of the Revolution.

[96] (London, 1776), p. 6.

Some Statistics on American Printing, 1764–1783

G. THOMAS TANSELLE

ᔡ᛬ ᔡ᛬ ᔡ᛬ ᔡ᛬ ᔡ᛬ ᔡ᛬ ᔡ᛬ ᔡ᛬ ᔡ᛬ ᔡ᛬ ᔡ᛬ ᔡ᛬ ᔡ᛬ ᔡ᛬ ᔡ᛬ ᔡ᛬

WHEN BENJAMIN FRANKLIN said of the Stamp Act, 'I think it will affect the Printers more than anybody,'[1] he was calling attention to the unique position in which American printers found themselves during the pre-Revolutionary years: the tax on imported paper posed a serious economic threat to their businesses, and at the same time the nature of their calling, involving the dissemination of ideas, gave them an opportunity to publicize the problem and stir up public feeling about it.[2] The role of the printers in this period has long been recognized as an important subject, and, after such books as Philip Davidson's *Propaganda and the American Revolution, 1763–1783* (1941) and Arthur M. Schlesinger's *Prelude to Independence: The Newspaper War on Britain, 1764–1776* (1958), the point no longer needs to be argued. It is surprising, therefore, given the amount of attention directed toward the recording of eighteenth-century American imprints, that so many of the generalizations about the output of the American press of this time are couched in vague terms and offer no concrete framework

---

[1] *The Papers of Benjamin Franklin*, ed. Leonard W. Labaree, 12 (New Haven, 1968): 65–66 (letter to David Hall, Feb. 14, 1765). Cf. Arthur M. Schlesinger, *The Colonial Merchants and the American Revolution, 1763–1776* (New York, 1918), pp. 69–70; and 'The Colonial Newspapers and the Stamp Act,' *New England Quarterly* 8 (1935): 63–83 (esp. 67).

[2] Bernard Bailyn, speaking not merely of the Revolutionary years, says that the printers, who were 'at once handicraftsmen, entrepreneurs, and cultural leaders' (p. 95), were 'second in importance only to the clergy as leaders of opinion and popular educators' (p. 93)—in *Education in the Forming of American Society: Needs and Opportunities for Study* (Chapel Hill, 1960).

for their interpretation. For instance, Moses Coit Tyler, writing in 1897, before Evans's *American Bibliography* was available, speaks of the 'rather notable' discovery that the Revolutionary period 'actually had a literary product very considerable in amount. Even in those perturbed years between 1763 and 1783,' he says, 'there was a large mass of literature produced in America.'[3] Daniel J. Boorstin, writing sixty years later, asserts, 'Considering the intellectual energy of colonial Americans, their output of books was strikingly small.'[4] The two statements are not necessarily contradictory, for the two writers are addressing themselves to different points: Tyler is speaking of literature in any form, and Boorstin is talking about books of some size, as opposed to pamphlets, newspapers, and broadsides. Nevertheless, the meaning of these statements depends on how the words 'large' and 'small' are defined in the context, and without some specific figures or relative proportions such statements cannot be very informative.

The historian who wishes, in the course of a larger discussion, to make a generalization about American printing of the Revolutionary period obviously cannot stop to examine and classify ten or eleven thousand items; the problem is that most of the specialized studies he might turn to for this information do not themselves offer statistical summaries that would furnish a convenient basis for generalization. The bibliographies and checklists that attempt to record all American imprints of the period or certain defined classes of them are of course the basic scholarly works for printing history, and Charles Evans's *American Bibliography*,[5] having the widest scope, is naturally the one that has the greatest potential for supplying the evidence for generalizations. Lawrence Wroth called Evans's work 'a Matrix of Histories': it is, he said, 'at once a guide to sources and a source itself, for nothing reveals more clearly the social and political development of the colonial era than a reflective reading of its titles as they present themselves in slowly unfolding chronological or-

---

[3] *The Literary History of the American Revolution, 1763–1783* (New York, 1897), 1: 7.

[4] *The Americans: The Colonial Experience* (New York, 1958), p. 319. In 1931 Margaret B. Stillwell called the output of the colonial press 'astonishing.' See *Incunabula and Americana, 1450–1800* (New York, 1931), p. 114.

[5] (Chicago, 1903–34), completed by vol. 13 (for 1799–1800), ed. Clifford K. Shipton (Worcester, 1955). Fuller citations of the bibliographies and checklists referred to here, as well as citations of other works relating to the printing of the Revolutionary years, can be found in my *Guide to the Study of United States Imprints*, 2 vols. (Cambridge, Mass., 1971).

der.'[6] Because Evans lists printed items, not manuscript documents, there is a limit to the kinds of historical writing for which it can serve as matrix; but there is no doubt that it contains the material out of which a great deal of pre-nineteenth-century American printing history can be constructed. Although Evans provided author and subject indexes to each volume, he did not set up any tables that would conveniently summarize the mass of material he had recorded. If one is investigating the output of a single year or a very small group of years or of a particular printer or writer, one can make a thorough examination of each relevant entry; but if one is dealing with a more extensive period or wishes to place a restricted subject against a larger background, one finds in Evans few aids to generalization and thus faces an arduous task of tabulation. To complicate matters, there have been many bibliographies since Evans that improve upon his work in certain fields, such as the imprints of a single state or locality or those of a particular class (like almanacs, newspapers, or political pamphlets), and a comprehensive supplement to Evans appeared in 1970.[7] In the absence of statistical summaries, this increase in knowledge has only exacerbated the problem of bringing together the evidence on which to base generalizations, when they are needed as background for more limited studies or as contributions to broadly conceived surveys.

The situation can be illustrated by Lawrence Wroth's discussion of the output of the press during the period 1638–1783 in *The Book in America*. Because he was writing a relatively brief (fifty-page) general account of all aspects of book production and distribution during this period, he could not have been expected to make any detailed analysis of Evans's 18,000 entries for these years. But the only statistical survey available to him was Arthur Berthold's University of Chicago master's thesis, 'American Colonial Printing as Determined by Contemporary Cultural Forces, 1639–1763' (1934), and therefore his section on 'Characteristics of the Output [of the press]'[8] is limited to those years, with no comment on the

[6] 'Evans's American Bibliography, a Matrix of Histories,' in *American Bibliography 1639–1729 by Charles Evans* (Boston, 1943). Wroth had earlier commented on the 'limitless' opportunities for study offered by Evans's bibliography in 'Recent Bibliographical Work in America,' *Library*, 4th ser. 9 (1928–29): 62.

[7] Roger P. Bristol, *Supplement to Charles Evans' American Bibliography* (Charlottesville, 1970).

[8] Hellmut Lehmann-Haupt, in collaboration with Lawrence C. Wroth and Rollo G. Silver, *The Book in America*, rev. ed. (New York, 1951), pp. 32–34.

last two decades, 1764–83. In Wroth's and Rollo Silver's treatment of the years 1784–1860 in the same volume, a brief analysis of two selected years, 1778 and 1798, is offered in tabular form, so that at least one year of the 1764–83 period is represented (pp. 122–23). Later writers of general accounts have been hampered in the same way and have either repeated the figures from *The Book in America*, as John Tebbel does,[9] or made vague generalizations, as Charles Madison does when he reports that 'every year during the 18th century made available a greater percentage of books dealing with subjects of mundane interest.'[10] A few scholars, in specialized studies, have presented somewhat more detailed figures, as when Carl Bridenbaugh lists the number of English and foreign-language Evans entries printed in five prominent cities in the periods 1743–60 and 1761–76.[11] And Harry B. Weiss has tabulated or summarized in graphs the material recorded in certain standard reference works, such as George L. McKay's directory of graphic artists in New York and Clarence Brigham's list of newspapers.[12] But for the most part little work of this kind has been done in the nearly four decades between Berthold's thesis and the recent writings of Mary Ann Yodelis. In discussing the economics of the Boston printers of newspapers, 1763–75, Yodelis has carefully worked out the statistics for characterizing the output of Boston printers in general during this period.[13] Yet even in this study,

[9] Tebbel, in *A History of Book Publishing in the United States*, 1 (New York, 1972), cites the Wroth–Silver figures for 1778 and 1798 on pp. 55–56.

[10] *Book Publishing in America* (New York, 1966), p. 5.

[11] *Cities in Revolt: Urban Life in America, 1743–1776* (New York, 1955), pp. 183, 386. He also makes good use of statistics in other works, such as 'The Press and the Book in Eighteenth Century Philadelphia,' *Pennsylvania Magazine of History and Biography* 65 (1941): 1–30. John T. Winterich, too, cites figures from Evans in surveying 'the printing field in America in 1763' in *Early American Books & Printing* (Boston, 1935), pp. 63–64.

[12] 'The Number of Persons and Firms Connected with the Graphic Arts in New York City, 1633–1820,' *Bulletin of the New York Public Library* 50 (1946): 775–86; 'A Graphic Summary of the Growth of Newspapers in New York and Other States, 1704–1820,' 52 (1948): 182–96. Weiss calls the latter 'a sort of analysis and readjustment of the entries and dates in Dr. Brigham's *Bibliography*' and says that it 'indicates the various historical uses that may be made of a complete and careful bibliography' (p. 182). Another example of a table derived from data in published bibliographies is Jesse H. Shera's on book catalogues, 1731–99, in 'The Beginnings of Systematic Bibliography in America, 1642–1799,' in *Essays Honoring Lawrence C. Wroth* (Portland, Me., 1951), p. 274.

[13] 'Who Paid the Piper? Publishing Economics in Boston, 1763–1775,' *Journalism Monographs* 38 (1975): 1–49, based upon Yodelis's dissertation, 'Boston's Second Ma-

with all its detail, it would have been helpful to have available for reference still other statistics (however unsophisticated compared to hers) for the rest of the country, in order to provide a basis for comparison.

Of course, detailed studies of limited areas generally form the soundest basis for more encompassing statistics; but the production of such studies is a slow process, and in the meantime it is useful to have provisional figures, even though based on less thorough investigation, to serve as a broad' background for the more specific discussions. With that in mind, I shall set forth here some figures for the two decades from the Sugar Act to the Treaty of Paris, in a sense extending the work of Berthold, which stopped with 1763, through the Revolutionary years. My intention is to try to show the kind of background that can be constructed without enormous effort from the standard bibliographies. Obviously the results, limited by the peculiarities and deficiencies of those bibliographies, must be taken as an approximation. More precise figures can come only from the critical examination of all the various entries for the 12,000 known items dated from 1764 through 1783. However, I think that the statistics that emerge can serve a useful interim purpose, by bringing together readily available data which are nevertheless too cumbersome to be amassed every time a writer wishes to make a generalization. In the process, certain needs for research will become evident—needs that in some cases result from the failure of previous bibliographers to present the statistics they were in the best position to present or from their negligence in providing the means for approaching their material in a sufficient variety of ways.

Before turning to the figures, one should be aware of certain limitations inherent in them. In the first place, they do not necessarily tell one very much about what was being read in America during these years, or even what was available in bookshops; their function is only to give some idea of what was being printed in America. Obviously something can be printed but not read very widely, and in addition many books were imported from England. A study of the availability of titles and of reading habits would have to draw on booksellers' and library catalogues and is

---

jor Paper War: Economics, Politics, and the Theory and Practice of Political Expression in the Press, 1763–1775' (Ph.D. diss., University of Wisconsin, 1971); and 'Genteel Rooms, Umbrilloes and Velvet Cords: Advertising in the Boston Press, 1763–1775,' *Journalism History* 3 (1976): 40–47.

an entirely different undertaking from the present one.[14] Second, the figures refer to entries in bibliographies and cannot be taken to represent the total number of items actually printed. Some bibliographers admit entries without seeing the items involved or having conclusive evidence that they once existed, and it is to be expected that certain items in such cases will turn out to be ghosts. At the same time, many other items, besides those that bibliographers have reported, must have been printed originally and either have not yet been found or have not survived in even a single copy. Lawrence Wroth estimated in 1931, on the basis of the Franklin & Hall Work Book for 1760–65, that the number of items originally printed was 4.7 times that presently known;[15] if he had been writing after the appearance of C. William Miller's *Benjamin Franklin's Philadelphia Printing, 1728–1766* (Philadelphia: American Philosophical Society, 1974), the figure might have been smaller, but his point nevertheless remains. Third, statistics based on numbers of entries do not necessarily reflect the amount of printing performed, because they do not take into account either the length of the works printed or the size of the editions.[16] Mary Ann Yodelis uses in her work the numbers of printed pages instead of the numbers of items and assumes that 'the printer who produced the most pages of printing per year probably earned the highest income from general printing.'[17] One may question whether this relationship would always hold, since some short pamphlets might sell in large quantities and be unusually profitable; in any case it is clear why pages are appropriate units for her to employ in discussing the economics of printing. But numbers of items are significant also, since each item, whether it is a broadside or a substantial volume, represents a distinct printing job; and certainly items are the more feasible units—because figures for them are more easily come by—to use in a broad survey of the kind attempted here. Both figures have their usefulness, and, where relevant, Yodelis's

[14] Robert B. Winans, who has written on 'The Reading of English Novels in Eighteenth-Century America, 1750–1800' (Ph.D. diss., New York University, 1972), is presently working on a study of this kind.

[15] *The Colonial Printer* (New York, 1931), p. 185. Repeated in the 2d edition (Portland, Me., 1938), p. 216; in *An American Bookshelf 1755* (Philadelphia, 1934), p. 4; and in *The Book in America*, p. 27.

[16] And, in the case of bibliographies that include newspapers, a single newspaper title is given a single entry, though it may represent a large number of issues. (For Wroth's comment on this situation, see *The Book in America*, pp. 26–27.)

[17] 'Who Paid the Piper?,' p. 3.

figures will be compared with mine. For all these reasons, the figures presented below can be regarded only as suggestive, not precise; those that express relationships (like percentages) can be taken as somewhat more reliable than those that express absolute quantities.

I

The first, and most basic, figures one might expect to derive from the published bibliographies are those for the total number of known printed items in each year. Of course, it is a simple matter of subtraction to come up with the total Evans entries for each year (adding at the proper points the items in the addenda to volume 6); for Bristol's supplement the procedure is somewhat less simple, but no great problem (there are deleted and interpolated entry numbers in Bristol, a section of addenda at the end of the volume, and several more in the *Proceedings of the American Antiquarian Society*—for April 1972 [82: 46–53]), October 1973 [83: 261–73], October 1977 [87: 409–15], and April 1978 [88: 102–14]). The resulting figures, however, are misleading for two reasons. First, it is now known that a great many of the Evans entries refer to items that never existed, as a result of his interpretation of titles announced in booksellers' advertisements and his assumption that publications in series (like almanacs) appeared in unbroken runs. Clifford K. Shipton estimated that about one in ten of Evans's entries 'is a ghost or contains a serious bibliographical error' and that when Evans was working against time 'one item in three is bad.'[18] Second, Bristol's supplement includes printed blank forms and other ephemera (such as tickets) which are excluded from Evans. It is misleading in itself to include in a volume of addenda material consciously excluded from the original work; in addition, the nature of this material is such that the recorded items are undoubtedly only a small fraction of those that have survived in various manuscript collections.[19] To adjust the Evans and Bristol totals in order to eliminate these peculiarities

[18] Shipton, 'Bibliotheca Americana,' *Papers of the Bibliographical Society of America* 62 (1968): 353; see also the 'Introduction' to his and James E. Mooney's *National Index of American Imprints through 1800: The Short-Title Evans* (Worcester and Barre, Mass., 1969), p. vi. An extensive evaluation of Evans's bibliography appears in chap. 14 of Edward G. Holley, *Charles Evans: American Bibliographer* (Urbana, Ill., 1963), pp. 307–21.

[19] Wroth, in *The Colonial Printer*, p. 223, illustrates the importance of job printing to the colonial printer by pointing out that nearly half the items recorded for 1765 in the Franklin & Hall Work Book are blank forms, bills, tickets, and the like.

would be an enormously time-consuming task. The means for correcting Evans exists, in Shipton and Mooney's *National Index*, which, as a by-product of the project for reproducing the contents of the imprints on Readex Microprint cards, involved the reexamination of every Evans entry. This work, as its introduction states, incorporates 'all of the tens of thousands of bibliographical corrections of the Evans entries turned up by the staff of the [American Antiquarian] Society in the course of fifty years of work' (p. v),[20] including the identification of ghosts. But the work is arranged alphabetically, so that to bring together the corrections for any given group of years would mean taking each consecutively numbered entry in Evans and looking it up alphabetically in Shipton-Mooney. A somewhat less arduous method would be to go consecutively through the Microprint cards (arranged by Evans number); but the task would still be formidable for any group of years after about 1750, and in any case the Shipton-Mooney volumes contain bibliographical information that turned up after the production of the cards. As for Bristol, the entries for ephemera can be eliminated only by going through his *Supplement* item by item. Because of the awkward interrelationships among these three basic works—Evans, Bristol, and Shipton-Mooney—it is still not possible, after all the decades of research on early American imprints, to establish without a great deal of work chronological statistics that would accurately reflect the number of located items.[21]

In the tables that follow, therefore, all references to Evans entries are to the original entries, not to any corrections of them that may be present in Shipton-Mooney. Figures based on Bristol are modified in two respects from the figures that would be obtained by the simple subtraction of entry numbers: (1) entries in the section of addenda in the *Supplement* as well as additions and deletions of entries reported in the Antiquarian

---

[20] See also Shipton's comment that the 'microprints have included the fruits of the fifty years of revision which had been made up to the time of publication' in *Proceedings of the American Antiquarian Society* 68 (1958): 186.

[21] Twenty years ago J. H. Powell, in *The Books of a New Nation: United States Government Publications, 1774–1814* (Philadelphia, 1957), said, 'It is a genuine handicap to the historian that there exists no single, authoritative bibliography of the literature of the American Revolution. Though a great many special studies have been made, they are so scattered through whole shelves of books and journals that we may properly say the systematic bibliographical recording and analysis of the literature of our birth as a nation is yet to be prepared' (p. 22). The situation has improved since then, but the 'single, authoritative bibliography of the literature of the American Revolution' does not yet exist.

Society *Proceedings* are taken into account, although some of the addenda are arbitrarily omitted from the count, in an attempt to offset the entries for dated blank forms; (2) entries for blank forms in the sections of entries datable only by decade are eliminated, and the remaining entries in those sections are arbitrarily distributed evenly throughout the decades involved. The number of blank forms that remains is probably not enough to affect the figures significantly; and no attempt has been made to locate the deleted and interpolated entries in the body of the *Supplement*, which in any case result in a net increase of only twenty items, as Bristol reports in a postscript (p. 635). When the Evans figures must remain approximate, there is no point in attempting to refine further the Bristol figures either.

Table 1A shows, first of all, that the number of recorded entries for these two decades totals 12,179, of which 8810 (or 72.3%) are supplied by Evans and 3369 (or 27.7%) by Bristol. The average number of entries per year listed in Evans is therefore 440.5 and in Bristol 168.45, making a total of 608.95 per year. Figuring the percentage of Evans entries (of the total for 1764–83) recorded for each year and making the same calculation for Bristol and for the Evans-Bristol totals enables one easily to see what effect the Bristol additions have on the overall picture. The years that show in Evans a greater than average percentage (the average would of course be 5% for each year of the twenty-year period) are 1773–79 and 1783; and, in spite of the fact that the Bristol percentages do not follow the same pattern, the percentages for the Evans-Bristol totals show precisely the same years to be above average as do the figures from Evans alone.[22] Furthermore, both in the Evans and the Evans-Bristol figures, 1775 is the year with the largest number of entries; and in both cases the two preceding years build up toward that climax and the three succeeding years show a gradual decline (with 1779 making a slight upturn). Whether the battles of Lexington and Concord and the other events of

---

[22] Another approach is to note the percentage increase or decrease each year shows over the one preceding. The year 1774 shows the greatest increase both in the Evans figures (52.41 percent) and in the Evans–Bristol figures (48.32 percent); and the next highest 3 years (1764, 1773, 1783) are the same for both sets of figures, though the 3 do not fall in the same order in each case. The years in which the Bristol entries produce the greatest differences between the Evans and the total increase/decrease percentages are 1764 (16.42 percent), 1783 (12.37 percent), 1769 (10.31 percent), and 1779 (10.27 percent). (In all other cases, the differences are under 10 points, or, except for 1773 and 1780, under 8.)

1775 caused more items to be printed or whether people saved more of the material printed in this year because of those events cannot now be stated with certainty. It is unquestionably true, however, that more items have survived from 1775 than from any other year during the Revolutionary period and that the years immediately before and after show a rising and falling pattern leading up to and away from the peak year.

TABLE 1A

Evans-Bristol Entries, 1764–1783, with Annual Percentages

	Number of entries			% of total			% Increase/Decrease		
	Evans	Bristol	E&B	Evans	Bristol	E&B	Evans	Bristol	E&B
1764	335	96	431	3.8	2.85	3.54	41.35	−11.11	24.93
1765	330	91	421	3.75	2.7	3.45	− 1.05	− 5.21	− 2.32
1766	313	90	403	3.55	2.67	3.31	− 5.15	− 1.1	− 4.28
1767	274	108	382	3.11	3.2	3.14	−12.46	20	− 5.21
1768	321	140	461	3.64	4.16	3.79	17.15	29.63	20.68
1769	414	133	547	4.7	3.95	4.49	28.97	− 5	18.66
1770	412	176	588	4.68	5.22	4.83	− .48	32.33	7.5
1771	342	113	455	3.88	3.35	3.74	−16.99	−35.8	−22.62
1772	339	94	433	3.85	2.79	3.55	− .88	−16.81	− 4.84
1773	456	169	625	5.18	5.02	5.13	34.51	79.79	44.34
1774	695	232	927	7.89	6.89	7.61	52.41	37.28	48.32
1775	852	267	1119	9.67	7.93	9.19	22.59	15.1	20.71
1776	590	251	841	6.7	7.45	6.91	−30.75	− 5.99	−24.84
1777	487	218	705	5.53	6.47	5.79	−17.46	−13.15	−16.17
1778	461	203	664	5.23	6.03	5.45	− 5.34	− 6.88	− 5.82
1779	525	163	688	5.96	4.84	5.65	13.88	−19.7	3.61
1780	394	180	574	4.47	5.34	4.71	−24.95	10.43	−16.57
1781	379	189	568	4.3	5.61	4.66	− 3.81	5	− 1.05
1782	372	221	593	4.22	6.56	4.87	− 1.85	16.93	4.4
1783	519	235	754	5.89	6.97	6.19	39.52	6.33	27.15
Total	8810	3369	12179	100	100	100			

In order to place these two decades in a larger context, Table 1B compares the number of entries by decade for the half-century 1744–93[23] and

[23] For convenience of reference the Evans–Bristol figures for before and after this

shows that the years 1764–83 do not present any major deviation from the general trend, which consists of an upward movement from an average of 223 entries per year in 1744–53 to 1084 in 1784–93. However, the record of percentage increases of each decade over the previous one

TABLE 1B

SUMMARY BY DECADES OF TOTAL EVANS-BRISTOL ENTRIES,
PERCENTAGES OF TOTAL PRE-1801 ENTRIES,
AND AVERAGE ENTRIES PER YEAR, 1744–1793

	Evans entries	*Bristol entries*	*Evans & Bristol*	*Percentage of total*	*Average entries per year*
1744–1753	1817	411	2228	4.42	222.8
1754–1763	2414	822	3236	6.43	323.6
1764–1773	3536	1210	4746	9.43	474.6
1774–1783	5274	2159	7433	14.76	743.3
1784–1793	8163	2677	10840	21.53	1084
1639–1700	967	209	1176	2.34	18.97
1701–1743	4357	1032	5389	10.7	125.33
1794–1800	12634	2664	15298	30.39	2185.43
Total	39162	11184	50346	100	

TABLE 1C

PERCENTAGE INCREASES IN ENTRIES PER DECADE, 1754–1793

	Evans	*Bristol*	*Evans & Bristol*
1754–1763	32.86	100	45.24
1764–1773	46.48	47.2	46.66
1774–1783	49.15	78.43	56.62
1784–1793	54.78	23.99	45.84

half-century are appended to the table in condensed form—showing, for instance, that the last 7 years of the 18th century contributed a larger percentage of the total entries (30.39 percent) than the entire 2 decades of 1764–83 (24.19 percent). The 125 years before 1764 represent less than a quarter (23.89 percent) of the total pre-1801 entries.

(shown in Table 1C) does exhibit a slight bulge for the 1774–83 decade: where the two preceding decades and the following one register a 45% or 46% increase, its increase amounts to 56.62%. Interestingly, the addition of the Bristol entries brings this situation about, for the Evans entries taken by themselves produce steadily rising percentage increases for these decades; it is the inclusion of the more erratic Bristol percentages that make the overall rates of increase fairly steady (not rising) except for the slight jump in 1774–83.

II

A second basic question, after an examination of the total figures for the period, is to ask for a characterization of that output by type of material. The only really satisfactory way to analyze the material by subject or genre is to go through all 12,000 items categorizing each one. Since Bristol does not provide subject entries in his index to Evans or to his own supplement,[24] the only shortcut available consists of the subject indexes in each volume of Evans. These are certainly less than ideal, but a tabulation of the number of entries Evans lists under each subject heading can at least serve to give an approximate picture. Because each of Evans's indexes applies to an entire volume and because he cites only entry numbers, without identifying the year each belongs to, annual statistics can be derived from his indexes only by the time-consuming process of assigning each cited number to the proper year. The figures in Table 2A, therefore, merely present the subject totals for each relevant volume of Evans: since volume 4 begins with 1765 and volume 6 ends with 1785 the figures for volumes 4, 5, and 6 cover approximately the period under consideration here (1764–83). The percentages do not add up to 100 because Evans's indexes do not include references to every entry number, and sometimes a single entry number is included under more than one heading;[25] the figures do not therefore offer a complete ac-

[24] Bristol's *Index* to Evans (Worcester, 1959) was published as vol. 14 of Evans's work; see also his *Index to Supplement to Charles Evans' American Bibliography* (Charlottesville, 1971).

[25] In two instances Evans simply refers the reader to his author index: for Bibles (under 'Theology') and for legislative journals and acts (under 'Law'). The figures given in Table 2A for 'Bible' and 'Law', therefore, include these items as listed in the author, rather than the subject, index—under 'Biblia' and the names of individual colonies (states). But since a single number is sometimes used in the author index to stand for a whole series of legislative journals or volumes of acts, it has sometimes been

count, but they do give an approximate sense of the relative attention devoted to certain subjects.

It is perhaps not surprising that theology remained, as it had been earlier, the leading subject; what is striking about the figures is the considerable decline they show in the number of entries relating to theology in the period 1774–78. Although theology was technically the leader even then, for practical purposes it was tied with political science and history, each of them representing about 9% of the entries for those years (as the summary table—Table 2B—helps to make clear). In the earlier and later groups of years, on the other hand, the percentage for theology was greater than that for political science and history combined. In so far as these figures can be relied on, they suggest that, while works on political science, history, and law maintained fairly evenly their substantial share (about 25%) of the total between 1765 and 1785, the attention given to theology sharply declined (from 29% to 10%) during the years around the time of the Declaration of Independence (and returned only to 18% in the next group of years). The fact that Evans's category of 'History' includes items dealing with current events perhaps helps to explain why this category increased in size during the years leading up to the break with England and the early years of the war and then yielded third place to works on law in the years that followed. It is instructive to compare the percentages for these four leading subjects in 1765–85 with the corresponding percentages for Evans's two preceding volumes, covering 1730–64:

	1730–1750	*1751–1764*
Theology	34.65	28.07
Political Science	3.02	3.55
History	3.34	9.67
Law	8.43	7.71

The contrast between the figures for theology and those for political science and history are much greater here than in the Revolutionary years.

---

necessary to turn to the entries themselves to achieve more reliable statistics. It was a simple matter, in the process, to count the other government documents entered under the colony and state names, and the resulting figures have been entered in the 'Government Publications' line in Table 2A; this line is the only place in the table where the figures represent a count of the entries themselves rather than a count of the entry numbers listed in the indexes. For additional treatment of government documents, see section IV below.

These figures support the view that the attention to theology was declining through the century, while that directed to current events and political discussion rose abruptly as the climate for rebellion developed. Whereas political science accounted for only about 3% of the entries in the thirty years before 1764, it accounted for 10 or 11% of the entries in the next twenty years; and historical works, 3% of the total in the two decades before 1750, jumped up to 9 or 10% for the next thirty years (and

TABLE 2A

SUBJECT AND GENRE ANALYSIS OF EVANS ENTRIES,
AS RECORDED IN EVANS'S INDEXES, 1765–1785

Subjects	1765–1773 Entries	%	1774–1778 Entries	%	1779–1785 Entries	%	Totals Entries	%
Bibliography	39	1.22	15	.49	37	1.13	91	.95
Biography	143	4.47	46	1.49	70	2.14	259	2.71
Funeral Sermons	97	3.03	28	.91	42	1.28	167	1.75
Other Biography	46	1.44	18	.58	28	.86	92	.96
Education	60	1.87	27	.88	28	.86	115	1.2
Geography	8	.25	22	.71	18	.55	48	.5
History	323	10.09	264	8.56	154	4.71	741	7.75
Language	57	1.78	28	.91	80	2.44	165	1.73
English	42	1.31	19	.62	59	1.8	120	1.26
Other	15	.47	9	.29	21	.64	45	.47
Law	219	6.84	162	5.25	273	8.34	654	6.84
Literature	126	3.94	143	4.64	137	4.19	406	4.25
Medicine	35	1.1	27	.88	22	.67	84	.88
Philosophy	5	.16	17	.55	17	.52	39	.41
Political Science	362	11.31	302	9.79	374	11.43	1038	10.86
Science	15	.47	6	.19	36	1.1	57	.6
Social Science	157	4.9	71	2.3	143	4.37	371	3.88
Theology	940	29.37	305	9.89	581	17.76	1826	19.1
Bible and Parts	32	1	14	.45	28	.86	74	.77
Church History	63	1.97	15	.49	63	1.93	141	1.48
Sermons	134	4.19	50	1.62	55	1.68	239	2.5
Other	711	22.21	226	7.33	435	13.29	1372	14.35
Useful Arts	85	2.66	101	3.27	124	3.79	310	3.24

Statistics on American Printing, 1764–1783

Genres	1765–1773 Entries	%	1774–1778 Entries	%	1789–1785 Entries	%	Totals Entries	%
Almanacs	302	9.43	200	6.48	222	6.78	724	7.57
Foreign-Language Books	110	3.43	87	2.82	68	2.08	265	2.77
German	84	2.62	72	2.33	55	1.68	211	2.21
Other	26	.81	15	.49	13	.4	54	.56
Government Publications	423	13.21	1067	34.59	1116	34.11	2606	27.27
Newspapers and Magazines (titles counted once per year)	55	1.72	73	2.37	107	3.27	235	2.46

TABLE 2B

PERCENTAGES OF EVANS ENTRIES IN THE EIGHT HIGHEST SUBJECT CATEGORIES, AS RECORDED IN EVANS'S INDEXES, 1765–1785

	1765–1773	1774–1778	1779–1785	1765–1785
Theology	29.37	9.89	17.76	19.1
Political Science	11.31	9.79	11.43	10.86
History	10.09	8.56	4.71	7.75
Law	6.84	5.25	8.34	6.84
Literature	3.94	4.64	4.19	4.25
Social Science	4.9	2.3	4.37	3.88
Useful Arts	2.66	3.27	3.79	3.24
Biography	4.47	1.49	2.14	2.71

then settled down again to the 4 or 5% range). Law remained more nearly constant (5–8%); but the three subjects taken together moved ahead of theology, for the first time, in 1774–78. Before that, the number of works on theology had surpassed the total for the other three categories, though by a rapidly decreasing margin (19.86% in 1730–50, 7.14% in 1751–64, and 1.13% in 1765–73).

No other subject equals the size of these four in Evans's classification, and only four others amount to more than 2% of the total for 1765–85:

literature (4.25%), social science (3.88%), what Evans calls 'Useful Arts'—military and naval science, agriculture, theater, music— (3.24%), and biography (2.71%). Figures based on Evans's subject indexes have some suggestive value, but, like any classification scheme, his system involves some subjective decisions which make his categories not directly comparable to those produced under other schemes. One has to be cautious, for example, about comparing Berthold's figures for the years through 1763 with those presented here for the next two decades. It is true that Berthold's figure of 37% for theology[26] fits well with the pattern that emerges from the Evans indexes, but Berthold finds that literature and law—not political science and history—come next. The explanation is not simply that a shift in priorities developed about 1764 (although apparently political science and history did begin to take on more importance); the real reason is a difference of classification, for Berthold includes almanacs and biography under 'Literature' and proclamations under 'Law,' whereas Evans does not.[27] As one can see from Table 2A, if the figures for almanacs and biography were added to those for literature, the category of literature would be in second place here, too, with an overall percentage of 14.53 (for 1774–78 it would be in first place); and if various other official documents besides acts and legislative journals were included in 'Law,' the percentage for that category would rise considerably. Because of the arbitrariness of such classifications, it is always important, when citing figures for particular categories, to notice related subjects that might overlap. With these cautions in mind, one can perhaps take the data in Table 2A to represent a preliminary characterization of the output of the press in the Revolutionary years, until such time as statistics based on a thorough analysis of each imprint are available.

III

A third approach to the material is geographical: it is useful to know how the total number of entries is distributed geographically, how one area compares with another in quantity of output. Evans's lists of printers and

[26] In his Table III, p. 29. The information from this table is repeated in *The Book in America*, p. 33.

[27] In the subject indexes to vols. 2 and 3, Evans does mention proclamations under 'Law' with a cross reference to the author index, but he does not do so in the next 3 volumes; since many of the proclamations in these volumes are indexed under other subject headings, they are not included in any of the figures given here for 'Law.'

booksellers at the end of each volume are arranged geographically, but they only record the dates of known imprints of each person and do not make reference to individual entry numbers; from these lists, therefore, one could calculate the number of printers operating in a particular place in a given year, but one could not get any idea of the number of imprints produced. A way of securing such figures, at least approximate ones, without examining each entry is offered by Bristol's indexes of printers and booksellers in Evans and in his own supplement to Evans.[28] Since his indexes helpfully indentify the year of each entry number listed, one can turn through, without investing an inordinate amount of time, and locate all the printers working during a given period, with the entry numbers for the items printed. The results of such a search, for 1764–83, are reported in Table 3A. It must be emphasized that the figures obtained in this way are necessarily approximate. For one thing, an imprint that includes two printers' names is naturally indexed in Bristol under both names, so a simple count of Bristol's references is misleading; I have attempted to eliminate such duplication of items in the figures given here, but certain errors arising from this situation are sure to remain. In the second place, a number of items are not assigned to any printer or bookseller in Evans's and Bristol's entries and thus cannot appear in Bristol's indexes of printers. As a result, the number of items recorded for each year in Table 3A falls short of the numbers listed in Table 1A. One can regard Table 3A, in other words, as offering a conservative estimate of the number of items produced in each colony or state in each year.

In these two decades as a whole, Pennsylvania was in first place, with 2877 items, or nearly 28% of the total for the country,[29] and Massachu-

---

[28] *Index of Printers, Publishers, and Booksellers Indicated by Charles Evans in His American Bibliography* (Charlottesville, 1961); the index to printers in Bristol's supplement is included in the same volume with his author-title index to the supplement (see note 24, above).

[29] That is, the total represented by the figures in Table 3A, based on Bristol's indexes, not the larger total shown in Table 1A, based on Evans–Bristol entries. It would be misleading to use the latter total without knowing the geographical distribution of the additional entries it contains. Thus all percentages in this section are based on Table 3A.

Mary Ann Yodelis has provided a table—based on the number of *pages* printed—of the percentage of total printing represented by Pennsylvania, Massachusetts, New York, and Connecticut in 1775–83, in 'The Press in Wartime: Portable and Penurious,' *Journalism History* 3 (1976): 2–6, 10. Her figures and mine frequently differ, but the general patterns they reveal are similar.

setts came second, with 2617, or 25%. This is a period, however, in which the leadership passed from Massachusetts to Pennsylvania, as an examination of the yearly record indicates. With the exception of 1764, Massachusetts led in the years through 1775, and Pennsylvania took over in 1776. Third, fourth, and fifth places alternated among New York, Connecticut, and Rhode Island, with New York holding third place for nine of the years (1764–66, 1768–69, 1774–77) and Connecticut for ten (1767, 1770–73, 1778, 1780–83). These top five accounted for nearly 83% of the total, and the top ten (including, in addition, Maryland, Virginia, South Carolina, New Jersey, and New Hampshire) accounted for 96%. The great extremes within these ten are suggested by the fact that in 1776 the figure for Pennsylvania was 272 items and for New Hampshire (in tenth place) only 13. The figures for some colonies (those with low production) seem relatively unaffected in the years of crisis, whereas the major printing centers showed a considerable increase: witness the figures over 200 for Massachusetts during 1773–75 and for Pennsylvania during 1775–79. (The geographical arrangement of the vertical columns in Table 3A makes it easy to see where the concentration of printing lay, for the largest figures fall in the columns from Massachusetts through Pennsylvania.) Because percentages are more immediately revealing than absolute figures, Table 3B presents a summary account in percentages. During the first of these decades Pennsylvania produced about a quarter of the total, while Massachusetts produced 32%; but in the second decade Pennsylvania moved up to 30% and Massachusetts fell to about 21%. New York and Connecticut generally hovered in the 10–14% range, and Rhode Island remained at 6% until the last five years of the period, moving up then to 9%. The other five of the top ten were characteristically in the 2–4% area, except when Maryland spurted up to 7% after 1778.

The number of towns and of printers or booksellers mentioned in imprints can also be tabulated from the Bristol indexes (Table 3C). Massachusetts had by far the largest number of towns with printing during these years; although no more than ten places are mentioned in the Massachusetts imprints of any single year, twenty-one different places are named in Massachusetts imprints during this twenty-year period. Pennsylvania, coming second, had only nine, followed by Connecticut and New Jersey with seven and New York with five. Only three colonies—Massachusetts, Pennsylvania, and Connecticut—had five or more towns appearing in the imprints of a single year during this period. The total

TABLE 3A

Geographical Analysis of Approximate Number of Entries Recorded in Bristol's Indexes of Printers and Publishers, 1764–1783

	NH	VT	MA	RI	CT	NY	NJ	PA	DE	MD	VA	NC	SC	GA	LA	Total
1764	9	—	84	28	20	33	7	170	8	5	18	5	8	3	2	400
1765	12	—	126	25	39	45	11	108	7	8	7	5	9	2	3	407
1766	11	—	132	23	38	62	4	77	4	11	10	6	18	3	—	399
1767	7	—	141	21	46	36	3	77	5	5	4	5	9	2	1	362
1768	10	—	151	31	45	54	4	71	3	14	11	5	15	2	5	421
1769	8	—	86	27	58	82	1	77	4	5	13	4	14	2	18	399
1770	9	—	136	32	59	43	11	125	9	10	8	4	13	4	4	467
1771	9	—	138	24	40	39	7	99	6	8	11	5	9	—	—	395
1772	5	—	122	25	46	27	7	99	6	5	15	2	9	2	—	370
1773	7	—	201	23	54	53	10	109	6	7	17	5	9	3	—	504
1774	8	—	220	42	80	142	7	194	7	22	28	11	18	9	—	788
1775	8	—	210	62	100	189	13	201	10	33	45	17	11	2	—	901
1776	13	—	158	47	63	67	12	272	6	35	24	3	25	—	—	725
1777	8	1	108	44	60	64	16	221	3	45	19	5	13	2	6	615
1778	8	7	100	24	64	53	7	192	8	18	20	11	11	—	5	528
1779	13	18	113	49	48	42	25	227	6	19	19	4	7	2	3	595
1780	11	6	102	48	61	37	31	106	5	17	10	—	13	2	3	452
1781	15	19	93	58	59	30	16	123	5	29	17	—	4	2	—	470
1782	3	10	98	40	50	36	20	130	15	33	11	2	8	1	—	457
1783	3	13	98	38	74	65	20	199	17	76	20	6	12	6	—	647
Total	177	74	2617	711	1104	1199	232	2877	140	405	327	105	235	49	50	10302
Percentage	1.72	.72	25.4	6.9	10.72	11.64	2.25	27.92	1.36	3.93	3.17	1.02	2.28	.48	.49	100

number of places of printing in any one year varied from about twenty to almost twice that number (thirty-seven), with the larger numbers generally occurring in the early war years. This geographical dispersion is to be accounted for in part by the removal of some city printers to smaller towns during the war: the clearest example is Massachusetts, where ten locations are recorded for 1776, though the output for that year was considerably smaller than for the previous year, when printing had occurred in only five places.

TABLE 3B

RELATIVE OUTPUT OF THE TEN LEADING COLONIES (STATES)
AS RECORDED IN BRISTOL'S INDEXES,
IN FIVE YEAR PERIODS, 1764–1783

(Expressed in approximate percentages of the total number of indexed entries)

	1764–1768	1769–1773	1774–1778	1779–1783	1764–1783
Pennsylvania	25	24	30	30	28
Massachusetts	32	32	22	19	25
New York	12	11	14	8	12
Connecticut	9	12	10	11	11
Rhode Island	6	6	6	9	7
Subtotal	84	85	82	77	83
Maryland	2	2	4	7	3.9
Virginia	3	3	4	3	3.2
South Carolina	3	3	2	2	2.28
New Jersey	1	2	2	4	2.25
New Hampshire	2	2	1	2	1.7
Total	95	97	95	95	96

The figures for the people refer principally to printers, but they include some booksellers as well. Since many of the imprints that state that the work is 'printed for' or 'sold by' a given person do not give the name of the printer, Bristol's index references to booksellers (publishers) have been included in the statistics. A number of these people of course worked in more than one location and are thus given more than one entry in Bristol's index; I have tried to consolidate such entries, so as not to inflate the number of persons involved. As one might expect, the colonies with the

TABLE 3c

Geographical Analysis of Approximate Number of Places of Printing and of Printers (or Booksellers) Recorded in Bristol's Indexes, 1764–1783

(Places precede the oblique lines; printers follow them)

	NH	VT	MA	RI	CT	NY	NJ	PA	DE	MD	VA	NC	SC	GA	LA	Total*
1764	1/2	—	2/22	2/3	3/3	1/6	1/1	3/11	1/1	1/1	1/2	2/2	1/2	1/1	1/1	21/53
1765	1/3	—	2/29	2/3	3/4	1/5	2/3	2/10	1/1	2/3	1/1	2/2	1/6	1/1	1/1	22/68
1766	1/5	—	2/25	2/5	3/4	1/10	1/2	3/13	1/1	1/1	1/3	2/2	1/5	1/1	—	20/71
1767	1/4	—	3/29	2/4	3/5	2/8	1/1	6/19	1/1	1/2	1/3	2/2	1/3	1/1	1/1	26/81
1768	2/3	—	4/25	2/7	3/4	1/6	1/1	2/12	1/1	2/3	1/3	3/3	1/3	1/1	1/1	25/70
1769	1/2	—	3/18	2/3	3/6	1/8	1/1	2/14	1/2	1/2	1/3	2/2	1/4	1/1	1/1	21/66
1770	1/2	—	4/26	2/2	3/6	1/8	1/1	2/19	1/2	1/2	1/3	2/2	1/6	1/1	1/1	22/78
1771	2/3	—	3/23	2/3	3/3	2/6	1/1	3/16	1/1	1/1	1/3	2/2	1/4	—	—	22/66
1772	1/2	—	3/29	2/3	3/3	2/6	1/1	3/18	1/2	1/1	1/3	2/2	1/3	1/1	—	22/74
1773	1/2	—	3/26	2/2	4/8	2/14	1/1	3/21	1/1	2/2	1/5	2/2	1/3	1/1	—	24/86
1774	2/3	—	3/34	2/3	4/9	2/18	1/1	3/25	1/2	2/4	2/6	2/2	1/6	1/1	—	26/109
1775	2/3	—	5/22	2/3	4/8	2/12	1/1	4/27	1/1	2/7	2/7	2/2	1/7	1/2	—	29/97
1776	3/5	—	10/25	3/6	4/8	2/7	2/2	3/21	1/1	2/3	1/6	1/1	1/4	—	—	33/82
1777	2/4	1/2	8/19	2/3	4/11	4/9	1/1	6/26	1/1	3/6	1/5	1/1	1/5	1/2	1/1	37/90
1778	2/3	1/2	6/18	2/4	4/10	3/7	2/1	3/23	1/1	2/3	1/6	1/1	1/5	—	1/1	30/79
1779	2/2	1/2	4/19	2/6	4/8	3/12	3/4	2/21	1/1	3/5	1/6	1/1	1/4	1/1	1/1	30/90
1780	2/2	1/2	6/20	2/4	4/7	3/11	2/2	2/15	1/1	3/4	2/4	—	1/6	1/2	1/1	31/77
1781	2/2	1/2	5/22	2/4	4/8	3/11	2/2	2/15	1/1	3/5	2/6	—	1/3	1/2	—	29/80
1782	1/1	1/2	3/22	2/4	5/11	4/11	2/2	2/19	1/1	3/5	2/5	1/1	2/5	1/1	—	30/88
1783	2/2	2/4	3/22	2/7	6/12	4/22	3/2	2/17	1/1	3/8	2/7	2/2	1/8	1/1	—	34/112
Total	4/11	4/6	21/94	3/22	7/29	5/48	7/8	9/91	1/4	3/18	5/18	4/6	2/26	1/6	1/2	77/335

*The totals of printers are adjusted to account for the printers who worked in more than one state.

largest output of printed items also show the largest number of names mentioned in imprints. Both Pennsylvania and Massachusetts imprints display about 90 or 95 names over these two decades, with New York showing half that many and Connecticut, South Carolina, and Rhode Island coming next with figures in the 20s. The largest number of printers working at one time seems to be 112 in the last year; but the highest years before that were 1774–75, the years of the First Continental Congress and the battles of Lexington and Concord. Altogether during these twenty years printed items were produced at something like seventy-seven places by a total of 335 or so persons.

Because the bulk of the printing was concentrated in a small number of these places, it is just as important to look at the relative output of the principal cities as it is to classify the imprints by colony or state. The three leading cities, of course, were Philadelphia, Boston, and New York, accounting for 55% of the output of these two decades. Since the majority of the imprints from Pennsylvania, Massachusetts, and New York came from these three cities, the patterns are roughly the same for these cities and colonies. One interesting difference, however, is that the lead passed from Boston to Philadelphia in 1775, one year earlier than it passed from Massachusetts to Pennsylvania. Boston was of course a city under siege, and all normal activities there, including printing, were disrupted. The movement of printers away from Boston at the beginning of the war, already suggested by the statistics relating to printing locations, is shown even more dramatically here. As Table 3D indicates, Boston's percentage of the total output of the country, after being 37% in 1773 and 23% in 1774 fell to 10% in 1775–76; but whereas Boston accounted for 92% and 83% of Massachusetts imprints in 1773–74, it accounted for only 41% and 44% in 1775–76. Thus Boston and Massachusetts did not decline simultaneously, showing that Massachusetts printing in 1775 simply shifted to locations outside of Boston. (As one can see in Table 3A, the number of Massachusetts imprints for 1775 was practically the same as that for 1774.) Of the top ten cities, the remaining seven (producing roughly 20% of the total output) do not entirely represent the other seven colonies on the list of the ten leading colonies (Table 3B), for the next five cities (Providence, Hartford, New Haven, New London, Newport) are located in only two colonies. They are followed by Williamsburg and Charleston, but Maryland, New Jersey, and New Hampshire are not represented. In 1766 these ten cities produced 89% of the total output, and even at the

TABLE 3D

RELATIVE OUTPUT OF THE TEN LEADING CITIES AS RECORDED IN BRISTOL'S INDEXES, 1764–1783

(Expressed in approximate percentages of the total number of indexed entries—and, for each of three cities, of the number of entries recorded for its colony or state)

	Philadelphia		Boston		New York City		Total for three cities	Providence	Hartford	New Haven	New London	Newport	Williamsburg	Charleston	Total for ten cities
	% of PA	% of country	% of MA	% of country	% of NY	% of country									
1764	91	39	96	20	100	8	67	2	.8	2.5	1.8	5	4.5	2	85.6
1765	94	25	98	30	100	11	66	2	2.7	3.9	2.9	4.2	1.7	2.2	85.6
1766	92	18	99	33	100	16	67	1.5	2.3	3.3	4	4.3	2.5	4.5	89.4
1767	82	17	91	36	97	10	63	1.7	5	3.6	4.1	4.1	1.1	2.5	85.1
1768	92	15	88	32	100	13	60	4.5	2.6	3.8	4.3	2.9	2.6	3.6	84.3
1769	91	18	88	19	100	21	58	1.8	3.8	4.8	5.8	5	3.3	3.5	86
1770	93	25	90	26	100	9	60	1.9	3.4	4.9	4.3	4.9	1.7	2.8	83.9
1771	91	23	91	32	97	10	65	3	3	2.8	4.3	3	2.8	2.3	86.2
1772	95	25	91	30	93	7	62	1.6	1.9	5.9	4.6	5.1	4.1	2.4	87.6
1773	91	20	92	37	91	10	67	.8	2.4	3.2	3	3.8	3.4	1.8	85.4
1774	89	22	83	23	99	18	63	1.9	2.7	2.5	1.6	3.4	3.3	2.3	80.7
1775	88	20	41	10	98	21	51	3.6	2.3	1.1	3.7	3.3	4.9	1.2	71.1
1776	92	34	44	10	79	7	51	4.6	1.5	1	2.2	1.7	3.3	3.4	68.7
1777	78	28	72	13	47	5	46	6.8	3.6	.7	3.4	.3	3.1	2.1	66
1778	70	26	65	12	74	7	45	3.6	4.4	1.7	2.7	.9	3.8	2.3	64.4
1779	97	37	81	15	69	5	57	7.4	4.5	.7	1.5	.8	3.2	1.3	76.4
1780	92	22	73	16	70	6	44	9.3	8.4	1.5	2	1.3	1.8	2.9	71.2
1781	98	26	77	15	80	5	46	11.7	8.1	.6	2.6	.6	—	.9	70.5
1782	95	27	72	16	47	4	47	7.7	4.6	2.4	2.4	1.1	—	.9	66.1
1783	99	30	68	10	69	7	47	4.6	4.2	2.8	2.3	1.2	—	1.9	64
Total	90	25	79	20	88	10	55	3.9	3.5	3.3	3	2.7	2.7	2.3	76.4

lowest points (1778, 1783) they still were responsible for 64%, achieving an overall figure of 76% for the twenty years.[30]

The individual firms that turned out the largest number of items were naturally located in these major cities, as Table 3E shows. Edes & Gill of Boston was the leader for the 1764–83 period, with about 565 imprints,[31] followed (at about 425 imprints) by John Dunlap of Philadelphia. John Holt (New York) and Timothy Green (and Green & Spooner, of New London and Norwich) were practically tied for third position, and the remaining places among the top twelve were occupied by four printers from Philadelphia and one each from New York, Providence, New Haven, and Boston. This distribution makes clear that the printing in Philadelphia was more evenly distributed among several prominent firms than was the case in the other cities: a Philadelphia printer was in second, but not first, place because Philadelphia also had the fifth-, tenth-, eleventh-, and twelfth-place firms; Boston, in contrast, had the first-place printer but only one other printer on the list, in ninth place, and New York printers occupied the third and sixth places. Whereas the five leading Philadelphia printers together produced only about 49% of Pennsylvania's output during these years, the two Green firms accounted for nearly 58% of Connecticut's output and the two leading New York City printers accounted for about 55% of that colony's total. John Carter of Providence, falling roughly in seventh place in the country as a whole, yet operating in the fifth-place colony, produced by himself 43% of the Rhode Island imprints of this period. It is interesting to note that Mary Ann Yodelis, using a different measure (the total number of pages printed), also places Edes & Gill in first position among Boston printers and Thomas & John Fleet (the only other Boston firm among the twelve in Table 3E) in second, and their percentages of total Boston printing come out about the same either way.[32] One can get some idea of the shifting posi-

---

[30] Bridenbaugh, *Cities in Revolt*, pp. 183, 386, has calculated, on the basis of Evans, that Boston, Philadelphia, New York, Newport, and Charleston accounted for 75 percent of the total output in 1743–60 (with Boston first) and 70 percent in 1761–76 (with Philadelphia first). In Table 3D, too, the percentage represented by these 5 cities from 1764 through 1776 averages 67.9 percent (but Boston's average for these years remains higher than Philadelphia's).

[31] This figure includes the work issued by the 2 men separately after 1775. But Edes would still be in first place (counting his Watertown imprints in 1775–76) even if the 80 or so Gill imprints of 1776–83 were deleted.

[32] 'Who Paid the Piper?,' pp. 5–6. Her figure for Edes & Gill's mean share of Boston printing, 1763–75, is 13 percent, and for Thomas & John Fleet's, 9 percent. The per-

tions of these printers over the years by noticing the difference between the standings for each of the two decades that make up this period. In the first decade, 1764–73, the Greens of Connecticut held the first two places, together producing about 9% of the total for the country, with Edes & Gill, Holt, Gaine, and Miller following. In the next decade, however, Edes & Gill jumped far out in front (6.7%), with Dunlap in second place (5.7%), Carter third (4.2%), and Holt fourth (3.2%). Dunlap was far

TABLE 3E

OUTPUT OF THE LEADING PRINTERS, MEASURED BY THE NUMBER OF ITEMS RECORDED IN BRISTOL'S INDEXES, 1764–1783

	1764–1773		1774–1783		Total		% of colony
	No.	%	No.	%	No.	%	
Edes & Gill (Boston)	153	3.71	412	6.67	565	5.48	21.6
John Dunlap (Philadelphia)	74	1.79	350	5.66	424	4.12	14.7
John Holt (New York)	148	3.59	200	3.24	348	3.38	29
Timothy Green (& Spooner) (New London and Norwich)	167	4.05	175	2.83	342	3.32	31
William & Thomas Bradford (Philadelphia)	131	3.18	183	2.96	314	3.05	11
Hugh Gaine (New York)	144	3.49	163	2.64	307	2.98	25.6
John Carter (Providence)	43	1.04	262	4.24	305	2.96	42.9
Thomas & Samuel Green (New Haven)	204	4.95	89	1.44	293	2.84	26.5
Thomas & John Fleet (Boston)	97	2.35	139	2.25	236	2.29	9
Hall & Sellers (Philadelphia)	110	2.67	123	1.99	233	2.26	8.1
Henry Miller (Philadelphia)	144	3.49	87	1.41	231	2.24	8
Robert Bell (Philadelphia)	42	1.02	158	2.56	200	1.94	7
Total	1457	35.33	2341	37.89	3798	36.86	

centages that result from my figures, based on the number of entries indexed, are, respectively, 14.5 percent and 8 percent.

down the list in the first decade, as the Greens were in the second. Thus the output of the most productive printers in the period of the Revolution itself was considerably greater than the output of the leading printers in the previous decade (twice as great, if one considers only the top three printers in each decade)—for the overall standings for the twenty years more nearly resemble those of the later than of the earlier decade.[33]

IV

After determining the approximate distribution of the entries for 1764–83 by subject and by place of printing, one naturally wishes to combine these two approaches and examine the subject distribution according to area. But the indexes to Evans and Bristol, unfortunately, do not provide a means for obtaining this information. For one important category of material, however, it is possible, without great effort, to derive a geographical classification directly from the body of Evans's and Bristol's works. Official colony (or state) documents are entered under the names of the colonies (states), and one can therefore easily count the number of entries of this kind for each colony (state) each year. For a more complete record of government documents, one would also have to examine the entries under 'Great Britain' and 'United States' and classify them according to place of printing. Table 4A offers the statistics for documents in the period 1764–83 resulting from such a procedure—which seems the most feasible approach, since the specialized checklists by Benjamin Perley Poore (federal documents) and by Richard R. Bowker (state documents) are far out of date (1885 and 1899–1908 respectively) and in any case difficult to use for this purpose (the former strictly chronological and without printers' names, and the latter divided first by state and then by type of document).[34] One could of course derive the information from Shipton-Mooney rather than Evans and Bristol and in the process take

[33] Some comments on the leading New England printers and listings of representative examples of their work can be found in a useful catalogue of an exhibition at the John Carter Brown Library, *New England Printers and the American Revolution* (Providence, 1975). Studies of the individual printers are listed in my *Guide to the Study of United States Imprints*.

[34] J. H. Powell in 1957 (*Books of a New Nation*) criticized the checklists of documents for this period; his remarks, as far as Evans is concerned, have been commented on by Holley, *Charles Evans*, pp. 315–17. Some statistics—based on the number of *pages* printed—on government printing in Boston, New York, Philadelphia, and Williamsburg are provided by Yodelis, 'Who Paid the Piper?'

TABLE 4A

GOVERNMENT PUBLICATIONS RECORDED IN EVANS-BRISTOL, 1764–1783

(Separate numbers and those preceding oblique lines refer to state documents; numbers following oblique lines refer to Great Britain or U.S. documents)

	NH	VT	MA	RI	CT	NY	NJ	PA	DE	MD	VA	NC	SC	GA	LA	Total
1764	4	—	18/1	10	5	9/1	3	11	2	3	9	3	2/1	4	—	86
1765	2	—	18/2	7	5/1	7/3	3/1	8/2	—	2/1	3	2	4	2	2	75
1766	3	—	24/1	7	6	10/2	2	5	1	5	6	3	5/1	3	—	84
1767	2/1	—	16/1	11	6	7/1	2	6	1	2	1	3	—	2	1	63
1768	5	—	16	7	6	7	3	8/1	—	3	3	1	7	2	4	73
1769	5	—	13/1	9	6	16/1	4	9	1	—	7	2	3	2	16	95
1770	2/1	—	22	8	4	4/2	9	8	3	4	3	3	1	2	4	80
1771	3	—	11	5	5	5	2	9	—	5	4	3	1	1	—	54
1772	3	—	11	7/1	8	5	4	6	1	3	7	—	—	1	—	57
1773	5	—	16/1	8	6	7	3	8	3	3	7	3	—	2	—	72
Sub-total	34/2	—	165/7	79/1	57/1	77/10	35/1	78/3	12	30/1	50	23	23/2	21	27	711/28
1774	7/2	—	25/22	15/4	13/9	16/9	3	13/22	1	6/2	10/2	3	1	5	—	190
1775	10/1	1	92/27	13/6	24/1	53/16	13	13/39	3	3/2	22	5/1	3	3	—	351
1776	12	—	73/14	27/3	39/3	27/16	10	42/53	4/1	10/7	12	2	15/2	—	—	372
1777	11/2	1/1	60/7	40/3	25/3	25/11	13	57/90	2	13/12	8/2	3	3	3	4	399
1778	9/3	4	38/6	39/3	19/1	11/15	9	29/74	10	4/5	7/2	7/1	2	1	3	302
1779	10/4	10	45/4	30	19/5	6/11	13	27/48	4/1	9/3	15	5	3	0/4	3	279
1780	7/2	5	44/1	33/3	26/4	7/8	25	19/34	4	11	7	2	1/10	—	2	255
1781	17/2	15	32/5	33/2	25	5	10	30/14	3	5	16	3	1	1	—	219
1782	7/1	5	22/1	21	16/3	10	8	12/23	14	7	7	1	9	1	1	169
1783	9/4	8	18/5	13/7	11/4	11/10	8/1	45/32	9/1	6/9	7/2	2	10	16	—	248
Sub-total (1774–83)	99/21	49/1	449/92	264/31	217/33	171/96	112/1	287/429	54/3	74/40	111/8	33/2	48/12	30/4	13	2011/773
Totals	133/23	49/1	614/99	343/32	274/34	248/106	147/2	365/432	66/3	104/41	161/8	56/2	71/14	51/4	40	2722/801
	156	50	713	375	308	354	149	797	69	145	169	58	85	55	40	3523

advantage of the additional research reflected there; but since the arrangement is not chronological under each state heading, one would have to search through all the pages devoted to documents—a quarter of the total.

What Table 4A shows is that roughly 3500 government documents (state, colony, Great Britain, and U.S., but not city) were printed in the twenty years 1764–83, the great majority (79%) in the second of the decades, especially in the peak years 1775–78, when over 300 documents were printed each year; approximately 75% of them were colony or state documents, the other 25% Great Britain or United States documents. In the first decade Massachusetts produced twice the number (172) of any other colony, with New York (87), Pennsylvania (81), and Rhode Island (80) all about equal; in the second decade Pennsylvania moved far ahead (716), with Massachusetts (541) second and with Rhode Island (295), New York (267), and Connecticut (240) following along in a group. The reason for Pennsylvania's sharp rise, of course, was Philadelphia's position as center of the federal government and the large number of United States documents printed there: nearly six times the number of United States documents were printed in Pennsylvania from 1774 through 1783 as in any other state (370, as opposed to 68 for Massachusetts and 43 for New York).[35] But if federal documents are excluded and only state documents considered, Massachusetts remained the leader (449) in the second decade as well, with Pennsylvania (287), Rhode Island (264), Connecticut (217), and New York (171) following at some distance.

The percentage of total printed output represented by government documents is set forth in Table 4B. The vertical column of national totals is somewhat more accurate than the figures for states because it shows the ratio of entries for government documents to the total number of Evans-Bristol entries. For the state columns, however, the only totals available are those in Table 3A, based on Bristol's indexes of printers and therefore falling short of the total number of items printed in each state. As a result, the percentages in the state columns in Table 4B are slightly exaggerated in most cases, and the figures for states with small output are less reliable than those for the more productive states. What the table does show are some broad trends: for example, the percentage of the total output de-

[35] The number of Great Britain documents are, respectively, 59, 24, and 53, bringing the totals to those shown in Table 4A.

TABLE 4B

GOVERNMENT PUBLICATIONS AS A PERCENTAGE OF THE INDEXED ENTRIES FOR EACH COLONY (STATE), 1764–1783

	NH	VT	MA	RI	CT	NY	NJ	PA	DE	MD	VA	NC	SC	GA	LA	Total*
1764	44.4	—	22.6	35.7	25	30.3	42.9	6.5	25	60	50	60	37.5	100	—	20
1765	16.7	—	15.9	28	15.4	22.2	36.4	9.3	—	37.5	42.9	40	44.4	100	66.7	17.8
1766	27.3	—	18.9	30.4	15.8	19.4	50	6.5	25	45.5	60	50	33.3	100	—	20.8
1767	42.9	—	12.1	52.4	13	22.2	66.7	7.8	20	40	25	60	—	100	100	16.5
1768	50	—	10.6	22.6	13.3	13	75	12.7	—	21.4	27.3	20	46.7	100	80	15.8
1769	62.5	—	16.3	33.3	10.3	20.7	100	11.7	25	—	53.8	50	21.4	100	88.9	17.4
1770	33.3	—	16.2	25	6.8	14	81.8	6.4	33.3	40	37.5	75	7.7	50	100	13.6
1771	33.3	—	8	20.8	12.5	12.8	28.6	9.1	—	62.5	36.4	60	11.1	100	—	11.9
1772	60	—	9	32	17.4	18.5	57.1	6.1	16.7	60	46.7	—	—	50	—	13.2
1773	71.4	—	8.5	34.8	11.1	13.2	30	7.3	50	42.9	41.2	60	—	66.7	—	11.5
1774	100	—	21.4	45.2	27.5	17.6	42.9	18	14.3	36.4	42.9	27.3	5.6	55.6	—	20.5
1775	100	100	56.7	30.6	25	36.5	100	25.9	30	15.2	48.9	35.3	27.3	100	—	31.4
1776	92.3	—	55.1	63.8	66.7	64.2	83.3	34.9	83.3	48.6	50	66.7	68	—	66.7	44.2
1777	100	100	62	97.7	46.7	56.3	81.3	66.5	66.7	55.6	52.6	60	23.1	100	60	56.6
1778	100	57.1	44	100	31.3	49.1	100	53.6	100	50	45	72.7	18.2	100	60	45.5
1779	100	55.5	43.4	61.2	50	40.5	52	33	83.3	63.2	78.9	100	42.9	100	100	40.6
1780	81.8	83.3	44	75	49.2	40.5	80.6	50	80	64.7	70	100	84.6	—	66.7	44.4
1781	100	78.9	39.8	60.3	42.4	16.7	62.5	35.8	60	17.2	94.1	100	25	50	—	38.6
1782	100	50	23.5	52.5	38	27.8	40	26.9	93.3	21.2	63.6	50	100	100	100	28.5
1783	100	61.5	23.5	52.6	20.3	32.3	45	38.7	58.8	19.7	45	33.4	83.3	100	—	32.9
Total	88	67.6	27.2	52.7	27.9	29.5	64.2	27.7	49.3	35.8	51.7	55.2	36.2	100	80	28.9

* This column is based on the totals in Table 1A, not those in Table 3A.

voted to government publications rose sharply in Massachusetts in 1775, in New York in 1776, and in Pennsylvania in 1777 and remained generally high for several years (through about 1780); in each of these states there was some point at which government documents accounted for more than 60% of the state's output. Altogether, documents amounted to about half the total number of items printed in the country during the early war years, 1776–80, and about 37% of the total for the decade 1774–83. The percentage for the previous decade was naturally much smaller, 15%, making the figure for the entire two decades close to 30% (28.9).

V

If Evans and Bristol do not offer an easy means for obtaining geographical statistics for other subjects or genres besides government documents, the more specialized bibliographies frequently offer no more help: bibliographies of imprints of a given genre often do not contain geographical indexes or tables, and bibliographies of imprints of a particular city or state generally do not have subject indexes. One way of proceeding, short of an item-by-item examination of the Evans-Bristol record, is to look into the bibliographies of certain prominent categories of material and construct a geographical analysis of the entries found there. While this plan will not of course produce a complete picture, it can at least show the geographical distribution of certain key materials. Three categories that are worth looking into for the Revolutionary period—and that have been provided with careful bibliographies—are almanacs, newspapers, and political pamphlets.

Milton Drake's *Almanacs of the United States* (New York: Scarecrow Press, 1962) arranges the entries first by state and then chronologically within each state, making a geographical analysis a simple matter (Table 5). Although Drake records the title dates only, I have assumed that each item was printed in the preceding year; thus the figures I list for 1764 apply to Drake's entries for 1765 almanacs, and so on.[36] Philip Davidson has called the almanacs 'the most widely read of all the printed material in the colonial period,'[37] although it is difficult to measure readership

[36] I have omitted in the counting a few entries that represent only minor variations from other entries and not separate editions.

[37] *Propaganda and the American Revolution, 1763–1783* (Chapel Hill, 1941), p. 223; he believes, however, that the almanacs were 'of little value to the propagandist.' The

TABLE 5

GEOGRAPHICAL DISTRIBUTION OF ALMANACS RECORDED IN DRAKE, 1764–1783

	NH	MA	RI	CT	NY	NJ	PA	DE	MD	VA	NC	SC	GA	Total
1764	1	4	3	4	7	—	11	2	1	1	—	3	—	37
1765	—	3	3	4	9	—	10	2	—	1	—	1	—	33
1766	2	8	2	5	10	—	12	2	2	3	—	1	—	47
1767	2	7	2	5	9	1	11	2	1	1	—	3	—	44
1768	1	19	6	6	10	1	11	2	1	2	—	4	1	64
1769	1	10	1	4	8	1	15	2	1	2	—	2	—	47
1770	1	10	3	5	6	1	13	2	1	2	—	3	—	47
1771	2	12	4	9	5	1	16	2	1	2	—	2	—	56
1772	—	10	2	10	3	1	16	2	1	2	—	5	—	52
1773	—	11	4	8	11	1	13	2	—	2	—	3	—	55
1774	—	13	2	8	14	1	16	2	—	3	—	2	—	61
1775	—	8	4	4	9	1	17	2	1	1	—	1	—	48
1776	—	9	2	5	4	2	16	2	—	1	—	1	—	42
1777	—	4	1	7	6	1	19	1	1	1	—	1	—	42
1778	—	11	1	8	6	1	18	1	1	2	—	2	—	51
1779	—	9	3	6	6	2	21	1	2	1	—	1	—	52
1780	1	10	9	7	7	3	16	1	2	1	—	3	—	60
1781	—	9	3	8	8	4	18	1	4	2	—	2	—	59
1782	1	12	3	11	7	3	17	1	3	1	—	2	1	62
1783	1	11	9	7	10	2	16	1	3	2	1	4	—	67
Total	13	190	67	131	155	27	302	33	26	33	1	46	2	1026
Percentage	1.27	18.52	6.53	12.77	15.11	2.63	29.43	3.22	2.53	3.22	.1	4.48	.19	100

precisely, especially without information on the sizes of editions. Table 5 cannot reveal anything about circulation, but it does show that the production of almanacs seems to have varied directly with the total amount of printing done in a given place. Pennsylvania, with over 300, had by far the largest number during this period, amounting to nearly 30% of the total; Massachusetts came next, with 19%, followed by New York (15%), Connecticut (13%), and Rhode Island (7%). The same

---

political comments in almanacs have been surveyed by Chester Noyes Greenough in 'New England Almanacs, 1766–1775, and the American Revolution,' *Proceedings of the American Antiquarian Society* 45 (1935): 288–316; and by Marion Barber Stowell, 'Revolutionary Almanac-Makers: Trumpeters of Sedition,' *Papers of the Bibliographical Society of America* 73 (1979): 41–61.

five colonies fell in the same order in regard to their total output (Table 3B), although the pattern in which Pennsylvania took over the lead from Massachusetts is not reflected in connection with almanacs, since Pennsylvania had the lead in them throughout this period (except for 1768). The total number of almanacs published in the early years of the war showed a decline, dropping to 48 in 1775 and 42 in 1776 and 1777; otherwise the annual figures from 1771 on never fell below 50 and sometimes rose into the 60s.

VI

The newspapers were a more important vehicle for political expression: in John C. Miller's words, 'The American Revolution was one of the first great popular movements in which the newspapers played a vital part.'[38] One measure of their importance has been suggested by Bruce Granger, who finds that of the 530 political satires published during this period 70% appeared in newspapers.[39] They have therefore received much attention, and some of the discussions—such as Davidson's and Schlesinger's—occasionally cite precise figures regarding the number and location of papers at a particular time.[40] One great advantage that students of early American newspapers have had is the availability for a long time of Clarence Brigham's excellent bibliography, first published serially between 1913 and 1927 and then in a revised edition in 1947.[41] The arrangement of Brigham's work, however, does not encourage a chronological approach to the material, for he takes up the newspapers in alphabetical order under each state and does not include a chronological index; as a result, it was a difficult task to locate all the papers of a particular year or period. Harry B. Weiss recognized this difficulty and published

[38] *Origins of the American Revolution* (Boston, 1943), p. 288. Pauline Maier, in *From Resistance to Revolution* (New York, 1972), also calls the newspapers 'the prime vehicle of uniting the population'—hence the 'special significance of printers' memberships in the Sons of Liberty' (p. 91).

[39] *Political Satire in the American Revolution, 1763–1783* (Ithaca, N.Y., 1960), pp. viii, 6.

[40] Davidson, *Propaganda and the American Revolution*, pp. 225–26, 394; Schlesinger, *Prelude to Independence: The Newspaper War on Britain, 1764–1776* (New York, 1958), pp. 67, 85.

[41] *History and Bibliography of American Newspapers, 1690–1820* (Worcester, 1947). Additions and corrections have been published in the *Proceedings of the American Antiquarian Society* 71 (1961): 15–62 and 87 (1977): 415–18. Brigham discusses the circulation of newspapers in the Revolutionary years in *Journals and Journeymen* (Philadelphia, 1950), pp. 19–22.

a 'graphic summary' of Brigham in 1948, but it showed the number of papers by state and year only in graphs and did not identify them precisely.[42] This problem has now been solved with the publication of Edward Connery Lathem's chronological tables,[43] which enable one to tell at a glance what papers were published in any given year through 1820. His tables make feasible the construction of a summary table, showing the number of newspapers and the number of places with newspapers in each colony during the Revolutionary years. Such a summary is offered in Table 6, based strictly on Lathem. The resulting figures may somewhat exaggerate the number of papers available at any given moment, since some titles do not run throughout calendar years: if, for instance, five titles were published in a particular colony during the course of a single year, that figure appears in the table, even though no more than three perhaps were being published at any one time during the year. Furthermore, changes of title which Brigham accords separate entry are treated as different papers in Lathem, although in some cases it might be possible to regard them as continuations of a single paper.

Figured on this basis, there were more newspapers (44) during 1775 than any other year before 1783, though several other years between 1775 and 1783 came close. In general, there was a steady increase in the number of papers over the first of these decades, running from 23 in 1764 to 34 in 1773, and in the number of places where the papers were published, running from 15 to 20; in the second decade the figures moved up and down more erratically, with the number of papers averaging about 41 and the places about 23. Altogether 137 papers were published in 44 locations during the course of these twenty years. New York accounted for the largest number (28), with Massachusetts (25) and Pennsylvania (23) close behind, the three together representing more than half (55%) the total. The figures for the three major cities in these colonies run as follows: New York City had a total of 23 different titles and averaged about 4 in any given year; Philadelphia's total was 18, with an average of slightly over 5; and Boston's total was 15, with an average of a little under 5. More papers were produced in Massachusetts outside of Boston than were produced in either of the other colonies outside their main cities; in 1775, when 10 papers were available in Massachusetts at some time during the year, only 5 were published in Boston (the same number

---

[42] See note 12, above.
[43] *Chronological Tables of American Newspapers, 1690–1820* (Barre, Mass., 1972).

TABLE 6

GEOGRAPHICAL ANALYSIS OF NUMBER OF PLACES WITH NEWSPAPERS AND NUMBER OF NEWSPAPERS, AS RECORDED IN LATHEM'S TABLES, 1764–1783

(Places precede the oblique lines; newspapers follow them)

	NH	VT	MA	RI	CT	NY	NJ	PA	MD	VA	NC	SC	GA	FL	Total
1764	1/1	—	1/4	2/2	3/3	1/3	—	2/4	1/1	1/1	1/1	1/2	1/1	—	15/23
1765	1/2	—	1/4	2/2	3/3	1/3	1/1	2/4	1/1	1/1	1/2	1/3	1/1	—	16/27
1766	1/2	—	1/4	2/2	3/3	1/4	—	2/5	1/1	1/2	1/1	1/3	1/1	—	15/28
1767	1/1	—	1/5	2/2	3/4	1/4	—	2/5	1/1	1/2	—	1/3	1/1	—	14/28
1768	1/1	—	2/7	2/2	3/4	1/4	—	2/5	1/1	1/2	1/1	1/3	1/1	—	16/31
1769	1/1	—	2/7	2/2	3/3	1/4	—	2/6	1/1	1/2	1/1	1/3	1/1	—	16/31
1770	1/1	—	2/7	2/2	3/3	1/4	—	2/5	1/1	1/2	2/2	1/3	1/1	—	17/31
1771	1/1	—	2/6	2/2	3/3	1/4	—	2/6	1/1	1/2	2/2	1/3	1/1	—	18/31
1772	1/1	—	2/6	2/2	3/3	2/4	—	2/6	1/1	1/2	2/2	1/3	1/1	—	18/31
1773	1/1	—	3/7	2/2	4/4	2/4	—	2/6	2/2	1/2	2/2	1/3	1/1	—	20/34
1774	1/1	—	3/8	2/2	4/4	1/3	—	2/6	2/2	2/3	2/2	1/3	1/1	—	21/35
1775	1/1	—	5/10	2/2	4/4	1/4	1/1	2/8	2/3	2/5	2/2	1/3	1/1	—	24/44
1776	2/3	—	4/8	2/2	4/4	1/4	2/2	2/7	2/3	1/3	1/1	1/3	1/1	—	23/39
1777	2/2	—	3/5	2/2	4/4	3/7	1/1	3/8	2/3	1/2	1/1	1/2	—	—	23/37
1778	2/3	—	2/7	2/2	4/4	3/5	2/2	2/10	1/3	1/2	1/1	1/3	—	—	21/42
1779	3/3	—	2/6	2/3	4/4	3/6	2/2	2/8	2/4	1/2	—	1/3	1/1	—	23/42
1780	1/1	—	2/6	2/4	4/4	3/6	2/2	1/5	2/2	2/3	—	1/4	1/1	—	20/38
1781	1/1	1/1	3/8	2/4	4/4	3/6	2/2	1/7	2/2	1/2	1/1	1/3	1/1	—	22/41
1782	1/1	—	4/8	2/2	4/4	4/8	2/2	1/7	2/2	1/2	—	2/3	1/1	—	24/40
1783	1/1	2/2	4/9	2/2	4/5	3/15	3/3	1/8	2/3	1/3	—	1/5	1/1	1/1	26/58
Total	3/6	3/3	6/25	2/5	4/6	5/28	7/7	3/23	2/5	3/10	2/4	2/12	1/2	1/1	44/137

as in the preceding four years), reflecting once again the removal of printers from Boston at the beginning of the war (in that year papers appeared
in five places in Massachusetts but in only two in Pennsylvania and one
in New York). These statistics do not in themselves, of course, reveal anything about the nature of the newspapers, but they can help to provide
a perspective for viewing more detailed information. For instance, Timothy M. Barnes's recent annotated checklist of loyalist newspapers of this
period records 27 items: 7 from New York and Pennsylvania, 5 from
Massachusetts, 3 from South Carolina, and 1 each from New Hampshire,
Rhode Island, Connecticut, Virginia, and Georgia.[44] Such figures have
more meaning when seen against the background of the total number of
papers. The most sophisticated statistical analysis of newspaper printers
during this period has been undertaken by Mary Ann Yodelis, and for
detailed statistics on Boston in particular her work should be consulted.[45]

VII

Probably the most significant category of printed matter in the Revolutionary years was the political pamphlet. Philip Davidson sums up the
matter: 'The thousands of pamphlets extant attest the fact that it was the
accepted medium on both sides of the Atlantic for the dissemination of
ideas. . . . The pamphlet in the prerevolutionary period was vitally and
peculiarly the medium through which was developed the solid framework of constitutional thought.'[46] Where were these 'thousands' of pamphlets printed, how many 'thousands' were there, and how did their output vary over the years? In 1940 Homer L. Calkin speculated, 'It is difficult to determine exactly the number of pamphlets written during the

[44] 'Loyalist Newspapers of the American Revolution, 1763–1783: A Bibliography,'
Proceedings of the American Antiquarian Society 83 (1973): 217–40. See also his Ph.D. dissertation, 'The Loyalist Press in the American Revolution, 1765–1781' (University
of New Mexico, 1970).

[45] See note 13, above. See also Gerald J. Baldasty, 'Flirting with Social Science:
Methodology and Virginia Newspapers, 1785–86,' *Journalism History* 1 (1974): 86–88;
and Dwight L. Teeter, 'A Legacy of Expression: Philadelphia Newspapers and Congress during the War for Independence 1775–1783' (Ph.D. diss., University of Wisconsin, 1966)—which points out, 'The lack of state and local studies of the press during the Revolution is so great that a satisfactory book [on newspapers during the Rev-
olution] could now be written only with great difficulty' (p. i). Warren E. Stickle III
discusses state financing of newspapers in 'State and Press in New Jersey during the
American Revolution,' *New Jersey History* 86 (1968): 158–70, 236–49.

[46] *Propaganda and the American Revolution*, pp. 209–10.

period from 1763 to 1783. It seems likely that there were between 1200 and 1500, possibly more, published during this period.'[47] He did not give a source for his figures but added that the most influential pamphlets appeared during 1765–66, 1768–69, and 1774–76. A quarter of a century later Bernard Bailyn, in his careful study of the pamphlets, had no figures other than Calkin's to turn to, although his own examination of over 400 pamphlets through 1776 enabled him to say that 'several hundred of them bearing on the Anglo-American controversy were published between 1750 and 1776.'[48] In the same year, however, the basis for an accurate accounting of the pamphlets in at least part of this period became available in Thomas R. Adams's admirable *American Independence*, which presents bibliographical descriptions of the pamphlets between 1764 and July 4, 1776.[49] Adams includes English pamphlets if they were reprinted in America or elicited a reply by an American, and he enters later editions of a pamphlet under the first edition, but with cross references under the proper years. Thus it is possible, by going through his pages, not only to see the chronological development of the controversy as reflected in the pamphlets but also to note which pamphlets went through the largest number of editions. Although he provides a table listing the most frequently reprinted pamphlets (Thomas Paine's *Common Sense* went through twenty-five American editions, more than twice as many as the second-place pamphlet), he does not offer any summary statistics or indexes showing the geographical distribution of the printers of the pamphlets. Table 7A has therefore been constructed to serve as one kind of summary of the data recorded by Adams. In using it one should remember that a number of pamphlet sermons not included by Adams (because their titles do not suggest that they are explicitly or largely concerned with political matters) do contain important political expression, and

[47] 'Pamphlets and Public Opinion during the American Revolution,' *Pennsylvania Magazine of History and Biography* 64 (1940): 23.

[48] *Pamphlets of the American Revolution, 1750–1776* (Cambridge, Mass., 1965), p. 8. Bailyn's extensive introduction to this collection of pamphlets has been published separately in revised form as *The Ideological Origins of the American Revolution* (Cambridge, Mass., 1967).

[49] *American Independence, The Growth of an Idea: A Bibliographical Study of the American Political Pamphlets Printed between 1764 and 1776 Dealing with the Dispute between Great Britain and Her Colonies* (Providence, 1965); supplemented by 'Additions and Corrections to *American Independence: The Growth of an Idea*,' *Papers of the Bibliographical Society of America* 69 (1975): 398–402. Any statistics derived from Adams in what follows take into account the information in the 'Additions and Corrections.'

TABLE 7A

Geographical Analysis of American-Printed Political Pamphlets
Recorded in Adams, 1764–1776

(First editions precede the oblique lines; later editions follow them)

	MA	RI	CT	NY	PA	DE	MD	VA	NC	SC	GA	Totals		Percentage
1764	5/0	—	1/0	—	—	—	—	1/0	—	—	—	7/0	7	1.8
1765	3/1	4/0	1/0	0/1	1/0	—	1/2	—	1/0	—	1/1	12/5	17	4.4
1766	6/5	3/0	4/1	1/2	4/1	—	1/0	1/1	—	0/1	—	20/11	31	8.1
1767	1/1	1/0	—	1/1	—	—	—	—	—	1/0	—	4/2	6	1.6
1768	0/3	1/0	—	1/3	4/2	—	—	—	—	—	—	6/8	14	3.6
1769	7/8	—	—	—	0/2	—	—	0/1	—	2/2	—	9/13	22	5.7
1770	5/7	—	1/0	—	1/0	—	—	—	—	—	—	7/7	14	3.6
1771	2/1	—	0/1	—	—	—	—	—	—	—	—	2/2	4	1
1772	2/1	—	—	—	—	—	—	—	—	—	1/0	3/1	4	1
1773	9/11	0/1	1/2	1/2	0/1	—	—	—	—	—	—	11/17	28	7.3
1774	12/14	0/2	2/5	12/7	8/11	0/1	—	3/1	—	3/0	—	40/41	81	21.1
1775	20/7	1/4	3/1	15/10	9/8	0/2	0/1	1/0	0/1	—	—	49/34	83	21.6
1776	6/9	0/7	4/5	3/6	11/19	0/1	—	1/0	—	0/2	2/1	25/49	74	19.2
Totals	78/68	10/14	17/15	34/32	38/44	0/4	2/3	7/3	1/1	6/5	2/1	195/190		
	146	24	32	66	82	4	5	10	2	11	3	385		
Percentage	37.9	6.2	8.3	17.2	21.3	1	1.3	2.6	.5	2.9	.8			100

the figures therefore do not take into account quite all the pamphlets that contributed to the political debate.

According to these figures, 195 pamphlets on the question of American independence were first published in America between 1764 and mid-1776 (Adams lists a total of 237 pamphlets, but 42 of them originated abroad). More than half (114, or 58%) appeared in the two and a half years 1774–76, and another 20% came out in 1764–66, at the time of the Sugar and Stamp Acts; during six and a half years of crisis, 1764–66 and 1773–76, 84% of the pamphlets first appeared, with the intervening six years (1767–72) producing only 16%. The number of reprinted pamphlets (that is, new editions of pamphlets previously published either in America or abroad) was nearly as large, amounting to 190 for these years; and roughly the same number of them (83%) as of the first editions appeared in 1764–66 and 1773–76, although the distribution was somewhat different, with a greater concentration (74%) falling in the 1773–76 period. By far the greatest number were produced in Massachusetts (146)—indeed, the number of pamphlets first printed there (78) is more than the number first printed in Pennsylvania and New York combined—with Pennsylvania coming second (82), followed by New York (66), Connecticut (32), and Rhode Island (24). Altogether these five colonies accounted for 91% of the total; and, as the solid block of figures in the lower left part of the table suggests, 65% of the total was produced in these five colonies during the three and a half years preceding the Declaration of Independence. Of the 117 first editions published in those five colonies during those years, 106 (or 91%) were contributed by Massachusetts, New York, and Pennsylvania (with New York, in this instance, coming second). One indication of Massachusetts's prominence as a source of new material is the fact that Massachusetts led by 16 over New York in the output of new pamphlets in 1773–76, whereas in the output of reprints it led only by two over Pennsylvania; or, stated another way, Pennsylvania's second-place position results more from its output of reprints than of first editions, whereas Massachusetts's output of first editions exceeds its output of later editions by a greater margin than in the case of any other colony.

Since Massachusetts, Pennsylvania, and New York dominated the production of political pamphlets, it is natural that the leading printers of pamphlets should have been in Boston, Philadelphia, and New York City. Table 7B compares the output of the most prolific firms. The Whig firm of Edes & Gill (Boston), in first place, produced 16% of the total for 1764–76, twice the number produced by the second-place (Tory) firm, James Rivington (New York); then there is another considerable drop, with the next four printers (two from Philadelphia, one from Boston, and one from New York) falling in the 3–4% range. Although Edes & Gill leads in the number both of first editions (34) and of later editions (28), the ranking of some other printers varies according to whether one looks at first or later editions. For example, William & Thomas Bradford (Philadelphia), in sixth place as far as total output of pamphlets is concerned, moves to third place if one considers only original pamphlets; and Robert Bell (Philadelphia), in third place for his total of 17 pamphlets, takes second place in regard to the number of reprinted pamphlets. The top eight printers of pamphlets, taken together, accounted for 42% of all the first editions in 1764–76 and 50% of all the later editions.

Two other measures of the importance of particular printers in producing political pamphlets are illustrated in Table 7C. The first approach is to note which firms produced the most often reprinted pamphlets. Here again Edes & Gill is clearly the leader: there were, during this period (1764–76), 23 later American editions and 27 foreign editions of pamphlets which were first printed by that firm. In second place comes not Rivington (who is second in number of pamphlets originated) but Bell, whose pamphlets went through a total of forty later editions in these years. The reason for Bell's prominence, using this standard, is that he was the printer of *Common Sense*, which by itself accounted for twenty-nine later editions (twenty-four American and five foreign). Rivington is a distant third, followed by two firms which were not among the top printers in Table 7B at all but which originated two often-reprinted pamphlets: Hall & Sellers (Philadelphia) first printed in pamphlet form John Dickinson's *Letters from a Farmer in Pennsylvania* (1768), which was reprinted ten times in this period;[50] and James Humphreys (Philadelphia) was the original printer of William Smith's *A Sermon on the Present Situation of American Affairs* (1775), which was reprinted fourteen times. By contrast Edes & Gill's position is all the more impressive, because it is not the result of one or two pamphlets that were reprinted in large numbers, but

[50] Dickinson's *Letters* and Paine's *Common Sense* are the only political pamphlets of this period included in Frank Luther Mott's list of best sellers in *Golden Multitudes* (New York, 1947), p. 304; he estimates that *Common Sense* sold 150,000 copies within the year 1776 (p. 51).

TABLE 7B

OUTPUT OF THE LEADING AMERICAN PRINTERS OF PAMPHLETS
RECORDED IN ADAMS, 1764–1776

	Original Pamphlets		Reprinted Pamphlets		Total	
	No.	%	No.	%	No.	%
Edes & Gill (Boston)	34	17.4	28	14.7	62	16.1
James Rivington (New York)	20	10.3	11	5.8	31	8.1
Robert Bell (Philadelphia)	5	2.6	12	6.3	17	4.4
Thomas & John Fleet (Boston)	5	2.6	11	5.8	16	4.2
John Holt (New York)	4	2.05	11	5.8	15	3.9
William & Thomas Bradford (Philadelphia)	9	4.6	5	2.6	14	3.6
John Dunlap (Philadelphia)	4	2.05	7	3.7	11	2.9
Solomon Southwick (Newport)	—	—	10	5.3	10	2.6
Total	81	41.5	95	50	176	45.7

TABLE 7C

AMERICAN PRINTERS WHOSE PAMPHLETS (PUBLISHED 1764–1776)
WERE REPRINTED MOST OFTEN: THE NUMBER OF
AMERICAN AND FOREIGN REPRINT EDITIONS, 1764–1776,
AND THE NUMBER OF PAMPHLETS INCLUDED IN BAILYN

	American	Foreign	Total	Bailyn
Edes & Gill (Boston)	23	27	50	14
Robert Bell (Philadelphia)	31	9	40	2
James Rivington (New York)	9	12	21	6
Hall & Sellers (Philadelphia)	10	6	16	1
James Humphreys (Philadelphia)	2	13	15	—
William & Thomas Bradford (Philadelphia)	8	4	12	4
Thomas & John Fleet (Boston)	4	8	12	1
John Dunlap (Philadelphia)	5	3	8	2
Total	92	82	174	30
Percentage	48	46	47	43

of a sizable group of pamphlets, each of which called for several editions.
All told, pamphlets originating with the eight printers listed in Table 7c
went through 174 later editions, or nearly half the total number of later

editions recorded in Adams.[51] A second measure of importance is based on present-day scholarly evaluation of the significance of individual pamphlets. For this purpose, one turns to Bernard Bailyn's selection of sixty-nine pamphlets dated 1764–76 for inclusion in his 1965 anthology.[52] Edes & Gill is again the unquestioned leader, for fourteen of the pamphlets were first printed by that firm; next is Rivington, with six, followed by the Bradfords, with four.[53]

One way of extending the coverage of pamphlets beyond Adams's ending date of 1776 is to analyze the entries in James E. Mooney's checklist of loyalist imprints, 1774–85.[54] Mooney's criteria for inclusion are of course quite different from Adams's: he admits broadsides, for example, as Adams does not, and his coverage in general is broader. But since he defines loyalist imprints as material 'written by, for, about, and against Loyalists,' and since the bulk of the items (aside from the broadsides) can be regarded as pamphlets, his list provides another approach to the genre of the political pamphlet, broadly conceived to include some government documents. Table 7D shows the geographical and annual breakdown of this material through 1783, with the broadsides recorded separately from the other items. Whether one looks at the non-broadside items or the totals, New York is in first place with 28%, followed by Pennsylvania (22.5% of non-broadside items), and then, at a considerable distance, Massachusetts (12.5%), Rhode Island (6.7%), Maryland (5.8%), and Connecticut (5%). Maryland's presence in this list is interesting because it has not been in the top five in the other approaches tabulated here. The years with the greatest output relating to loyalists are, not surprisingly, the 1770s (1775 in particular), with the numbers falling off noticeably in the early 1780s. Although New York and Boston dominated in the production of loyalist pamphlets in 1774–75, New York's leadership was

[51] Only 3 pamphlets first printed in England went through more than 8 later editions (the figure for Dunlap, the last figure in Table 7C): they are Adams 134 (10 later editions), 141 (15), and 224 (25).

[52] This work contains 72 pamphlets, but 3 of them are from before 1764.

[53] Although Bailyn's text for pamphlet 53 (Adams 125), Charles Lee's *Strictures* (1774), is based on Timothy Green's New London 1775 edition, it is here counted for the Bradfords, who printed the first edition.

[54] 'Loyalist Imprints Printed in America, 1774–1785,' *Proceedings of the American Antiquarian Society* 84 (1974): 105–218. Evans, Bristol, and Shipton-Mooney numbers are supplied; but the list includes several items that are not recorded in those 3 works —see pp. 125 (4th complete entry), 132 (2nd), 154 (2nd), 161 (3rd), 179 (1st), and 216 (5th).

TABLE 7D

GEOGRAPHICAL ANALYSIS OF LOYALIST IMPRINTS RECORDED IN MOONEY, 1774–1783

(Broadsides precede the oblique lines; books of more than one page follow them)

	NH	VT	MA	RI	CT	NY	NJ	PA	DE	MD	VA	NC	SC	GA	np	Totals		%
1774	3/0	—	10/8	2/1	2/3	21/20	—	3/6	—	—	4/1	—	0/2	5/0	0/2	50/43	93	10.8
1775	1/0	1/6	26/18	4/2	4/1	35/25	—	8/12	—	6/3	4/4	2/0	—	—	7/6	98/77	175	20.3
1776	—	1/0	6/1	2/1	2/1	13/6	—	16/16	—	—	1/2	—	0/2	—	2/1	43/30	73	8.5
1777	1/0	1/0	4/3	2/0	3/4	12/11	—	35/12	—	2/1	0/1	1/0	0/2	1/5	3/1	65/40	105	12.2
1778	1/0	0/1	1/5	2/2	0/3	1/18	1/3	24/18	0/1	1/5	—	1/1	0/1	—	3/1	35/59	94	10.9
1779	—	0/1	1/5	2/8	0/2	10/11	0/2	8/11	—	4/7	0/4	0/2	0/1	6/0	0/1	31/55	86	10
1780	0/1	0/1	1/4	0/2	0/2	9/16	0/2	7/11	—	0/4	0/1	0/2	6/4	0/1	2/1	25/52	77	9
1781	—	0/1	1/2	1/2	3/4	4/9	0/2	6/3	1/0	0/2	0/1	—	1/0	—	0/1	17/27	44	5.1
1782	—	—	2/3	1/8	0/1	2/7	0/1	2/8	3/0	3/2	0/1	0/2	1/2	0/1	—	14/36	50	5.8
1783	0/1	0/1	3/9	1/5	0/2	7/8	—	0/7	—	1/3	0/3	0/1	2/1	2/3	6/0	20/44	64	7.4
Totals	6/2	3/11	55/58	17/31	14/23	112/131	1/10	109/104	4/1	17/27	9/18	4/8	10/15	14/10	23/14	398/463	861	100
	8	14	113	48	37	243	11	213	5	44	27	12	25	24	37			
Percentage	.9	1.6	13.1	5.6	4.3	28.2	1.3	24.7	.6	5.1	3.1	1.4	2.9	2.8	4.3			

shared with Philadelphia from 1776 on (a shift reflecting the changing locations of the British army). Altogether Mooney records 861 loyalist items from 1774 through 1783, of which 398 (46%) are broadsides.

VIII

One could, in a similar manner, go through checklists of other classes of material, working out the geographical distribution of the entries for 1764–83. It is rare to encounter a listing that, like Drake's on almanacs, provides for ready access both by chronology and by geography. Ray O. Hummel's *Southeastern Broadsides before 1877* (Richmond: Virginia State Library, 1971) is one such, with the entries divided first by state and then arranged chronologically; from his book, therefore, it is easy to determine that, among the southern colonies, the one with the largest number of located and dated broadsides during this period is Virginia (thirty-three), followed by South Carolina (twenty-four) and Georgia (twelve).[55] Another bibliography admirable in this respect is Irving Lowens's *A Bibliography of Songsters Printed in America before 1821* (Worcester: American Antiquarian Society, 1976); its basic arrangement is chronological, but it is exemplary in providing tables of geographical statistics in the introduction (pp. xiv–xv) and in furnishing an index of printers arranged geographically and specifying the date of each cited entry. Thus one can determine immediately that twenty-five songsters were printed in the 1764–83 period, principally in New York (nine), Philadelphia (eight), and Boston (five). Generally, however, chronological lists are neither subdivided according to location nor supplied with geographical indexes or statistics. One subject of natural interest in this period is military books, and from John Henry Stanley's list[56] one can quickly calculate that of the 125 military manuals printed in America during this period, 74 (or 59%) appeared in the space of four years (1774–77) and 92 (or 73%) within six years (1774–79); but an analysis of each entry would be required to discover the geographical distribution.[57] In the case of Bibles, Margaret

---

[55] Various categories are excluded, such as blank forms, maps, music, and official publications. Hummel has supplemented the Virginia section with *More Virginia Broadsides before 1877* (Richmond, 1975), which includes 44 more dated broadsides for the 1764–83 period.

[56] 'Preliminary Investigation of Military Manuals of American Imprint Prior to 1800' (master's thesis, Brown University, 1964).

[57] Similarly, Jacob B. Lishchiner's 'Bibliography of American Published Sources, Military Literature: 1645–1799,' in typescript at the American Antiquarian Society,

T. Hills's work,[58] which is arranged chronologically, contains a geographical index of printers, from which one can learn the names for a given area to look up in the alphabetical index of printers. Of course, since the numbers are small for this period, each entry can quickly be checked: Hills records thirteen Bibles for the six years 1777–82 (none in 1783), with eight printed in Philadelphia, three in Trenton, and one each in Boston and Wilmington. A different situation is represented by Louis C. Karpinski's record of mathematics books.[59] As in Adams's bibliography of political pamphlets, later editions of a work are listed following the entry for the first edition; but whereas Adams is dealing with only a few years, Karpinski covers a long period, making it difficult to locate all the imprints of any given shorter period. One can immediately see that between 1764 and 1783 there are six first editions of mathematical works recorded (three from Boston, two from Philadelphia, and one from Portsmouth), but the only way to learn how many other editions there were is either to go through all the entries preceding 1764 or to go through the entire index of printers (for this period the former method is easier, yielding a total of fourteen, with six from Boston and three from both Philadelphia and New York).

Other listings are basically alphabetical but offer chronological indexes or lists. Thus, despite the alphabetical arrangement of the main entries, one can easily learn from Frank Pierce Hill's *American Plays Printed 1714–1830* (Stanford: Stanford University Press, 1934) that thirty plays are recorded for 1764–83 (eight of them in 1775–76, the only years with more than two); from Robert B. Austin's *Early American Medical Imprints . . . 1668–1820* (Washington: U.S. Department of Health, Education, and Welfare, Public Health Service, 1961) that 107 items are known for these twenty years; and from Donald L. Hixon's *Music in Early America: A Bibliography of Music in Evans* (Metuchen, N.J.: Scarecrow Press, 1970) that 65 pieces with music notation are listed for these two de-

---

records 863 items for 1764–83, of which 435 (50 percent) appeared in the 3 years 1775–77.

[58] *The English Bible in America: A Bibliography of Editions of the Bible & the New Testament Published in America, 1777–1957* (New York, 1961).

[59] *Bibliography of Mathematical Works Printed in America through 1850*, with the cooperation of Walter F. Shenton (Ann Arbor, 1940); supplemented in *Scripta Mathematica* 8 (1941–42): 233–36; 11 (1945): 173–77; 20 (1954): 197–202.

cades.[60] But there is no provision for geographical, as well as chronological, access.

Theoretically, another approach to a geographical subject analysis would be through the geographical imprint bibliographies. The works that list imprints of particular states or towns, like those devoted to subjects, can be expected to be more detailed and thorough (because they are more specialized) than those of great breadth, like Evans and Bristol. But there are some difficulties with using them for this purpose. For one thing, although they are generally arranged chronologically, they frequently do not provide subject indexing or even, surprisingly, indexes of printers, and they almost never present any statistical summaries. Lawrence Wroth, for instance, did excellent pioneer work on the imprints of Maryland through 1776,[61] but he did not provide a directory of printers and only included some subjects in his regular index. It is no task to ascertain that he records 144 Maryland imprints for the thirteen years 1764–76, but to generalize about the number and location of printers involved or the kind of material produced would require an item-by-item analysis. Rarely does one find the kind of tabulation presented by Douglas C. McMurtrie in his *Eighteenth Century North Carolina Imprints, 1749–1800* (Chapel Hill: University of North Carolina Press, 1938), which lists the printers (with dates) by location and specifies for each the number of located items with imprints and without imprints and the number of unlocated items; but even this work does not offer any statistics on the types of material printed.

A second problem in using the regional imprint lists as a basis for a geographical subject analysis of the country as a whole is their great unevenness. Some states, such as Rhode Island and Vermont, have been given exemplary coverage for this period in separate bibliographies (by John E. Alden and Marcus A. McCorison),[62] whereas others, such as Massachusetts and New York, have been given none at all (or, as in the case of Pennsylvania, were treated so long ago that the record has been superseded by Evans and Bristol).[63] Lists published after Evans can be ex-

[60] What amounts to a chronological index in Hixon is a 'Numerical Index,' pp. 591–607, recording Evans numbers in numerical order.

[61] *A History of Printing in Colonial Maryland, 1686–1776* (Baltimore, 1922).

[62] Alden, *Rhode Island Imprints, 1727–1800* (New York, 1950); McCorison, *Vermont Imprints, 1778–1820* (Worcester, 1963).

[63] Charles R. Hildeburn, *A Century of Printing: The Issues of the Press of Pennsylvania, 1685–1784* (Philadelphia, 1885–86).

pected to have supplemented his work, but if they were published before 1970 they have presumably been incorporated into (and indeed supplemented by) Bristol. The number of entries recorded by Wroth for Maryland, 1764–76, is 144, and by McMurtrie for North Carolina, 1764–83, is 73, whereas the corresponding numbers found in Table 3A, based on Evans and Bristol combined, are 168 and 105. It would be misleading, in other words, to bring together figures for different colonies which were based on bibliographies produced at widely separated times and perhaps with differing standards for inclusion.

The tables and comments I have set out in the preceding pages not only have presented certain information but also in the process have implied, I hope, some of the shortcomings of the present state of eighteenth-century American bibliography. The figures given are at best rough approximations, and some of the data one wishes to know are still not readily available in the reference works, after all these decades of study. Two recent books, which are outstanding contributions, illustrate the situation. D'Alté A. Welch's *A Bibliography of American Children's Books Printed Prior to 1821* (Worcester: American Antiquarian Society and Barre Publishers, 1972) is arranged alphabetically but has no chronological index; there is an index of printers, giving the inclusive dates for each, but it does not identify the dates of the cited entries. If one wished to study the children's books of a particular decade or generation, then, one would first have to look up all the indexed entry numbers for printers operating during the right period, or else just search methodically through the entire bibliography. The introduction is 'A Chronological History of American Children's Books' (pp. xxi–xliv), but it does not give precise figures for different periods.[64] Frederick E. Bauer, Jr., of the American Antiquarian Society, was recently preparing a paper on the children's books of the Revolutionary years, and in order to find out what the body of material consisted of he had to make a time-consuming search through Welch. It is clearly wasteful of effort for each person with this kind of topic to have to go through all the entries, when one time through could result in a chronological index. Another important publication, Elizabeth Carroll Reilly's *A Dictionary of Colonial American Printers' Ornaments & Illustrations* (Worcester: American Antiquarian Society, 1975), reveals a some-

---

[64] Instead, generalizations of this kind are made: 'After the American Revolution, especially after 1785, there was a marked increase in the production of children's books' (p. xxvii).

what different problem of chronology. It does contain a chronological index; but a tabulation based on that index would not serve as a fair indication of the quantity of illustrated items produced in a given period, because the *Dictionary* records for any printer only 'the first appearance of the given ornament or illustration in each year of its use by that printer.'[65] The work of course fulfills its aim of reproducing each ornament and illustration, but it could so easily have provided at the same time a record of all the printed pieces containing those devices. Both these books are excellent in many other ways, so one regrets all the more that the work has not been carried to its logical conclusion.

It is surprising how often American imprint bibliographies for the eighteenth century—which by their nature are historical reference works —fail to satisfy the demands of certain basic kinds of historical research. In his foreword to McCorison's bibliography of Vermont imprints, Clifford K. Shipton describes a printed item as 'a witness which we can call to the stand to answer our questions about the past.' The Vermont bibliography, therefore, becomes 'a roll of the witnesses of the first period of Vermont history. Using it, the historian can call them up and, with their testimony, revise the history of the State' (pp. ix–x). Shipton is principally concerned here with the content of the listed items, but those items, as pieces of printing, are also witnesses to printing history, and we might have revised the history of early American printing more than we have if the bibliographies in general had been more accommodating. What needs to be undertaken now is a systematic first-hand examination of the printed material (and not merely for the Revolutionary period), using Shipton-Mooney as a guide, in order to record various kinds of information in such a form that they can be retrieved by computer. In addition to the basic elements of an entry (author, brief title, place, printer, bookseller, year, pages, Evans number) and a subject classification, certain physical characteristics should be noted: format, paper, type, system of signatures employed, presence of press figures, inclusion of bookseller's advertisements, nature of running titles, and the like. One could then not merely locate all items of a given year according to subject, city, or printer but also be in a position to learn in detail how the physical appearance of the printed product changed over time or from one part of the country to another, whether certain formats were associated with

---

[65] What is meant by 'first' here is not the earliest use during the year but the lowest relevant Evans or Bristol number—that is, merely the first item alphabetically.

particular subjects, whether the printers of one area or period preferred a specific pattern of signature notation, and so on. Such study of the localization of printed matter not ony contributes to printing history but helps in assigning dates or printers to previously unidentified items.[66] Furthermore, the recording of such details may aid in the discovery of unrecognized variants; as Edwin Wolf has effectively pointed out, the comparison of multiple copies of American printed items of historical, rather than literary, significance has been a largely neglected activity but one that promises to yield a great deal of new bibliographical information.[67] That kind of analysis has been applied extensively to English books of the Renaissance because of the importance of many of the texts in those books; while it is true that there are considerably fewer eighteenth-century American books of interest for their texts, such analysis is not simply an aid to editing but a means of uncovering significant historical facts about printers' methods of operation. What must be coupled with this kind of data, of course, in order to achieve a fuller picture, is information about the economics of the printing trade and the sizes of editions—information which is not easy to come by but which does turn up in occasional contracts or day books which have survived.[68]

A fully comprehensive project of this sort would result in far more reliable and detailed statistics than are now possible on a large scale. In the meantime, one can derive certain very rough approximations from published bibliographies, as I have done here. One can see, for example, that the magnitude of printed matter during the Revolutionary years was something on the order of 600 items per year, with 1775 and the immedi-

[66] For a good example of this kind of study, devoted to European books, see R. A. Sayce, 'Compositorial Practices and the Localization of Printed Books, 1530–1800,' *Library*, 5th ser. 21 (1966): 1–45.

[67] 'Historical Grist for the Bibliographical Mill,' *Studies in Bibliography* 25 (1972): 29–40.

[68] See, for example, Rollo G. Silver, 'Three Eighteenth-Century American Book Contracts,' *Papers of the Bibliographical Society of America* 47 (1953): 381–87 (all later than 1783), and his 'Government Printing in Massachusetts, 1751–1801,' *Studies in Bibliography* 16 (1963): 161–200; and Marcus A. McCorison, 'The Wages of John Carter's Journeyman Printers, 1771–1779,' *Proceedings of the American Antiquarian Society* 81 (1971): 273–303 (Carter's account book 'shows dramatically the difficulties caused by the disruptions of the American War of Independence'). This kind of information, in turn, must be studied in relation to the figures set forth in such works as Stella H. Sutherland, *Population Distribution in Colonial America* (New York, 1936), and Anne Bezanson, *Prices and Inflation during the American Revolution: Pennsylvania 1770–1790* (Philadelphia, 1951).

ately surrounding years forming a peak; that the dominant position of religious works in the printed output declined sharply in these years, with the percentage devoted to political science, history, and law surpassing theology for the first time in the early war years; that Pennsylvania took over from Massachusetts during this period as the leading source of printed material, with the two together accounting for more than half the total number of items; that the cities of Philadelphia, Boston, and New York produced about 55% of the total; that 300 or more printers were engaged in business during these two decades at something like six dozen towns (more towns in Massachusetts than in any other single colony); that the geographical concentration of printing in the New England and middle colonies was such that five of them (Pennsylvania, Massachusetts, New York, Connecticut, and Rhode Island) turned out over 80% of the total; that the Boston firm of Edes & Gill was the leading printer in America at this time, both in number of items printed and probably in influence as well, judging from the number and importance of the political pamphlets originating with it; that two firms, John Dunlap of Philadelphia along with Edes & Gill, were responsible for nearly 10% of the total output of these years; that the production of government publications increased greatly in the decade 1774–83, averaging about 37% of the total; and that well over half of the political pamphlets on the question of independence appeared in the two and a half years preceding the Declaration. Although such statistics as these tell one nothing about the number of copies printed or the money involved, they do serve to fill in, with broad strokes, some of the background against which the work of individual printers or the activity in particular localities must be viewed. Their suggestiveness, in fact, makes one look forward to the time when they are superseded by figures of greater refinement and dependability.

Afterword: The Legacy of the Press in the American Revolution

JAMES RUSSELL WIGGINS

A MERE HANDFUL of weekly newspapers, in the closing decades of the eighteenth century, helped rouse the American colonies of Great Britain to flaming resentment at the arbitrary acts of the British ministry, then fanned that resentment into rebellion, shaped it toward Revolution, turned it to a demand for Independence, and joined statesmen in building a new nation.

If they were the collaborators of patriots and politicians in these great tasks, they were the chief architects of one aspect of the new nation they helped to build. That nation's concept of freedom of the press was in large part their own especial handiwork.

EDITOR'S NOTE: The author of this Afterword has spent his working life following the vocation of a newspaperman, while pursuing the avocation of history. He began his newspaper career at the age of eighteen as a reporter for the *Rock Country Star* in his native Luverne, Minnesota, and after that served in a variety of high positions with the *St. Paul Dispatch* and *Pioneer Press*, the *New York Times*, and the *Washington Post*. He was the *Post*'s editor and executive vice-president from 1960 to 1968.

President Lyndon B. Johnson appointed Mr. Wiggins United States ambassador to the United Nations, a position he occupied in 1968 and 1969. Since then, Mr. Wiggins has been editor and publisher of the *Ellsworth American*, a lively weekly newspaper located near his home in Brooklin, Maine.

Mr. Wiggins's deep interest in American history led to his election in 1963 to membership in the American Antiquarian Society. He served as president of the Society from 1969 to 1977.

Mr. Wiggins has long been concerned with the rights of newspapermen in all countries, especially for the need for full access by journalists to the proceedings of governments. In 1956 he published an important book on this subject, entitled *Freedom or Secrecy*, and he has continued in recent years to write and speak on this theme. His Afterword in the present volume of essays renews his consideration of the issues of press freedom. It is the work of an eminent twentieth-century journalist seeking current meaning in the legacy left by his Revolutionary predecessors.

They derived these concepts, which went far beyond those propounded in England by Blackstone and Fox, from the experience in making a revolution. They had gained, in their struggle, a truer understanding of the inseparable relationship between a free society and a free press than that possessed by any other people. That conception, so far in advance of their own time, and so little understood in many portions of the world now, two centuries later, is their unique and distinctive bequest to American society.[1]

They understood very well that if a society is to have freedom of the press, it must allow (1) access to information; (2) the right to print without prior restraint; (3) the right to print without sanguinary reprisal for publication alleged to be wrongful; (4) the right of access to the means of publication; and (5) the right to distribute printed material.

The right to get information about their own government was a continuing colonial effort. The notion that secrecy should envelop even legislative bodies had a long tradition in England, and it attended colonial governments to this hemisphere. The English House of Commons, in the sixteenth century, closed its proceedings to protect members from the reprisals of the monarch. In the seventeenth century the House habitually concluded enactments by warning that only the parliamentary printer was to publish any of its proceedings. Parliament did not relinquish this secrecy until the Wilkes case in 1771.

As late as 1725 (May 13), the Massachusetts Council passed an order to the effect that 'the printers of the newspapers in Boston be ordered upon their peril not to insert in their prints anything of public affairs of this province relating to the war without the order of government.' Assemblies generally met in secret. Slowly, a different view took over in the colonies. By 1747, the New York General Assembly had passed this declaration: 'Resolved that it is the undoubted right of the people of this colony to know the proceedings of their representatives in General Assembly and that any attempt to prevent their proceedings being printed or published is a violation of the rights and liberties of the people of this colony.'

The proceedings of the Massachusetts General Court were opened to

---

[1] On the subject of freedom of the press, see the extended treatment in this volume by Richard Buel, Jr., 'Freedom of the Press in Revolutionary America: The Evolution of Libertarianism, 1760–1820.' The essay by Stephen Botein, 'Printers and the American Revolution,' above, also bears on this subject.

the public on June 3, 1766, so citizens might hear the debates, on the motion of James Otis. Samuel Adams had written the *Public Advertiser* of Boston, at a very early period, 'Whoever acquaints us that we have no right to examine into the conduct of those who, though they derive their power from us to serve the common interests, make use of it to impoverish and ruin us, is in a degree a rebel—to the undoubted rights and liberties of the people.'[2]

The struggle for access to government proceedings was always lively in Massachusetts, but sharpened as revolution approached. When the Massachusetts Council received Governor Francis Bernard's plan for quartering British troops, in 1768, the Council headed by James Bowdoin, in spite of the governor's wishes, made the plans public. The governor said 'no civilized Government upon earth' could function when its intimate deliberations were 'canvassed by Tavern politicians and censured by News Paper Libellers.'

In 1769 Governor Bernard's confidential letters to the British ministry were printed by the *Boston Gazette* and the *Evening-Post*, creating such indignation in Boston that he sailed for England on August 1, 1769, never to return.

In 1773, Governor Thomas Hutchinson's confidential letters to Thomas Whately, former undersecretary of treasury in Grenville's ministry, were revealed to a closed session of the Massachusetts Assembly, under an injunction that they were not to be published. Benjamin Franklin had obtained them from a source never divulged to this day. He sent them to the Speaker of the Massachusetts House on December 2, 1772, with instructions that they were not to be copied, but shown only to the Committee of Correspondence and some specified persons. The package reached Boston in March 1773. Rumors about them circulated quickly. Sam Adams had them read aloud to the whole House. The *Massachusetts Spy*, on June 3, wrote of 'amazing discoveries' in the letters. By June 15, all restraints broke down and Edes and Gill of the *Boston Gazette* printed the incriminating letters in pamphlet form. They destroyed Hutchinson as the Bernard letters had destroyed the earlier governor, for they appeared to disclose that he had advocated secretly measures prejudicial to the freedom of the citizens of Massachusetts. Hutchinson complained that the letters had been selected and edited to damage him and he was

2 William V. Wells, *The Life and Public Services of Samuel Adams*, 3 vols. (Boston, 1865), 1:17.

stoutly defended by some, but his reputation did not survive the odium that the disclosed correspondence heaped upon him.[3]

The printers who had hammered at the doors of colonial assemblies and sought access to the proceedings of Governor's Councils, persisted in their effort to find out about the transactions of their own government, after the American Revolution. State after state provided for the access to legislative proceedings. In the first Congress under the Constitution, the House was open but the Senate did not regularly admit the public to either legislative or executive sessions until February 20, 1794. The present-day expansion of the 'people's right to know' grows from the beginnings made by small weekly newspapers in the closing decades of the eighteenth century.

Government's right to prior restraint was accepted in the colonies, as it had been accepted in England. The Massachusetts General Court in October 1662 passed the first formal act of censorship of the press in the following terms: 'for the prevention of irregularities and abuse to the authority of this country by the printing presse, it is ordered that henceforth no copie shall be printed but by the allowance, first had and obtained under the hands of Cpt. Daniel Gookin & Jonathan Mitchel, until this Court shall take further order therein.'[4] The American colonists rapidly shed such restraints. After 1765, they invoked William Blackstone, whose commentaries had the widest legal currency in the colonies. By the time the government was established under the United States Constitution, if there was one settled principle about the press, it was that prior restraint was improper. At the height of the Federalist attacks on the press, in the John Adams administration, even the most extreme Federalist senators disavowed any intention to impose prior restraint. They had, by that time, come to the view that press freedom meant only immunity to prior restraint.[5]

The precarious position of a press without access to the physical means of publication was borne in upon American newspapers and students of the press by the plight of the press from the start of the American Revolution. The English common press, the staple printing apparatus of the

---

[3] Bernard Bailyn, *The Ordeal of Thomas Hutchinson* (Cambridge, Mass., 1974), p. 221.

[4] Clyde A. Duniway, *The Development of Freedom of the Press in Massachusetts* (New York, 1906), p. 41.

[5] For a more detailed discussion of the breakdown of prior restraint, see Buel, 'Freedom of the Press.'

period, could be obtained only in England. The repairs for it had to be purchased in England. There were few typefounders, no type designers. Paper was scarce—so scarce that Washington's tents at Morristown went to make paper after the Continental Army wintered there. Keeping printing plants going, physically, challenged American printers. There is an amusing story of Benjamin Franklin making a timely visit in Worcester and helping repair Isaiah Thomas's failing common press. This was a case of scarcity induced by natural conditions. But society has had to learn that access to printing materials can be reduced by bureaucracies and governments that wish to suppress information and inhibit opinion—which is what happened in Argentina in the years of Perón, when, for example, deferred duties on newsprint were used to close *La Prensa*. The people's access to the means of publication no longer can be fulfilled by the simple availability of the raw materials of publishing. That access to the raw material of opinion, to factual information, to the means of voicing opinion, should not be obstructed is a principle not as easily made effective under modern conditions. But the anxiety to provide access underlies the statutes creating the Federal Communications Commission. An increasingly sensitive federal attitude toward monopoly of the press also reflects a certain nervous realization that the principle grows more difficult to implement. But the impress of the colonial experience remains. Modern American lawmakers would be extremely cautious about imposing any restraints on access by printers to the raw materials of publication. And they would be nervous about press measures exhibiting an indifference to the deliberate exclusion of any segment of public opinion from the columns of newspapers or the channels of the electronic media.

Reprisal for publication disliked by authority was a commonplace in the whole colonial experience. The most celebrated case in the American experience was that of John Peter Zenger who was acquitted of libeling Governor William Cosby after Andrew Hamilton's brilliant defense. But the Zenger case by no means put an end to governmental reprisal. In Massachusetts, Governors Bernard and Hutchinson were repeatedly induced to seek legal reprisal for publications they disliked. Printers were accustomed to this kind of intervention. It was a commonplace of their trade. As the tension grew between the people and the royal governors, however, newspapers got the courage and the strength to make a popular resistance that the governments were reluctant to defy.

Reprisal outside the law and in spite of the law is something else, but the colonial experience gave Americans a familiarity with that, too.[6] Printers like John Mein, of the *Boston Chronicle*, experienced the inhibiting effect of lawless reprisal for unwelcome printed utterance. Mein outraged Whig opinion in Boston by his attacks on 'patriots' who had secretly violated nonimportation agreements. The windows of his shop were broken. His personal safety was threatened. He went about armed. Finally, a mob attacked him on the street. In terror of his life, he fled to a ship in the harbor and went to England. His strong loyalist paper suspended publication on June 25, 1770. The press of James Rivington, loyalist editor of *The New-York Gazetteer*, was demolished and his type was carried away by a mob in 1775, and Rivington fled to England. *The Massachusetts Gazette and Boston News-Letter*, another loyalist paper, published in Boston while the British occupation lasted but thereafter suspended, but no violence was visited upon Margaret Draper.

Much as the patriot newspapers spoke of freedom of the press, a real clash of opinion hostile to the Revolution and that supporting it did not take place in the war years. The patriot editors had no patience with nor sympathy for the Tory press.

Nevertheless, the violence visited upon them, and upon newspapers that dissented from prevailing opinion in subsequent periods of history, took its place in American history as nothing to be applauded and may have had a curious obverse effect as an example of suppression, by extralegal means.

The importance to press freedom of the right to distribute was very forcefully impressed on this country by another experience of the Revolutionary period. Postal service in the American colonies had reached a high level of efficiency by 1764. Mail moved three times a week between Philadelphia and New York, and the royal post office system, under Benjamin Franklin as deputy postmaster general, was both effective and profitable. As the struggle for independence proceeded, the patriot press became increasingly annoyed by the postal establishment. The British system was suspected of interfering with the delivery of patriot newspapers and of opening mail. The *Boston Gazette* and the *Massachusetts Spy* both decried interference with the distribution of their papers.

[6] See Buel, 'Freedom of the Press,' which shows how such extralegal repression of the press during the Revolutionary period may be understood in the context of the ideology of republicanism.

The *New-York Journal* and the *Pennsylvania Journal* protested the refusal of the mail service to handle their papers. William Goddard, editor of the *Maryland Journal* and the *Pennsylvania Chronicle*, in February 1774 commenced the organization of a colonial postal system. On July 26, 1775, the Continental Congress took over the system Goddard had set up and made Benjamin Franklin the postmaster general. On Christmas Day 1775, British postal headquarters in New York canceled all deliveries and left the field.

The principle of unobstructed postal service was thus born before the country was born. It has not always been respected. It was rudely interrupted by Southern postmasters in the days before the Civil War when abolitionist journals were destroyed. It has been disregarded on other occasions. But, thanks to the experience of patriot printers who called forth a new postal service, there is in our society no sanction for intervention with the mails for ideological and political reasons.

The weekly press of the American colonies was certainly not even dimly aware of forming a coherent and related doctrine of freedom of the press. They proceeded pragmatically to its principles as successive challenges arose.[7] Their doctrine of press freedom got no worldwide welcome from contemporary society. It was no more welcome than other theories of liberty that emerged in the struggle for Independence.

The world climate of opinion was very well described by one American patriot, the Reverend Samuel Williams, of Salem, Massachusetts, in his *Discourse on the Love of Our Country* in 1775. Williams said:

> Throughout the whole continent of Asia people are reduced to such a degree of abusement and degradation that the very idea of liberty is unknown among them. In Africa, scarce any human beings are to be found but barbarians, tyrants, and slaves: all equally remote from the true dignity of human nature and from a well-regulated state of society. Nor is Europe free from the curse. Most of her nations are forced to drink deep of the bitter cup. And in those in which freedom seems to have been established, the vital flame is going out. Two kingdoms, those of Sweden and Poland, have been betrayed and enslaved in the course of one year. The free towns of Germany can remain free no longer than their potent neighbors shall

---

[7] The printers' essentially pragmatic response to changing business and political conditions in the Revolutionary period is emphasized in Botein, 'Printers and the American Revolution.'

please to let them. Holland has got the forms if she has lost the spirit of a free country. Switzerland alone is in the full and safe possession of her freedom.

These were times as inhospitable to freedom—and especially to press freedom—as our own. Few countries in Asia could alter this gloomy estimate by their present plight, made more melancholy by the decline of liberty in Vietnam, Laos, Cambodia, Thailand, and by the suppression of the press in India in the last year of the administration of Prime Minister Indira Gandhi. The United Nations Educational and Social Council, meeting in Nairobi in October 1977, confronted and affronted liberal world opinion with a Soviet-sponsored convention calling for governmental control of the foreign press of all countries. The proposal was shelved for the time being, but it led to continued demands for 'a new information order' from Third World delegates in 1978. In the United States, access to information about local, state, and federal systems of criminal justice have been obstructed by measures in Congress and in the states, inspired by the desire to preserve privacy. Access to judicial proceedings, regarded as unassailable in this country, has been obstructed to an unprecedented degree in the name of impartial justice.

The small weekly newspapers of the eighteenth-century American colonies did not forever fasten freedom of the press, or any other freedom, upon the institutions of the world; but they demonstrated its efficacy as a revolutionary force, its indispensability as an element in a really free society, and its compatibility with orderly government.

The press was not free in many countries then. It is not free in many countries now. Two hundred years of the American experience with press freedom, however, have made suspect political systems that deny press freedom. A handful of weekly newspapers, printed on the hand-operated English common press, launched an experiment in freedom of the press on this continent two hundred years ago, so successful in the furtherance of human liberty in every society where it has been imitated that no arbitrary government would dare commence the suppression of any human freedom without extinguishing this freedom first.

372

The Editors and Contributors

WILLI PAUL ADAMS is Professor of North American History, John F. Kennedy-Institut für Nordamerikastudien, Freie Universität, Berlin, West Germany.

BERNARD BAILYN is Winthrop Professor of History at Harvard University.

STEPHEN BOTEIN is Assistant Professor of History at Michigan State University

RICHARD BUEL, JR., is Professor of History at Wesleyan University.

ROBERT M. CALHOON is Professor of History at the University of North Carolina at Greensboro.

JOHN B. HENCH is Alden Porter Johnson Research and Publication Officer at the American Antiquarian Society.

PAUL LANGFORD is Fellow and Tutor in Modern History at Lincoln College, Oxford University.

MARCUS A. McCORISON is Director and Librarian of the American Antiquarian Society.

JANICE POTTER is Sessional Lecturer in Canadian–American Relations at the University of Saskatchewan.

G. THOMAS TANSELLE is Vice-president of the John Simon Guggenheim Memorial Foundation.

ROBERT M. WEIR is Professor of History at the University of South Carolina.

JAMES RUSSELL WIGGINS is Editor and Publisher of *The Ellsworth* (Maine) *American*.

Index

375

*Designed, composed, printed, and bound
in Lunenburg, Vermont, at
The Stinehour Press*